THIS
BIBLE
BELONGS
TO

_____

_____

_____

THIS

BIBLE

BELONGS

TO

MARRIAGES

BIRTHS

BIRTHS

BIRTHS

DEATHS

DEATHS

THE READER'S DIGEST BIBLE

LARGE-TYPE EDITION

THE READER'S DIGEST BIBLE

CONDENSED FROM
THE REVISED STANDARD VERSION
OLD AND NEW TESTAMENTS

LARGE-TYPE EDITION
VOLUME I

General Editor
BRUCE M. METZGER
Ph.D., D.D., L.H.D., D.Theol.
Princeton Theological Seminary

Published by
Reader's Digest Fund for the Blind, Inc.
with permission of
THE READER'S DIGEST ASSOCIATION
PLEASANTVILLE, NEW YORK
LONDON, MONTREAL, SYDNEY, CAPE TOWN, HONG KONG

Note:
The full-length text of
the Revised Standard Version
is available from the following:

Holman Bible Publishers
Thomas Nelson Publishers
Oxford University Press Inc.
World Bible Publishers Inc.
The Zondervan Corporation

© 1982 by The Reader's Digest Association, Inc.
Copyright © 1982 by The Reader's Digest
Association (Canada) Ltd.
Copyright © 1982 by Reader's Digest Association
Far East Limited
Philippines copyright 1982 by
Reader's Digest Association Far East Limited

Eighth Printing 1994

This condensation is based upon
the Revised Standard Version of the Bible,
© 1971 The Division of Christian Education of the
National Council of the Churches of Christ
in the U.S.A., by permission of the copyright holder.

Reader's Digest is a registered trademark of
The Reader's Digest Association, Inc.,
Pleasantville, New York.

The Reader's Digest Bible, Large-Type Edition,
was first published in hard cover in 1986.

CONTENTS

PREFACE

The age-old effort to spread knowledge of the Bible and its message has today entered a new era. The twentieth century, in fact, has witnessed a near revolution in the field, and the Bible may now be read in a remarkable variety of versions and editions. There are any number of new translations made from the ancient Hebrew and Greek originals. There are paraphrases, adaptations, updatings, amplifications, abridgments, selections, modernizations. While in each case the manner of presentation differs, all these editions are designed for a single purpose: in one way or another to reduce the formidable length, complexity, or obscurity of the Scriptures and thus to bring them ever closer to the mind and heart of the general reader.

Prompted by this atmosphere of ferment

and renewal, Reader's Digest some ten years ago took up a task it had long contemplated, condensation of the Bible as a whole. For many years the Digest has been aware that in the experience and skills of its editors it possessed a literary method for producing a version of the Scriptures that could be of unique value: a text significantly shortened and clarified, yet which retains all sixty-six books, carefully preserves every incident, personality, and teaching of substance, and keeps as well the true essence and flavor of the language. Such an unprecedented version could be achieved only through the condensation methods developed by Reader's Digest during more than half a century of use on all types of writing, including some of the world's foremost literature.

As practiced by the Digest, condensation is basically different from other methods of reducing the length of a text, such as abridgment. Condensation concerns itself with every individual word of the text, every phrase, sentence, paragraph, and chapter, as well as the larger portions or blocks of text, in relation both to the immediate context and to the whole. At the same time infinite care is taken to leave the essential fabric intact. By contrast, abridgment merely eliminates whole books or sizable sections of books, or brings together selected passages.

Though it is the inspired word of God, the Bible is still a written document—actually a library of many books—employing the language of mortals. Like all things mortal, language, too, is subject to change. Forms of literary expression, habits of thought, structure of language, preferences in vocabulary have altered considerably over the centuries. The device of repetition in word, thought, and incident, and the multiplying of words for rhetorical effect were practices favored in ancient times. Today they tend to confuse and exhaust the reader's attention. Also, of course, a certain percentage of the Old Testament text, particularly details concerning the ritual and history presented in some of the earlier books, holds a less immediate relevance for Christian belief and practice. The special technique of condensation employed by the Digest smooths away such features and frees for the modern reader a text that shines forth with simplicity and directness, without in the least reshaping its fundamental character.

The task of producing such a version of the Bible was one which, in all its subtle complexity, went far beyond anything that Digest editors had faced before. Consequently, the first approaches were made with unusual care. Exhaustive preliminary studies of the text were carried out, and special problems were isolated and analyzed. In repeated experiment, methods were carefully tested, book by book, and were modified where necessary. As the work of condensation progressed, the editors made constant reference to standard commentaries on the Bible, in order to be guided by the best approved opinion.

Serving in the capacity of General Editor was the Reverend Bruce M. Metzger,

Ph.D., D.D., L.H.D., D.Theol., Professor of New Testament Language and Literature, Princeton Theological Seminary. Dr. Metzger was actively involved at every stage of the work, from the initial studies on each of the sixty-six books through all subsequent editorial reviews. The finished condensation has received his full approval. Nothing has been changed, he states, nothing added to or removed from the text that in any way diminishes its spirit, its teachings, or the familiar ring of its language. Further, he certifies that the work has been thoroughly objective, without bias toward or against any particular set of beliefs. Finally, he provided the Introductions to the Old and New Testaments and to each individual book.

In this condensed version the Biblical text has been reduced by an overall figure of some forty percent. The Old Testament, with its greater variety in form and language, understandably offered larger scope than the New Testament for reduction. It has been shortened by approximately one half, different books permitting different percentages of reduction. The New Testament, much sparer in form and language, was brought down by about one quarter. Apart from the preliminary studies, the actual work of condensation required a total time of three years and involved a team of seven editors.

The basic text of *The Reader's Digest Bible* is the Revised Standard Version, the New Testament of which was first published in 1946 and the Old Testament in 1952. This version was chosen for several reasons: it is in wide use, its scholarship is impeccable, it enjoys an established familiarity, and it is directly linked to the King James Version, a relationship that gives it a strong echo of that elevated and dignified tone cherished by so many generations. The King James Version itself, published in 1611, took notice of those English translations that had preceded it, including that of William Tyndale, the first English translation to be made directly from the original Hebrew and Greek. Later, the King James

Version underwent extensive revision, emerging in 1901 as the American Standard Version, of which the present RSV is the authorized revision.

Not in any way intended to replace the full Biblical text, which will always remain available, *The Reader's Digest Bible* offers the general reader a more direct means of becoming intimately acquainted with the *whole* body of the Scriptures. It can be read more rapidly and with swifter comprehension, for inspiration, for instruction, even for pure heart-lifting enjoyment—the Bible is, after all, an unsurpassed collection of marvelous and stirring events linked to the divine will and purpose, compelling tales of men and women caught up in a courageous effort to live good and godly lives.

The Reader's Digest Bible is presented in the confident hope that readers, young and old, will find its quickened pace, its sharper focus, its smoothly flowing narratives an irresistible invitation to draw closer to the spiritual heart of the greatest book mankind possesses.   —The Editors

THE
OLD TESTAMENT

GENESIS–JOB

INTRODUCTION
TO THE
OLD TESTAMENT

The phrase "Old Testament" is the Christian name for a collection of sacred books that records the religious life and faith of ancient Israel—in short, the Jewish Bible. Composed at different times and places, by many different hands, over a period of some thousand years, these books set forth the mighty drama of divine revelation against a kaleidoscopic human background. From the very start of Christianity they have been an integral part of the Christian Scriptures, because in them is prefigured much of the religious teaching that reached the full flower of its development in the New Testament. "The New Testament was in the Old concealed," Saint Augustine explained, "the Old Testament is in the New revealed."

In the pages of the Old Testament may be found a wide variety of literary forms: prose, poetry, folktales, history, religious and secular laws, proverbs of the wise, oracles of the prophets, sacred hymns, a superb love song, laments, allegories, and much more. Originally written almost entirely in Hebrew, the Old Testament had a long history even after leaving the hands of the writers or editors who gave the separate books their present form. Until well into the Christian era it was the practice in writing the Hebrew text to represent only the consonants. As a result, depending on which vowels were supplied by the reader, some passages could yield more than one sense (in English, for example, the three consonants G-R-T might be read as GReaT, GReeT, GiRT, GRiT, GRaTe, eGReT, GRoaT). About A.D. 600 the manuscripts were supplied with strokes and dots, called vowel points, thus fixing the traditional Hebrew reading. This pointed text, known as the Masoretic text (from the Hebrew word for tradition), became the standard Hebrew Scriptures.

In the Hebrew Bible the separate books are grouped into three sections: the Law (consisting of the first five books, known collectively as the Pentateuch), the Prophets, and the Writings. Of these three, the Law (Torah) is regarded by Jews as most important, but Christians view the Old Testament in a different light. All of its books are accepted as being equally inspired, and no gradation of rank or sacredness is imposed. Their sequence in the Christian Bible is also arranged differently, according to a more systematic plan.

In ancient times translations of the Jewish Scriptures were made for those who could not read the original Hebrew. The earliest of these was the Old Greek, called the Septuagint (after the seventy translators who supposedly worked on the Pentateuch). The Septuagint became the Old Testament of the early Christian Church, and later versions were made from it or patterned after it. Included in the Septuagint were certain books not found in the

Masoretic text, and these books have since been regarded as canonical by the Roman Catholic Church. At the Reformation, however, Protestants refused to recognize the canonicity of these books, and to set them apart, translators grouped them in a section following the Old Testament, which they entitled the Apocrypha. Thus the Protestant canon of the Old Testament is exactly like the Masoretic, though with a difference in the order of the books.

The true sequence of the books of the Old Testament, as established by modern scholars on the basis of internal clues, differs greatly from their actual order as they stand in the Bible. This is so not only for the books as a whole, but also as regards their parts, for many of the books are of composite authorship. The process of compiling and editing occupied many centuries, and though in ancient times traditions of authorship became attached to some of the books, firm identification of the different authors is seldom possible. In most cases, material that existed much earlier was recast by one or more later writers and editors before reaching final form. These men—great creative artists who produced masterpieces of literature—were unconcerned about their own names being preserved. Above all, it was important to them that readers should be guided in understanding God's will and in gaining a fuller appreciation of his purpose.

Until recently the oldest known manuscripts containing major sections of the Hebrew Bible dated from only the ninth and tenth centuries of the Christian era, with the oldest dated manuscript of the entire Hebrew Bible coming from A.D. 1008. But discoveries made during the mid-twentieth century, in caves at Qumran near the Dead Sea, have brought to light much older manuscripts, most of them fragmentary, of all the books of the Old Testament except Esther. Several of these "Dead Sea Scrolls," as they are now called, go back to the second century B.C. or even earlier.

Frequently New Testament writers

quote from the Old Testament, a practice that forms an obvious bond between the two parts of the Bible. Some of these quotations are direct, some are vague and allusive, while still others show considerable variation from the wording of the older Scriptures. For the variations there are several causes: first, the New Testament writers all apparently quoted from the Greek of the Septuagint; second, many of them must frequently have quoted from memory; third, they sometimes abridged or expanded the original, in order to gain force of expression or derive a new meaning.

The remarkable variety of the Old Testament is evident even to the casual reader. Yet running as a golden thread through all this wide-ranging diversity there is a unifying, never failing sense of the presence and activity of the living God, who reveals himself to his people and who desires their fellowship. And in both Testaments it is the selfsame God who is revealed, a circumstance that is memorably expressed in the opening words of the Letter to the Hebrews: "In many and various ways God spoke of old to our fathers by the prophets; but in these last days he has spoken to us by a Son."

GENESIS

Although Genesis is silent as to its author, Jewish and Christian thought had long accepted it as the work of Moses. However, nearly all modern scholars agree that, like the other books of the Pentateuch, it is a composite of several sources, embodying traditions that go back in some cases to Moses. The book falls into two parts. The first includes the stories of the creation, the Garden of Eden, Cain and Abel, Noah and the Flood, and the Tower of Babel. The second deals with the "fathers" of Israel. It begins with God's call to Abram (later renamed Abraham) to leave his own country for one that God would give him. He is promised an innumerable posterity, among whom chief attention is given to Joseph. The lengthy saga of Joseph explains how the Israelites came to be in Egypt, thus providing the background for the narrative of their deliverance, recounted in the next book, Exodus.

Theologically, Genesis is basic to both the Old and the New Testament. The covenant between God and his chosen people, expressed in the promises given to Abraham and renewed to Isaac and to Jacob, is fundamental to the Old Testament as a whole. New Testament writers, who frequently refer to Genesis, presuppose its accounts of creation and of the fall, and reiterate the covenant-keeping character of God.

———

IN THE BEGINNING God created the heavens and the earth. The earth was without form and void, and darkness was upon the face of the deep; and the Spirit of God was moving over the face of the waters.

God said, "Let there be light"; and there was light. And God saw that the light was good; and God separated the light from the darkness. God called the light Day, and the darkness he called Night. And there was evening and morning, one day.

God said, "Let there be a firmament in the midst of the waters." And God made the firmament and separated the waters which were under the firmament from the waters which were above it. And God called the firmament Heaven. And there was evening and morning, a second day.

God said, "Let the waters under the heavens be gathered together, and let the dry land appear." And it was so. God called the dry land Earth, and the waters he called Seas. God said, "Let the earth put forth vegetation, plants yielding seed, and trees bearing fruit in which is their seed, each according to its kind." It was so, and God saw that it was good. And there was evening and morning, a third day.

God said, "Let there be lights in the firmament of the heavens to separate day from night; let them be for signs and seasons and days and years, and let them give light upon the earth." God made the two great lights, the greater to rule the day, the lesser to rule the night; he made the stars also, and set them in the heavens. God saw that it was good. And there was evening and morning, a fourth day.

God said, "Let the waters bring forth swarms of living creatures, and let birds fly across the heavens." So God created the great sea monsters and every living creature with which the waters swarm, and every winged bird. And God saw that it was good, and blessed them, saying, "Be fruitful and multiply." And there was evening and morning, a fifth day.

God said, "Let the earth bring forth living creatures: cattle and creeping things and beasts of the earth." So God made the beasts of the earth, and the cattle, and everything that creeps upon the ground according to its kind. And God saw that it was good.

Then God said, "Let us make man in our image, after our likeness; and let them have dominion over all the earth." So God created man in his own image, in the image of God he created him; male and female he created them. And God blessed them, saying, "Be fruitful and multiply, and fill the earth and subdue it; and have dominion over the fish of the sea and the birds of the air and every living thing that moves upon the earth." And God said, "Behold, I have given you every plant yielding seed, and every tree with seed in its fruit; you shall have them for food. And to every beast and every bird, to everything that has the breath of life, I have given every green plant for food." And it was so. God saw that everything he had made was very good. And there was evening and morning, a sixth day.

Thus the heavens and the earth were finished, and on the seventh day God rested from all his work. God blessed and hallowed the seventh day, because on it he rested from all his work of creation.

WHEN THE LORD God made the earth and heavens, no plant was yet in the earth, no herb of the field had yet sprung up—for the LORD God had not caused it to rain upon the earth, and there was no man to till the ground; but a mist went up from the earth and watered the ground— then the LORD God formed man of dust from the ground, and breathed into his nostrils the breath of life; and man became a living being.

To the east, in Eden, the LORD God planted a garden. Out of the ground he made to grow every tree that is pleasant to the sight and good for food, the tree of life also, in the midst of the garden, and the tree of the knowledge of good and evil. A river flowed out of Eden to water the garden, and there it divided and became four rivers. The first is the Pishon, which flows around the land of Havilah, where there is gold; the second is the Gihon, which flows around the land of Cush; the third is the Tigris, which flows east of Assyria. The fourth river is the Euphrates.

The LORD God took the man and put him in the garden of Eden to till it and keep it. He commanded the man, saying, "You may freely eat of every tree of the garden; but of the tree of the knowledge of good and evil you shall not eat, for in the day that you eat of it you shall die."

Then the LORD God said, "It is not good that the man should be alone; I will make a helper fit for him." Out of the ground he formed every beast and bird, and brought them to the man; and whatever the man called every living creature, that was its name. The man gave names to all cattle, to the birds of the air, and to every beast of the field; but there was not found a helper fit for him. So the LORD God caused a deep sleep to fall upon the man, and while he slept took one of his ribs and closed up its place with flesh; and the rib which the LORD God had taken from the man he made into a woman and brought her to the man. "This at last is bone of my bones and flesh of my flesh," the man said. "She shall be called Woman, because she was taken out of Man." Therefore a man leaves his father and mother and cleaves to his wife, and they become one flesh. The man and his wife were both naked, and were not ashamed.

Now the serpent was more subtle than any other wild creature that the LORD God had made. He said to the woman, "Did God say, 'You shall not eat of any tree of the garden'?" The woman replied, "We may eat fruit, but God said, 'You shall not eat fruit from the tree in the midst of the garden, lest you die.' "

"You will not die," the serpent said. "God knows that when you eat of it your eyes will be opened, and you will be like God, knowing good and evil." So the woman, seeing that the tree was good for food and was to be desired to make one wise, ate of its fruit. She gave some to her husband, and he also ate. Then the eyes of both were opened, and they knew that they were naked, and they sewed fig leaves together and made aprons for themselves.

In the cool of the day they heard the LORD God walking in the garden, and hid themselves among the trees. But the LORD God called to the man, "Where are you?" The man said, "I heard thee in the garden, and was afraid, because I was naked; and I hid myself." God said, "Who told you that you were naked? Have you eaten of the tree of which I commanded you not to eat?" The man replied, "The woman whom thou gavest to be with me gave me the fruit, and I ate." Then the LORD God said to the woman, "What is this you have done?" The woman said, "The serpent beguiled me, and I ate."

"Because you have done this," the LORD

God said to the serpent, "you are cursed above all animals. Upon your belly you shall go, and you shall eat dust all your life. I will put enmity between you and the woman, and between your seed and her seed; he shall bruise your head, and you shall bruise his heel." To the woman he said, "In pain you shall bring forth children, yet your desire shall be for your husband, and he shall rule over you." To Adam he said, "Because you have listened to the voice of your wife, and have eaten of the tree of which I commanded you not to eat, cursed is the ground because of you. In toil you shall eat of it all your life, and it shall bring forth thorns and thistles to you. In the sweat of your face you shall eat bread till you return to the ground, for out of it you were taken; you are dust, and to dust you shall return." The man called his wife's name Eve, because she was the mother of all living, and the LORD God made garments of skins for them and clothed them.

Then the LORD God said, "Man has become like one of us, knowing good and evil. Now he might eat also of the tree of life, and live for ever." So the LORD God drove man out of the garden of Eden, to till the ground from which he was taken. East of Eden he placed the cherubim, and a flaming sword which turned every way, to guard the way to the tree of life.

Adam knew Eve his wife, and she conceived and bore Cain, saying, "I have gotten a man with the help of the LORD." Again, she bore his brother Abel. Now Abel was a keeper of sheep, and Cain a tiller of the ground. In the course of time Cain brought to the LORD an offering of the fruit of the ground, and Abel brought the firstlings of his flock and of their fat portions. The LORD had regard for Abel and his offering, but not for Cain and his. So Cain was very angry. "Why are you angry?" the LORD said to him. "If you do well, will you not be accepted? If you do not do well, sin is couching at the door; its desire is for you, but you must master it."

Cain said to Abel, "Let us go out to the field," and when they were there, Cain rose up against his brother and killed him. "Where is Abel?" the LORD asked Cain. "I do not know," he replied. "Am I my brother's keeper?" The LORD said, "What have you done? The voice of your brother's blood is crying to me from the ground. Now you are cursed from the ground, which has opened its mouth to receive your brother's blood from your hand. When you till the ground, it shall no longer yield to you its strength; you shall be a wanderer on the earth."

"My punishment is greater than I can bear," said Cain. "I shall be hidden from thy face, a fugitive. Whoever finds me will slay me." But the LORD said, "Not so! If any one slays Cain, vengeance shall be taken on him sevenfold." He put a mark on Cain, lest any who came upon him should kill him. Then Cain went away from the presence of the LORD, and dwelt in the land of Nod, east of Eden.

Cain knew his wife, and she conceived and bore Enoch. And Cain built a city, and named the city after his son, Enoch. To Enoch was born Irad; and Irad was the father of Mehujael, and Mehujael the father of Methushael, and Methushael the father of Lamech. Lamech took two wives, Adah and Zillah. Adah bore Jabal; he was the father of those who dwell in tents and have cattle. His brother Jubal was the father of those who play the lyre and pipe. Zillah bore Tubal-cain, the forger of all instruments of bronze and iron.

THIS IS THE book of the generations of Adam. When God created man, he made him in the likeness of God. Male and female he created them, and he blessed them and named them Man. When Adam had lived a hundred and thirty years, he became the father of a son in his own likeness, after his image, and named him Seth. The days of Adam after he became the father of Seth were eight hundred years; and he had other sons and daughters. Thus all the days that Adam lived were nine hundred and thirty years; and he died.

Seth became the father of Enosh, and also had other sons and daughters. All the days of Seth were nine hundred and twelve years; and he died. Enosh became the father of Kenan, and also had other sons and daughters. All the days of Enosh were nine hundred and five years; and he died. Kenan became the father of Mahalalel, and also had other sons and daughters. All the days of Kenan were nine hundred and ten years; and he died. Mahalalel became the father of Jared, and also had other sons and daughters. All the days of Mahalalel were eight hundred and ninety-five years; and he died. Jared became the father of Enoch, and also had other sons and daughters. All the days of Jared were nine hundred and sixty-two years; and he died.

Enoch became the father of Methuselah, and also had other sons and daughters. All the days of Enoch were three hundred and sixty-five years. Enoch walked with God; and then he was not, for God took him.

Methuselah became the father of Lamech, and also had other sons and daughters. All the days of Methuselah were nine hundred and sixty-nine years; and he died. Lamech became the father of a son, and called him Noah, saying, "Out of the ground which the LORD has cursed this one shall bring us relief from our toil." All the days of Lamech were seven hundred and seventy-seven years; and he died. After Noah was five hundred years old, he became the father of Shem, Ham, and Japheth.

WHEN MEN BEGAN to multiply on earth, and daughters were born to them, the sons of God saw that the daughters of men were fair, and took to wife such as they chose. The LORD said, "My spirit shall not abide in man for ever, for he is flesh; his days shall be a hundred and twenty years." The Nephilim were on the earth in those days, and also afterward, when the sons of God came in to the daughters of men, who bore children to them. These were the mighty men of old, men of renown.

Now the LORD saw that the wickedness of man was great, and his every imagination continually evil. It grieved him to his heart that he had made man on earth, so he said, "I will blot out man from the face of the earth, man and beast and creeping things and birds, for I am sorry I made them." But Noah found favor in the eyes of the LORD. A righteous man, blameless in his generation, Noah walked with God.

The earth was corrupt in God's sight, and filled with violence; for all flesh had corrupted their way upon the earth. God said to Noah, "I have determined to destroy all flesh, for the earth is filled with violence through them. You are to make an ark of gopher wood, and cover it with pitch. Make it four hundred and fifty feet long, seventy-five feet wide, and forty-five feet high. Make a roof for the ark, and set the door of the ark in its side; make it with lower, second, and third decks. For I will bring a flood upon the earth, and everything shall die. But I will establish my covenant with you, and you shall come into the ark, you, your sons, your wife, and your sons' wives. You shall bring two, male and female, of every living thing into the ark, to keep them alive with you: birds, animals, creeping things, according to their kinds. Also take with you every sort of food, and store it up for you and them." Noah did all that God commanded him.

In the six hundredth year of Noah's life, in the second month, on the seventeenth day of the month, all the fountains of the deep burst forth, and the windows of the heavens were opened. On the very same day Noah and his wife, his sons, Shem and Ham and Japheth, and their wives entered the ark. Every beast, all the cattle, every creeping thing, and bird of every sort went into the ark with Noah, two and two, male and female, as God had commanded, and the LORD shut them in.

The flood continued. Rain fell upon the earth for forty days and forty nights. The waters increased, and bore up the ark, and it rose high above the earth, floating on the face of the waters. The waters prevailed so mightily that all the high mountains were covered more than twenty feet deep. All flesh died; everything on dry land in whose nostrils was the breath of life died. Man and animals, creeping things and birds— all were blotted out from the earth. Only Noah and those with him in the ark were left. The waters prevailed upon the earth a hundred and fifty days, but God remembered Noah and all with him in the ark. He made a wind blow, and the waters subsided. The rain was restrained, the waters receded, and in the seventh month, on the seventeenth day of the month, the ark came to rest upon the mountains of Ararat. The waters continued to abate until, on the first day of the tenth month, the tops of the mountains were seen.

Noah opened the window of the ark and sent forth a raven; to and fro it went until the waters were dried up from the earth. Then Noah sent forth a dove, to see if the waters had subsided; but the dove, finding no place to set her foot, returned. So he put forth his hand and brought her into the ark. He waited seven days, and again sent the dove out. She came back in the evening, and in her mouth was a freshly plucked olive leaf, so Noah knew that the waters had subsided from the earth. He waited another seven days, then again sent forth the dove, and she did not return any more.

Removing the covering of the ark, Noah looked about. The ground was dry. God said to Noah, "Go forth from the ark with your wife, your sons and their wives. Bring forth with you every living thing, that they may be fruitful and multiply upon the earth." So they all went forth by families out of the ark, and Noah built an altar to the LORD, and offered burnt offerings. When the LORD smelled the pleasing odor, he said in his heart, "I will never again curse the ground because of man, for the imagination of man's heart is evil from his youth; neither will I ever again destroy every living creature. While the earth remains, seedtime and harvest, cold and heat, summer and winter, day and night, shall not cease."

God blessed Noah and his sons, saying, "Be fruitful and multiply, and fill the earth. The fear and dread of you shall be upon every beast of the earth, and every bird of the air, upon everything that creeps on the ground and all the fish of the sea; into your hand they are delivered. Every moving thing that lives shall be food for you; and as I gave you the green plants, I give you everything. Only you shall not eat flesh with its life, that is, its blood. For your lifeblood I will surely require a reckoning; of every beast I will require it and of man. Whoever sheds the blood of man, by man shall his blood be shed; for God made man in his own image."

Then God said to Noah and his sons, "I establish my covenant with you and your descendants, and every living creature for all future generations. Never again shall there be a flood to destroy the earth. This is the sign of the covenant: I set my bow in the cloud. When I bring clouds over the earth and the bow is in the clouds, I will look upon it and remember my covenant; and the waters shall never again become a flood to destroy all flesh."

Noah was the first tiller of the soil. He planted a vineyard, drank of the wine, became drunk, and lay uncovered in his tent. Ham, the father of Canaan, saw the nakedness of his father, and told his two brothers. Shem and Japheth laid a garment upon both their shoulders, walked backward, their faces turned away, and covered the nakedness of their father. When Noah awoke from his wine and knew what his youngest son had done to him, he said, "Cursed be Canaan; a slave shall he be to his brothers. Blessed by the LORD my God be Shem, and let Canaan be his slave. God enlarge Japheth, and let Canaan be his slave." After the flood Noah lived three hundred and fifty years, and all his days were nine hundred and fifty years. From the families of his sons the nations spread abroad on the earth after the flood.

Now the whole earth had one language

and few words. As men migrated from the east, they settled on a plain in the land of Babylon. "Come," they said to one another, "let us make bricks, and burn them thoroughly." Then they had brick for stone, and bitumen for mortar. "Let us build a city," they said, "and a tower with its top in the heavens, and let us make a name for ourselves."

The LORD came down to see the city and the tower which the sons of men had built. "Behold," he said, "they are one people with one language, and this is only the beginning. Nothing they propose to do will now be impossible for them. Let us confuse their language, that they may not understand one another." So the LORD scattered them abroad over the face of the earth, and they stopped building the city; it was called Babel, because there the LORD confused their language and from there he scattered them over all the earth.

THESE ARE THE descendants of Shem, who became the father of Arpachshad two years after the flood: Arpachshad became the father of Shelah, Shelah the father of

Eber, and Eber the father of Peleg. Peleg became the father of Reu, Reu the father of Serug, Serug the father of Nahor, and Nahor the father of Terah. Terah became the father of Abram, Nahor, and Haran. Haran became the father of Lot, and died before his father, Terah, in the land of his birth, Ur of the Chaldeans. Abram and Nahor took wives. Abram's wife was Sarai, and Nahor's wife was Milcah, the daughter of Haran. Abram's wife, Sarai, was barren; she had no child. Terah took his son Abram, his daughter-in-law Sarai, and his grandson Lot, the son of Haran, and they went forth together from Ur to go into the land of Canaan. But when they came to Haran, they settled there, and Terah died in Haran.

Now the LORD said to Abram, "Go from your country and your kindred to the land I will show you. I will make of you a great nation, and make your name great. I will bless you and those who bless you, and curse him who curses you. By you all the families of the earth shall be blessed." So Abram, who was seventy-five years old, departed from Haran with Sarai his wife,

Lot his brother's son, and all their possessions, and the persons that they had gotten in Haran. When they came to Canaan, Abram passed through the land to the oak of Moreh near Shechem. There the LORD appeared to him and said, "To your descendants I will give this land." So Abram built an altar to the LORD at Shechem; then he moved on to the mountain east of Bethel, pitched his tent, and built another altar and called on the name of the LORD. Then he journeyed on, still going toward the Negeb.

There was a famine in the land, so Abram went down to Egypt to sojourn there. As they were about to enter Egypt, Abram said to Sarai, "When the Egyptians see that you are a woman beautiful to behold, they will say, 'This is his wife.' Then they will kill me, but let you live. Say you are my sister, that it may go well with me because of you, and my life may be spared."

In Egypt the princes of Pharaoh saw that Sarai was very beautiful, and they praised her to Pharaoh, who took her into his house. For her sake Pharaoh dealt well with Abram, giving him sheep, oxen, asses, servants, and camels. But because of Sarai the LORD afflicted Pharaoh and his house with great plagues. So Pharaoh called Abram. "What is this you have done to me?" he said. "Why did you say, 'She is my sister,' so that I took her for my wife? Now, take her, and be gone." And Pharaoh's men set Abram on the way, with his wife and all that he had.

Abram, very rich in cattle, silver, and gold, went up from Egypt, he and his wife, and Lot with him, into the Negeb. They journeyed on as far as Bethel, to the place where Abram's tent had been, and where he had made an altar. Now Lot also had many flocks, herds, and tents. So great were the possessions of Abram and Lot that the land could not support both of them dwelling together, and there was strife between their herdsmen.

"Let there be no strife between you and me," Abram said to Lot, "for we are kinsmen. Is not the whole land before you? Separate yourself from me. If you take land to the left, then I will go right; if you go right, I will go to the left." Lot saw that the Jordan valley was well watered everywhere like the garden of the LORD, like the land of Egypt, so he chose for himself all the Jordan valley, and journeyed east. Thus they separated. Abram dwelt in the land of Canaan, while Lot dwelt among the cities of the valley and moved his tent as far as Sodom, where the men were wicked, great sinners against the LORD.

"Lift up your eyes," the LORD said to Abram after Lot had gone. "From where you are, look northward, southward, eastward, and westward. I will give all the land you see to you and your descendants for ever. I will make your descendants as the dust of the earth; if one can count the dust, your descendants also can be counted. Arise. Walk the length and the breadth of the land, for I will give it to you." So Abram moved his tent, and dwelt by the oaks of Mamre, at Hebron; and there he built an altar to the LORD.

Now AMRAPHEL KING of Babylon, Arioch king of Ellasar, Chedorlaomer king of Elam, and Tidal king of Goiim made war with the Canaanite kings of Sodom, Gomorrah, Admah, Zeboiim, and Zoar. For twelve years the Canaanite kings had served Chedorlaomer, but in the thirteenth year they rebelled. When Chedorlaomer and the kings who were with him came and subdued all the country as far as the border of the wilderness, the Canaanite kings went out and joined battle, five kings against four, in the Valley of Siddim (that is, the Salt Sea). But the Valley of Siddim was full of bitumen pits, and as the forces of the kings of Sodom and Gomorrah fled, some fell into them; the rest fled to the mountain. So the enemy took all the goods of Sodom and Gomorrah, and they captured Lot, Abram's kinsman who dwelt in Sodom, took his goods, and departed.

Then one who had escaped came and told Abram, living by the oaks of Mamre, that his kinsman had been taken captive. Abram led forth his trained men, born in his house, three hundred and eighteen of them, and went in pursuit as far as Dan. He divided his forces against the enemy by night, routed them, and pursued them to Hobah, north of Damascus. He brought back all the goods, and Lot with his goods and people.

As Abram was returning, the king of Sodom came out to meet him at the King's Valley. And Melchizedek, king of Salem and priest of God Most High, brought out bread and wine, and blessed him, saying, "Blessed be Abram by God Most High, maker of heaven and earth; and blessed be God Most High, who has delivered your enemies into your hand!" And Abram gave him a tenth of everything.

The king of Sodom said to Abram, "Give me the persons, but take the goods for yourself." But Abram said, "I have sworn to the LORD God Most High, maker of heaven and earth, that I would not take a thread or a sandal-thong of yours, lest you should say, 'I have made Abram rich.' I will take nothing but what the young men have eaten."

After these things the word of the LORD came to Abram in a vision: "Fear not, Abram, I am your shield; your reward shall be very great." But Abram said, "O Lord GOD, what wilt thou give me? For I continue childless, and Eliezer of Damascus, a slave in my house, will be my heir." Then the word of the LORD came: "This man shall not be your heir; your own son shall be your heir." The LORD brought Abram outside and said, "Look toward heaven, and number the stars, if you are able to. So shall your descendants be." Abram believed, and the LORD reckoned it to him as righteousness, and said, "I am the LORD who brought you from Ur of the Chaldeans, to give you this land to possess. Your descendants will be sojourners in a land not theirs. They will be slaves there, oppressed for four hundred years; but I will bring judgment on the nation which they serve. Afterward they shall come out with great possessions, and come back here in the fourth generation. As for your-self, you shall go to your fathers in peace, and be buried in a good old age."

ABRAM HAD DWELT ten years in the land of Canaan, and Sarai, his wife, had borne him no children. "The LORD has prevented me from bearing children," she said to Abram. "Go in to my maid, Hagar; it may be that I shall obtain children by her."

Abram hearkened to Sarai's voice, so Sarai took Hagar, her Egyptian maid, and gave her to Abram as a wife. He went in to Hagar, and she conceived; and then she looked with contempt on her mistress. "May the wrong done to me be on you!" Sarai said to Abram. "I gave my maid to your embrace, and when she conceived, she looked on me with contempt." Abram said, "Your maid is in your power. Do to her as you please." Then Sarai dealt harshly with Hagar, and Hagar fled. But the angel of the LORD found her by a spring of water in the wilderness, and he said, "Hagar, where have you come from and where are you going?" She replied, "I am fleeing from my mistress Sarai."

"Return and submit to your mistress," the angel said, "and I will so greatly multiply your descendants that they cannot be numbered. You are with child, and shall bear a son. Call his name Ishmael, because the LORD has given heed to your affliction. He shall be a wild ass of a man, his hand against every man and every man's hand against him; and he shall dwell over against all his kinsmen." Hagar said, "Have I really seen God and remained alive after seeing him?" And Hagar bore Abram a son, and Abram called him Ishmael.

When Abram was ninety-nine, the LORD appeared to him and said, "I am God Almighty; walk before me, and be blameless. My covenant is with you. No longer shall your name be Abram, but your name shall be Abraham, for I have made you the father of a multitude of nations. I will establish my covenant between me and you, an everlasting covenant, to be God to you and to your descendants, and I will give to you and your descendants all the land of Canaan for an everlasting possession. As a sign of the covenant between us, you and your descendants, every male among you, shall be circumcised in the flesh of your foreskins. He that is eight days old shall be circumcised; every male throughout your generations, both he that is born in your house and he that is bought with your money. Any uncircumcised male shall be cut off from his people; he has broken my covenant.

"As for your wife, you shall not call her

Sarai, but Sarah shall be her name. I will bless her, and give you a son by her. She shall be a mother of nations; kings shall come from her."

Abraham fell on his face and laughed, and said to himself, "Shall a child be born to a man who is a hundred years old? Shall Sarah, who is ninety years old, bear a child?" To God he said, "O that Ishmael might live in thy sight!" God said, "I have heard you. I will bless Ishmael and make him fruitful; I will make him a great nation. But Sarah your wife shall bear you a son at this season next year, and you shall call his name Isaac. I will establish my covenant with him as an everlasting covenant for his descendants after him." When God had finished talking with him, Abraham took Ishmael his son and all the male slaves in his house, and he circumcised them that very day.

THE LORD APPEARED to Abraham by the oaks of Mamre, as he sat at the door of his tent in the heat of the day. Abraham lifted up his eyes, and there before him stood three men. He ran to meet them, and bowed, saying, "My lords, do not pass by your servant. Let a little water be brought. Wash your feet, and rest under the tree, while I fetch food. Refresh yourselves, and after that you may pass on." Abraham ran to the herd, took a tender calf, and gave it to the servant to prepare. Then he took curds, milk, and the prepared calf, set it before the men, and stood by them under the tree while they ate.

"Where is Sarah your wife?" they asked. And Abraham said, "She is in the tent." The LORD said, "I will surely return to you in the spring, and Sarah your wife shall have a son." Sarah was listening at the tent door, and she laughed to herself, saying, "After I have grown old, and my husband is old, shall I have pleasure?"

"Why did Sarah laugh?" the LORD said to Abraham. "Is anything too hard for the LORD?" But Sarah denied it, saying, "I did not laugh," for she was afraid. "No, but you did laugh," the LORD said.

The men set out toward Sodom, and Abraham went with them to set them on their way. "Shall I hide from Abraham what I am about to do," the LORD asked himself, "seeing that he shall become a great and mighty nation? No, for I have chosen him and his household after him to keep the way of the LORD by doing righteousness and justice." So the LORD said to Abraham, "The outcry against Sodom and Gomorrah is great. I will go down to see whether their sin is as grave as the outcry which has come to me."

The men turned toward Sodom, but Abraham, still standing before the LORD, drew near, and said, "Wilt thou indeed destroy the righteous with the wicked? Suppose there are fifty righteous within the city; wilt thou not spare it for the fifty righteous? Far be it from thee to slay the righteous with the wicked! Shall not the Judge of all the earth do right?" The LORD said, "If I find at Sodom fifty righteous, I will spare the whole place for their sake."

"Behold," Abraham said, "I who am but dust and ashes have taken upon myself to speak to the Lord. Suppose only forty righteous are found. Wilt thou destroy the whole city?" The LORD replied, "For the sake of forty I will not do it." Abraham said, "Suppose thirty are found." The

LORD answered, "I will not do it, if I find thirty." Abraham said, "Suppose twenty are found." The LORD replied, "For the sake of twenty I will not destroy it." Abraham said, "Let not the LORD be angry, and I will speak again but this once. Suppose ten are found." The LORD answered, "For the sake of ten I will not destroy it." Then the LORD went his way, and Abraham returned to his place.

When the two angels came to Sodom in the evening, Lot was sitting in the city gate. He rose, bowed, and said, "My lords, turn aside to your servant's house and spend the night. Then you may rise up early and go on your way."

"No," they said, "we will spend the night in the street." But Lot urged them strongly, so they entered his house where he made a feast for them, and they ate. But before they lay down, the men of the city of Sodom, both young and old, surrounded the house and called to Lot, "Where are the men who came to you tonight? Bring them out, that we may know them."

Lot went out, shut the door after him, and said, "I beg you, my brothers, do not act so wickedly. I have two daughters who have not known man; let me bring them out to you. Do to them as you please; only do nothing to these men under the shelter of my roof."

"This fellow would play the judge!" the men of Sodom said. "We will deal worse with you than with them." They pressed hard against Lot, and drew near to break down the door. But the angels put forth their hands, brought Lot into the house, and shut the door. They struck with blindness the men outside, so that they wearied themselves groping for the door.

When morning dawned, the angels urged Lot to leave. "Take your wife, your two daughters, and any one else you have here, lest you be consumed in the punishment of the city, for the LORD has sent us to destroy it." But Lot lingered. The angels seized him and his wife and daughters by the hand, the LORD being merciful to him, and they brought them forth and set them outside the city. "Flee for your life," the angels said. "Do not look back or stop anywhere in the valley; flee to the hills, lest you be consumed."

"You have shown me great kindness in saving my life," said Lot, "but I cannot flee to the hills, lest disaster overtake me. Let me escape to yonder city—is it not a little one?—and my life will be saved!" The LORD said, "I grant you this favor also. I will not overthrow that city. Make haste, escape; for I can do nothing till you arrive there." The city was called Zoar, and the sun had risen when Lot came there.

Then the LORD rained on Sodom and Gomorrah brimstone and fire out of heaven; and he overthrew the valley, and all the inhabitants of the cities. But Lot's wife, behind him, looked back, and she became a pillar of salt. Early in the morning Abraham went to the place where he had stood before the LORD, and looked down toward Sodom and Gomorrah, and lo, the smoke of the land of the valley went up like the smoke of a furnace. So it was that, when God destroyed the cities of the valley, he remembered Abraham, and sent Lot out of the midst of the overthrow.

Lot was afraid to dwell in Zoar, so he went up to the hills and dwelt in a cave with his two daughters. "Our father is old," the first-born daughter said to the younger, "and there is not a man to come in to us after the manner of all the earth. Let us make our father drink wine, and we will lie with him, that we may preserve offspring through him." So they made their father drink wine that night, and the first-born went in, and lay with him; he did not know when she lay down or when she arose. The next night they made their father drink wine also, and the younger arose, and lay with him. Thus both the daughters of Lot were with child by their father. The first-born bore a son, and called him Moab; he is the father of the Moabites to this day. The younger also bore a son, and called him Ben-ammi; he is the father of the Ammonites to this day.

THE LORD VISITED Sarah and did as he had promised, and Sarah conceived and bore Abraham a son when he was a hundred years old. Abraham called his son Isaac, and he circumcised him when he was eight days old, as God had commanded. "God has made laughter for me," said Sarah.

"Who would have said Sarah would suckle children? Yet I have borne Abraham a son in his old age."

The child grew, and Abraham made a great feast on the day Isaac was weaned. But Sarah saw Ishmael, the son of Hagar the Egyptian, playing with her son Isaac. "Cast out this slave woman with her son," Sarah said to Abraham, "for he shall not be heir with my son Isaac." This was very displeasing to Abraham, but God said to him, "Be not displeased. Do as Sarah tells you, for through Isaac shall your descendants be named. And I will make a nation of Hagar's son also, because he is your offspring." So Abraham took bread and a skin of water, and gave it to Hagar, putting it on her shoulder, and sent her away with the child, and they wandered in the wilderness of Beer-sheba.

When the water in the skin was gone, Hagar cast Ishmael under a bush, and sat down a good way off, saying, "Let me not look upon the death of my child." The lad lifted up his voice and wept. God heard, and the angel of God called to Hagar from heaven, "What troubles you, Hagar? Fear not; for God has heard the voice of the lad. Arise, lift him up, and hold him fast with your hand; for I will make him a great nation." God opened her eyes, and she saw a well of water. She filled the skin with water, and gave the lad a drink. And God was with Ishmael. He grew up, lived in the wilderness of Paran, and became an expert with the bow. His mother took a wife for him from the land of Egypt, and his sons dwelt opposite Egypt in the direction of Assyria.

AFTER THESE THINGS God tested Abraham, and said to him, "Take your son Isaac, whom you love, and go to the land of Moriah. Offer him there as a burnt offering upon one of the mountains of which I shall tell you." So Abraham rose early in the morning, cut wood for the burnt offering, saddled his ass, took two young men with him, and his son Isaac, and went toward the place of which God had told him. On the third day he saw the place afar off. "Stay here with the ass," he said to his young men. "The lad and I will go yonder and worship, and come again to you." He laid the wood on Isaac, and took in his hand the fire and the knife. "My father," Isaac said, "I behold the fire and the wood, but where is the lamb for a burnt offering?" Abraham said, "God will provide the lamb, my son."

When they came to the place of which God had told him, Abraham built an altar and laid the wood in order. He bound Isaac and laid him on the altar, upon the wood. Then he took the knife to slay his son. But the angel of the LORD called from heaven, "Abraham! Abraham! Do not lay your hand on the lad, for now I know that you fear God, seeing you have not withheld your son from me."

Abraham lifted up his eyes and looked, and there behind him was a ram, caught in a thicket by his horns. He took the ram, and offered it up as a burnt offering instead of his son. Then he called that place The LORD will provide; as it is said to this day, "On the mount of the LORD it shall be provided."

The angel of the LORD called to Abraham a second time, "Because you have done this, I will indeed bless you. I will multiply your descendants as the sand on the seashore. They shall possess the gate of their enemies, and all the nations of the earth shall be blessed by them, because you have obeyed my voice." So Abraham returned to his young men, and they went together to Beer-sheba, where Abraham dwelt.

SARAH LIVED A hundred and twenty-seven years; she died at Hebron, in the land of Canaan. Abraham mourned and wept for her, and buried her in the cave of the field of Machpelah, east of Mamre. And the field and the cave that is in it were sold to Abraham by the Hittites, the people of the land, as a burying place.

Now Abraham was old, and the LORD had blessed him in all things. To his oldest servant, who had charge of all that he had, Abraham said, "Swear by the LORD, the God of heaven and earth, that you will not take a wife for my son from the daughters of the Canaanites. Go to my country and to my kindred, and take a wife for Isaac."

"Perhaps the woman may not be willing to follow me to this land," the servant replied. "Must I then take your son back to the land from which you came?"

"Do not take my son back there," said Abraham. "The LORD, who took me from the land of my birth, spoke to me and swore, 'To your descendants I will give this land.' He will send his angel before you, and you shall take a wife for my son from there. If the woman is not willing to follow you, you will be free from this oath." So the servant swore to Abraham concerning this matter. Then he took ten of his master's camels, with all sorts of choice gifts, and departed.

The servant went to Mesopotamia, to Haran, the city of Abraham's brother, Nahor. Outside the city, he made the camels kneel down by the well at evening time when women go out to draw water. "O LORD, God of my master Abraham," he said, "grant me success today, and show steadfast love to my master. I am standing by the spring, and the daughters of the city are coming out to draw water. Let the maiden to whom I shall say, 'Pray let down your jar that I may drink,' and who shall say, 'Drink, and I will water your camels'—let her be the one whom thou hast appointed for thy servant Isaac."

Before he had done speaking, Rebekah, a virgin, very fair to look upon, and the granddaughter of Nahor, came out with her water jar upon her shoulder. She went down to the spring and filled her jar. As she came up, the servant ran to meet her, saying, "Pray give me a little water to drink from your jar." Rebekah said, "Drink, my lord," and she quickly let down her jar. Then she said, "I will draw for your camels also," and emptying her jar into the trough, she ran again to the well.

The man gazed at her in silence, and when the camels had done drinking, he took a gold ring and two bracelets for her arms and said, "Tell me whose daughter you are." Rebekah said, "I am the daughter of Bethuel who is the son of Nahor." Bowing his head, the servant said, "Blessed be the LORD, who has not forsaken his steadfast love toward my master, and has led me to the house of my master's kinsmen."

The maiden ran and told her mother's household about these things. When Rebekah's brother, Laban, saw the ring and the bracelets, and heard his sister's words, he went to the man standing by the camels at the spring. "Come in," he said. "Why do you stand outside? I have prepared the house and a place for the camels." So the man came into the house. Laban gave him straw and provender for the camels, and water to wash his feet. Food was set before him, but he said, "I will not eat until I have told my errand. I am Abraham's servant. The LORD has greatly blessed my master, and has given him flocks and herds, silver and gold, menservants and maidservants, camels and asses. Sarah my master's wife bore him a son when she was old; to this son he has given all he has. My master made me swear not to take a wife for his son from the daughters of the Canaanites, but from his kindred." Then the servant told everything that had happened at the well, and said to Rebekah's father and brother, "Now, tell me if you will deal loyally and truly with my master."

"This comes from the LORD," Laban and Bethuel answered. "Behold, Rebekah

is before you. Take her and go, and let her
be the wife of your master's son." When
Abraham's servant heard their words, he
bowed himself to the earth before the
LORD. Then he brought forth jewelry of
silver and gold, and raiment, and gave
them to Rebekah; he also gave costly orna-
ments to her brother and mother. He ate
and drank, and spent the night there.

When they arose in the morning, the
servant said, "Send me back to my master." Rebekah's brother and mother said,
"Let the maiden remain with us a few
days. Then she may go." But he said, "Do
not delay me, since the LORD has prospered my way." So they called Rebekah
and said to her, "Will you go with this
man?" She said, "I will go." Then they
blessed her, and she and her maids arose,
and rode upon the camels, following Abraham's servant.

Now Isaac was dwelling in the Negeb.
One evening when he went out to meditate
in the field, he lifted up his eyes and behold, there were camels coming. When Rebekah saw Isaac, she said to the servant,
"Who is the man yonder, walking in the

field to meet us?" The servant said, "It is my master's son." Rebekah alighted from the camel, took her veil, and covered herself. The servant told Isaac all that he had done; then Isaac brought Rebekah into the tent. She became his wife, and he loved her. So Isaac was comforted after his mother's death.

ABRAHAM BREATHED HIS last and died at the age of a hundred and seventy-five, and was gathered to his people. His sons, Isaac and Ishmael, buried him in the cave of Machpelah with Sarah his wife. After the death of Abraham God blessed Isaac.

Isaac was forty years old when he took to wife Rebekah, and he prayed to the LORD for his wife, because she was barren. The LORD granted his prayer, and Rebekah conceived. Within her, the children struggled together, and she said, "If it is thus, why do I live?" She inquired of the LORD, and the LORD said, "Two nations are in your womb. Two peoples, born of you, shall be divided. One shall be stronger than the other, and the elder shall serve the younger."

When Rebekah's days to be delivered were fulfilled, there were twins in her womb. The first came forth red, all his body hairy; so they called him Esau. Afterward his brother came forth, and his hand had taken hold of Esau's heel; so he was called Jacob (that is, he supplants). When the boys grew up, Esau was a skilful hunter, a man of the field, while Jacob was a quiet man, dwelling in tents. Isaac loved Esau, because he ate of his game; but Rebekah loved Jacob.

Once when Jacob was boiling pottage, Esau came in from the field. "Let me eat some of that," he said, "for I am famished!" But Jacob said, "First sell me your birthright." Esau said, "Here I am about to die. Of what use is a birthright to me?" Jacob said, "Swear to me first." So Esau swore, and sold his birthright to Jacob. Then Jacob gave bread and pottage of lentils to Esau, who ate and drank, and went his way. Thus Esau despised his birthright.

When Esau was forty years old, he took to wife Judith and Basemath, daughters of the Hittites, and Esau's wives made life bitter for Isaac and Rebekah.

ISAAC WAS OLD and his eyes were dim so that he could not see. "I am old," he said to Esau his older son. "I do not know the day of my death. Take your quiver and bow, and go out and hunt game for me. Prepare savory food, such as I love, and bring it to me to eat, that I may bless you before I die." Rebekah was listening, so when Esau went to hunt game, she told Jacob what she had heard. "Therefore, my son," she said, "obey my word. Go to the flock, and fetch me two good kids, that I may prepare savory food for your father. You shall bring it to him to eat, so that he may bless you before he dies." But Jacob said, "My brother Esau is a hairy man, and I am a smooth man. Perhaps my father will feel me. I shall seem to be mocking him, and bring a curse upon myself, not a blessing."

"Upon me be your curse, my son," Rebekah replied. "Go. Fetch the kids to me." So Jacob brought them to his mother, and she prepared savory food, such as his father loved. Then she took the best garments of Esau and put them on Jacob. She put the skins of the kids upon his hands and the smooth part of his neck. Then she gave him the food she had prepared, and Jacob went in to his father. "My father," he said.

"Here I am," said Isaac. "Who are you, my son?" Jacob said, "I am Esau your first-born. I have done as you told me. Sit up and eat of my game, that you may bless me." But Isaac said, "How did you find it so quickly, my son?"

"God granted me success," Jacob answered. "Come near," Isaac said, "that I may feel you, to know whether or not you are really my son Esau." So Jacob went near, and his father felt his hands, which were hairy like his brother Esau's hands. "Are you really Esau?" Isaac asked, and Jacob answered, "I am."

"The voice is Jacob's," Isaac said, "but these are the hands of Esau. Bring the game to me, that I may eat of it and bless you." So Jacob brought the food, and Isaac ate; Jacob brought him wine, and he drank. Then Isaac said, "Come, kiss me, my son." When Jacob came near and kissed him, Isaac smelled his garments, and said, "See, the smell of my son is as the smell of a field which the LORD has blessed!" And Isaac blessed Jacob, saying, "May God give you of the dew of heaven, of the fatness of the earth, and plenty of grain and wine. Let peoples serve you, and nations bow down to you. Cursed be those who curse you, and blessed be those who bless you!"

Jacob had scarcely left Isaac's presence when Esau came in from his hunting. Esau also prepared savory food, and brought it to his father, saying, "Arise and eat of your son's game, that you may bless me." But Isaac said, "Who are you?" Esau answered, "I am your son, your first-born, Esau."

"Who was it then that hunted game and brought it to me?" Isaac asked, trembling. "I ate it all before you came, and I have blessed him—yes, and he shall be blessed." When Esau heard these words, he cried out bitterly, "Bless me, even me also, O my father!" But Isaac said, "Your brother came with guile, and he has taken away your blessing."

"Is he not rightly named Jacob?" Esau said. "For he has twice supplanted me. He has taken away my birthright, and now my blessing. Have you but one blessing, my father? Bless me also." And Esau lifted up his voice and wept. "Away from the fatness of the earth," Isaac answered, "shall your dwelling be, and away from the dew of heaven. By your sword you shall live, and you shall serve your brother; but when you break loose you shall break his yoke from your neck."

Now Esau hated Jacob because his father had blessed him. "The days of mourning for my father are approaching," Esau said to himself. "Then I will kill my brother Jacob." But his words were told to Rebekah, so she called Jacob. "Your brother Esau comforts himself by planning to kill you," she said. "Flee to Laban my brother in Haran. Stay with him until your brother's fury turns away, and he forgets what you have done to him."

Then Rebekah said to Isaac, "I am weary of my life because of the Hittite women. If Jacob marries one of them, what good will my life be to me?" So Isaac called Jacob, and charged him, "You shall not marry a Hittite. Go to Haran to the house of

Bethuel your mother's father, and take as wife one of the daughters of Laban your mother's brother. God Almighty bless you and make you fruitful. May he give the blessing of Abraham to you and your descendants, that you may possess the land God gave to Abraham!"

Thus Isaac sent Jacob away; and Jacob went toward Haran. He came to a certain place, and stayed there that night, because the sun had set. Taking a stone, he put it under his head and lay down to sleep. Jacob dreamed that a ladder was set up on earth; its top reached to heaven, and the angels of God were ascending and descending on it! The LORD stood above it and said, "I am the LORD, the God of Abraham and Isaac. The land on which you lie I will give to you and your descendants, and you shall spread abroad to the west, east, north, and south; by you shall all the families of the earth be blessed. Behold, I am with you and will keep you wherever you go, and bring you back to this land." Jacob awoke and said, "Surely the LORD is in this place, and I did not know it." And he was afraid. "How awesome is this place!" he said. "This is none other than the house of God, and this is the gate of heaven."

Jacob took the stone he had put under his head, set it up for a pillar, and poured oil on the top of it. He called the place Bethel (that is, the house of God), vowing, "If God will be with me and keep me, and give me bread to eat and clothing to wear, so that I come again to my father's house in peace, then the LORD shall be my God. This stone, set up for a pillar, shall be God's house; and of all that thou givest me I will give the tenth to thee."

JACOB JOURNEYED ON to the land of the people of the east. There, in a field, he saw three flocks of sheep lying beside the well where they were watered. The stone on the well's mouth was large, and when all the flocks were gathered there, the shepherds would roll the stone from the mouth of the well, water the sheep, and put the stone back in place. "Where do you come from, my brothers?" Jacob asked the shepherds. When they said, "We are from Haran," Jacob asked, "Do you know Laban?" The shepherds said, "We know him. And see, Rachel his daughter is coming with the sheep which she keeps for her father!"

When Jacob saw Rachel the daughter of his mother's brother, he rolled the stone from the well's mouth, and watered the flock of Laban. Then Jacob kissed Rachel, and wept aloud. He told her that he was her father's kinsman, Rebekah's son, and Rachel ran and told her father. When Laban heard the tidings of his sister's son, he went to Jacob, embraced him, and brought him to his house, saying, "Surely you are my bone and my flesh."

Jacob stayed with Laban a month. Then Laban said, "Because you are my kinsman, should you therefore serve me for nothing? Tell me, what shall your wages be?" Now Laban had two daughters; the older was Leah, and the younger was Rachel. Leah's eyes were weak, but Rachel was beautiful, and Jacob loved her. "I will serve you seven years," he said, "for your younger daughter Rachel." Laban said, "It is better that I give her to you than to any other man. Stay with me." So Jacob served seven years for Rachel, and they seemed to him but a few days because of the love he had for her.

"My time is completed," he then said to Laban. "Give me my wife, that I may go in to her." So Laban made a feast. But in the evening he brought his daughter Leah, covered with her veil, to Jacob; and Jacob went in to her. Next morning, when Jacob saw that it was Leah, he said to Laban, "What is this you have done to me? Did I not serve with you for Rachel? Why then have you deceived me?"

"It is not so done in our country," said Laban, "to give the younger daughter before the first-born. Complete the marriage week of this one, and we will give you the other also in return for serving me another seven years." Jacob did so, completing Leah's week. Then Laban gave him Rachel to wife, so Jacob served Laban for another seven years. And he loved Rachel more than Leah.

When the LORD saw that Leah was hated, he opened her womb, but Rachel was barren. Leah conceived and bore four sons: first Reuben, then Simeon, then Levi, and then Judah; then she ceased bearing. But Rachel bore Jacob no children. She envied her sister, and said to Jacob, "Give me children, or I shall die!" This kindled Jacob's anger against Rachel. "Am I in the place of God," he said, "who has withheld from you the fruit of the womb?"

"Here is my maid Bilhah," said Rachel. "Go in to her, that I may have children through her." So Jacob went in to Bilhah, and she conceived and bore Jacob a son. "God has heard my voice," said Rachel, "and given me a son." She called his name Dan. Rachel's maid Bilhah conceived again and bore Jacob a second son; Rachel called him Naphtali.

When Leah saw that she had ceased bearing children, she gave her maid Zilpah to Jacob as a wife. Zilpah bore Jacob a son, and Leah named him Gad. Zilpah bore Jacob a second son, and Leah named him Asher. Then God hearkened to Leah, and she conceived again. She bore Jacob a fifth son, Issachar, and a sixth son, Zebulun. "Now my husband will honor me," Leah said, "because I have borne him six sons." Afterwards she bore a daughter, and called her name Dinah.

Then God remembered Rachel, and opened her womb. Rachel conceived and bore a son, and she called his name Joseph, saying, "May the LORD add to me another son!"

AFTER RACHEL HAD borne Joseph, Jacob said to Laban, "Give me my wives and children for whom I have served you, and let me go to my own home and country." But Laban said, "The LORD has blessed me because of you. Name your wages, and I will give it."

"You know how I have served you, and how your cattle have fared," said Jacob. "For you had little before I came, and it has increased abundantly. The LORD has blessed you wherever I turned. Now when shall I provide for my own household also?" But Jacob saw that Laban did not regard him with favor as before. Then the LORD said to Jacob, "Return to the land of your fathers and to your kindred, and I will be with you." So Jacob arose, set his sons and his wives on camels, and fled with all he had, to go to the land of Canaan to his father Isaac. Laban had gone to shear his sheep, and Jacob did not tell him that he intended to flee. Crossing the Euphrates, Jacob set his face toward the hill country of Gilead.

When Laban heard that Jacob had fled, he pursued him for seven days. But God came to Laban in a dream by night, and said, "Take heed that you say not a word to Jacob, either good or bad." Laban overtook Jacob in the hill country where Jacob had pitched his tent. "Why have you cheated me," he said, "and carried away my daughters like captives of the sword? Why did you not permit me to kiss them farewell?" Jacob answered, "Because I was afraid, for I thought you would take your daughters from me by force." Laban replied, "The daughters are my daughters, the children are my children, the flocks are my flocks, and all that you see is mine. But what can I do this day to these my daughters, or to their children? Come now, let us make a covenant, you and I. The LORD watch between you and me, when we are absent one from the other. If you ill-treat my daughters, or if you take wives besides my daughters, although no man is with us, remember, God is witness between you and me." Jacob offered a sacrifice on the mountain, and they ate bread and tarried there all night. Early in the morning Laban arose, kissed his grandchildren and his daughters, and blessed them. Then he departed and returned home.

Jacob went on his way and sent messengers before him to Esau his brother in the land of Seir, the country of Edom, instructing them to tell Esau that Jacob sought favor in his sight. The messengers returned, saying that Esau was coming with four hundred men. Jacob, greatly afraid, prayed to the LORD, saying, "Deliver me from the hand of my brother Esau, for I fear him, lest he come and slay us all, the mothers with the children. I am not worthy of thy steadfast love, but thou didst say, 'Return to your country and your kindred, and I will do you good.' "

That night Jacob took a present for Esau: droves of goats, ewes, rams, camels, cows, bulls, and asses. These he delivered into the hands of his servants, and said, "Pass on before me, and when Esau my brother meets you, you shall say, 'These are a present sent by your servant Jacob to my lord Esau.' " For Jacob thought, "I may appease Esau with the present, and afterwards, when I see his face, perhaps he will accept me." So the present passed on before him. The same night Jacob sent his two wives, his two maids, his eleven children, and everything he had across the ford of the river Jabbok. He was left alone in the camp. A man wrestled with him until the breaking of the day, but he did not prevail against Jacob. Then the man touched the hollow of Jacob's thigh, and it was put out of joint. "Let me go," he said to Jacob, "for the day is breaking." But Jacob said, "I will not let you go, unless you bless me."

"What is your name?" the man asked, and when Jacob told him, he said, "Your name shall no more be called Jacob, but Israel, for you have striven with God and with men, and have prevailed." Jacob asked him, "Tell me, I pray, your name." But the man said, "Why is it you ask my name?" And there he blessed Jacob. So Jacob called the name of the place Peniel, saying, "I have seen God face to face, and yet my life is preserved."

The sun rose upon Jacob as he passed
on, limping because of his thigh. Then he
lifted up his eyes and saw Esau coming
with four hundred men. So he divided the
children among Leah and Rachel and the
two maids, putting Rachel and Joseph last
of all. He himself went on before them,
bowing himself to the ground as he came
near to his brother. But Esau ran to meet
him, and embraced him, and kissed him,
and they wept.

"Who are these with you?" Esau asked,
and Jacob said, "The children whom God
has graciously given me." Then Esau asked,
"And what did you mean by all this company I met?" Jacob answered, "To find
favor in the sight of my lord." But Esau
said, "I have enough, my brother; keep
what you have for yourself." Jacob said,
"No, I pray you accept my present, for truly
to see your face is like seeing the face of
God, with such favor have you received
me. My gift is brought to you, because God
has dealt graciously with me, and because I
have enough." So Esau took it, and returned that day to Edom. But God said to
Jacob, "Go to Bethel, and make there an

altar to the God who appeared to you when you fled from your brother Esau." So Jacob and all the people with him went to Bethel, and there he built an altar.

They journeyed on, and when they were still some distance from Ephrath (that is, Bethlehem), Rachel travailed, and she had hard labor. "Fear not," the midwife said, "for now you will have another son." As her soul was departing (for she died), Rachel named the boy Ben-oni, but his father called him Benjamin. So Rachel died, and was buried, and Jacob set up a pillar upon her grave, the pillar of Rachel's tomb. And now the sons of Jacob were twelve.

Israel journeyed on, and came to his father Isaac at Mamre, where Abraham and Isaac had sojourned. Now the days of Isaac were a hundred and eighty years when he died and was gathered to his people. His sons Esau and Jacob buried him. Then Esau returned to the hill country of Edom, and Jacob dwelt in the land of his father's sojournings, in Canaan.

THIS IS THE history of the family of Jacob.

Joseph, being seventeen years old, was

shepherding the flock with his brothers, and he brought an ill report of them to their father. Now Israel loved Joseph, the son of his old age, more than his other children, and he made him a long robe with sleeves. Because of this, Joseph's brothers hated him, and could not speak to him peaceably. When Joseph told his brothers of a dream he had, they only hated him the more. "I dreamed we were binding sheaves in the field," he said. "My sheaf arose and stood upright; and your sheaves gathered round it, and bowed down to my sheaf." His brothers said, "Are you indeed to have dominion over us?" Joseph dreamed another dream, and told it to his father and his brothers, saying, "The sun, the moon, and eleven stars were bowing down to me." His brothers were jealous, and his father rebuked him. "What is this dream? Shall we indeed come to bow before you?" But his father kept the saying in mind.

One day Israel sent Joseph to Shechem, where his brothers had gone to pasture their father's flock. "Go see if it is well with your brothers and the flock," he told

Joseph, "and bring me word." When Joseph came to Shechem, a man found him wandering in the fields, and asked, "What are you seeking?" Joseph said, "I am seeking my brothers, who are pasturing the flock." The man said, "They have gone away. I heard them say, 'Let us go to Dothan.'" So Joseph went after his brothers and found them at Dothan.

They saw him afar off, and conspired against him. "Here comes this dreamer," they said to one another. "Let us kill him and throw him into one of the water pits, and say that a wild beast has devoured him. Then we shall see what will become of his dreams." But Reuben, hoping to rescue Joseph, said, "Do not take his life. Shed no blood. Cast him into this empty pit here in the wilderness, but lay no hand upon him." So when Joseph came to his brothers, they stripped him of his long robe, and they cast him into the empty pit.

As the brothers sat down to eat, they saw a caravan of Ishmaelites approaching, their camels bearing gum, balm, and myrrh. "Let us sell our brother to the Ishmaelites," Judah said, "and let not our hand be upon him." His brothers heeded him, and when the caravan passed by, they drew Joseph up out of the pit, and sold him to the Ishmaelites for twenty shekels of silver. Then the brothers killed a goat, and dipped Joseph's robe in the blood, and brought the robe to their father, saying, "This we have found. Is it your son's robe?" Jacob recognized it, and said, "It is my son's. A wild beast has devoured him; Joseph is without doubt torn to pieces." Jacob rent his garments, and put sackcloth upon his loins, and mourned for his son many days. All Jacob's sons and daughters rose up to comfort him; but he refused to be comforted.

JOSEPH WAS TAKEN down to Egypt, where Potiphar, the captain of Pharaoh's guard, bought him from the Ishmaelites. The LORD was with Joseph, and he became a successful man in the house of his Egyptian master. Potiphar saw that the LORD caused all that Joseph did to prosper, so he made him his overseer, putting him in charge of all that he had.

Joseph was handsome, and after a time his master's wife cast her eyes upon him. "Lie with me," she said. But Joseph refused, saying, "My master has put everything that he has in my hand except yourself, because you are his wife. How then can I do this great wickedness, and sin against God?" Although she spoke to Joseph day after day, he would not lie with her. Then one day, when he came into the house to do his work, she caught him by his garment, saying, "Lie with me." But Joseph fled out of the house, leaving his garment in her hand. She called to the men of her household. "See how this Hebrew insults us," she said. "He came in to lie with me, and when I cried out, he left his garment and fled." When her husband came home, she told him the same story, and his anger was kindled. He took Joseph and put him into prison. But the LORD was with Joseph, showing him steadfast love, and giving him favor in the sight of the keeper of the prison, who committed to Joseph's care all the other prisoners. Whatever Joseph did, the LORD made it prosper.

Some time after this, Pharaoh was angry

with his chief butler and chief baker, and he put them in the prison where Joseph was confined. They were placed in Joseph's care, and continued for some time in custody. One night the butler and the baker both dreamed—each his own dream with its own meaning. When Joseph came to them in the morning, he saw that they were troubled. "Why are your faces downcast today?" he asked. "We have had dreams," they said, "and there is no one to interpret them." Joseph said, "Do not interpretations belong to God? Tell them to me, I pray you."

"In my dream," said the butler, "there was a vine with three branches. It budded, blossomed, and the clusters ripened into grapes. Pharaoh's cup was in my hand. I took the grapes, pressed them into the cup, and placed it in Pharaoh's hand." Joseph said, "This is its interpretation: the three branches are three days. Within three days Pharaoh will restore you to your office, and you shall place Pharaoh's cup in his hand as formerly. Remember me then, I pray you. Mention me to Pharaoh. For I was stolen out of the land of the Hebrews, and I have done nothing that they should put me into the dungeon." When the baker saw that the interpretation was favorable, he said to Joseph, "I also had a dream: there were three cake baskets on my head. In the uppermost basket was food baked for Pharaoh, but the birds were eating it." Joseph answered, "This is its interpretation: the three baskets are three days. Within three days Pharaoh will lift up your head—from you!—and hang you on a tree; and the birds will eat the flesh from you." On the third day, which was Pharaoh's birthday, he made a feast for all his servants. He restored the chief butler to his butlership; but he hanged the chief baker, as Joseph had interpreted. Yet the chief butler did not remember Joseph.

Two YEARS LATER, Pharaoh dreamed one night he was standing by the Nile, and seven cows, sleek and fat, came up out of the Nile to feed in the reed grass. Seven other cows, gaunt and thin, came up after them, and ate up the seven fat cows. Pharaoh awoke, but he fell asleep and dreamed a second time: seven ears of grain, plump and good, were growing on one stalk, and after them sprouted seven ears, thin and blighted. The thin ears swallowed up the plump ears. In the morning his spirit was troubled, so he sent for all of Egypt's wise men, and told them his dream. None could interpret it. Then the chief butler said, "I remember my faults today. When Pharaoh was angry with his servants, and put me and the chief baker in custody, we dreamed on the same night, each having a different dream. A young Hebrew was with us, and he interpreted our dreams, and as he interpreted, so it came to pass; I was restored to my office, and the baker was hanged."

Pharaoh sent for Joseph, and they brought him hastily out of the dungeon. When he had shaved himself and changed clothes, he came in before Pharaoh, who said, "I have heard that you can interpret dreams." Joseph answered, "It is not in me; God will give Pharaoh a favorable answer." So Pharaoh told Joseph his dream of the seven thin cows that ate the seven fat cows. "But when they had eaten them," Pharaoh said, "they were still as gaunt as at the beginning." He then told his dream of the seven good ears of grain and the seven blighted ears. "There is no one," Pharaoh said, "who can explain this to me."

"The dreams are one," Joseph said. "The seven good cows and seven good ears are seven years. The seven lean cows and seven blighted ears are also seven years. God has shown Pharaoh what he is about to do. There will come seven years of great plenty throughout Egypt, but after them will come seven years of famine, and the famine will consume the land. The doubling of Pharaoh's dream means that the thing is fixed by God, and will shortly come to pass. Therefore, let Pharaoh select a man discreet and wise, and set him over the land of Egypt. Let Pharaoh appoint overseers to lay up a fifth of the produce of the land of Egypt during the seven plenteous years that are coming. Let it be a reserve against the seven years of famine, so that the land may not perish."

This proposal seemed good to Pharaoh and to all his servants. "Can we find such a man as this," he asked, "in whom is the

Spirit of God?" Then he said to Joseph, "Since God has shown you all this, there is none so discreet and wise as you. I shall set you over all the land of Egypt, and my people shall do as you command." He took his signet ring from his hand and put it on Joseph's hand. He arrayed Joseph in garments of fine linen, put a gold chain about his neck, and made him ride in his second chariot. Moreover, he gave to Joseph in marriage Asenath, the daughter of Potiphera, priest of On.

When Joseph entered the service of Pharaoh, he was thirty years old. During the seven plenteous years, he went through all of Egypt gathering and storing up grain in great abundance until, like the sand of the sea, it could not be measured. Before the years of famine came, Asenath bore Joseph two sons. The first-born he named Manasseh, and the second son he called Ephraim. After the seven years of plenty, the seven years of famine began to come. When all the land of Egypt was famished, the people cried to Pharaoh for bread, and Pharaoh said, "Go to Joseph." So Joseph opened all the storehouses, and sold to the Egyptians.

Moreover, all the earth came to Egypt to buy grain, because the famine was severe everywhere.

WHEN JACOB LEARNED that there was grain in Egypt, he said to his sons, "Go down to Egypt and buy grain for us, that we may not die." So ten of Joseph's brothers, the sons of Israel, went down to buy grain in Egypt. But Jacob did not send Joseph's brother Benjamin, for he feared that harm might befall him.

Now Joseph was governor over the land. When his brothers came and bowed themselves before him, they did not know him, but Joseph knew them, and remembered the dreams he had dreamed of them. Yet he treated them like strangers and spoke roughly to them. "Where do you come from?" he said. They replied, "From the land of Canaan, to buy food." Joseph said, "You are spies. You have come to see the weakness of the land." But they said, "No, my lord, your servants come to buy food. We are all honest men, not spies. We are twelve brothers, the sons of one man in the land of Canaan. The youngest is this day with our father, and one is no more."

"Surely you are spies," said Joseph, "but by this shall your words be tested: if you are honest men, let one of your brothers remain here, confined in prison. Let the rest carry grain to your households. Then bring your youngest brother to me, so your words will be verified." And Joseph took Simeon from his other brothers and bound him before their eyes.

"Now comes a reckoning for Joseph's blood," the brothers said to one another, "for in truth we are guilty concerning him, in that we saw the distress of his soul when he besought us and we would not listen." They did not know that Joseph understood them, for there was an interpreter between them. And Joseph turned away from them and wept. Then he gave orders to fill their bags with grain, and to give them provisions for the journey. This was done, and the brothers departed. When they came to the land of Canaan, they told their father all that had befallen them. "You have bereaved me of my children," Jacob said. "Joseph is no more. Simeon is no more. Now you would take Benjamin.

Why did you tell the man you had another brother?"

"The man, the lord of the land, took us to be spies and spoke roughly to us," they replied. "He questioned us carefully about ourselves and our kindred, and we answered. Could we know he would say, 'Bring your brother down'?"

"Benjamin shall not go with you," said Jacob, "for his brother is dead, and he only is left. If harm should befall him, you would bring down my gray hairs with sorrow to the grave."

But the famine continued. When they had eaten the grain brought from Egypt, Jacob said to his sons, "Go again. Buy us a little food." But Judah said to him, "The man who is lord of the land solemnly warned us, saying, 'Bring your youngest brother. Then I shall know you are not spies, and will deliver your other brother to you.' If you will not send Benjamin, we will not go. But if you send the lad with me, I will be surety for him. If I do not bring him back to you, then let me bear the blame for ever."

"If it must be so," said Jacob, "do this:

carry a present down to the man, a little balm, a little honey, gum, myrrh, pistachio nuts, and almonds. Take also your brother Benjamin, and may God Almighty grant you mercy before the man, that he may send back your other brother, Simeon, and Benjamin. If I am bereaved of my children, I am bereaved."

So they took the present and Benjamin, and went down to Egypt. When Joseph saw Benjamin with them, he said to his steward, "Bring the men to my house, for they are to dine with me at noon." The steward did as he was bidden but the brothers were afraid. "We are brought here," they said, "so that he may make slaves of us." But the steward said, "Do not be afraid." Then he brought Simeon to them, and gave them water to wash their feet, and provender for their asses.

When Joseph came home, they gave him the present they had brought, and bowed down to him. "Is your father well," Joseph inquired, "the old man of whom you spoke?" They said, "Our father is well." And they bowed their heads and made obeisance. Then Joseph saw his brother

Benjamin, and his heart yearned for him. "Is this your youngest brother?" he asked. "God be gracious to you, my son!" And he made haste to enter his chamber, and wept there. Then he washed his face and came out. Controlling himself he said, "Let food be served." His brothers sat before him, the first-born according to his birthright and the youngest according to his youth. They looked at one another in amazement, and they drank and were merry with him.

Then Joseph commanded the steward of his house, "Fill the men's sacks with food, as much as they can carry, and put my cup, the silver cup, in the sack of the youngest." The steward did so, and as soon as the morning was light, the men were sent away with their asses. When they had gone but a short distance from the city, Joseph said to his steward, "Overtake the men, and say to them, 'Why have you returned evil for good? Why have you stolen the silver cup from which my lord drinks and by which he divines?' " When the steward overtook the brothers and spoke these words, they said, "Far be it from your servants to do such a thing! If it be found with one of us, let him die, and we also will be my lord's slaves." Then every man quickly lowered his sack to the ground, and opened it. The steward searched, beginning with the eldest and ending with the youngest, and the cup was found in Benjamin's sack. The brothers rent their clothes, and returned to Joseph's house, falling to the ground before him. "What deed is this you have done?" Joseph said. "Do you not know that such a man as I can indeed divine?" Judah said, "What shall we say? How can we clear ourselves? God has found out the guilt of your servants; behold, we are my lord's slaves, both we and he also in whose hand the cup has been found." But Joseph said, "Only that man shall be my slave. As for you, go in peace to your father."

Then Judah went up to Joseph and said, "O my lord, let your servant speak, and let not your anger burn against me. When our father said, 'Go again, buy us a little food,' we said, 'We cannot go unless our youngest brother is with us.' My father said, 'You know that my wife bore me two sons; one left me, and he has surely been torn to pieces. I have never seen him since. If you take this one also from me, and harm befalls him, you will bring down my gray hairs in sorrow to the grave.' Then I became surety for the lad to my father. Therefore, let me, I pray you, remain instead of the lad as a slave to my lord. How can I go back if the lad is not with me? I fear to see the evil that would come upon my father." Joseph could not control himself before all those who stood by him. He sent out all but his brothers, and he wept aloud as he made himself known. "I am your brother, Joseph, whom you sold into Egypt," he said. But they could not answer him, for they were dismayed.

"Now do not be distressed," Joseph said, "or angry with yourselves because you sold me. God sent me before you to preserve life in these years of famine, and to keep alive for you a remnant of survivors on earth. It was not you who sent me here, but God; and he has made me lord of Pharaoh's house and ruler over all the land. Go and bring my father to me. Do not tarry. You shall dwell near me in the land of Goshen, you and your children and your children's children, your flocks, and your herds. There I will provide for you, for there are yet five years of famine to come." Then he fell upon Benjamin's neck, and he kissed all his brothers and wept.

When Pharaoh heard that Joseph's brothers had come, he was pleased. "Say to your brothers," he told Joseph, "that the best of all the land of Egypt is theirs." So Joseph gave his brothers grain and provisions, and wagons for their wives and little ones and for his father on the journey. Then he sent them away, saying, "Do not quarrel on the way." When they came to the land of Canaan, they told their father that Joseph was still alive, and was ruler over all the land of Egypt. And Jacob's heart fainted, for he did not believe them. But when he saw the wagons which Joseph had sent to carry him, his spirit revived. "Joseph my son is alive," he said. "I will go and see him before I die."

So the sons of Israel carried their father, their little ones, and their wives in the wagons. They took their cattle and their goods, and came into Egypt. All the persons of the house of Jacob were seventy. Then Jacob sent Judah to Joseph, and Joseph made ready his chariot and went up and presented himself to his father in the land of Goshen. "Now let me die," said Jacob, "since I have seen your face and know that you are still alive." Joseph brought his father to Pharaoh, and Jacob blessed Pharaoh. And Joseph settled his father and his brothers, and gave them a possession in the land of Egypt, in the best of the land, as Pharaoh had commanded.

JACOB DWELT IN Egypt, in the land of Goshen, for seventeen years. When the days of his life were a hundred and forty-seven years, the time drew near that he must die. So Joseph, told that his father was ill, took his two sons, Manasseh and Ephraim, and went to him. Summoning his strength, Jacob sat up in bed. "God Almighty appeared to me," he said, "at Bethel in the land of Canaan. He blessed me and said he would give that land to my descendants for an everlasting possession. Now your two sons, Ephraim and Manasseh, shall be mine, as Reuben and Simeon are. The offspring born to you after them shall be yours, but shall be called by the name of their brothers in their inheritance."

Then Jacob called all his sons. "Gather yourselves together," he said, "that I may tell you what shall befall you in days to come. Assemble and hearken to Israel your father. Reuben, you are my first-born. Pre-eminent in pride and power, you are unstable as water. You shall not have pre-eminence. Simeon and Levi are brothers; weapons of violence are their swords. Cursed be their anger, for it is fierce; and their wrath, for it is cruel! I will divide them in Jacob and scatter them in Israel. Judah, your brothers shall praise you; your hand shall be on the neck of your enemies. Judah is a lion's whelp; from the prey, my son, you have gone up. He stooped down, he couched as a lion; who dares rouse him up? The scepter shall not depart from Judah, until he comes to whom it belongs; and to him shall be the obedience of the peoples.

"Zebulun shall dwell at the shore of the

sea, a haven for ships, and his border shall be at Sidon. Issachar is a strong ass, crouching between the sheepfolds. He saw that a resting place was good, the land pleasant, so he bowed his shoulder and became a slave at forced labor. Dan shall judge his people as one of the tribes of Israel. He shall be a serpent in the path, that bites the horse's heels so that the rider falls backward. Raiders shall raid Gad, but he shall raid at their heels. Asher's food shall be rich, and he shall yield royal dainties. Naphtali is a hind let loose, that bears comely fawns.

"Joseph is a fruitful bough by a spring; his branches run over the wall. The archers fiercely attacked him, yet his bow remained unmoved. His arms were made agile by the Mighty One of Jacob (by the name of the Shepherd, the Rock of Israel), the God of your father who will help you, and bless you with blessings of heaven above. Benjamin is a ravenous wolf, in the morning devouring the prey, and at even dividing the spoil."

All these are the twelve tribes of Israel, and thus their father Jacob blessed them.

Then he said to his sons, "I am to be gathered to my people. When I came from Haran, Rachel to my sorrow died in the land of Canaan when there was still some distance to go; and I buried her there on the way to Ephrath. But bury me with my fathers in the cave that is in the field at Machpelah, to the east of Mamre, in the land of Canaan. There they buried Abraham and Sarah; there they buried Isaac and Rebekah; and there I buried Leah." When he had finished, Jacob drew up his feet into the bed, and breathed his last. Joseph fell on his father's face and wept over him, and kissed him. Then he commanded the physicians to embalm his father. Forty days were required for it, and the Egyptians wept for Jacob seventy days.

When the days of weeping were past, Joseph spoke to Pharaoh. "If now I have found favor in your eyes," he said, "let me go up to the land of Canaan and bury my father; then I will return." Pharaoh agreed. So with all the servants of Pharaoh, all the elders of Egypt, and all his own household, Joseph went up to Canaan. There were chariots and horsemen; it was a very great company. When the Canaanites saw this, they said, "This is a grievous mourning to the Egyptians." Thus Jacob's sons did for him as he had commanded, and buried him in the cave of the field at Machpelah. Then Joseph returned to Egypt with his brothers and all who had gone up with him.

Joseph's brothers, knowing that their father was dead, said, "It may be that Joseph will hate us and pay us back for all the evil we did to him." They sent a message to Joseph, praying for his forgiveness, and they came and fell down before him, saying, "Behold, we are your servants." But Joseph said to them, "Fear not, for am I in the place of God? You meant evil against me; but God meant it for good, that many people should be kept alive, as they are today. Do not fear; I will provide for you and your little ones." Thus he reassured and comforted them.

So Joseph dwelt in Egypt. He saw Ephraim's children of the third generation, and children of the son of Manasseh were born upon his knees. And Joseph said to his brothers, "I am about to die; but God will visit you, and bring you up out of this land to the land which he swore to Abraham, to Isaac, and to Jacob." Then Joseph took an oath of the sons of Israel, saying, "God will visit you, and you shall carry up my bones from here." So Joseph died, being a hundred and ten years old; and they embalmed him, and he was put in a coffin in Egypt.

EXODUS

At the book's opening, several hundred years have passed since the close of Genesis, and the Israelites in Egypt are suffering as slaves under an oppressive new regime. First recounted is the story of Moses: his birth, his divine commission to free his fellow slaves, the ten plagues called down upon Egypt, the institution of Passover, and the miraculous escape of the Israelites through the Red Sea. The date of this "exodus" from Egypt has been calculated as between 1580 B.C. and 1215 B.C., with present opinion favoring the mid-thirteenth century B.C.

The narrative continues with the establishment, at Mount Sinai, of the covenant between God and his people. It is at the summit of this mountain, against the backdrop of a majestic theophany, that Moses receives the Ten Commandments from God.

Elsewhere in the Old Testament this deliverance of the Israelites from bondage is celebrated as the outstanding instance of God's love for his chosen people. It also plays a part in the New Testament, where the imagery of the Passover is applied to the sacrifice of Christ on Calvary. As with Genesis, several strands of literary tradition, some very ancient, some as late as the sixth century B.C., were combined in the makeup of the book.

––––––––

JOSEPH DIED, AND all his brothers, and all that generation, but the descendants of Jacob were fruitful and increased greatly in Egypt for four hundred years; they multiplied and grew exceedingly strong, so that the land was filled with them. Now there arose a new king over Egypt, who did not know Joseph, and to his people he said, "The people of Israel are too many and too mighty for us. Come, let us deal shrewdly with them, lest, if war befall us, they join our enemies, fight against us, and escape from the land." So the Egyptians set task-masters over the people of Israel to afflict them with heavy burdens, and make their lives bitter with hard service in mortar and brick, and work in the field, building for Pharaoh the store-cities of Pithom and Rameses. But the more the people of Israel were oppressed, the more they multiplied and spread abroad. And the Egyptians were in dread of them.

Then Pharaoh said to the Hebrew mid-wives, Shiphrah and Puah, "When you serve the Hebrew women, and see them upon the birthstool, if it is a son, you shall kill him; but if it is a daughter, she shall live." But the midwives feared God, and did not do as Pharaoh commanded. He then called them and said, "Why have you let the male children live?" The midwives said, "Because the Hebrew women are not like Egyptian women; they are vigorous and are delivered before the midwife comes to them." So God dealt well with the midwives, giving them families. And the people of Israel multiplied and grew so strong that Pharaoh then commanded all his people, "Every son born to the Hebrews shall be cast into the Nile, but let every daughter live."

Now Amram, a man from the house of Levi, had taken to wife Jochebed, a daughter of Levi, who conceived and bore a son. She saw that he was a goodly child, and hid him three months. Then, when she could hide him no longer, she took a basket made of bulrushes, daubed it with bitumen and pitch, put the child in it, and placed it among the reeds at the river's brink. The child's sister stood at a distance to see what would happen.

Soon the daughter of Pharaoh came down to bathe at the river. She saw the basket among the reeds, sent her maid to fetch it, opened it, and saw the child. The babe was crying, and she took pity on him. "This is one of the Hebrews' children," she said. Then his sister approached, saying, "Shall I go call a nurse from the Hebrew women to nurse the child for you?" Pharaoh's daughter said, "Go." So the girl called the child's mother. "Take this child away, and nurse him for me," Pharaoh's daughter told the mother, "and I will give you wages." The woman took the child, nursed him, and he grew; and then she brought him back. Thus the child became the son of Pharaoh's daughter; and she named him Moses.

ONE DAY, WHEN Moses was grown, he went out to his people, looked on their burdens, and saw an Egyptian beating a Hebrew. Moses looked around, and seeing no one near, he killed the Egyptian and hid him in the sand. Next day he went out again and saw two Hebrews struggling together. "Why do you strike your fellow?" Moses asked the man that did wrong. "Who made you a judge over us?" the man answered. "Do you mean to kill me as you killed the Egyptian?" Then Moses was afraid. "Surely the thing is known," he thought. And when Pharaoh heard of it, he sought to kill Moses.

But Moses fled from Pharaoh to the land of Midian. There he sat down by a well, and soon the seven daughters of Jethro, the priest of Midian, came and drew water for their father's flock. Shepherds came then, and drove the girls away; but Moses stood up and helped them, and watered their flock. When they returned to their father, he said, "How did you finish so soon to-day?" They replied, "An Egyptian delivered us from the shepherds, and even drew water for us and watered the flock." Jethro said, "Where is this man? Call him, that he may eat bread." And Moses stayed there, content to dwell with them. Jethro gave Moses his daughter Zipporah in marriage, and she bore him two sons. The first he named Gershom, that is, Sojourner, for he said, "I have been a sojourner in a foreign land," and the second Eliezer, "My God, my help."

IN THE COURSE of time the king of Egypt died, but the people of Israel still groaned under their bondage, and cried out for help. And God heard, and he remembered his covenant with Abraham, with Isaac, and with Jacob. Now Moses was keeping the flock of his father-in-law. He led it to the west side of the wilderness and came to Sinai, the mountain of God. There the angel of the LORD appeared to him in a flame of fire out of the midst of a bush. When Moses saw that the bush was burning yet was not consumed, he said, "I will turn aside and see this great sight." God called to him out of the bush, saying, "Moses, Moses!" Moses said, "Here am I." God said, "Do not come near; put off your shoes, for you are standing on holy ground. I am the God of your father, the God of Abraham, Isaac, and Jacob." And Moses hid his face, afraid to look at God.

Then the LORD said, "I have seen the affliction of my people in Egypt, and have heard their cry. I know their sufferings, and I have come down to deliver them out of that land to a good and broad land, flowing with milk and honey, to the place of the Canaanites. Come, I will send you to Pharaoh that you may bring forth my people, the sons of Israel, out of Egypt." But Moses said, "Who am I that I should go to Pharaoh?" Then God said, "I will be with you; and this shall be the sign for you, that I have sent you: when you have brought the people out of Egypt, you shall serve God upon this mountain."

Moses said, "If I say to the people of

Israel, 'The God of your fathers has sent me,' and they ask, 'What is his name?' what shall I say to them?" God said, "I AM WHO I AM. Say this to the people of Israel, 'I AM has sent me to you.' This is my name for ever, and thus I am to be remembered throughout all generations. Say to the elders of Israel, 'The LORD, the God of your fathers, the God of Abraham, Isaac, and Jacob, has appeared to me, and promised to bring you up out of the affliction of Egypt, to the land of Canaan, a land flowing with milk and honey.' You and the elders shall go to Pharaoh and say, 'The LORD, the God of the Hebrews, has met with us; and now, we pray you, let us go a three days' journey into the wilderness, that we may sacrifice to the LORD our God.' "

"But the people will not believe me," Moses said. The LORD said to him, "Cast your rod on the ground." Moses did so, and the rod became a serpent; and Moses fled from it. But the LORD said, "Put out your hand, and take it by the tail." Moses did so, and the serpent became a rod in his hand. And God said, "If they will not believe that the LORD, the God of their fathers, has appeared to you, they may believe signs, and then they will heed your voice."

But Moses said, "Oh, my Lord, I am not eloquent. I am slow of speech and tongue." The LORD replied, "Who has made man's mouth? Who makes him dumb, or deaf, or seeing, or blind? Is it not I, the LORD? Now go. I will teach you what you shall speak." Moses said, "Oh, my Lord, send, I pray, some other person." Then the anger of the LORD was kindled against Moses and he said, "Aaron, your brother, can speak well; he is coming out to meet you, and when he sees you, he will be glad. You shall speak to him and put the words in his mouth. I will be with you and teach you. He shall speak for you to the people; he shall be a mouth for you, and you shall be to him as God. Take in your hand this rod, with which you shall do before Pharaoh all the miracles I have put in your power."

So Moses went to Jethro his father-in-law. "Let me go back to my kinsmen in Egypt," he said, "and see whether they are still alive." And Jethro said, "Go in peace." And the LORD said to Moses, "Go back to Egypt, for all the men who were seeking your life are dead." So Moses took his wife and his sons and set them on an ass, and went back to the land of Egypt; in his hand Moses took the rod of God.

THEN THE LORD said to Aaron, "Go into the wilderness to meet Moses." So Aaron went, and met him at the mountain of God, and kissed him; and Moses told Aaron all that the LORD had charged him to do. Then they gathered together all the elders of the people of Israel, and Aaron spoke the words which the LORD had spoken to Moses, and did the signs, and the people believed. When they heard that the LORD had visited the people of Israel and had seen their affliction, they bowed their heads and worshiped.

Afterward Moses and Aaron went to Pharaoh and said, "The LORD, the God of Israel, has met with us and says, 'Let my people go that they may hold a feast to me in the wilderness.'" But Pharaoh said, "Who is the LORD, that I should heed his voice? I do not know the LORD, and I will not let Israel go." They said, "Let us go, we pray, a three days' journey into the wilderness, and sacrifice to the LORD our God, lest he fall upon us with pestilence or sword." Pharaoh said, "Moses and Aaron, why do you take the people away from their work? Get to your burdens." The same day Pharaoh commanded his task-masters and their foremen, "You shall no longer give the people of Israel straw to make bricks. Let them gather straw for themselves. But do not lessen the daily number of bricks which they must make. For they are idle; therefore they cry, 'Let us go and offer sacrifice to our God.' Let heavier work be laid upon them."

The taskmasters and foremen told the people of Pharaoh's words, and the people were scattered throughout the land to gather straw. "Complete your work, your daily task," the taskmasters urged. And the foremen, whom Pharaoh's taskmasters had set over the people of Israel, were beaten, and were asked, "Why have you not done all your task of making bricks today, as hitherto?" The foremen, seeing they were

in evil plight, went to Moses and Aaron
and said, "The LORD look upon you and
judge. You have made us offensive to
Pharaoh and his servants, and have put a
sword in their hands to kill us."

"O LORD," Moses prayed, "why didst
thou ever send me? For since I came to
Pharaoh to speak in thy name, he has done
evil to thy people, and thou hast not delivered them at all." The LORD replied, "Now
you shall see what I will do to Pharaoh; for
with a strong hand he will send them out;
he will drive them out of his land. I am the
LORD; tell Pharaoh all that I say to you.
But I will harden Pharaoh's heart, and
though I multiply my signs and wonders,
Pharaoh will not listen to you; then I will
lay my hand upon Egypt and bring forth
my people, the sons of Israel, out of Egypt
by great acts of judgment. For the Egyptians shall know that I am the LORD. When
Pharaoh says to you, 'Prove yourselves by
working a miracle,' then you shall say to
Aaron, 'Cast your rod down before Pharaoh, that it may become a serpent.' "

So Moses and Aaron went to Pharaoh
and did as the LORD commanded. But

when Aaron cast down his rod before Pharaoh and it became a serpent, Pharaoh summoned the wise men and sorcerers of Egypt, and they did the same by their secret arts. Every man cast down his rod, and the rods became serpents. Then Aaron's rod swallowed up their rods. Still Pharaoh's heart was hardened, as the LORD had said, and he would not listen to them.

Then the LORD said to Moses, "Go to Pharaoh in the morning, as he is going out to the water; wait for him by the river's brink, and say to him, 'The LORD, the God of the Hebrews, sent me to you, saying, "Let my people go and serve me in the wilderness." You have not obeyed. Now the LORD says, "By this you shall know that I am the LORD: the water in the Nile shall be turned to blood; the fish in the Nile shall die, and it shall become foul and loathsome." ' Tell Aaron to stretch out his rod over the waters of Egypt, over their canals, ponds, and pools, that they may become blood; and there shall be blood throughout all the land of Egypt."

Moses and Aaron did as the LORD commanded; in the sight of Pharaoh and his servants, all the water in the Nile turned to blood. There was blood throughout Egypt. But the magicians of Egypt did the same by their secret arts; so Pharaoh's heart remained hardened, and he would not listen, as the LORD had said. Pharaoh turned and went into his house, and the Egyptians dug round about the Nile for water, for they could not drink from the Nile.

SEVEN DAYS PASSED. Then the LORD said to Moses, "Go tell Pharaoh the LORD says, 'If you refuse to let my people go and serve me, I will plague your country with frogs. The Nile shall swarm with frogs which shall come up into your houses, and bedchambers, and beds, and into your ovens and kneading bowls; the frogs shall come up on you and all your people.' And tell Aaron to stretch out his rod, and cause frogs to come." So Aaron stretched out his hand over the waters of Egypt, and frogs came up and covered the land. But the magicians did the same by their secret arts.

Then Pharaoh called Moses and Aaron. "Entreat the LORD to take away the frogs," he said, "and I will let the people go to sacrifice." Moses said, "It shall be as you say, so that you may know there is no one like the LORD our God. The frogs shall depart." Moses and Aaron went out from Pharaoh; and Moses cried to the LORD concerning the frogs. The frogs died out of the houses and courtyards and fields; they were gathered together in heaps, and the land stank. But when Pharaoh saw there was a respite, he hardened his heart, as the LORD had said.

Then the LORD said to Moses, "Tell Aaron to strike with his rod the dust of the earth, that it may become gnats throughout all Egypt." Aaron struck the dust, and it became gnats on man and beast throughout the land. The magicians tried by their secret arts to bring forth gnats. When they could not, they said to Pharaoh, "This is the finger of God." But Pharaoh's heart was hardened, and he would not listen.

So the LORD said to Moses, "Rise up early in the morning, and tell Pharaoh the LORD says, 'If you will not let my people go, I will send swarms of flies on you and your people. But there shall be no swarms of flies in the land of Goshen, where my people dwell. So that you may know that I am the LORD, I will thus put a division between my people and your people. By tomorrow shall this sign be.' " And the LORD did so; all the land of Egypt was ruined by great swarms of flies.

Then Pharaoh called Moses and Aaron. "Go," he said. "Sacrifice to your God within the land." But Moses said, "It would not be right. For we shall sacrifice animals to our God—offerings abominable to the Egyptians. Will they not stone us? We must go three days' journey into the wilderness to sacrifice." Pharaoh said, "I will let you go and sacrifice in the wilderness, only not far away. Make entreaty for me." Moses said, "I will pray to the LORD that the swarms of flies may depart tomorrow; only let not Pharaoh deal falsely again." So Moses went out and prayed to the LORD, and the LORD removed the swarms of flies; not one remained. But Pharaoh hardened his heart this time also. He did not let the people go.

Then the LORD said to Moses, "Go tell

Pharaoh that the LORD, the God of the Hebrews, says, 'Let my people go and serve me. If you refuse, a severe plague will fall upon your cattle which are in the field, the horses, asses, and camels, all your herds and flocks. But the LORD will make a distinction between the cattle of Israel and of Egypt; nothing that belongs to the people of Israel shall die.' " The LORD set a time, saying, "Tomorrow the LORD will do this." And on the morrow all the cattle of the Egyptians died, yet not one of the cattle of the Israelites died. But Pharaoh did not let the people go.

The LORD then said to Moses and Aaron, "Take handfuls of ashes from the kiln. Throw them toward heaven in the sight of Pharaoh, to become fine dust over all the land, and cause boils to break out on man and beast throughout Egypt." So they took ashes, stood before Pharaoh, and Moses threw them toward heaven. Boils broke out on man and beast; the magicians could not stand before Moses, for boils were upon them and all Egyptians. But the LORD hardened the heart of Pharaoh, and he did not listen.

Then the LORD said to Moses, "Rise up early, stand before Pharaoh, and tell him the God of the Hebrews says, 'Let my people go, or this time I will send all my plagues upon your heart, so that you may know there is none like me in all the earth. By now I could have struck you and your people with pestilence, and cut you off from the earth; but I have let you live, to show you my power, so my name may be declared throughout the earth. You are still exalting yourself against my people. Tomorrow I will cause very heavy hail to fall, such as never has been in Egypt. Get your cattle into safe shelter; for every man and beast in the field shall die.' " Then those among Pharaoh's servants who feared the word of the LORD made their slaves and cattle flee into the houses; but those who did not, left slaves and cattle in the field.

And the LORD said to Moses, "Stretch forth your hand toward heaven, that there may be hail." Moses stretched forth his rod, and the LORD sent thunder and hail upon the land, and fire flashing continually in the midst of the very heavy hail. The hail struck down every plant in the field. (The flax in the bud and the barley in the ear were ruined. But the wheat, which is late coming up, was not ruined.) The hail struck down every man and beast in the field throughout Egypt, and it shattered every tree. Only in the land of Goshen, where the people of Israel were, was there no hail.

Then Pharaoh sent for Moses and Aaron. "I have sinned this time," he said. "The LORD is right. Entreat the LORD, for there has been enough hail. I will let you go." Moses said, "I will stretch out my hands to the LORD; there will be no more hail, that you may know that the earth is the LORD'S. But I know you do not yet fear the LORD God." So Moses went out of the city, and stretched out his hands to the LORD; the thunder and hail ceased. But when Pharaoh saw this, he sinned yet again, and did not let the people of Israel go.

MOSES AND AARON again went in to Pharaoh, and told him, "The LORD says, 'How long will you refuse to humble yourself before me? If you refuse to let my people go, behold, tomorrow I will bring locusts into your country, as neither your fathers nor your grandfathers have seen. The locusts shall cover the face of the land, fill your houses, and eat every plant that is left after the hail.'" Then Moses and Aaron turned and went out.

"How long shall this man be a snare to us?" Pharaoh's servants said to him. "Let the men go and serve the LORD their God. Do you not understand that Egypt is ruined?" So Moses and Aaron were brought back. "Go, serve the LORD your God," Pharaoh said, "but who are to go?" Moses said, "Our young and old, our sons and daughters, and our flocks and herds, for we must hold a feast to the LORD." But Pharaoh said, "The LORD be with you, if ever I let you and your little ones go! No! You have some evil purpose in mind. Let the men among you go and serve the LORD, for that is what you desire." And they were driven out from Pharaoh's presence.

Then the LORD said to Moses, "Stretch out your hand, that the locusts may come." So Moses stretched forth his rod, and the LORD brought an east wind upon the land all that day and night; and the east wind brought locusts over all of Egypt. Such a dense swarm of locusts had never been before. They darkened the whole land, eating all plants and the fruit of all trees; not a green thing remained. In haste, Pharaoh called Moses and Aaron. "I have sinned against your God, and against you," he said. "Forgive my sin, I pray, and entreat the LORD your God to remove this death from me." So Moses entreated the LORD, and the LORD sent a very strong west wind, which lifted the locusts and drove them into the Red Sea; not a single locust was left. But Pharaoh did not let the children of Israel go.

The LORD then said to Moses, "Stretch out your hand toward heaven to bring darkness over Egypt, a darkness to be felt." So Moses stretched out his hand, and there was thick darkness in all the land. The Egyptians did not see one another nor rise from their places for three days; but the people of Israel had light where they dwelt. Then Pharaoh called Moses. "Go, serve the LORD," he said. "Your children may go with you; only let your flocks and herds remain behind." But Moses said, "We must take our cattle, for we do not know with what sacrifices and burnt offerings we must serve the LORD until we arrive there." Then the LORD hardened Pharaoh's heart, and Pharaoh said to Moses, "Get away from me. Never see my face again, or you shall die." Moses said, "As you say!"

But the LORD said to Moses, "Yet one plague more I will bring upon Pharaoh and Egypt. Afterwards he will let you go; he will drive you away. Speak now in the hearing of the people, that they ask, every man of his neighbor and every woman of her neighbor, jewelry of silver and of gold."

And Moses said to Pharaoh, "Thus says the LORD: 'About midnight I will go forth in Egypt, and all the first-born in the land shall die, from the first-born of Pharaoh upon his throne, to the first-born of the maidservant behind the mill, even to all the first-born of the cattle. There shall be a great cry throughout Egypt, such as has never been, nor shall be again. But against any of the people of Israel, either man or beast, not a dog shall growl; thus you will know that the LORD makes a distinction between the Egyptians and Israel.' And all your servants shall come and bow down to me, saying, 'Get out, you and all who follow you.' And after that I will go."

Moses then went out from Pharaoh in hot anger. And the LORD said to Moses, "Pharaoh will not listen to you, so that my wonders may be multiplied in the land of Egypt." Thus the LORD hardened Pharaoh's heart, and he did not let the people of Israel go.

THE LORD SAID to Moses and Aaron, "This month shall be for you the first month of the year. Tell all of Israel that on the tenth day of this month they shall take a lamb for each household, a lamb without blemish, a male a year old. Keep it until the fourteenth day of this month, when the whole congregation of Israel shall kill their lambs in the evening. Then they shall take some of the blood, and put it on the two doorposts and the lintel of the house in which they eat them. They shall eat the flesh that night, roasted; with unleavened bread and bitter herbs they shall eat it. Eat with your loins girded, your sandals on, your staff in hand; and eat in haste. It is the LORD's passover. For I will pass through the land of Egypt that night, and smite all the first-born, both man and beast; on the gods of Egypt I will execute judgments: I am the LORD. The blood shall be a sign for you; when I see blood upon your houses, I will pass over you, and no plague shall destroy you.

"This shall be a memorial day; keep it throughout your generations as a feast to the LORD. Seven days you shall eat unleavened bread; no leaven shall be found in your houses, for if any one eats what is leavened, that person shall be cut off from Israel. On the first day and on the seventh you shall hold a holy assembly; no work shall be done on those days. And you shall observe the feast of unleavened bread as an ordinance for ever."

Then Moses called all the elders of Israel. "Select and kill lambs for yourselves," he said, "according to your families. Dip a bunch of hyssop in the blood which is in the basin, and touch the lintel and door-posts; and none of you shall go out of his house until morning. For the LORD will pass through to slay the Egyptians; and when he sees the blood, he will pass over the door, and will not allow the destroyer to enter your houses to slay you. You shall observe this rite for ever. When you come to the land which the LORD will give you, as he has promised, you shall keep this service. And when your children say, 'What do you mean by this service?' you shall say, 'It is the sacrifice of the LORD's passover, for he passed over our houses and spared the people of Israel in Egypt, when he slew the Egyptians.' " And the people of Israel bowed their heads and worshiped. Then they did as the LORD had commanded.

At midnight the LORD smote all the first-born in the land of Egypt, from the first-born of Pharaoh to the first-born of the captive in the dungeon, even to the first-born of the cattle. Pharaoh rose up in the night, he, and all his servants; and there was a great cry in Egypt, for there was not a house where one was not dead. And he summoned Moses and Aaron by night and said, "Go forth, both you and the people of Israel. Go, serve the LORD, as you have said. Take your flocks and herds, and be gone; and bless me also!" So the people of Israel took their dough before it was leavened, their kneading bowls being bound up in their mantles on their shoulders. They had also done as Moses told them, and had asked of the Egyptians jewelry of silver and of gold, and clothing. And the LORD had given them favor in the sight of the Egyptians; moreover, Moses was very great in the sight of Pharaoh's servants. So the Egyptians let them have what they asked.

The people of Israel journeyed from Rameses to Succoth, about six hundred thousand men on foot, besides women and children. A mixed multitude also went with them, and many cattle, flocks, and herds. And they baked unleavened cakes of the dough which they had brought when they were thrust out of Egypt and could not tarry, neither had they prepared for themselves any provisions.

The people of Israel had dwelt in Egypt four hundred and thirty years. And at the end of that time, on that very day, all the hosts of the LORD went out from the land of Egypt. It was a night of watching by the LORD, to bring them out; so this same night is a night of watching kept to the LORD by all the people of Israel throughout their generations.

WHEN PHARAOH LET the people go, God did not lead them to Canaan by way of the land of the Philistines, although that was near; for God said, "If the people see war, they might repent and return to Egypt." So God led the people round by way of the wilderness toward the Red Sea. They went out of Egypt equipped for battle. And Moses took the bones of Joseph with him; for Joseph had solemnly sworn the people of Israel, saying, "God will visit you; carry my bones with you from here." They moved on from Succoth, and encamped at Etham, on the edge of the wilderness. The LORD led them by day in a pillar of cloud, and by night in a pillar of fire to give them light, that they might travel by day and by night, and he did not depart from before the people.

Then the LORD said to Moses, "Tell the people of Israel to turn back and encamp in front of Pihahiroth, by the sea. For Pharaoh will say, 'The people of Israel are entangled in the land; the wilderness has shut them in.' Then he will pursue them, and I will get glory over Pharaoh; the Egyptians shall know that I am the LORD." And the people did so.

Now when Pharaoh and his servants were told that the people of Israel had fled, their minds were changed toward them. "What is this we have done," they said, "to let Israel go from serving us?" So Pharaoh made ready his chariot and took his army with him, and six hundred picked chariots and all his horses and horsemen. He pursued the people of Israel, and overtook them encamped at the sea, by Pihahiroth. When the people of Israel saw that the Egyptians were marching after them, in great fear they cried out to the LORD; and they said to Moses, "Is it because there are no graves in Egypt that you have brought us out to die? What have you done to us? It would have been better for us to serve the Egyptians than to die in the wilderness."

"Fear not," said Moses, "stand firm, and see the salvation that the LORD will work for you today; for the Egyptians whom you see today, you shall never see again. The LORD will fight for you, and you have only to be still." Then the LORD said to Moses, "Tell the people of Israel to go forward. Lift up your rod over the sea and divide it, that the people may go through on dry ground. And I will harden the hearts of the Egyptians so that they shall go in after them. The Egyptians shall know that I am the LORD, when I have gotten glory over Pharaoh, his chariots, and his horsemen."

Then the angel of God who went before the host of Israel moved behind them; and the pillar of cloud moved from before them and stood behind them, coming between them and the host of Egypt. And there was darkness; and the night passed without one coming near the other. Moses stretched out his hand over the sea, and the LORD drove the sea back by a strong east wind all night, and made the sea dry land; the waters were divided. The people of Israel went into the midst of the sea on dry ground, the waters being a wall to them on their right hand and their left. The Egyptians pursued, and went in after them into the midst of the sea, all Pharaoh's horses, chariots, and horsemen. And at the morning watch the LORD in the pillar of fire and of cloud looked down upon the host of the Egyptians, and discomfited them, clogging their chariot wheels so that they drove heavily; and the Egyptians said, "Let us flee; for the LORD fights for Israel against us."

Then the LORD said to Moses, "Stretch out your hand over the sea, that the water may come back upon the Egyptians." Moses stretched forth his hand, and the sea returned to its wonted flow when the morning appeared; and the LORD routed the Egyptians. The waters covered their chariots and horsemen and all the host of Pharaoh; not so much as one of them remained. But the people of Israel walked on dry ground through the sea.

Thus the LORD saved Israel that day from the hand of the Egyptians; Israel saw them dead upon the seashore. And the people saw the great work which the LORD did, and they feared the LORD, and believed in him and in his servant Moses.

THEN MOSES AND the people of Israel sang this song:

I will sing to the LORD, for he has
    triumphed gloriously;
  the horse and his rider he has thrown
    into the sea.
The LORD is my strength and my song,
    and he has become
  my salvation; this is my God, and I
    will praise and exalt him.
The LORD is a man of war;
  the LORD is his name.

Pharaoh's chariots, his host, and his
    picked officers
  are sunk in the Red Sea.
The floods cover them; they went down
    into the depths like a stone.

Thy right hand, O LORD, glorious in
    power, shatters the enemy.
In thy majesty thou overthrowest thy
    adversaries;
      thou sendest forth thy fury; it
      consumes them like stubble.
At the blast of thy nostrils the waters
    piled up;
      the floods stood up in a heap;
      the deeps congealed in the heart of
      the sea.
The enemy said, "I will pursue,
    overtake, divide the spoil;
      my desire shall have its fill of them.
      I will draw my sword, my hand shall
      destroy them."
Thou didst blow with thy wind, the sea
    covered them;
      they sank as lead in the mighty waters.
Who is like thee, O LORD, among the
    gods?
Majestic in holiness, terrible in glorious
    deeds, doing wonders?
Thou didst stretch out thy right hand,
    the earth swallowed them.
Thou hast led in thy steadfast love the
    people whom thou hast redeemed.

Thou wilt bring thy people in, and plant
　　them on thy own mountain,
　　the place, O LORD, which thou hast
　　　made for thy abode,
　　the sanctuary which thy hands have
　　　established.
The LORD will reign for ever and ever.

Then Aaron's sister Miriam, the prophetess, took a timbrel in her hand; all the women went out after her with timbrels and dancing. And Miriam sang:

Sing to the LORD, for he has triumphed
　　gloriously;
　　the horse and his rider he has thrown
　　into the sea.

THEN MOSES LED Israel onward from the Red Sea, three days into the wilderness of Shur, and they found no water. They came to Marah, but could not drink the water there because it was bitter, and the people murmured against Moses. "What shall we drink?" they said. Moses cried to the LORD; and the LORD showed him a tree; he threw it into the water, and the water became sweet. There the LORD made for them an ordinance to prove them, saying, "If you will hearken to the LORD your God, doing what is right in his eyes and keeping his statutes, I will put none of the diseases upon you which I put upon the Egyptians; for I am the LORD, your healer." Then they came to Elim, where there were springs and palm trees, and encamped by the water.

After Elim, on the fifteenth day of the second month after they had departed from Egypt, they came to the wilderness of Sin. And the whole congregation of Israel murmured against Moses and Aaron, saying, "Would that we had died by the hand of the LORD in Egypt, when we sat by the fleshpots and ate bread to the full. You have brought us out into this wilderness to kill us with hunger." Then the LORD said to Moses, "Behold, I will rain bread from heaven. The people shall gather a day's portion every day, that I may prove them, whether they will walk in my law or not. On the sixth day what they bring in will be twice as much as they gather daily."

And Moses said to Aaron, "Say to the

people of Israel, 'Come near before the LORD, for he has heard your murmurings.' " The whole congregation looked, and the glory of the LORD appeared in the cloud. The LORD said to Moses, "I have heard the murmurings of the people; say to them, 'At twilight you shall eat flesh, and in the morning you shall be filled with bread; then you shall know that I am the LORD your God.' " So Moses and Aaron said to the people, "At evening you shall know that it was the LORD who brought you out of the land of Egypt, and in the morning you shall see his glory, because he has heard your murmurings against him. For what are we, that you murmur against us? Your murmurings are not against us but against the LORD."

In the evening, quails came up and covered the camp; in the morning, dew lay round about the camp. When the dew had gone, a flake-like thing, fine as hoarfrost, was left on the ground. "What is it?" the people asked. Moses said, "It is the bread which the LORD has given you to eat. The LORD has commanded: 'Gather of it, every man, as much as he can eat; a measure apiece according to the number of persons each has in his tent.' " And the people of Israel did so; some gathered more, some less. But when they measured it, he that gathered much had nothing over, and he that gathered little had no lack. And Moses said to them, "Let no man leave any till the morning." But they did not listen; some left part till the morning, and it bred worms and became foul; and Moses was angry with them.

Morning by morning they gathered the bread, but when the sun grew hot, it melted. On the sixth day they gathered twice as much. And Moses said to them, "The LORD has commanded: 'Tomorrow is a day of rest, a holy sabbath to the LORD; bake and boil what you will, and keep all the bread that is left over till the morning.' " So they laid it by till morning, and it did not become foul. Moses said, "Eat it today, for today is the seventh day, a sabbath to the LORD; today you will not find it in the field." Still some people went out to gather, and found none. The LORD said to Moses, "How long do you refuse to keep my laws? The LORD has given you the sabbath, therefore on the sixth day he gives you bread for two days. Let no man go out of his place on the seventh day." So the people rested on the seventh day.

Now the house of Israel called the bread manna; it was like coriander seed, white, and tasting like wafers made with honey. And Moses said, "The LORD has commanded: 'Let a measure of it be kept throughout your generations, that they may see the bread I fed you when I brought you out of Egypt.' " (And the people of Israel ate the manna forty years, till they came to a habitable land, to the border of the land of Canaan.)

The congregation of Israel then moved on from the wilderness of Sin by stages, according to the LORD's commandment. They camped at Rephidim, but there was no water to drink, and the people found fault with Moses. "Why do you find fault with me?" he said. "Why do you put the LORD to the proof?" But the people murmured against Moses. "Why did you bring us up out of Egypt," they said, "to kill us and our children and our cattle with thirst?" So Moses cried to the LORD,

"What shall I do? These people are almost ready to stone me." The LORD replied, "Pass on before the people, taking with you some of the elders, and take your rod with which you struck the Nile. Go. I will stand before you there on the rock. Strike the rock, and water shall come out of it, that the people may drink." And Moses did so, in the sight of the elders of Israel. And he called the name of the place Massah (that is, Proof), and Meribah (that is, Contention), because the children of Israel put the LORD to the proof by saying, "Is the LORD among us or not."

Then came Amalek and fought with Israel at Rephidim. To Joshua, Moses said, "Choose men and go out and fight with Amalek; tomorrow I will stand on the top of the hill with the rod of God in my hand." So Joshua fought with Amalek; and Moses, Aaron, and Hur went up the hill. Whenever Moses held up his hand, Israel prevailed; whenever he lowered his hand, Amalek prevailed. But Moses' arms grew weary, so they took a stone and put it under him, and he sat upon it, and Aaron and Hur held up his hands, one on each side, until the going down of the sun. And Joshua mowed down Amalek and his people with the sword. And the LORD said to Moses, "Write this as a memorial in a book and recite it in the ears of Joshua, that I will utterly blot out the remembrance of Amalek from under heaven." Then Moses built an altar and called the name of it, The LORD is my banner, saying, "A hand upon the banner of the LORD! The LORD will have war with Amalek from generation to generation."

JETHRO, THE PRIEST of Midian, Moses' father-in-law, heard of all that God had done, how the LORD had brought Israel out of Egypt. Now Zipporah, Moses' wife, and Gershom and Eliezer, her two sons, were with Jethro, and he came with them to where Moses was encamped in the wilderness. Moses went out to meet him, and did obeisance and kissed him; and they asked each other of their welfare, and went into the tent. Then Moses told his father-in-law all that the LORD had done to Pharaoh, all the hardship that had come upon them in the way, and how the LORD had delivered them. And Jethro said, "Blessed be the LORD, who has delivered you out of the hand of the Egyptians. Now I know that the LORD is greater than all gods." And Jethro offered a burnt offering and sacrifices to God; and Aaron came with all the elders of Israel to eat bread with Jethro before God.

On the morrow Moses sat to judge the people, from morning till evening. "What is this you are doing, and why do you sit alone, and all the people stand about you from morning till evening?" Jethro asked. "The people come to me to inquire of God, when they have a dispute. I make them know the statutes of God and his decisions," Moses replied. "The thing is too heavy for you," Jethro said. "I will give you counsel. You shall represent the people before God, and teach them the statutes and decisions. But choose able men from all the people, such as fear God, men who are trustworthy and hate a bribe; and place such men over the people as rulers of thousands, of hundreds, of fifties, and of tens. Every great matter they shall bring to you, but any small matter they shall decide themselves; they will bear the burden with you. Then all this people will go to their place in peace."

So Moses gave heed to the voice of his father-in-law and did all that he had said, choosing able men out of all Israel. Then Moses let Jethro depart, and he went his way to his own country.

On the day of the third new moon after the people of Israel had gone forth out of Egypt, they came into the wilderness of Sinai, and encamped before the mountain. Moses went up, and the LORD called to him out of the mountain, saying, "These words you shall speak to the people of Israel: 'You have seen what I did to the Egyptians, how I bore you on eagles' wings and brought you to myself. Now, if you will obey my voice and keep my covenant, you shall be my own possession among all peoples; for all the earth is mine, and you shall be to me a kingdom of priests and a holy nation.' "

So Moses called the elders, and set before them the LORD's words. And the people answered, "All that the LORD has spoken we will do." Moses reported their words to the LORD, and the LORD said, "Lo, I am coming to you in a thick cloud, that the people may hear when I speak with you, and may believe you for ever. Go to the people, consecrate them, let them wash their garments and be ready; for on the third day the LORD will come down upon Mount Sinai in sight of the people. Set bounds for them, saying, 'Take heed that you do not go up into the mountain; whoever touches the mountain shall be put to death.' When the trumpet sounds a long blast, they shall come up to the mountain." So Moses went down from the mountain, and consecrated the people. On the morning of the third day there were thunders, lightnings, a thick cloud upon the mountain, and a very loud trumpet blast, so that all in the camp trembled. Moses brought the people out of the camp to meet God, and they took their stand at the foot of the mountain. Mount Sinai was wrapped in smoke, because the LORD descended upon it in fire; and the whole mountain quaked greatly. As the sound of the trumpet grew louder, Moses spoke, and God answered him in thunder. The

LORD called Moses to the top of the mountain, and Moses went up.

And God spoke these words:

"I am the LORD your God, who brought you out of the land of Egypt, out of the house of bondage.

"You shall have no other gods before me.

"You shall not make for yourself a graven image, or any likeness of anything that is in heaven above, or that is in the earth beneath, or that is in the water under the earth; you shall not bow down to them or serve them; for I the LORD your God am a jealous God, visiting the iniquity of the fathers upon the children to the third and the fourth generation of those who hate me, but showing steadfast love to thousands of those who love me and keep my commandments.

"You shall not take the name of the LORD your God in vain; for the LORD will not hold him guiltless who takes his name in vain.

"Remember the sabbath day, to keep it holy. Six days you shall labor, and do all your work; but the seventh day is a sabbath to the LORD your God; in it you shall not do any work, you, or your son, or your daughter, your manservant, or your maidservant, or your cattle, or the sojourner who is within your gates; for in six days the LORD made heaven and earth, the sea, and all that is in them, and rested the seventh day; therefore the LORD blessed the sabbath day and hallowed it.

"Honor your father and your mother, that your days may be long in the land which the LORD your God gives you.

"You shall not kill.

"You shall not commit adultery.

"You shall not steal.

"You shall not bear false witness against your neighbor.

"You shall not covet your neighbor's house; you shall not covet your neighbor's wife, or his manservant, or his maidservant, or his ox, or his ass, or anything that is your neighbor's."

Now when the people perceived the thunderings, the lightnings, the sound of the trumpet, and the mountain smoking, they trembled with fear and stood afar off. "You speak to us, and we will hear," they said to Moses, "but let not God speak to us, lest we die." And Moses replied, "Do not fear; for God has come to prove you, that the fear of him may be before your eyes, that you may not sin."

WHILE THE PEOPLE stood afar off, Moses drew near to the thick darkness where God was, and the LORD said, "Thus you shall say to the people of Israel: 'You have seen for yourselves that I have talked with you from heaven. You shall not make for yourselves gods of silver or gold. Make for me an altar of earth and sacrifice on it your burnt offerings and peace offerings; in every place where I cause my name to be remembered I will come to you and bless you.' "

And the LORD said, "Now these are ordinances which you shall set before them: When you buy a Hebrew slave, he shall serve six years, and in the seventh he shall go out free. If he comes in single, he shall go out single; if he comes in married, then his wife shall go out with him.

"Whoever wilfully attacks a man so that he dies shall be put to death. Whoever strikes his father or his mother shall be put to death. Whoever curses his father or his mother shall be put to death. When a man strikes his slave, male or female, with a rod and the slave dies under his hand, he shall be punished. When a man strikes the eye of his slave and destroys it, he shall let the slave go free for the eye's sake. If he knocks out the tooth of his slave, he shall let the slave go free for the tooth's sake. When an ox gores a man or a woman to death, the ox shall be stoned; but the owner of the ox shall be clear. But if the ox has gored in the past, and its owner has not kept it in, and it kills a man or a woman, the ox shall be stoned, and its owner put to death.

"When one man's ox hurts another's, so that it dies, then they shall sell the live ox and divide the price of it; and the dead beast also they shall divide. If a man steals an ox or sheep, and kills or sells it, he shall pay five oxen for an ox, and four sheep for a sheep. He shall make restitution; if he has nothing, then he shall be sold for his theft. When a man lets his beast loose and it feeds in another man's field or vineyard, he shall make restitution from the best in his own field and vineyard. When fire breaks out and catches in thorns so that stacked or standing grain in the field is consumed, he that kindled the fire shall make full restitution. If a man borrows anything of his neighbor, and it is hurt or dies, he shall make full restitution. If you meet your enemy's ox or his ass going astray, you shall bring it back to him.

"You shall not permit a sorceress to live. Whoever lies with a beast shall be put to death. You shall not wrong a stranger or oppress him; you know the heart of a stranger, for you were strangers in Egypt. You shall not afflict any widow or orphan. If you do, I will surely hear their cry, and my wrath will burn; I will kill you, and your wives shall become widows and your children fatherless. If you lend money to any of my people who is poor, you shall not exact interest. If you take your neighbor's garment in pledge, you shall restore it to him before the sun goes down, for that is his only covering; in what else shall he sleep? And if he cries to me, I will hear, for I am compassionate. You shall not re-

vile God, nor curse a ruler of your people.
You shall not utter a false report. You
shall not follow a multitude to do evil; nor
shall you bear witness in a suit, turning
aside after a multitude, so as to pervert
justice; nor shall you be partial to a poor
man in his suit. You shall take no bribe,
for a bribe blinds officials, and subverts
the cause of those in the right.

"For six years you shall sow your land
and gather in its yield; but the seventh year
you shall let it lie fallow, that the poor may
eat; and what they leave the wild beasts
may eat. You shall do likewise with your
vineyard and olive orchard. Three times in
the year you shall keep a feast to me. You
shall keep the feast of unleavened bread,
as I commanded you when you came out
of Egypt. You shall keep the feast of harvest, of the first fruits of what you sow.
You shall keep the feast of ingathering at
the end of the year, when you gather in
from the field the fruit of your labor. Three
times in the year shall all your males appear before the Lord GOD.

"Behold, I send an angel before you, to
guard you and bring you to the place I

have prepared. Give heed to him, and do not rebel against him, for my name is in him. But if you hearken to his voice and do all that I say, then I will be an enemy to your enemies. I will bless your bread and your water; I will take sickness away from the midst of you. I will send my terror before you, and throw into confusion all the people against whom you shall come. And I will send hornets before you, which shall drive out the Canaanites. Little by little I will drive them out, until you possess the land from the Red Sea to the sea of the Philistines, and from the wilderness to the Euphrates. I will deliver the inhabitants of the land into your hand, and you shall drive them out before you. You shall make no covenant with them or with their gods, but you shall break the pillars of their gods in pieces. They shall not dwell in your land, lest they make you sin against me; for if you serve their gods, it will surely be a snare to you."

And God said to Moses, "Come up to the LORD with Aaron and his sons, Nadab and Abihu, and seventy elders of Israel, and worship. Moses alone shall come near to the LORD; but the others shall worship afar off, and the people shall not come up with him."

WHEN MOSES TOLD the people all the words of the LORD and all the ordinances, with one voice they said, "All the words which the LORD has spoken we will do." Then Moses wrote all the words of the LORD, and he built an altar at the foot of the mountain, and twelve pillars, according to the twelve tribes of Israel. He sent young men of Israel, who offered burnt offerings and sacrificed peace offerings of oxen to the LORD. Moses put half of the blood in basins, and half of the blood he threw against the altar. Then he took the book of the covenant, and read it in the hearing of the people; they said, "All that the LORD has spoken we will do, and we will be obedient."

Taking the blood, Moses threw it upon the people. "Behold the blood of the covenant," he said, "which the LORD has made with you in accordance with these words."

Then Moses and Aaron, Nadab and Abihu, and seventy of the elders of Israel went up, and saw the God of Israel. Under his feet was a pavement like sapphire stone, like the very heaven for clearness. He did not lay his hand on the chief men of the people of Israel; they beheld God, and ate and drank.

The LORD said to Moses, "Come up to me on the mountain, and wait there; I will give you tables of stone, with the law and the commandment, which I have written for their instruction." So Moses rose with his young servant Joshua to go up into the mountain of God. He said to the elders, "Tarry here, until we come to you again. Aaron and Hur are with you; let whoever has a cause go to them."

Then Moses went up on the mountain, and the cloud covered it. The glory of the LORD settled on Mount Sinai; the cloud covered it six days, and on the seventh day the LORD called to Moses out of the midst of the cloud. Now the glory of the LORD was like a devouring fire on the top of the mountain in the sight of the people of Israel. And Moses entered the cloud, up on the mountain. And Moses was on the mountain forty days and forty nights.

The LORD said to Moses, "Speak to the people of Israel, that they take for me an offering, from every man whose heart makes him willing. And this is the offering you shall receive from them: gold, silver, and bronze, blue and purple and scarlet stuff and fine twined linen, goats' hair, tanned rams' skins, goatskins, acacia wood, oil for lamps, spices for anointing oil and for fragrant incense, and onyx stones for setting. Let them make me a sanctuary, that I may dwell in their midst. According to all that I show you concerning the pattern of the tabernacle, and of all its furniture, so you shall make it.

"Make an ark of acacia wood, forty-five inches long, twenty-seven inches wide, and twenty-seven inches high. Overlay it with pure gold, within and without. Cast four rings of gold for it and put two on one side and two on the other. Make poles of acacia wood, and overlay them with gold, and put them into the rings, to carry the ark. Make a mercy seat of pure gold, with two cherubim of gold on the two ends, their faces one to another, and put the mercy seat on the top of the ark. And in the ark you shall put the tables of the law that I shall give you. There I will meet with you, and from above the mercy seat I will speak with you. Make the tabernacle (the tent of meeting to enclose the ark) with ten curtains of fine twined linen and blue and purple and scarlet stuff, with cherubim skilfully worked. Make curtains of goats' hair for a tent over the tabernacle, and a covering for the tent of tanned rams' skins and goatskins. Make upright frames for the tabernacle of acacia wood. Make a veil of blue and purple and scarlet stuff and fine twined linen, embroidered with cherubim; and hang it in the tabernacle upon four pillars of acacia wood overlaid with gold. Bring the ark within the veil; and the veil shall separate for you the holy place from the most holy.

"Make a table of acacia wood, and overlay it with pure gold; and you shall set the bread of the Presence on the table before me always. Make a lampstand of pure gold, with six branches, three on each side; and make seven lamps for it. Make an altar of acacia wood for burnt offerings, and overlay it with bronze. Make an altar to burn incense upon, of acacia wood overlaid with pure gold. And you shall also make a laver of bronze, with its base of bronze, for washing hands and feet.

"Make the court of the tabernacle, enclosed with hangings of fine twined linen. The length of the court shall be a hundred and fifty feet, the breadth seventy-five, and the height of the hangings seven and a half feet. Command the people that they bring pure beaten olive oil, that a lamp may be set up to burn continually. Aaron and his sons shall tend it from evening to morning before the LORD. It shall be a statute for ever to be observed by the people of Israel. And you shall make holy garments for Aaron your brother, for glory and for beauty. And you shall speak to all who have ability, whom I have endowed with an able mind, that they make Aaron's garments, to consecrate him for my priesthood, and also for his sons. Make a breastpiece of judgment, in skilled work, of gold, blue and purple and scarlet stuff and fine twined linen. Set in it twelve stones, for the twelve tribes of Israel, set in gold filigree. And you shall make a robe all of blue; on its skirts pomegranates, with bells of gold between them, a golden bell and a pomegranate, a golden bell and a pomegranate, round about on the skirts of the robe. And it shall be upon Aaron when he ministers, and its sound shall be heard when Aaron goes into the holy place before the LORD, and when he comes out.

"I will consecrate the tent of meeting and the altar. There I will meet with the people of Israel, and it shall be sanctified by my glory; Aaron also and his sons I will consecrate, to serve me as priests. I will dwell among the people of Israel, and they shall know that I am the LORD their God, who brought them forth out of the land of Egypt, that I might dwell among them; I am the LORD their God."

And the LORD said to Moses, "See, I have called by name Bezalel, of the tribe of Judah: and I have filled him with the Spirit of God, and with ability, intelligence, knowledge, and craftsmanship, to devise artistic designs, to work in gold, silver, and bronze, in cutting stones for setting, and in carving wood. I have appointed with him Oholiab, of the tribe of Dan; and I have given to all able men ability to make all that I command you. This they shall do."

When the LORD finished speaking with Moses upon Mount Sinai, he gave him the two tables of the law, tables of stone, written with the finger of God.

WHEN THE PEOPLE saw that Moses delayed to come down from the mountain, they gathered together and said to Aaron, "Make gods to go before us. As for this Moses, who brought us out of Egypt, we do not know what has become of him." And Aaron said, "Take off the golden earrings of your wives, sons, and daughters, and bring them to me." So all the people brought their golden earrings to Aaron. He received the gold, fashioned it with a graving tool, and made a molten calf; and the people worshiped it. Seeing this, Aaron built an altar before the golden calf, and made proclamation: "Tomorrow shall be a feast to the LORD." The people rose early on the morrow, offered burnt offerings and brought peace offerings; and they sat down to eat and drink, and rose up to play.

The LORD said to Moses, "Go down; for

your people have corrupted themselves, turning quickly from the way which I commanded them. They have made for themselves a molten calf, have worshiped it and sacrificed to it. Behold, this is a stiff-necked people; now therefore let me alone, that my wrath may burn hot against them and that I may consume them; but of you I will make a great nation."

But Moses besought the LORD, saying, "O LORD, why does thy wrath burn hot against thy people, whom thou hast brought out of Egypt with a mighty hand? Why should the Egyptians say, 'With evil intent did he bring them forth, to slay them in the mountains, and to consume them from the face of the earth'? Turn from thy fierce wrath. Remember Abraham, Isaac, and Jacob, thy servants, to whom thou didst say, 'I will multiply your descendants as the stars of heaven, and all this land I will give to your descendants for ever.'" And the LORD repented of the evil which he thought to do to his people.

Then Moses went down from the mountain with the two tables of the law in his hands, tables that were the work of God;

on both sides were they written, and the writing graven upon the tables was the writing of God. Joshua, hearing the people as they shouted, said to Moses, "There is a noise of war in the camp." But Moses said, "It is not shouting for victory, or the cry of defeat, but the sound of singing that I hear." As he came near the camp and saw the calf and the dancing, Moses' anger grew hot. He threw down the two tables and broke them at the foot of the mountain. He took the calf they had made, burnt it, ground it to powder, scattered it upon the water, and made the people of Israel drink it.

"What did this people do to you," Moses asked Aaron, "that you have brought a great sin upon them?" Aaron said, "Let not the anger of my lord burn hot; you know the people are set on evil. 'Make gods to go before us,' they said to me, 'for we do not know what has become of Moses.' I said, 'Let any who have gold take it off.' So they gave it to me, I threw it into the fire, and out came this calf."

And when Moses saw that the people were out of control (for Aaron had let them get out of control, to their shame among their enemies), Moses stood in the gate of the camp, saying, "Who is on the LORD's side? Come to me." All the sons of Levi gathered to him, and he said, "Thus says the LORD God of Israel, 'Let every man put on his sword, and go from gate to gate throughout the camp, and slay his brother, his companion, and his neighbor.'" The sons of Levi did according to the word of Moses, and three thousand of the people fell that day. "Today you have ordained yourselves for the service of the LORD," Moses said, "each one at the cost of son and brother, that the LORD may bestow a blessing upon you."

On the morrow Moses said to the people, "You have sinned a great sin. I will go up to the LORD; perhaps I can make atonement for your sin." So Moses returned to the LORD and said, "Alas, this people have made for themselves gods of gold. But now, if thou wilt, forgive their sin—and if not, blot me, I pray, out of thy book of life." The LORD said, "Whoever has sinned against me, him will I blot out of my book. But go now, lead the people to the place of which I have spoken. Nevertheless, I will visit their sin upon them." And the LORD sent a plague upon the people, because of the calf Aaron made.

NOW MOSES USED to take a tent and pitch it far off from the camp. When he entered the tent, the pillar of cloud would descend and stand at the door, and the LORD would speak with him. And when the people saw the cloud at the door, they would all rise up and worship, every man at his tent door. Thus the LORD used to speak to Moses face to face, as a man speaks to his friend.

Then Moses said to the LORD, "Thou sayest to me, 'Bring up this people.' But thou hast not let me know whom thou wilt send with me. I pray thee, show me now thy ways, that I may know thee. Consider too that this nation is thy people. If thy presence will not go with me, do not carry us up from here. For is it not in thy going with us that we are distinct, I and thy people, from all other people upon the face of the earth?" And the LORD said, "My presence will go with you, and I will give you rest. This I will do; for you have found favor in my sight, and I know you by name."

Moses said, "I pray thee, show me thy glory." And the LORD said, "I will make all my goodness pass before you, and will proclaim before you my name 'The LORD'; and I will be gracious to whom I will be gracious, show mercy on whom I will show mercy. But you cannot see my face; for man shall not see me and live. There is a place where you shall stand upon the rock. While my glory passes by I will put you in a cleft of the rock, and cover you with my hand until I have passed by. Then I will take away my hand, and you shall see my back; but my face shall not be seen."

The LORD said to Moses, "Cut two tables of stone like the first; I will write upon them the words that were on the first tables, which you broke. Be ready in the morning, and come up to Mount Sinai. Present yourself to me on the top of the mountain. No man shall come with you, and let no man be seen throughout the mountain; let no flocks or herds feed before that mountain." So Moses cut two tables of stone, and early in the morning he took them up on Mount Sinai. The LORD descended in the cloud and stood with him; then the LORD passed before him, and proclaimed his name: "The LORD, a God merciful and gracious, slow to anger, and abounding in faithfulness, keeping steadfast love for thousands, forgiving iniquity and transgression and sin, but who will by no means clear the guilty, visiting the iniquity of the fathers upon the children and the children's children, to the third and the fourth generation." Moses bowed his head toward the earth, and worshiped, saying, "If now I have found favor in thy sight, O Lord, I pray thee, go in the midst of us, although it is a stiff-necked people; pardon our iniquity and sin, and take us for thy inheritance."

The LORD said, "Behold, I make a covenant. Before all your people I will do marvels, such as have not been wrought in all the earth; and all the people among whom you are shall see the work of the LORD; for it is a terrible thing that I will do with you."

When Moses came down from Mount Sinai, with the two tables of the law in his hand, he did not know that the skin of his face shone because he had been talking with God. When Aaron and all the people of Israel saw this, they were afraid to come near him. But Moses called to them; and he talked with Aaron and the leaders of the congregation. Then all the people came near, and Moses gave them in commandment all that the LORD had spoken. When he finished, he put a veil on his face. Whenever Moses went in before the LORD, he took the veil off; when he came out and told the people what he was commanded, they saw that the skin of Moses' face shone; and Moses would put the veil on again, until he went in to speak with the LORD.

AFTER MOSES TOLD the congregation what the LORD had said concerning the sanctuary, all the men and women whose heart moved them to bring anything for the work brought it as their freewill offering to the LORD. Moses called Bezalel and Oholiab and every able man in whose mind the

LORD had put ability, and they came to do the work. When the work was finished, the people of Israel brought to Moses the tabernacle, the tent, the veil, the ark of the tables of the law and the mercy seat, the table and the bread of the Presence, the lampstand, the golden altar, the oil and incense, the bronze altar and the laver, the hangings of the court, all the utensils for the service of the tabernacle, and the finely worked holy garments for Aaron and his sons to serve as priests. Moses saw all the work, and behold, the people of Israel had done it as the LORD had commanded. And Moses blessed them.

The LORD said to Moses, "On the first day of the first month you shall erect the tabernacle of the tent of meeting, and set its arrangements in order. Set up the court round about. Then take the anointing oil, anoint the tabernacle and all that is in it, and consecrate it and all its furniture; it shall become holy. Consecrate the altar; it shall be most holy. Then bring Aaron and his sons to the door of the tent of meeting, and wash them with water. Put upon Aaron the holy garments, anoint him, and consecrate him, that he may serve me. Put coats on his sons and anoint them: and their anointing shall admit them to a perpetual priesthood throughout their generations."

On the first day of the first month in the second year, the tabernacle was erected. Moses laid its bases, set up its frames, and raised up its pillars. He put the tables of the law into the ark, and set the mercy seat on the ark; he brought the ark into the tabernacle, and set up the veil. He put the table in the tent of meeting, and set the bread in order on it before the LORD. He set up the lampstand and put the golden altar before the veil, and burnt fragrant incense upon it. He set the altar of burnt offering at the door of the tabernacle, and offered upon it the burnt offering. He set the laver between the tent of meeting and the altar, and put water in it for washing; when Moses and Aaron and his sons went into the tent of meeting and approached the altar, they washed their hands and feet, as the LORD had commanded. And Moses erected the court round the tabernacle and altar. So he finished the work.

Then the cloud covered the tent of meeting; and Moses was not able to enter, because the cloud abode upon it, and the glory of the LORD filled the tabernacle. Throughout their journeys, whenever the cloud was taken up from over the tabernacle, the people of Israel would go onward; but they did not go onward till the day that it was taken up. For throughout all their journeys the cloud of the LORD was upon the tabernacle by day, and fire was in it by night, in the sight of all the house of Israel.

LEVITICUS

The word Leviticus means "pertaining to the Levites," and the book contains the system of laws, administered by the Levitical priesthood, under which the Israelites lived. Included are regulations concerning kinds of sacrifices, the consecration of priests to their office, the distinction between clean and unclean, the ceremony for the annual Day of Atonement, and various precepts concerning Israel's life as a holy people *("You shall be holy; for I the Lord your God am holy")*.

The language and theology of Leviticus are reflected in the words and ideas of certain New Testament writers, notably in the Letter to the Hebrews. There the priesthood of Jesus Christ is contrasted with the Levitical priesthood. It is also significant that of all the many precepts contained in this book, Jesus singled out the command *"You shall love your neighbor as yourself"* as second only to the primary command of love toward God. The oldest part is probably the Code of Holiness (pages 174–186), which was combined with other traditional material in the sixth century B.C.

————

THE LORD CALLED Moses, and spoke to him from the tent of meeting, saying, "Speak to the people of Israel, and say, When any man of you brings an offering to the LORD, bring cattle from the herd or from the flock. If it is a burnt offering from the herd, offer a male without blemish; offer it at the door of the tent of meeting, to be accepted before the LORD; lay your hand upon its head, and it shall be accepted to make atonement for you. Then kill the bull before the LORD; Aaron's sons the priests shall present the blood, and throw it round about against the altar at the door of the tent of meeting. Flay the burnt offering and cut it into pieces; the sons of Aaron shall put fire on the altar, lay wood upon the fire, and lay the pieces, the head, and the fat, in order upon the wood. The entrails and legs shall be washed with water, and the priest shall burn the whole on the altar, as a burnt offering, an offering by fire, a pleasing odor to the LORD.

"If the burnt offering is from the flock, sheep or goats, offer a male without blemish; kill it on the north side of the altar before the LORD, and the priests shall throw its blood against the altar round about. Cut it into pieces, and the priest shall lay them upon the wood that is on the fire. The entrails and legs shall be washed with water, and the priest shall offer the whole, and burn it on the altar; it is a burnt offering, a pleasing odor to the LORD.

"If your offering is a burnt offering of birds, then bring a turtledove or young pigeon. The priest shall bring the offering to the altar and wring off its head. Its blood shall be drained out on the side of the altar, and its crop, with the feathers, cast beside the altar in the place for ashes. Tear it by its wings, but do not divide it asunder. The priest shall burn it on the altar, an offering by fire, a pleasing odor to the LORD.

"When any one brings a cereal offering to the LORD, it shall be of fine flour; pour oil upon it, and put frankincense on it, and bring it to Aaron's sons the priests. Take from it a handful which the priest shall burn as its memorial portion upon the altar, an offering by fire, a pleasing odor to the LORD. What is left of the cereal offering shall be for Aaron and his sons, a most holy part of the offerings by fire to the LORD. No cereal offering shall be made with leaven; you shall burn no leaven or honey as an offering by fire to the LORD. Season all your cereal offerings with salt; do not let the salt of the covenant with your God be lacking from your cereal offering; with all your offerings you shall offer salt.

"If you offer a cereal offering of first fruits to the LORD, offer crushed new grain from fresh ears, parched with fire. Put oil upon it, lay frankincense on it, and the priest shall burn its memorial portion as an offering by fire to the LORD.

"If, as a sacrifice of peace offering, you offer an animal from the herd, male or female, offer it without blemish before the LORD. Lay your hand upon its head and kill it at the door of the tent of meeting; Aaron's sons the priests shall throw the blood against the altar round about. Offer the fat that is on the entrails, the two kidneys with the fat on them, and the appendage of the liver. Aaron's sons shall burn them on the altar upon the burnt offering, which is upon the wood on the fire; it is an offering by fire, a pleasing odor to the LORD.

"If your sacrifice of peace offering is an animal from the flock, male or female, offer it without blemish. If it is a lamb, offer it before the LORD, laying your hand upon its head and killing it before the tent of meeting; Aaron's sons shall throw its blood against the altar, and the priest shall burn its fat as food offered by fire to the LORD. All fat is the LORD's. It shall be a perpetual statute throughout your generations, that you eat neither fat nor blood."

The LORD said to Moses, "If any one of

the common people sins unwittingly in doing any of the things which the LORD has commanded not to be done, he shall offer a female goat without blemish for the sin which he has committed. He shall lay his hand on the head of the sin offering, and kill it. The priest shall burn it upon the altar, and make atonement for him, and he shall be forgiven.

"If any one commits a breach of faith against the LORD by deceiving his neighbor in a matter of deposit, or through robbery, or if he has oppressed his neighbor, or has found what was lost and lied about it, swearing falsely—in any of these sins of which men become guilty, he shall restore what he took by robbery, or got by oppression, or the deposit committed to him, or the lost thing he found, or anything about which he has sworn falsely; he shall restore it in full, add a fifth to it, and give it to him to whom it belongs, on the day of his guilt offering. He shall bring to the priest his guilt offering to the LORD, a ram without blemish out of the flock; the priest shall make atonement for him before the LORD, and he shall be forgiven."

The LORD said to Moses, "Command Aaron and his sons, saying, This is the law of the burnt offering: it shall be on the hearth upon the altar all night, and the fire of the altar shall be kept burning. In the morning the priest shall put on his linen garments, take up the ashes of the burnt offering, and put them beside the altar. Then he shall put off his garments, and put on other garments, and carry the ashes outside the camp to a clean place. The fire on the altar shall be kept burning continually; it shall not go out."

THE LORD SAID to Moses, "Take Aaron and his sons; take the garments, the anointing oil, the bull of the sin offering, two rams, and the basket of unleavened bread; and assemble the congregation at the door of the tent of meeting."

Moses did as the LORD commanded him, and said to the assembled congregation, "This the LORD has commanded be done." Then he washed Aaron and his sons with water. He put on Aaron the coat, the girdle, and the robe; he put the priestly apron upon him, girding him with its skilfully woven band. He placed the breastpiece on him, and he set the turban upon his head. On the turban he set the golden plate, the holy crown, as the LORD commanded. Then Moses took the anointing oil, and sprinkled it on the tabernacle and on all that was in it, and on the altar and all its utensils, to consecrate them. He poured some of the oil on Aaron's head, consecrating him, and he clothed Aaron's sons with coats, girded them, and bound caps on them, as the LORD commanded.

Then Moses brought the bull of the sin offering, and Aaron and his sons laid their hands upon its head. Moses killed it, and with his finger put some of the blood on the horns of the altar round about to purify it. He poured out the rest of the blood at the base of the altar to consecrate and make atonement for it. Then he took the fat on the entrails, the appendage of the liver, the two kidneys with their fat, and burned them on the altar. But the bull, its skin, its flesh, and its dung, Moses burned outside the camp, as the LORD commanded. Then Moses presented the ram of the burnt offering; Aaron and his sons laid their hands on its head, and Moses killed it, and threw the blood upon the altar. The ram was cut into pieces, and Moses burned it on the altar, a pleasing odor, an offering by fire to the LORD, as the LORD commanded.

Then Moses presented the other ram, the ram of ordination; Aaron and his sons laid their hands on its head. Moses killed it, and put some of its blood on the tip of Aaron's right ear, the thumb of his right hand, and the great toe of his right foot. He put blood on the tips of the right ears of Aaron's sons, on the thumbs of their right hands, and on the great toes of their right feet; then Moses threw the blood upon the altar. He took the fat tail, the fat on the entrails, the appendage of the liver, the two kidneys with their fat, and the right thigh; out of the basket of unleavened bread he took one unleavened cake, one cake of bread with oil, and one wafer, and placed them on the fat and on the right thigh; he put all these in the hands of Aaron and his sons, and waved them before the altar as a wave offering to the LORD. Then Moses took them from their hands, and burned them on the altar as an ordination offering to the LORD. Moses took the breast, and waved it before the altar; it was Moses' portion of the ram of ordination, as the LORD commanded.

Moses took anointing oil and some of the blood which was on the altar, and sprinkled it upon Aaron and his sons, consecrating them. "Boil the flesh of the ram at the door of the tent of meeting," Moses said to them, "and eat it there with the bread that is in the basket of ordination offerings. What remains you shall burn. Do not go out of the tent of meeting for seven days, for it will take seven days to ordain you. The LORD has commanded what has been done today, to make atonement for you. Remain at the door of the tent of meeting day and night for seven days, performing what the LORD has charged, lest you die; for so I am commanded." And Aaron and his sons did all the things the LORD commanded by Moses.

On the eighth day Moses called Aaron and his sons and the elders of Israel. "Take a bull calf for a sin offering," he said to

Aaron, "and a ram for a burnt offering, both without blemish; offer them before the LORD. Say to the people of Israel, Take a male goat for a sin offering, a calf and a lamb, both without blemish, for a burnt offering, and an ox and a ram for peace offerings, to sacrifice before the LORD, and a cereal offering mixed with oil; for today the LORD will appear to you." They brought what Moses commanded before the tent of meeting, and the congregation drew near and stood before the LORD. "Draw near to the altar," Moses said to Aaron, "and offer your sin offering and burnt offering to make atonement for yourself; then bring the people's offering and make atonement for them, as the LORD has commanded."

So Aaron drew near to the altar. He presented his offering and the people's offering according to the ordinances. Then he lifted up his hands toward the people and blessed them; he came down from the altar and, with Moses, went into the tent of meeting. When they came out they blessed the people, and the glory of the LORD appeared to all. Fire came forth from before the LORD and consumed the offerings upon the altar; and the people, seeing it, shouted and fell on their faces.

Now NADAB AND Abihu, sons of Aaron, each took a censer, put fire in it, laid incense on it, and offered unholy fire before the LORD, such as he had not commanded them. Fire came forth from the presence of the LORD, devouring them, and they died. "This," Moses said to Aaron, "is what the LORD has said: 'I will show myself holy among those who are near me, and before all the people I will be glorified.' " Aaron held his peace.

Then Moses called Mishael and Elzaphan, sons of Uzziel, Aaron's uncle. "Draw near," he said to them. "Carry your brethren from before the sanctuary out of the camp." So they carried them out in their coats, as Moses had said. Then Moses said to Aaron and his sons, Eleazar and Ithamar, "Do not let your hair hang loose, and do not rend your clothes in mourning, lest you die, and wrath come upon the congregation; but your brethren, the house of Israel, may bewail the burning which the LORD has kindled. And do not go out of the tent of meeting, lest you die; for the anointing oil of the LORD is upon you." They did according to the word of Moses.

The LORD said to Aaron, "Drink no wine nor strong drink, you nor your sons, when you go into the tent of meeting, lest you die; it shall be a statute throughout your generations. You are to distinguish between the holy and the common, between the unclean and the clean; and you are to teach the people of Israel the statutes which the LORD has spoken to them by Moses."

THE LORD SAID to Moses and Aaron, "Say to the people of Israel, These are the living things which you may eat among all the beasts on earth. Whatever parts the hoof and is cloven-footed and chews the cud, you may eat. Nevertheless, among animals that chew the cud or part the hoof, you shall not eat these: the camel, the rock badger, and the hare. Because they chew the cud but do not part the hoof, they are unclean to you. The swine, because it parts the hoof and is cloven-footed but does not chew the cud, is unclean to you.

"These you may eat, of all that are in the waters: everything that has fins and scales, whether in the seas or in the rivers. But anything that has not fins and scales is an abomination to you. Of their flesh you shall not eat, and their carcasses you shall have in abomination.

"And these you shall have in abomination among the birds, they shall not be eaten: the eagle, the vulture, the osprey, the kite, the falcon, every raven according to its kind, the ostrich, the nighthawk, the sea gull, the hawk, the owl, the cormorant, the ibis, the water hen, the pelican, the carrion vulture, the stork, the heron, the hoopoe, and the bat.

"All winged insects that go upon all fours are an abomination to you. Yet among them you may eat those which have legs above their feet, with which to leap on the earth. Of them you may eat: the locust, the bald locust, the cricket, and the grasshopper according to its kind. But all other winged insects which have four feet are an abomination to you.

"And by these you shall become unclean; whoever touches their carcass shall be unclean until evening; whoever carries any part of their carcass shall wash his clothes and be unclean until evening. Every animal which parts the hoof but is not cloven-footed or does not chew the cud is unclean to you; every one who touches them shall be unclean. All that go on their paws, among animals that go on all fours, are unclean to you; whoever touches their carcass shall be unclean, and he who carries their carcass shall wash his clothes and be unclean until evening.

"These are unclean to you among the swarming things upon the earth: the weasel, the mouse, the great lizard, the gecko, the land crocodile, the lizard, the sand lizard, and the chameleon. Whoever touches them when they are dead shall be unclean until evening. Anything upon which any of them falls when they are dead shall be unclean, whether it is an article of wood, a garment, a skin or a sack, any vessel used for any purpose; it must be put into water, and it shall be unclean until evening; then it shall be clean. And if any part of their carcass falls into any earthen vessel, all that is in the vessel shall be unclean, and you shall break it. Any food in it, upon which water may come, shall be unclean; and all drink which may be drunk from every such vessel shall be unclean. Nevertheless, a spring or a cistern holding water shall be clean. And if any part of their carcass falls upon any seed that is to be sown, it is clean; but if water is put on the seed and any part of their carcass falls on it, it is unclean to you.

"If any animal of which you may eat dies, he who touches its carcass shall be unclean until evening; he who eats of its carcass shall wash his clothes and be unclean until evening; he also who carries the carcass shall wash his clothes and be unclean until evening.

"Whatever goes on its belly, whatever goes on all fours, whatever has many feet, all the swarming things that swarm upon the earth, you shall not eat; for they are an abomination. You shall not defile yourselves with them, lest you become unclean. For I am the LORD your God; consecrate yourselves therefore, and be holy, for I am holy. I brought you up out of Egypt, to be your God; you shall be holy, for I the LORD your God am holy."

This is the law pertaining to beast and bird and every living creature that moves through the waters and swarms upon the earth, to make a distinction between the unclean and the clean, between the living creature that may be eaten and the living creature that may not be eaten.

THE LORD SAID to Moses, "Say to the people of Israel, If a woman conceives, and bears a male child, then she shall be unclean seven days, as at the time of her menstruation. On the eighth day the flesh of the child's foreskin shall be circumcised. Then she shall continue for thirty-three days in the blood of her purifying; she shall not touch any hallowed thing, nor come into the sanctuary, until the days of her purifying are completed. But if she bears a female child, she shall be unclean two weeks, as in her menstruation, and she shall continue in the blood of her purifying for sixty-six days.

"When the days of her purifying are completed, whether for a son or a daughter, she shall bring to the priest at the door of the tent of meeting a year-old lamb for a burnt offering, and a young pigeon or turtledove for a sin offering; the priest shall offer it before the LORD, and make atonement for her; then she shall be clean from the flow of her blood. This is the law for her who bears a child, male or female. If she cannot afford a lamb, she shall take two turtledoves or two young pigeons, one for a burnt offering and the other for a sin offering; the priest shall make atonement for her, and she shall be clean."

THE LORD SAID to Moses, "This shall be the law of the leper for his day of cleansing. He shall be brought to the priest, and the priest shall go out of the camp and make an examination. If the leprous disease is healed, the priest shall command that two living clean birds, some cedarwood, scarlet thread, and hyssop be taken for him who is to be cleansed. One of the birds shall be killed in an earthen vessel over running water, and the priest shall dip the living bird, with the cedarwood, the scarlet thread, and the hyssop, in the blood of the bird that was killed; the priest shall sprinkle the blood seven times upon him who is to be cleansed of leprosy, then pronounce him clean, and let the living bird go into the open field. He who is to be cleansed shall wash his clothes, shave off all his hair, bathe himself in water, and he shall be clean; after that he shall come into the camp, but shall dwell outside his tent seven days. On the seventh day he shall shave off all his hair, his beard, and his eyebrows. Then he shall wash his clothes and bathe his body, and he shall be clean.

"On the eighth day the man who is to be cleansed shall take two male lambs and a year-old ewe lamb without blemish, a cereal offering, and a measure of oil. The priest shall offer these things to the LORD, to make atonement for him, and he shall be clean.

"But if he is poor and cannot afford so much, then he shall take one male lamb, a cereal offering, a measure of oil, and two turtledoves or two young pigeons, such as he can afford. On the eighth day he shall bring them to the priest, and the priest shall offer these and make atonement before the LORD for him who is being cleansed. This is the law for him in whom is a leprous disease, who cannot afford the offerings for his cleansing."

The LORD said to Moses and Aaron, "When you come into the land of Canaan, which I give you for a possession, and I put a leprous disease in a house there, the priest shall command that the house be emptied, lest all that is in it be declared unclean; then he shall examine the house. If the disease is in the walls with greenish or reddish spots, and if it appears to be deeper than the surface, the priest shall shut up the house seven days. On the seventh day he shall come again and look; if the disease has spread in the walls, the priest shall command that the diseased stones be taken and thrown into an unclean place outside the city; the inside of the house shall be scraped, and the plaster poured into an unclean place outside the city; then other stones shall be put in the place of those stones, and other plaster used to plaster the house.

"If the disease breaks out again, and

spreads, it is a malignant leprosy in the house; it is unclean. He who owns the house shall break it down, and carry its stones, timber, and plaster out of the city to an unclean place. But if the priest makes an examination, and the disease has not spread after the house was plastered, then the priest shall make atonement for the house, and it shall be clean."

This is the law for any leprous disease: to show when it is unclean and when it is clean.

THE LORD SPOKE to Moses, after the death of Aaron's two sons, when they drew near before the LORD and died. The LORD said, "Tell Aaron your brother not to come at all times into the holy place within the veil, before the mercy seat which is upon the ark, lest he die; for I will appear in the cloud upon the mercy seat. But thus shall Aaron come into the holy place: with a young bull for a sin offering and a ram for a burnt offering. He shall bathe his body, put on the holy linen coat and breeches, be girded with the linen girdle, and wear the linen turban; these are the holy garments.

He shall take from the congregation of the people of Israel two male goats for a sin offering, and one ram for a burnt offering.

"Aaron shall offer the bull as a sin offering, and make atonement for himself and for his house. Then he shall take the two goats, and set them before the LORD at the door of the tent of meeting; he shall cast lots upon the two goats, one lot for the LORD and the other for Azazel. Aaron shall offer the goat on which the lot fell for the LORD as a sin offering for the people. He shall kill it and sprinkle its blood upon and before the mercy seat; thus he shall make atonement for the holy place, because of the uncleannesses of the people of Israel, and because of all their sins; and so he shall do for the tent of meeting, which abides with them in the midst of their uncleannesses. There shall be no man in the tent of meeting when he enters the holy place, or until he comes out, after having made atonement for himself, for his house, and for all of Israel. Then he shall go out to the altar before the LORD and make atonement for it, sprinkling some blood of the bull and of the goat upon it with his finger seven times, to cleanse and hallow it from the uncleannesses of the people of Israel.

"When Aaron has made an end of atoning for the holy place and the tent of meeting and the altar, he shall present before the LORD the goat on which the lot fell for Azazel. He shall lay both his hands upon the head of the live goat, and confess over it all the iniquities of the people of Israel, all their transgressions, all their sins; he shall put these upon the head of the goat, and send it into the wilderness by the hand of a man who is in readiness. The goat shall bear the people's iniquities to a solitary land, and there it shall be let go. Then Aaron shall come into the tent of meeting, put off the linen garments, and leave them there; he shall bathe, put on his garments, come forth, offer his burnt offering and the burnt offering of the people, and make atonement for himself and for the people.

"And it shall be a statute for ever that on the tenth day of the seventh month, you shall fast, and do no work, either the native or the stranger who sojourns among you; for on this day shall atonement be made for you; from all your sins you shall be clean before the LORD. It is a sabbath of solemn rest to you. The priest, wearing the holy linen garments, shall make atonement for the sanctuary, for the tent of meeting, for the altar, for the priests, and for all the people of the assembly. This shall be an everlasting statute for you, that atonement may be made for the people of Israel once in the year because of all their sins." And Moses did as the LORD commanded him.

THE LORD SAID to Moses, "Say to the people of Israel, You shall be holy; for I the LORD your God am holy. Every one of you shall revere his mother and his father, and you shall keep my sabbaths. Do not turn to idols or make for yourselves molten gods: I am the LORD your God.

"You shall not steal, nor lie to one another. And you shall not swear by my name falsely, and so profane the name of your God. You shall not oppress your neighbor or rob him. The wages of a hired servant shall not remain with you all night until the morning. You shall not curse the deaf or put a stumbling block before the blind, but you shall fear your God: I am the LORD.

"You shall do no injustice in judgment; you shall not be partial to the poor or defer to the great, but in righteousness shall you judge your neighbor. You shall not hate your brother in your heart. You shall not take vengeance or bear any grudge against the sons of your own people, but you shall love your neighbor as yourself. And when a stranger sojourns with you in your land, you shall not do him wrong. He shall be to you as the native among you, and you shall love him as yourself; for you were strangers in the land of Egypt: I am the LORD your God.

"You shall do no wrong in judgment, in measures of length or weight or quantity. You shall have just balances, just weights. I am the LORD your God, who brought you out of the land of Egypt. You shall observe all my statutes and all my ordinances, and do them: I am the LORD."

THE LORD SAID to Moses, "Say to the people of Israel, My appointed feasts which you shall proclaim as holy convocations are these. Six days shall work be done; but on the seventh day, a sabbath of solemn rest, you shall do no work; it is a sabbath to the LORD in all your dwellings.

"These are the holy convocations, which you shall proclaim at the appointed time. On the fourteenth day of the first month, in the evening, is the LORD'S passover. On the fifteenth day of the same month begins the feast of unleavened bread to the LORD; seven days you shall eat unleavened bread. On the first day you shall have a holy convocation; you shall do no laborious work. But you shall present an offering by fire to the LORD seven days; on the seventh day also there shall be a holy convocation; you shall do no laborious work."

The LORD said to Moses, "Say to the people of Israel, When you come into the land which I give you and reap its harvest, bring the sheaf of the first fruits of your harvest to the priest; on the morrow after the sabbath he shall wave it before the LORD, that you may find acceptance. On that day you shall offer a male lamb a year old without blemish as a burnt offering to the LORD. A cereal offering of fine flour mixed with oil shall be offered with it by fire to the LORD, a pleasing odor; the drink offering with it shall be of wine. You shall eat neither bread nor grain, parched or fresh, until you have brought the offering of your God: it is a statute for ever in all your dwellings.

"Count from the day you brought the sheaf of the wave offering seven full weeks, counting fifty days to the morrow after the seventh sabbath; then present a cereal offering of new grain to the LORD. Bring from your dwellings two loaves of bread to be waved, made of fine flour and baked with leaven, as first fruits to the LORD. Present also seven lambs, one young bull, and two rams as a burnt offering, a pleasing odor to the LORD. Offer one male goat for a sin offering, and two male lambs a year old as a sacrifice of peace offerings. The priest shall wave them before the LORD with the bread of the first fruits; they shall be holy to the LORD for the priest. You shall make proclamation on the same day, and hold a holy convocation, and do no laborious work: it is a statute for ever throughout your generations.

"When you reap the harvest, you shall not reap your field to its very border, nor shall you gather the gleanings after your harvest; leave them for the poor and for the stranger: I am the LORD your God."

The LORD said to Moses, "Say to the people of Israel, On the first day of the seventh month, observe a day of solemn rest, a memorial proclaimed with blast of trumpets, a holy convocation. You shall do no laborious work, and you shall present an offering by fire to the LORD.

"On the tenth day of this seventh month is the day of atonement, a time of holy convocation; you shall fast, present an offering by fire to the LORD, and do no work on this day; for it is a day of atonement, to make atonement for you before the LORD your God. Whoever does not fast on this day shall be cut off from his people; whoever does any work, that person I will destroy from among his people. It shall be to you a sabbath of solemn rest; on the ninth day of the month, beginning at evening, from evening to evening shall you keep your sabbath.

"On the fifteenth day of this seventh

month, when you have gathered in the produce of the land, you shall keep the feast of booths to the LORD for seven days; on the first and eighth days shall be a solemn rest. Take on the first day the fruit of goodly trees, branches of palm trees, boughs of leafy trees, and willows of the brook; rejoice before the LORD your God seven days. It is a statute for ever; keep it as a feast to the LORD seven days in the seventh month. All Israel shall dwell in booths for seven days, that your generations may know that I made the people of Israel dwell in booths when I brought them out of Egypt: I am the LORD your God."

Thus Moses declared to the people of Israel the appointed feasts of the LORD.

Now AN ISRAELITE woman's son, whose father was an Egyptian, quarreled in the camp with a man of Israel, and her son blasphemed the Name, and cursed. The people brought him to Moses, and put him in custody, till the will of the LORD should be declared to them.

The LORD said to Moses, "Bring out of

the camp him who cursed; let all who heard him lay their hands upon his head, and let the congregation stone him. Say to the people of Israel, Whoever curses his God shall bear his sin. The sojourner as well as the native, when he blasphemes the name of the LORD, shall be put to death; all the congregation shall stone him.

"And he who kills a man shall be put to death. He who kills a beast shall make it good, life for life. When a man causes a disfigurement in his neighbor, as he has done it shall be done to him, fracture for fracture, eye for eye, tooth for tooth. You shall have one law for the sojourner and for the native; for I am the LORD your God." So Moses spoke to the people of Israel; and they brought him who had cursed out of the camp, and stoned him. Thus the people did as the LORD commanded Moses.

THE LORD SAID to Moses on Mount Sinai, "Say to the people of Israel, When you come into the land which I give you, the land shall keep a sabbath to the LORD. Six years you shall sow, prune, and gather, but the seventh year you shall not; it shall be a year of solemn rest for the land.

"You shall count seven times seven years, forty-nine years. Then you shall send abroad the loud trumpet on the day of atonement. And you shall hallow the fiftieth year, and proclaim liberty throughout the land; it shall be a jubilee for you, when each of you shall return to his property and to his family. For the land shall not be sold in perpetuity; the land is mine, and you are strangers and sojourners with me. In all the country you possess, you shall grant a redemption of the land.

"If your brother becomes poor, sells part of his property, and has not sufficient means to get it back, then what he sold shall remain in the hand of him who bought it until the year of jubilee; then it shall be released, and he shall return to his property. If your brother becomes poor, and cannot maintain himself, you shall maintain him; as a stranger and a sojourner he shall live with you. Take no interest from him or increase, but fear your God; that your brother may live beside you.

"And if your brother becomes poor beside you, and sells himself to you, you shall not make him serve as a slave: he shall be as a hired servant and a sojourner. He shall serve with you until the year of the jubilee; then he shall go out from you, he and his children with him, and go back to his own family, returning to the possession of his fathers. For to me the people of Israel are servants, my servants whom I brought forth out of the land of Egypt: I am the LORD your God.

"YOU SHALL MAKE for yourselves no idols, erect no graven image or pillar to bow down to; for I am the LORD your God. You shall keep my sabbaths and reverence my sanctuary: I am the LORD.

"If you walk in my statutes and observe my commandments, I will give you rains in their season, and the land shall yield its increase, the trees shall yield their fruit. Your threshing shall last to the time of vintage, and the vintage shall last to the time for sowing; you shall eat bread to the full, and dwell in your land securely. I will give peace, and none shall make you afraid; I will remove evil beasts, and the sword shall not go through your land. You shall chase your enemies, and they shall fall before you. I will make you fruitful, and will confirm my covenant with you. I will make my abode among you; my soul shall not abhor you. I will be your God, and you shall be my people. I am the LORD your God, who brought you out of Egypt, that you should not be slaves; I have broken the bars of your yoke and made you walk erect.

"But if you will not do all these commandments, if you spurn my statutes, if your soul abhors my ordinances, so that you break my covenant, I will appoint over you sudden terror, consumption, and fever that waste the eyes and cause life to pine away. You shall sow your seed in vain, for your enemies shall eat it; I will set my face against you, and you shall be smitten before your enemies; those who hate you shall rule you, and you shall flee when none pursues. If in spite of this you will not hearken to me, then I will chastise you again sevenfold; I will break the pride of your power, and make your heavens like iron and your earth like brass; your strength shall be spent in vain, for your land shall not yield its increase, and the trees shall not yield their fruit.

"Then if you will not hearken to me, I will bring more plagues upon you, seven-fold as many as your sins. I will let loose the wild beasts among you, to rob you of your children, destroy your cattle, and make you few in number. And if by this discipline you are not turned to me, but walk contrary to me, then I also will walk contrary to you; I myself will smite you. I will bring a sword upon you, that shall execute vengeance for the covenant; if you gather within your cities, I will send pestilence among you. When I break your staff of bread, ten women shall bake your bread in one oven, and you shall eat, but not be satisfied.

"If in spite of this you will not hearken to me, but walk contrary to me, then I, in fury, will chastise you myself sevenfold for your sins. You shall eat the flesh of your sons and daughters. I will destroy your high places, cut down your incense altars, and cast your dead bodies upon the dead bodies of your idols; my soul will abhor you. I will make your sanctuaries desolate, and I will not smell your pleasing odors. I will devastate the land, so that your enemies who settle in it shall be astonished at it. And I will scatter you among the nations; your land shall be a desolation, and your cities shall be a waste.

"Then, while you are in your enemies' land, the land shall enjoy its sabbaths. It shall have rest, the rest it had not when you dwelt upon it. As for those of you that are left, I will send faintness into your hearts in the lands of your enemies; at the sound of a driven leaf you shall flee as one flees from the sword, stumbling over one another and falling though none pursues. You shall have no power to stand before your enemies. You shall perish among nations, and the land of your enemies shall eat you up. Those of you that are left shall pine away in your enemies' lands because of your iniquity and the iniquities of your fathers.

"But if you confess your iniquity and the treachery of your fathers, committed against me; if your uncircumcised heart is humbled and you make amends; then I will remember my covenant with Jacob, with Isaac, and with Abraham, and I will remember the land. I will not spurn you, neither will I abhor you so as to destroy you utterly and break my covenant; for I am the LORD your God; I will remember the covenant with your forefathers, whom I brought forth out of the land of Egypt in the sight of the nations, that I might be your God: I am the LORD."

These are the statutes and ordinances and laws which the LORD commanded Moses for the people of Israel on Mount Sinai.

NUMBERS

Prior to their arrival at the border of the Promised Land, the Israelites wandered in the wilderness for nearly forty years, mostly in the vicinity of an oasis near Kadesh. The Book of Numbers relates the varied experiences of these years, including the often discontented murmuring of the people. The unknown compiler of these traditions emphasizes that God, though he disciplined the Israelites for their faithlessness, was at the same time marvelously guiding and sustaining them throughout their long and difficult journey. In addition, within the narrative there are miscellaneous laws and ceremonial ordinances, which supplement the Sinaitic code and anticipate the settlement in Canaan. The New Testament has several references to the events in this book, including the bronze serpent, the revolt of Korah and its consequences, the prophecies of Balaam, and the water that Moses brought gushing from the rock. The book derives its name from the account, at the beginning, of the census or numbering of the Israelite people.

———

THE LORD SPOKE to Moses in the wilderness of Sinai, in the tent of meeting, on the first day of the second month, in the second year after they had come out of Egypt, saying, "Take a census of the people of Israel, by families, by fathers' houses, every male, from twenty years old and upward; all in Israel who are able to go forth to war, you and Aaron shall number them, company by company. There shall be with you a man from each tribe, each being the head of the house of his fathers. And these are the men who shall attend you: from the tribe of Reuben, Elizur; from the tribe of Simeon, Shelumiel; from Judah, Nahshon; from Issachar, Nethanel; from Zebulun, Eliab; from the sons of Joseph, from

Ephraim, Elishama, and from Manasseh, Gamaliel; from Benjamin, Abidan; from Dan, Ahiezer; from Asher, Pagiel; from Gad, Eliasaph; and from Naphtali, Ahira." These were the chosen leaders of their ancestral tribes, the heads of the clans of Israel.

So Moses and Aaron assembled the congregation, and with the help of the leaders of Israel, they numbered them. And their whole number was six hundred and three thousand five hundred and fifty. But the Levites were not numbered by their ancestral tribe. For the LORD said to Moses, "You shall not take a census of the tribe of Levi among the people of Israel; but appoint the Levites over the tabernacle of the testimony; they are to carry and tend the tabernacle and all its furnishings, and they shall encamp around it. When the tabernacle is to set out, the Levites shall take it down; and when the tabernacle is to be pitched, they shall set it up. If any one else comes near, he shall be put to death. The people of Israel shall pitch their tents by their companies, every man by his own camp and his own standard; but the Levites shall encamp around the tabernacle of the testimony, and keep charge of it, that there may be no wrath upon the congregation." And the people of Israel did all that the LORD commanded Moses.

The LORD said to Moses and Aaron, "The people of Israel shall encamp, each with the ensign of his fathers' house, facing the tent of meeting on every side. Those to encamp on the east side toward the sunrise shall be of the standard of the camp of Judah by their companies, the leader of the people of Judah being Nahshon, and his host as numbered being seventy-four thousand six hundred. Next to him shall encamp the tribe of Issachar, their leader being Nethanel, and their number being fifty-four thousand four hundred. Then the tribe of Zebulun, led by Eliab, and numbering fifty-seven thousand four hundred. The whole camp of Judah, by their companies, is a hundred and eighty-six thousand four hundred. They shall set out first on the march.

"On the south side shall be the camp of Reuben by their companies, the leader of the people of Reuben being Elizur, his host being forty-six thousand five hundred. Next to him shall encamp the tribe of Simeon, led by Shelumiel, his host numbering fifty-nine thousand three hundred. Then the tribe of Gad, led by Eliasaph, and numbering forty-five thousand six hundred and fifty. The whole camp of Reuben is a hundred and fifty-one thousand four hundred and fifty. They shall set out second.

"Then the tent of meeting shall set out, with the camp of the Levites in the midst of the other camps; as they encamp, so shall they set out, each in position.

"On the west side shall be the standard of the camp of Ephraim, the leader of the people of Ephraim being Elishama, his host being forty thousand five hundred. Next to him shall be the tribe of Manasseh, their leader being Gamaliel, and their number being thirty-two thousand two hundred. Then the tribe of Benjamin, led by Abidan, and numbering thirty-five thousand four hundred. The whole camp of Ephraim, numbering a hundred and eight thousand one hundred, shall set out third on the march.

"On the north side shall be the camp of

Dan, the leader of the people of Dan being
Ahiezer, his host being sixty-two thousand
seven hundred. Next to him shall encamp
the tribe of Asher, led by Pagiel, and numbering forty-one thousand five hundred.
Then the tribe of Naphtali, their leader
being Ahira, and their number being fifty-
three thousand four hundred. The whole
camp of Dan, numbering a hundred and
fifty-seven thousand six hundred, shall set
out last, standard by standard."

Thus the people of Israel, according to
all that the LORD commanded Moses, encamped by their standards, and so they set
out, every one according to his fathers'
house.

THE LORD SAID to Moses, "Command the
people of Israel to put out of the camp
every leper, every one having a discharge,
and every one unclean through contact
with the dead; put out both male and female, that they may not defile their camp,
in the midst of which I dwell." And the
people drove them outside the camp, as
the LORD said.

The LORD said to Moses, "Say to the

people of Israel, When a man or woman sins, breaking faith with the LORD, that person shall confess the sin committed, and make full restitution, adding a fifth to it, and giving it to him to whom he did the wrong. But if there is no kinsman to whom restitution may be made, the restitution shall go to the LORD for the priest, in addition to the ram of atonement. Every offering, all the holy things that the people of Israel bring to the priest, shall be his."

The LORD said to Moses, "Say to the people of Israel, If any man's wife goes astray and acts unfaithfully, if a man lies with her carnally, hidden from the eyes of her husband, and there is no witness against her, since she was not taken in the act; and if the spirit of jealousy comes upon the husband whose wife has defiled herself; or if he is jealous of his wife, though she has not defiled herself; then the man shall bring his wife to the priest, with a cereal offering of jealousy. The priest shall set her before the LORD; then he shall take holy water in an earthen vessel, and put some of the dust from the floor of the tabernacle into the water. He shall unbind the woman's hair, and place in her hands the cereal offering of jealousy. In his hand the priest shall have the water of bitterness that brings the curse. Then the priest shall make her take the oath of the curse, saying to her, 'If no man has lain with you, be free from this water of bitterness that brings the curse. But if you have gone astray, though you are under your husband's authority, and if some man other than your husband has lain with you, then the LORD make you an execration among your people; may this water that brings the curse pass into your bowels and make your body swell and your thigh fall away.' And the woman shall say, 'Amen, Amen.'

"Then the priest shall write these curses in a book, and wash them off into the water of bitterness. He shall take the cereal offering of jealousy out of the woman's hand, wave it before the LORD, and burn a handful of it upon the altar as its memorial portion. Afterward he shall make the woman drink the water of bitterness that brings the curse; if she has acted unfaithfully against her husband, the water shall enter into her and cause bitter pain; her body shall swell, her thigh shall fall away, and she shall become an execration among her people. But if the woman has not defiled herself, then she shall be free and shall conceive children."

The LORD said to Moses, "Say to the people of Israel, When a man or woman makes the vow of a Nazirite, to separate himself to the LORD, he shall separate himself from wine and strong drink; he shall drink no vinegar made from wine, shall drink no juice of grapes, and shall eat no grapes, fresh or dried. All the days of his separation he shall eat nothing produced by the grapevine. All the days of his vow no razor shall come upon his head; until the time of his separation to the LORD is completed, he shall be holy, letting his hair grow long. While he separates himself he shall not go near a dead body. Neither for his father nor mother, nor for brother or sister, if they die, shall he make himself unclean; because his separation to God is upon his head. He is holy to the LORD. If any man dies suddenly beside him, defiling his consecrated head, then he shall shave his head on the day of his cleansing; on the seventh day he shall shave it. On the eighth day he shall bring two turtledoves or two young pigeons to the tent of meeting, and the priest shall offer one for a sin offering and the other for a burnt offering, and make atonement for him. He shall consecrate his head that same day, and separate himself to the LORD for the days of his separation; but the former time shall be void, because his separation was defiled.

"This is the law for the Nazirite, when his time of separation has been completed: he shall be brought to the door of the tent of meeting, and he shall offer his gift to the LORD, one male lamb for a burnt offering, one ewe lamb as a sin offering, one ram as a peace offering, and a basket of unleavened bread, cakes, and wafers. The priest shall present the offerings before the LORD and shall offer also cereal and drink offerings. The Nazirite shall shave his consecrated head at the door of the tent of meeting, and put the hair on the fire under the sacrifice of the peace offering. The priest shall put the shoulder of the ram, when it is boiled, one unleavened cake, and one unleavened wafer upon the hands of the Nazirite after he has shaven. Then the priest shall wave them for a wave offering before the LORD; they are a holy portion for the priest; and after that the Nazirite may drink wine. This is the law for the Nazirite in accordance with his vow."

The LORD said to Moses, "Say to Aaron and his sons, Thus you shall bless the people of Israel: you shall say to them, The LORD bless you and keep you; the LORD make his face to shine upon you, and be gracious to you; the LORD lift up his countenance upon you, and give you peace. So shall they put my name upon the people of Israel, and I will bless them."

ON THE DAY Moses finished setting up the tabernacle, after he had anointed and consecrated it with all its furnishings, the leaders of Israel, heads of their fathers' houses, brought their offerings before the LORD: six covered wagons and twelve oxen. They offered them before the tabernacle, and the LORD said to Moses, "Accept these to be used in doing the service of the tent of meeting, and give them to the Levites." So Moses took the wagons and the oxen, and gave them to the Levites.

Then the leaders offered offerings for the dedication of the altar. The LORD said to Moses, "They shall offer their offerings, one leader each day, for twelve days." At the end of the twelve days, this was the dedication offering for the altar from the leaders of Israel: twelve silver plates, twelve silver basins, twelve golden dishes, each silver plate weighing a hundred and thirty shekels and each basin seventy, the twelve golden dishes, full of incense, weighing ten shekels apiece according to the shekel of the sanctuary; all the cattle for the burnt offering: twelve bulls, twelve rams, twelve male lambs a year old, with their cereal offering; twelve male goats for a sin offering; and all the cattle for the sacrifice of peace offerings: twenty-four bulls, sixty rams, sixty male goats, and sixty male lambs a year old. And when Moses went into the tent of meeting to speak with the LORD, he heard the voice speaking to him from above the mercy seat upon the ark of the testimony.

Now the LORD said to Moses, "Take the Levites from among the people of Israel, and cleanse them. Sprinkle the water of expiation upon them, and let them shave all their body, wash their clothes, and cleanse themselves. Then let them take a young bull and its cereal offering, and you shall take another young bull for a sin offering. Present the Levites before the tent of meeting, and assemble the congregation. The people of Israel shall lay their hands upon the Levites, and Aaron shall offer the Levites before the LORD as a wave offering from the people of Israel, to do the service of the LORD. Then the Levites shall lay their hands upon the heads of the bulls; and you shall offer one for a sin offering and the other for a burnt offering, to make atonement for the Levites. And the Levites shall attend Aaron and his sons.

"Thus you shall separate the Levites to do service at the tent of meeting. They are wholly given to me from among the people of Israel, instead of all that open the womb. For the first-born of Israel, both man and beast, are mine; on the day I slew all the first-born in Egypt I consecrated them for myself, and I have taken the Levites instead of all the first-born of Israel. I have given the Levites to Aaron and his sons, to do service at the tent of meeting, and to make atonement, that there may be no plague among the people of Israel in case the people should come near the sanctuary."

Thus Moses, Aaron, and the congregation did all that the LORD commanded Moses concerning the Levites. And the Levites went in to do their service in the tent of meeting. The LORD said to Moses, "From twenty-five years old and upward the Levites shall perform work in the tent of meeting; and from the age of fifty years they shall withdraw and serve no more, but minister to their brethren in the tent of meeting, to keep the charge."

THE LORD SPOKE to Moses in the wilderness of Sinai, in the first month of the second year after they had come out of Egypt, saying, "Let the people of Israel keep the passover at its appointed time, on the fourteenth day of this month, in the evening, according to all its ordinances."

So Moses told the people of Israel, and they kept the passover in the wilderness of Sinai, according to all that the LORD commanded. But certain men were unclean through touching a dead body, so they could not keep the passover. They came before Moses and Aaron on that day, and said, "We are unclean through touching the dead body of a man; why are we kept from offering the LORD's offering at its appointed time?" Moses answered, "Wait, that I may hear what the LORD will command concerning you."

The LORD said to Moses, "Say to the people, If any of you is unclean through touching a dead body, or is afar off on a journey, he shall still keep the passover to the LORD, not in the first month, but in the second month on the fourteenth day in the evening. But the man who is clean and is not on a journey, yet refrains from keeping the passover at its appointed time, shall be cut off from his people; he shall bear his sin. And if a stranger sojourns among you, and will keep the passover to the LORD, according to its ordinance, so shall he do; have one statute for both sojourner and native."

On the day the tabernacle was set up, the cloud covered the tent of the testimony; at evening it was over the tabernacle like the appearance of fire until morning. So it was continually; the cloud by day, and the appearance of fire by night. Whenever the cloud was taken up, the people of Israel set out; and in the place where the cloud settled down, the people of Israel encamped. Even if the cloud continued over the tabernacle many days, they remained in camp; and when the cloud was taken up, they set out.

The LORD said to Moses, "Make two silver trumpets of hammered work; use them for summoning the congregation, and for breaking camp. The sons of Aaron, the priests, shall blow the trumpets. When both trumpets are blown, the congregation shall assemble at the tent of meeting. But if only one is blown, the leaders, the heads of the tribes of Israel, shall gather. An alarm is to be sounded whenever the tribes are to set out. When the first alarm is blown, the camps on the east side shall set out, and when the second is blown, the camps on the south side shall set out. The trumpets shall be a perpetual statute throughout your generations. When you go to war, sound an alarm, that you may be remembered before the LORD your God, and be saved from your enemies. On the day of your gladness also, at your appointed feasts, and at the beginnings of your months, blow the trumpets over your burnt offerings and peace offerings; they shall serve you for remembrance before your God: I am the LORD your God."

IN THE SECOND year, on the twentieth day of the second month, the cloud was taken up from over the tabernacle, and the people of Israel set out by stages from the wilderness of Sinai. The ark of the covenant of the LORD went before them, to seek out a resting place. The cloud of the LORD was over them by day, whenever they set out from the camp. And whenever the ark set out, Moses said, "Arise, O LORD, and let thy enemies be scattered; let them that hate thee flee before thee." And when it rested, he said, "Return, O LORD, to the ten thousand thousands of Israel."

Now the people complained about their misfortunes; and when the LORD heard, his anger was kindled, and the fire of the LORD burned among them, and consumed outlying parts of the camp. Then the people cried to Moses, who prayed to the LORD, and the fire abated. So that place was called Taberah, that is, Burning, because the fire of the LORD burned there.

But the rabble that was among them had a strong craving; and the people of Israel also wept again, and said, "O that we had meat to eat! We remember the fish we ate in Egypt, the cucumbers, melons, leeks, onions, and garlic; but now there is nothing but this manna to look at." The manna was like coriander seed; it fell, with the dew, on the camp in the night. The people gathered it, ground it in mills or beat it in mortars, boiled it, and made cakes of it which tasted like cakes baked with oil.

Moses heard the people weeping; the anger of the LORD blazed hotly, and Moses was displeased. He said to the LORD, "Why dost thou lay the burden of all this people upon me? Did I conceive them? Did I bring them forth, that thou shouldst tell me to carry them in my bosom, as a nurse carries the sucking child, to the land which thou didst swear to give their fathers? Where am I to get meat to give to all who weep before me? I am not able to carry all this people alone, the burden is too heavy. If thou wilt deal thus with me, kill me at once, that I may not see my wretchedness."

The LORD said to Moses, "Gather seventy of the elders of Israel; bring them to the tent of meeting, and I will come down and talk with you there. I will take some of the spirit which is upon you and put it upon them; and they shall bear the burden of the people with you. Say to the people, Consecrate yourselves for tomorrow, and you shall eat meat; for you have wept in the hearing of the LORD, saying, 'Who will give us meat to eat?' Therefore the LORD will give you meat, and you shall eat, not one or two days, or five or ten or twenty days, but a whole month, until it comes out at your nostrils and becomes loathsome to you, because you have rejected the LORD who is among you, saying, 'Why did we come forth out of Egypt?' " But Moses said, "The people number six hundred thousand on foot; and thou hast said, 'I will give them meat to eat for a whole month!' Shall flocks and herds be slaughtered to suffice them? Or shall all the fish of the sea be gathered to suffice them?" The LORD said, "Is the LORD's hand shortened? You shall see whether my word will come true or not."

So Moses told the people the words of the LORD, and he gathered seventy elders in the tent. Then the LORD came down in the cloud, and took some of the spirit that was upon Moses and put it upon the seventy; and when the spirit rested upon them, they prophesied. But they did not do so again.

Now two men, Eldad and Medad, had not gone to the tent, but had remained in the camp. And the spirit rested upon them, so they prophesied in the camp. A young man ran and told Moses, "Eldad and Medad are prophesying in the camp." And Joshua the son of Nun, the minister of Moses, one of his chosen men, said, "My lord Moses, forbid them." But Moses said, "Are you jealous for my sake? Would that all the LORD's people were prophets, that the LORD would put his spirit upon them!" And Moses and the elders of Israel returned to the camp.

Then there went forth a wind from the LORD, and it brought quails from the sea, and let them fall round about the camp. All that day, all night, and all the next day the people gathered the quails. Each gathered at least one hundred bushels, which they spread out to dry in the sun, all around the camp. While the meat was yet between their teeth, the anger of the LORD was kindled against the people, and the LORD smote them with a very great plague. That place was called Kibroth-hattaavah, that is, Graves of craving, because there they buried the people who had the craving. From Kibroth-hattaavah the people journeyed to Hazeroth, where they remained.

MIRIAM AND AARON spoke against Moses because he had married a Cushite woman. "Has the LORD indeed spoken only through Moses?" they said. "Has he not spoken through us also?" And the LORD heard, and his anger was kindled against them. Now Moses was very meek, more than all men on earth. And the LORD said to Moses, Aaron, and Miriam, "Come, you three, to the tent of meeting." They came, and the LORD came down in a pillar of cloud, stood at the door of the tent, and called Aaron and Miriam. When they came forward, he said, "Hear my words: If there is a prophet among you, I the LORD make myself known to him in a vision, I speak with him in a dream. Not so with my servant Moses. With him I speak mouth to mouth, clearly, and not in dark speech; and he beholds the form of the LORD. Why then were you not afraid to speak against Moses?" Then the LORD departed, and when the cloud removed from over the tent, behold, Miriam was leprous, as white as snow. Aaron, seeing this, said to Moses, "Oh, my lord, do not punish us because we have sinned. Let her not be as one dead, of whom the flesh is half consumed." Moses cried to the LORD, "Heal her, O God, I beseech thee." But the LORD said, "If her father had but spit in her face, should she not be shamed seven days? Let her be shut up outside the camp seven days; after that she may be brought in." So Miriam was shut up seven days; and the people did not march till she returned. Then they set out from Hazeroth, and encamped in the wilderness of Paran.

The LORD said to Moses, "Send men to spy out the land of Canaan, which I give to Israel; from each tribe of their fathers send one man, every one a leader." So Moses sent from the wilderness of Paran, according to the LORD's command, these men who were heads of the people of Israel: from the tribe of Reuben, Shammua; from the tribe of Simeon, Shaphat; from Judah, Caleb; from Issachar, Igal; from Ephraim, Joshua; from Benjamin, Palti; from Zebulun, Gaddiel; from Manasseh, Gaddi; from Dan, Ammiel; from Asher, Sethur; from Naphtali, Nahbi; and from Gad, Geuel. "Go up into the Negeb yonder," Moses said to them. "Go up into the hill country, and see what the land is, whether it is good or bad, rich or poor, whether the people who dwell in it are strong or weak, few or many, and whether their cities are camps or strongholds. Be of good courage, and bring back some of the fruit of the land." It was the season of the first ripe grapes.

So the men of Israel spied out the land from the wilderness of Zin to Rehob; they went up into the Negeb, and came to Hebron, where they saw the descendants of Anak, men of great stature. In the Valley of Eshcol they cut down a branch with a single cluster of grapes, which they carried on a pole between two of them; they brought also some pomegranates and figs. At the end of forty days they returned, and came to Moses, Aaron, and all the congregation in the wilderness of Paran, at Kadesh. They showed them the fruit of the land, but gave an evil report. "The land to which you sent us flows with milk and honey," they told Moses, "and this is its fruit. Yet the people who dwell there are strong, and the cities are fortified and very large; and besides, we saw the descendants of Anak there." But Caleb quieted the people. "Let us go up at once, and occupy the land," he said, "for we are well able to overcome it." Then the men who had gone up with him said, "We are not able to, for the people are stronger than we. All that we saw there are men of great stature, such as the sons of Anak; we seemed to ourselves like grasshoppers, and so we seemed to them."

That night the people of Israel wept, and murmured against Moses and Aaron. "Would that we had died in Egypt or in this wilderness!" they said. "Why does the LORD bring us here to fall by the sword? Our wives and little ones will become a prey. Let us choose a captain, and go back to Egypt." Then Moses and Aaron fell on their faces before the assembly. Joshua and Caleb, who were among those who had spied out the land, rent their clothes, saying, "The land we passed through is exceedingly good. If the LORD delights in us, he will bring us into this land which flows with milk and honey. Only, do not rebel against the LORD; and do not fear the people of the land; their protection is removed, and the LORD is with us." But the congregation said to stone them. Then the glory of the LORD appeared to the people of Israel. And the LORD said to Moses, "How long will this people despise me and not believe in me, in spite of all the signs I have wrought among them in Egypt and in the wilderness? I will strike them with pestilence and disinherit them, and I will make of you a nation greater than they."

But Moses said to the LORD, "Then the Egyptians will hear of it, and they will tell the inhabitants of this land, who have heard that thou, O LORD, art in the midst of this people. If thou dost kill this people, then the nations will say, 'Because the LORD was not able to bring them into the land he swore to give to them, he has slain them in the wilderness.' Now, I pray thee, let the power of the LORD be great as thou hast promised, saying, 'The LORD is slow to anger, and abounding in steadfast love, forgiving iniquity and transgression, but he will by no means clear the guilty, visiting the iniquity of fathers upon children, to the third and fourth generation.' Pardon the iniquity of this people, I pray thee, according to the greatness of thy steadfast love, as thou hast forgiven them from Egypt until now."

Then the LORD said, "I have pardoned, according to your word; but truly, as I live, none of the men who have seen my glory and my signs, and yet have not hearkened to my voice, shall see the land I swore to give to their fathers; none of those who despised me shall see it. Now, since the Canaanites dwell in the valleys, turn to-morrow and set out for the wilderness by way of the Red Sea. Tell the people of Israel, Of all your number, numbered from twenty years old and upward, who have murmured against me, not one shall come into the land where I swore that I would make you dwell, except Caleb and Joshua, who have followed me fully. But your little ones, who you said would become a prey, I will bring in; they shall know the land which you have despised. As for you, your dead bodies shall fall in this wilderness. Your children shall be shepherds in the wilderness forty years, suffering for your faithlessness until the last of your dead bodies lies in the wilderness. You shall bear your iniquity a year for every day of the forty days you spied out the land. For forty years you shall know my displeasure.

"I, the LORD, have spoken; surely this will I do to this wicked congregation gathered together against me: in this wilderness they shall die."

And the men whom Moses sent to spy out the land, and who returned bringing an evil report, died by plague before the LORD. Only Joshua and Caleb remained alive.

Moses told the LORD's words to the people of Israel, and they mourned greatly. They rose early in the morning, and went up toward the hill country, saying, "We will go up to the place which the LORD has promised; for we have sinned." But Moses said, "Why now are you transgressing the command of the LORD, for that will not succeed? Do not go lest you be struck down before your enemies, for the LORD is not among you. The Canaanites are before you, and you shall fall by the sword, because you have turned back from following the LORD." But they presumed to go, although neither the ark of the covenant of the LORD, nor Moses, departed out of the camp. Then the Canaanites who dwelt in that hill country came down, and defeated them and pursued them, even to Hormah.

Now KORAH, A son of Levi, and Dathan, Abiram, and On, sons of Reuben, rose up before Moses, with two hundred and fifty leaders of the congregation. They assembled themselves together against Moses and Aaron, and said, "You have gone too far! For all the congregation are holy, every one of them, and the LORD is among them; why then do you exalt yourselves above the assembly of the LORD?" When Moses heard this, he said to Korah and his company, "The LORD will show who is his, and who is holy, and will cause him to come near to him. Do this: take censers, put fire in them, and put incense upon them before the LORD. The man whom the LORD chooses shall be the holy one. You have gone too far, you sons of Levi! Is it too small a thing for you that the God of Israel has separated you from the congregation, to bring you near to himself, to do service in the tabernacle of the LORD, and to minister to the congregation? Would you seek the priesthood also? It is against the LORD that you have gathered together; what is Aaron, that you murmur against him?"

Then Moses summoned Dathan and Abiram, but they said, "We will not come up. Is it a small thing that you, having brought us out of a land flowing with milk and honey, to kill us in the wilderness, must also make yourself a prince over us? Moreover you have not brought us into a land flowing with milk and honey, nor given us inheritance of fields and vineyards. We will not come up." Moses was very angry, and said to the LORD, "Do not respect their offering. I have not taken one ass from them, and I have not harmed them."

Moses then said to Korah, "Be present, you and all your company, before the LORD; and every one of you bring his censer, two hundred and fifty censers." So every man took his censer, put fire in it, and laid incense upon it, and they stood at the entrance of the tent of meeting with Moses and Aaron. Then Korah assembled all the congregation against them, and the glory of the LORD appeared. The LORD said to Moses and to Aaron, "Separate yourselves from this congregation, that I may consume them." But Moses and Aaron fell on their faces. "O God," they said, "if one man sins, wilt thou be angry with all the congregation?"

Then the LORD said to Moses, "Say to the congregation, Get away from the dwellings of Dathan and Abiram." So Moses rose and went to Dathan and Abiram. The elders of Israel followed him, and Moses said, "Depart from the tents of these wicked men; touch nothing of theirs, lest you be swept away with all their sins." Then Dathan and Abiram came out and stood at the door of their tents, with their wives, sons, and little ones. Moses said, "Hereby you shall know that the LORD has sent me to do these works, and that it has not been of my own accord. If these men die the common death of all men, then the LORD has not sent me. But if the ground opens its mouth, and swallows them up alive, with all that belongs to them, then you shall know that these men have despised the LORD." As he finished speaking, the ground under Dathan and Abiram split asunder; the earth swallowed them up, with their households and all their goods. It closed over them, and they perished. All

Israel that were round about them fled at their cry.

Then fire came forth from the LORD, and consumed Korah and his company, the two hundred and fifty men offering the incense. The LORD said to Moses, "Tell Eleazar, the son of Aaron the priest, to take the censers out of the blaze, and scatter the fire far and wide. For the censers of these men who have sinned at the cost of their lives are holy; they were offered before the LORD. Let them be hammered into plates as a covering for the altar, to be a sign to the people of Israel." So Eleazar the priest took the bronze censers, and they were hammered out as a covering for the altar, to remind the people that no one who is not a priest, a descendant of Aaron, should burn incense before the LORD, lest he become as Korah and his company.

But on the morrow all the congregation of Israel murmured against Moses and Aaron, saying, "You have killed the people of the LORD." And behold, the cloud covered the tent of meeting, and the glory of the LORD appeared. The LORD said to Moses, "Get away from the midst of this congregation, that I may consume them." Moses and Aaron fell on their faces, and Moses said to Aaron, "Take your censer, put fire from the altar therein, and lay incense on it; carry it quickly to the congregation, and make atonement for them, for wrath has gone forth from the LORD; the plague has begun." So Aaron took the censer and ran into the midst of the assembly. He stood between the dead and the living; and the plague was stopped. But fourteen thousand seven hundred died by the plague, besides those who died in the affair of Korah. When the plague was stopped, Aaron returned to Moses.

The LORD said to Moses, "Speak to the people of Israel; get from their leaders twelve rods, one rod for the head of each fathers' house. Write each man's name upon his rod, and write Aaron's name upon the rod of Levi. Deposit the rods in the tent of meeting before the testimony, where I meet with you. The rod of the man whom I choose shall sprout; thus I will make to cease the murmurings of the people of Israel against you." Moses spoke to the people, and each leader gave him a rod. The rod of Aaron was among them, and Moses deposited the rods before the LORD in the tent.

On the morrow Moses went into the tent, and behold, the rod of Aaron for the house of Levi had sprouted, put forth buds, produced blossoms, and it bore ripe almonds. Moses brought out all the rods; the people of Israel looked, and each man took his rod. But the LORD said to Moses, "Put back the rod of Aaron before the testimony, to be kept as a sign for the rebels to make an end to their murmurings against me, lest they die." As the LORD commanded, so Moses did.

THE PEOPLE OF Israel, the whole congregation, came into the wilderness of Zin in the first month, and the people stayed in Kadesh; and Miriam died there, and was buried there.

Now there was no water for the congregation. They assembled themselves against Moses and Aaron, and contended with Moses, saying, "Would that we had died when our brethren died before the LORD! Why have you brought the assembly of the

LORD into this wilderness, that we should die here, both we and our cattle? Why have you made us come up out of Egypt, to bring us to this evil place? It is no place for grain, or figs, or vines, or pomegranates; and there is no water to drink." Then Moses and Aaron went from the presence of the assembly to the tent of meeting, and fell on their faces. The glory of the LORD appeared to them, and the LORD said to Moses, "Take the rod, and assemble the congregation, you and Aaron your brother, and tell the rock before their eyes to yield its water; so you shall bring water out of the rock; so you shall give drink to the congregation and their cattle." Moses took the rod as the LORD commanded, and he gathered the assembly before the rock.

"Hear now, you rebels," Moses said, "shall we bring forth water for you out of this rock?" He lifted up his hand and struck the rock with his rod twice; water came forth abundantly, and the congregation drank, and their cattle. But the LORD said to Moses and Aaron, "Because you did not believe in me, to sanctify me in the eyes of the people, you shall not bring this assembly into the land which I have given them." These are the waters of Meribah, where the people of Israel contended with the LORD, and he showed himself holy among them.

Moses sent messengers from Kadesh to the king of Edom, saying, "You know all the adversity that has befallen us, your brother Israel: how our fathers went down to Egypt, and the Egyptians dealt harshly with us; and when we cried to the LORD, he heard our voice, and brought us forth out of Egypt; and here we are in Kadesh, a city on the edge of your territory. Now let us pass through your land. We will not pass through field or vineyard; we will go along the King's Highway, and will pay if we drink of your water; let us pass through on foot, nothing more." But the king said, "You shall not pass through," and Edom came out against them with a strong force of many men, and refused to give Israel passage.

So the people of Israel turned away, and journeyed from Kadesh to Mount Hor. The LORD said to Moses and Aaron, "Aaron shall be gathered to his people. He shall not enter the land I have given to Israel, because both of you rebelled at the waters of Meribah. Bring Aaron and Eleazar his son up to Mount Hor; strip Aaron of his garments, and put them upon Eleazar; and Aaron shall die there." Moses did as the LORD commanded; they went up Mount Hor in the sight of all the congregation, and Aaron died there. Then Moses and Eleazar came down, and all the house of Israel wept for Aaron thirty days.

From Mount Hor they set out by the way to the Red Sea, to go around the land of Edom. On the way, the people became impatient, and spoke against God and Moses. "Why have you brought us up out of Egypt to die in the wilderness? For there is no water, and we loathe this worthless food." Then the LORD sent fiery serpents among them, and the serpents bit the people, so that many Israelites died. The people came to Moses, and said, "We have sinned, for we have spoken against the LORD and against you; pray to the LORD, that he take away the serpents from us." So Moses prayed for the people. And the LORD said to Moses, "Make a fiery serpent, and set it on a pole; every one who is bitten, when he sees it, shall live." So Moses made a bronze serpent, and set it on a pole; and if a serpent bit any man, the man would look at the bronze serpent and live.

The people of Israel went on to the valley lying in the region of Moab by the top of Pisgah, which looks down upon the desert. Then Israel sent messengers to Sihon the king of the Amorites, who dwelt at Heshbon, saying, "Let us pass through your land." But Sihon would not allow Israel to pass. He gathered his men and went out and fought against them. And Israel slew him, and took possession of the land of the Amorites. Then they turned and went up by the way to Bashan; and Og the king of Bashan came out to battle against them at Edrei. But the LORD said to Moses, "Do not fear him, for I have given him into your hand; and you shall do to him as you did to Sihon." So they slew him, and all his people; and they possessed his land.

THEN THE PEOPLE of Israel encamped in the plains of Moab beyond the Jordan at Jericho. Balak the king of Moab saw all that

Israel had done to the Amorites, and
Moab was in great dread of the people of
Israel, because they were many. The Moabites said to the elders of Midian, "This
horde will now lick up all that is round
about us, as the ox licks up the grass of
the field." So Balak sent messengers to
call Balaam the son of Beor at Pethor,
which is near the river Euphrates, saying,
"Behold, a people has come out of
Egypt; they cover the face of the earth,
and are dwelling opposite me. Come,
curse this people, for they are too mighty
for me; perhaps I shall be able to drive
them from the land; for I know that he
whom you bless is blessed, and he whom
you curse is cursed."

So the elders of Moab and Midian departed with the fees for divination in their
hand. When they gave Balak's message to
Balaam, he said to them, "Lodge here this
night. I will bring back word to you, as the
LORD speaks to me." So they stayed, and
God came to Balaam and said, "Who are
these men?" Balaam said, "Balak the king
of Moab has sent them to me, saying, 'A
people has come out of Egypt, and covers

the face of the earth; come, curse them for me; perhaps I shall be able to drive them out.' " God said to Balaam, "You shall not go; you shall not curse the people, for they are blessed." Balaam rose in the morning, and said to the elders, "Go to your own land; the LORD has refused to let me go with you." So they returned to Balak, and said, "Balaam refuses to come."

Once again Balak sent messengers to Balaam, saying, "Let nothing hinder you from coming, for I will surely do you great honor, and whatever you say to me I will do. Come, curse this people for me." But Balaam said to the servants of Balak, "Though Balak were to give me his house full of silver and gold, I could not go beyond the command of the LORD my God. Pray tarry here this night also, that I may know what more the LORD will say to me." And God came to Balaam at night and said, "If the men have come to call you, rise, go with them; but do only what I bid you."

So Balaam rose in the morning, saddled his ass, and went with the elders of Moab. But God's anger was kindled, and the angel of the LORD took his stand in the way as Balaam was riding. The ass saw the angel of the LORD standing in the road, with a drawn sword in his hand, and turned aside into the field; so Balaam struck the ass, to turn her into the road. Then the angel stood in a narrow path between the vineyards, with a wall on either side. When the ass saw the angel, she pushed against the wall, pressing Balaam's foot against it; so he struck her again. Then the angel went ahead, and stood in a place so narrow there was no way to turn. When the ass saw this, she lay down under Balaam. Balaam's anger was kindled, and he struck the ass with his staff. Then the LORD opened the mouth of the ass. "What have I done to you," she said to Balaam, "that you have struck me these three times?" And Balaam said, "You have made sport of me. If I had a sword in my hand, I would kill you." But the ass said, "Am I not your ass, upon which you have ridden all your life? Was I ever accustomed to do so to you?" And Balaam said, "No."

Then the LORD opened Balaam's eyes;

he saw the angel standing with drawn sword, and he bowed his head, and fell on his face. "Why have you struck your ass these three times?" the angel said. "Behold, I have come to withstand you, because your way is perverse before me. If the ass had not turned aside, I would have slain you." Then Balaam said, "I have sinned, for I did not know that thou didst stand in the road against me. If it is evil in thy sight, I will go back." But the angel said, "Go with the men; but speak only the words which I bid you." So Balaam went on with the servants of Balak.

When Balak heard that Balaam had come, he went out to meet him, and said, "Why did you not come to me? Am I not able to honor you?" Balaam answered, "Lo, I have come to you! Have I now any power at all to speak anything? The word that God puts in my mouth, that must I speak."

On the morrow Balak took Balaam up into the high places, and from there he saw the people of Israel. "Build for me here seven altars," Balaam said to Balak, "and provide seven bulls and seven rams."

Balak did so, and they offered on each altar a bull and a ram. "Stand beside your burnt offering," Balaam said, "and I will go yonder; perhaps the LORD will meet me, and whatever he shows me I will tell you." So Balaam went to a bare height, and God met him. The LORD put words in Balaam's mouth, and said, "Return to Balak, and speak thus."

Balaam returned, and found Balak and all the princes of Moab standing beside his burnt offering. Balaam took up his discourse, saying, "From Mesopotamia Balak has brought me: 'Come, curse Israel for me!' How can I curse whom God has not cursed? From the top of the mountains I see a people dwelling alone, and not reckoning itself among the nations! Who can count the dust of Israel? Let me die the death of the righteous, and let my end be like his!"

Then Balak said to Balaam, "What have you done to me? I took you to curse my enemies, and you have done nothing but bless them." Balaam answered, "Must I not speak what the LORD puts in my mouth?" Balak said, "Come with me to another place, from which you may see only the nearest of the people of Israel, not all of them; then curse them for me from there." He took Balaam to the top of Pisgah, and built seven altars, and offered a bull and a ram on each. "Stand here beside your burnt offering," Balaam said, "while I meet the LORD yonder." The LORD again put words in Balaam's mouth. He returned to Balak and the princes of Moab, and took up his discourse, saying, "Rise, Balak, and hear: God is not man, that he should lie, or a son of man, that he should repent. Has he spoken, and will he not fulfil it? He has blessed, and I cannot revoke it. He has not beheld misfortune in Israel. The LORD their God is with them, and the shout of a king is among them. God brings them out of Egypt; they have as it were the horns of the wild ox. There is no divination against Israel; now it shall be said of Israel, 'What has God wrought!' Behold, a people! As a lioness it rises up; it devours the prey, and drinks the blood of the slain."

Then Balak said to Balaam, "Neither curse them, nor bless them." But Balaam answered, "Did I not tell you, 'All that the LORD says, that I must do'?" And Balak said, "Come now, I will take you to another place; perhaps it will please God that you may curse them for me from there." So Balak took Balaam to the top of Peor, that overlooks the desert. Balak built seven altars there, and offered a bull and a ram on each. When Balaam saw that it pleased the LORD to bless Israel, he did not go, as at other times, to look for omens, but set his face toward the wilderness. He lifted up his eyes, and saw Israel encamping tribe by tribe. The Spirit of God came upon him, and he said, "The oracle of Balaam, the man whose eye is opened, the oracle of him who hears the words of God: how fair are your encampments, O Israel! Like valleys that stretch afar, like gardens beside a river. Water shall flow from his buckets, and his kingdom shall be exalted. God brings him out of Egypt; he shall eat up his adversaries, break their bones in pieces, and pierce them with his arrows. He lay down like a lion; who will rouse him up? Blessed be those who bless you, and cursed be those who curse you."

Balak's anger was kindled; he struck his hands together, and said to Balaam, "I called you to curse my enemies, and you have blessed them these three times. Now flee to your place; I said I would honor you, but the LORD has held you back from honor." Balaam replied, "Did I not tell your messengers I would not be able to do either good or bad of my own will? What the LORD speaks, that will I speak. Now I am going to my people; but come, I will let you know what this people will do to your people in the latter days." And he took up his discourse, saying, "The oracle of Balaam, the man whose eye is opened, the oracle of him who knows the knowledge of the Most High: I see him, but not now; I behold him, but not nigh: a star shall come forth out of Jacob, and a scepter shall rise out of Israel; it shall crush the forehead of Moab, and Edom also shall be dispossessed. By Israel shall dominion be exercised, and the survivors of cities be destroyed!" Then Balaam rose, and went back to his place; and Balak also went his way.

WHILE ISRAEL DWELT in Shittim, the people began to play the harlot with the daughters of Moab, who invited them to the sacrifices of their gods. They ate, and bowed down to Baal of Peor. And the LORD, his anger kindled against Israel, said to Moses, "Take all the chiefs of the people, and hang them in the sun before the LORD." So Moses said to the judges of Israel, "Every one of you slay his men who have yoked themselves to Baal of Peor."

And behold, one of the people of Israel brought a Midianite woman to his family, in the sight of Moses and the whole congregation at the tent of meeting. When Phinehas the son of Eleazar, son of Aaron the priest, saw it, he left the congregation, took a spear, went after them into the inner room, and pierced both of them through her body. Thus the plague which the LORD had sent was stayed from the people of Israel. Nevertheless twenty-four thousand died. The LORD said to Moses, "Phinehas, jealous with my jealousy, has turned back my wrath from the people of Israel. Therefore I give my covenant of peace to him and his descendants, the cov-

enant of a perpetual priesthood, because
he was jealous for his God, and made
atonement for the people of Israel." The
slain man was Zimri, a Simeonite, and the
Midianite woman who was slain with him
was Cozbi, daughter of a prince of Midian.
And the LORD said to Moses, "Harass the
Midianites, and smite them; for they have
harassed you with their wiles in the matter
of Peor, and of Cozbi, their sister, who
was slain on the day of the plague."

After the plague the LORD said to Moses
and to Eleazar the son of Aaron, "Take
another census of the people of Israel,
from twenty years old and upward, by
their fathers' houses, all who are able to go
forth to war." Moses and Eleazar did as
the LORD commanded; and the people
numbered six hundred and one thousand
seven hundred and thirty. The LORD said
to Moses, "To these the land shall be divided for inheritance; according to the
names of the tribes of their fathers they
shall inherit." But not a man of these, except Caleb and Joshua, was among those
numbered by Moses and Aaron in the wilderness. For the LORD had said of them,

"They shall die in the wilderness."

Then drew near the daughters of Zelophehad, of the tribe of Manasseh. Their names were: Mahlah, Noah, Hoglah, Milcah, and Tirzah. They stood before Moses and Eleazar, and all the congregation at the tent of meeting, saying, "Our father died in the wilderness; he was not among those who gathered together against the LORD in the company of Korah, but died for his own sin; and he had no sons. Why should the name of our father be taken away from his family, because he had no son? Give to us a possession among our father's brethren."

Moses brought their case before the LORD. And the LORD said, "The daughters of Zelophehad are right; you shall cause the inheritance of their father to pass to them. Say to the people of Israel, If a man dies, and has no son, then his inheritance shall pass to his daughter. If he has no daughter, give his inheritance to his brothers; if he has no brothers, give it to his father's brothers; and if his father has no brothers, then give his inheritance to the next kinsman of his family. This shall be to the people of Israel a statute and ordinance."

Then the LORD said to Moses, "Go up into the mountains of Abarim, and see the land which I have given to the people of Israel. When you have seen it, you also shall be gathered to your people, as Aaron was, because you rebelled against my word at the waters of Meribah." Moses said, "Let the LORD, the God of the spirits of all flesh, appoint a man over the congregation, who shall lead them out and bring them in; that the congregation of the LORD may not be as sheep with no shepherd." And the LORD said, "Take Joshua the son of Nun, a man in whom is the spirit, and lay your hand upon him; cause him to stand before Eleazar the priest, and commission him in the sight of all the congregation. Invest him with some of your authority, that the people of Israel may obey; at his word they shall go out and come in, all the people with him, the whole congregation." And Moses did as the LORD directed.

THE LORD SAID to Moses, "Avenge the people of Israel on the Midianites; afterward you shall be gathered to your people." So Moses said to the people, "Arm men for war, that they may execute the LORD's vengeance on Midian. Send a thousand from each of the tribes of Israel." So there were provided twelve thousand armed men, and Moses sent them to the war, together with Phinehas the son of Eleazar, with the vessels of the sanctuary and the trumpets for the alarm in his hand. They warred against Midian, as the LORD commanded, and slew every male. They slew the five kings of Midian; and they also slew Balaam the son of Beor with the sword. They took captive the women of Midian and their little ones; and they took as booty all their cattle, flocks, and goods. They burned their cities and all their encampments. Then they brought the captives and the booty to Moses and Eleazar the priest, and to the congregation of the people of Israel, at the camp on the plains of Moab by the Jordan at Jericho.

Moses, Eleazar, and the leaders of the congregation went to meet them outside the camp. And Moses was angry with the officers of the army who had come from service in the war. "Have you let all the women live?" he said. "These caused the people of Israel, by the counsel of Balaam, to act treacherously against the LORD at Peor, and so the plague came. Now therefore, kill every male among the little ones, and kill every woman who has known man by lying with him. But keep alive for yourselves all the young girls who have not known man. Encamp outside the camp seven days; whoever of you has killed any person, or touched any slain, purify yourselves and your captives on the third day and on the seventh day. You must wash your clothes on the seventh day, and afterward you shall be clean and shall come into the camp."

The LORD said to Moses, "Count the booty that was taken, both of man and of beast, and divide it into two parts, between the warriors who went out to battle and all the congregation. Levy for the LORD a tribute from the men of war; from their half take one out of five hundred, both of persons and of beasts, to give to Eleazar the priest as an offering to the LORD. From the people of Israel's half take one of every fifty, both of persons and of beasts, and give them to the Levites who have charge of the tabernacle of the LORD." Moses and Eleazar did as the LORD commanded Moses, and divided the booty remaining of the spoil that the men of war had taken, which was: six hundred and seventy-five thousand sheep, seventy-two thousand cattle, sixty-one thousand asses, and thirty-two thousand women who had not known man by lying with him.

Now THE SONS of Reuben and the sons of Gad had a multitude of cattle; and when they saw that the lands of Jazer and Gilead were a good place for cattle, they came to Moses and Eleazar, and to the leaders of the congregation, and said, "If we have found favor in your sight, let this land be given to us for a possession; do not take us across the Jordan." But Moses said to them, "Shall your brethren go to the war while you sit here? Will you discourage the people of Israel from going over into the land which the LORD has given them?

Thus did your fathers in the wilderness of Paran, when I sent them from Kadesh to see the land. They discouraged the heart of the people. The LORD's anger was kindled that day, and he swore that none of the men who came up out of Egypt would see the land promised to Abraham, Isaac, and Jacob; none except Caleb and Joshua, who had wholly followed the LORD. And the LORD made Israel wander in the wilderness forty years. Now you have risen in your fathers' stead, a brood of sinful men, to increase still more the LORD's fierce anger! For if you turn away, he will again abandon Israel in the wilderness; and you will destroy this people."

But the sons of Gad and of Reuben said, "We will build sheepfolds here for our flocks, and cities for our little ones. Then we will take up arms and go with Israel. Our little ones, our wives, our flocks and cattle, shall remain in the fortified cities of Gilead, but we will not return to our homes until we have brought all the people of Israel to their place. For we will not inherit with them on the other side of the Jordan; our inheritance has come to us here on the east side." So Moses said to them, "If you will do this, if you will take up arms to go before the LORD for the war; then after that you shall return here, and this land shall be your possession before the LORD. But if you will not do so, you have sinned against the LORD, and your sin will find you out. Build cities now, and folds for your sheep, and do what you have promised." And they said to Moses, "Your servants will do as my lord commands." So Moses gave to the sons of Gad and of Reuben, and to the half-tribe of Manasseh, the kingdom of the Amorites and the kingdom of Bashan, the land and its cities throughout the country. And the sons of Gad and of Reuben, and of Machir the son of Manasseh, built fortified cities, and folds for sheep. They gave names to the cities which they built; they took villages, and dispossessed the people, and they settled there.

WHEN THE PEOPLE of Israel had gone forth out of the land of Egypt under the leadership of Moses and Aaron, Moses had written down their starting places, stage by stage, by command of the LORD. These are their stages according to their starting places. They set out from Rameses on the fifteenth day of the first month, the day after the passover. They went out triumphantly in the sight of the Egyptians, while the Egyptians were burying all their first-born, whom the LORD had struck down. They encamped at Succoth, then at Etham on the edge of the wilderness, then turned back to Pihahiroth, by the Red Sea. They passed through the midst of the sea, went a three days' journey in the wilderness of Shur, and encamped at Marah, then came to Elim, where there were twelve springs of water and seventy palm trees, and encamped there. They set out from Elim, encamped by the Red Sea, then in the wilderness of Sin, and then at Rephidim, where there was no water for the people to drink. They set out from Rephidim, encamped in the wilderness of Sinai, then at Kibroth-hattaavah, and then at Hazeroth. They set out from Hazeroth, and encamped at Rithmah, and at Eziongeber, and in the wilderness of Zin (that is, Kadesh). Then they set out from Kadesh, and encamped at Mount Hor, on the edge of the land of Edom.

Aaron the priest went up Mount Hor at the command of the LORD, and died there, in the fortieth year after the people of Israel had come out of Egypt. Aaron was a hundred and twenty-three years old when he died.

The people of Israel set out from Mount Hor, and entered the territory of Moab. They encamped in the mountains of Abarim, before Mount Nebo, and then in the plains of Moab by the Jordan at Jericho. The LORD said to Moses, "Say to the people of Israel, When you pass over the Jordan into the land of Canaan, drive out all the inhabitants of the land, destroy their figured stones and molten images, and demolish all their high places; take possession of the land and settle in it, for I have given it to you. You shall inherit the land by lot according to the tribes of your fathers. But if you do not drive out the inhabitants of the land, those whom you let remain shall be as pricks in your eyes and thorns in your sides. And I will do to you as I thought to do to them."

The Lord said to Moses in the plains of Moab, "Command the people of Israel to give from their inheritance forty-two cities to the Levites, for them to dwell in, and pasture lands round about the cities for their livestock. In addition, give them six cities of refuge. Give three cities beyond the Jordan, and three in the land of Canaan. These six cities shall be for the people of Israel, for the stranger, and for the sojourner among them, that any one who kills without intent may flee there.

"But if any one strikes a person down with an instrument of iron, a stone in the hand, or a weapon of wood, so that the person dies, he is a murderer and shall be put to death. The avenger of blood shall himself put the murderer to death, when he meets him. And if any one stabs a person from hatred, or hurls at him, lying in wait, or in enmity strikes him down with his hand, so that he dies, then he who struck the blow shall be put to death; he is a murderer; the avenger of blood shall put him to death, when he meets him.

"But if any one kills without intent, the congregation shall judge, in accordance with these ordinances, and shall rescue him from the hand of the avenger of blood; and he shall live in his city of refuge until the death of the high priest. But if the man-slayer shall at any time go beyond the bounds of his city of refuge, and the avenger of blood finds him, and slays him, the avenger shall not be guilty of blood. For the man must remain in his city of refuge until the death of the high priest, after which he may return to the land of his possession.

"These things shall be a statute to you throughout your generations. If any one kills a person, the murderer shall be put to death on the evidence of witnesses; but no person shall be put to death on the testimony of one witness. Accept no ransom for the life of a murderer; he shall be put to death. For blood pollutes the land, and no expiation can be made for blood that is shed, except by the blood of him who shed it. You shall not defile the land in which you live, for I the LORD dwell in the midst of the people."

THE HEADS OF the families of the tribe of Manasseh came and spoke before Moses and the leaders of the people of Israel. "The LORD commanded my lord to give land for inheritance by lot to the people," they said, "and to give the inheritance of Zelophehad, our brother, to his daughters. But if they marry sons of other tribes, then their inheritance will be taken from the inheritance of our fathers, and added to the inheritance of the other tribe. When the year of jubilee comes, their inheritance will be added to the inheritance of the tribe to which they belong, and taken from the inheritance of the tribe of our fathers."

And Moses commanded the people of Israel according to the word of the LORD, saying, "The tribe of Manasseh is right concerning the daughters of Zelophehad. Let them marry whom they think best; only, they shall marry within the family of the tribe of their father. The inheritance of the people of Israel shall not be transferred from one tribe to another. Every daughter who possesses an inheritance in any tribe shall be wife to one of the family of the tribe of her father, so that every one of the people may possess the inheritance of his fathers. Each of the tribes shall cleave to its own inheritance."

The daughters of Zelophehad did as the LORD commanded Moses; for Mahlah, Tirzah, Hoglah, Milcah, and Noah married sons of their father's brothers. They were married into the families of the sons of Manasseh, and their inheritance remained in the tribe of their father.

These are the ordinances which the LORD commanded by Moses to the people of Israel in the plains of Moab by the Jordan at Jericho.

DEUTERONOMY

The Israelites have now almost reached the land of Canaan, where they are to settle, and Moses speaks to them for the last time. He reviews the mighty acts of the Lord, solemnly warns of the temptations to be found in Canaan, and pleads for fidelity to God as the condition for life in the Promised Land.

Deuteronomy, which means "second law," amplifies the law proclaimed at Mount Sinai, and repeats some Israelite history from earlier books. Its compilation is generally assigned to the seventh century B.C., though it rests upon much older tradition, some of it from Moses' time. The distinctive oratorical style of the book, in which absolute monotheism is strongly emphasized, sets it apart from the other Pentateuchal writings. At the emergence of

Christianity, Deuteronomy shared with the Psalms a preeminent position among Old Testament books. Jesus quoted from it in overcoming his threefold temptation in the desert, and in explaining the first and greatest commandment: *"The Lord our God is one Lord; and you shall love the Lord your God with all your heart, and with all your soul, and with all your might."*

THESE ARE THE words that Moses spoke to all Israel beyond the Jordan in the wilderness, in the land of Moab. In the fortieth year, on the first day of the eleventh month, Moses undertook to explain to the people all the law that the LORD had given him in commandment to them, saying, "The LORD our God said to us at Sinai, 'You have stayed long enough at this mountain; turn and take your journey to the hill country of the Amorites, and to all their neighbors in the lowland, and in the Negeb, and by the seacoast, the land of the Canaanites, and Lebanon, as far as the great river Euphrates. Go take possession of the land which the LORD swore to give to your fathers, Abraham, Isaac, and Jacob, and to their descendants.'

"At that time I said to you, 'The LORD your God has multiplied you, and behold, you are as the stars of heaven. May the LORD make you a thousand times as many as you are, and bless you, as he has promised! But how can I bear alone the burden of you and your strife? Choose wise, understanding, and experienced men, according to your tribes, and I will appoint them as your heads.' And you answered, 'That is good for us to do.' So I set wise and experienced men over you, throughout your tribes. I charged your judges, 'Hear cases between your brethren, and judge righteously. Do not be partial; hear the small and the great alike. Do not be afraid of the face of man, for the judgment is God's; the case that is too hard for you, bring to me, and I will hear it.' And I commanded you at that time all the things that you should do.

"We set out from Sinai, and after going through that great and terrible wilderness,

as the LORD commanded us, we came to
Kadesh. 'You have come to the hill country of the Amorites,' I said. 'Behold, the
LORD your God has set the land before
you; go up, take possession, as the LORD
has told you; do not fear or be dismayed.'
But you said, 'Let us send men before us
to explore the land, and bring word of the
way by which we must go up and the cities
into which we shall come.' So I sent twelve
men, one for each tribe, into the hill country to spy it out. They returned, bringing in
their hands some of the fruit of the land,
and said, 'It is a good land which the LORD
our God gives us.'

"Yet you would not go up, but rebelled
against the command of the LORD, and
murmured in your tents. 'Because the
LORD hated us,' you said, 'he has brought
us forth out of Egypt, to give us into the
hand of the Amorites, to destroy us. Our
brethren have made our hearts melt, saying that the people are greater and taller
than we, for the sons of the Anakim are
there; and their cities are fortified up to
heaven.' Then I said to you, 'Do not be in
dread of them. The LORD your God who

goes before you will himself fight for you, just as he did in Egypt, and in the wilderness. You have seen how the LORD bore you, as a man bears his son, all the way to this place, going before you to show you the way, in fire by night, and in the cloud by day.' Yet in spite of this you did not believe.

"The LORD heard your words, and was angered, and he swore, 'Not one man of this evil generation shall see the good land I swore to give to your fathers, except Caleb and Joshua, who have wholly followed the LORD!' The LORD was angry with me also on your account, and said, 'You also shall not go in there; encourage Joshua, who stands before you, for he shall cause Israel to inherit it. Moreover your little ones, who you said would become a prey, shall go in and possess the land. But as for you, turn, and journey into the wilderness.'

" 'We have sinned against the LORD,' you answered; 'we will go up and fight, as the LORD commanded us.' You girded on weapons, and thought it easy to go up into the hill country. The LORD told me to say to you, 'Do not go up or fight, lest you be defeated, for I am not in the midst of you.' But you would not hearken; you were presumptuous and went up into the hill country. The Amorites who lived there came out against you and chased you as bees do and beat you. Returning, you wept before the LORD; but the LORD did not give ear to you. So we remained at Kadesh many days.

"Then we turned, and journeyed into the wilderness in the direction of the Red Sea, as the LORD told me; and for many days we went about Mount Seir. And the LORD said, 'You have been going about this mountain country long enough; turn northward. But do not contend with your brethren the sons of Esau, who live in Edom; for I will not give you any of their land, no, not so much as for the sole of the foot to tread on, because I have given Edom to Esau as a possession.' So we turned in the direction of the wilderness of Moab, away from our brethren the sons of Esau. And the LORD said, 'Do not harass Moab or contend with them in battle, for I will not give you any of their land. I have given it to the sons of Lot for a possession.

Now rise up, and go over the brook Zered.' So we went over. Thirty-eight years
had passed from the time we left Kadesh
until we crossed the brook Zered, and the
entire generation, the men of war, had perished from the camp, as the LORD had
sworn.

"When all the men of war were dead,
the LORD said to me, 'This day you are to
pass over the boundary of Moab. When
you approach the frontier of the sons of
Ammon, do not contend with them, for I
will not give you any of their land. I have
given it also to the sons of Lot. Take your
journey over the valley of the Arnon; behold, I have given into your hand Sihon,
the Amorite king, and his land; contend
with him in battle, and take possession of
it. This day I will begin to put the fear of
you upon the peoples that are under the
whole heaven, who shall hear the report of
you and shall tremble and be in anguish.'

"So I sent messengers to Sihon, with
words of peace, saying, 'Let me pass
through your land; I will go only by the
road, and will not turn aside. Sell me food
and water, and let me pass through on

foot, and I will go over the Jordan into the land which the LORD our God gives to us.' But Sihon would not let us pass, for the LORD hardened his spirit, that he might give him into our hand. Sihon and all his people came out to battle against us, and the LORD gave him over to us, and we defeated him. We captured all his cities and utterly destroyed the men, women, and children; we left none remaining; only the cattle we took as spoil.

"Then we turned and went up to Bashan; and Og the king of Bashan and all his people came out to battle against us. But the LORD gave them into our hand also. There was not a city we did not take from them—sixty cities, the whole kingdom of Bashan, all fortified with high walls, gates, and bars—besides very many unwalled villages. We utterly destroyed them, as we did Sihon the king of the Amorites, until no survivor was left. But all the cattle and the spoil of the cities we took as booty. And behold, the iron bedstead of Og the king of Bashan was thirteen and a half feet long, and six feet wide.

"So we took the land of the two kings,

from the valley of the Arnon to Mount Hermon, all Gilead and all Bashan. To the Reubenites and the Gadites I gave the territory which is on the edge of the valley of the Arnon, and half the hill country of Gilead; the rest of Gilead and all Bashan I gave to the half-tribe of Manasseh. 'The LORD has given you this land,' I said to them. 'Your wives, your little ones, and your cattle (I know you have many cattle) shall remain in the cities. But all your men of valor shall pass over armed before your brethren, the people of Israel, until the LORD gives rest to them, as to you, and they also occupy the land which the LORD gives them beyond the Jordan. Then you shall return to this possession which I have given you.'

"I besought the LORD at that time, saying, 'O Lord GOD, thou hast only begun to show thy servant thy greatness; for what god is there in heaven or on earth who can do such mighty acts as thine? Let me go over, I pray, and see the good land beyond the Jordan.' But the LORD was angry with me on your account, and would not hearken. 'Speak no more of this matter,' he said to me. 'Go up to the top of Pisgah, and lift up your eyes westward, northward, southward, and eastward, and behold the land; for you shall not go over this Jordan. Encourage and strengthen Joshua, for he shall lead this people and put them in possession of the land which you shall see.' So we remained in the valley opposite Beth-peor."

"AND NOW, O Israel," said Moses, "give heed to the statutes and ordinances I teach you. You shall not add to the word which I command you, nor take from it; that you may keep the commandments of the LORD. Your eyes have seen how the LORD destroyed all who followed the Baal of Peor; but you who held fast to the LORD your God are alive this day. Behold, I have taught you statutes and ordinances, as the LORD commanded me. Keep them and do them in the land which you are entering, for that will be your wisdom in the sight of the peoples, who, when they hear all these statutes, will say, 'Surely this great nation is a wise and understanding people.' For what great nation has a god so near to it as the LORD our God is to us, whenever we call upon him? And what great nation has statutes and ordinances so righteous as all this law which I set before you this day?

"Only take heed, lest you forget the things your eyes have seen. Make them known to your children and your children's children—how, at Sinai, the LORD said to me, 'Gather the people to me, that I may let them hear my words, so they may learn to fear me all the days that they live, and may teach their children so.' And you came near and stood at the foot of the mountain, which was wrapped in darkness, cloud, and gloom, and burned with fire to the heart of heaven. The LORD spoke to you out of the midst of the fire; you heard the words, but saw no form; there was only a voice. He declared his covenant, the ten commandments, for you to perform; and he wrote them upon two tables of stone.

"Therefore take heed. Since you saw no form on the day that the LORD spoke to you at Sinai, beware lest you act corruptly by making a graven image for yourselves, in the form of any figure, male or female, the likeness of any beast on earth, any bird that flies, anything that creeps on the ground, or any fish in the water under the earth. And beware lest you lift up your eyes to heaven, and seeing the sun, moon, and stars, be drawn away to worship them, things which the LORD has allotted to all peoples under the whole heaven. Take heed, lest you forget the covenant of the LORD. For the LORD your God is a devouring fire, a jealous God.

"When you beget children and children's children, and have grown old in the land, if you act corruptly by doing what is evil in the sight of the LORD, I call heaven and earth to witness against you this day, that you will soon utterly perish from the land which you are going over the Jordan to possess. The LORD will scatter you, and you will be left few in number among the nations where the LORD will drive you. There you will serve gods of wood and stone, the work of men's hands, that neither see, nor hear, nor eat, nor smell. But from there you will seek the LORD your God, and you will find him, if you search after him with all your heart and with all your soul. When you are in tribulation, and these things come upon you, you will return to the LORD and obey his voice, for the LORD your God is merciful; he will not fail you or destroy you or forget the covenant with your fathers.

"For ask now, since the day God created man upon the earth, whether such a great thing as this has ever happened. Did any people ever hear the voice of a god speaking out of the midst of the fire, as you have heard, and still live? Or has any god ever attempted to take a nation for himself from the midst of another nation, by trials, by signs, by wonders, and by war, by a mighty hand and an outstretched arm, and by great terrors, as the LORD your God did for you in Egypt? To you it was shown, that you might know that the LORD is God; there is no other besides him. Out of heaven he let you hear his voice, that he might discipline you; and on earth he let you see his great fire. He loved your fathers and chose their descendants, and brought you out of Egypt with his own presence, driving out before you nations mightier than yourselves, to give you their land for an inheritance. Know therefore this day, and lay it to your heart, that the LORD is God in heaven above and on the earth beneath; there is no other. Keep his commandments, that it may go well with you, and with your children, and that you may prolong your days in the land which the LORD your God gives you for ever."

Then Moses set apart three cities of refuge east of the Jordan, that the manslayer who kills his neighbor unintentionally might flee to one of them and save his life: Bezer on the tableland for the Reubenites, Ramoth in Gilead for the Gadites, and Golan in Bashan for the Manassites.

THIS IS THE law, these are the testimonies, statutes, and ordinances, which Moses spoke to the children of Israel east of the Jordan in the valley opposite Beth-peor, under the slopes of Pisgah. Summoning all Israel, he said, "Hear, O Israel, the statutes which I speak this day; learn them and be careful to do them. The LORD our God made a covenant with us at Sinai. Out of the midst of the fire he spoke, saying, 'I am the LORD your God, who brought you out of the land of Egypt, out of the house of bondage.

" 'You shall have no other gods before me.

" 'You shall not make for yourself a graven image, or any likeness of anything that is in heaven above, or that is on the earth beneath, or that is in the water under the earth; you shall not bow down to them or serve them; for I the LORD your God am a jealous God, visiting the iniquity of the fathers upon the children to the third and fourth generation of those who hate me, but showing steadfast love to thousands of those who love me and keep my commandments.

" 'You shall not take the name of the LORD your God in vain: for the LORD will not hold him guiltless who takes his name in vain.

" 'Observe the sabbath day, to keep it holy, as the LORD your God commanded you. Six days you shall labor, and do all your work; but the seventh day is a sabbath to the LORD your God; in it you shall not do any work, you, or your son, or your daughter, or your manservant, or your maidservant, or your ox, or your ass, or any of your cattle, or the sojourner who is within your gates, that your manservant and your maidservant may rest as well as you. You shall remember that you were a servant in the land of Egypt, and the LORD your God brought you out thence with a mighty hand and an outstretched arm; therefore the LORD your God commanded you to keep the sabbath day.

" 'Honor your father and your mother, as the LORD your God commanded you; that your days may be prolonged, and that it may go well with you, in the land which the LORD your God gives you.

" 'You shall not kill.

" 'Neither shall you commit adultery.

" 'Neither shall you steal.

" 'Neither shall you bear false witness against your neighbor.

" 'Neither shall you covet your neighbor's wife; and you shall not desire your neighbor's house, his field, or his manservant, or his maidservant, his ox, or his ass, or anything that is your neighbor's.'

"These words the LORD spoke to all your assembly at the mountain out of the midst of the fire, with a loud voice; and he added no more. When you heard the voice, you came to me, saying, 'Behold, the LORD our God has shown us his glory. But this great fire will consume us; if we hear the voice of the LORD any more, we shall die. For who of all flesh has heard the voice of the living God, as we have, and still lived? Go near, and hear all that the LORD will say; then speak it to us, and we will hear and do it.'

"And the LORD said to me, 'I have heard the words of this people; they have rightly spoken. Oh that they had such a mind always, to fear me and keep my commandments, that it might go well with them and with their children for ever! Let them return to their tents, but you, stand here by me, and I will tell you all the statutes and ordinances which you shall teach them, that they may do them in the land which I give them to possess.'

"Now these are the statutes and ordinances which the LORD commanded me to teach you. Hear therefore, and do them; that you may multiply greatly, as the LORD, the God of your fathers, has promised you, in a land flowing with milk and honey.

"Hear, O Israel: The LORD our God is one LORD; and you shall love the LORD your God with all your heart, and with all your soul, and with all your might. These words shall be upon your heart; teach them diligently to your children, and talk of them when you sit in your house, when you walk by the way, when you lie down, and when you rise. Bind them as a sign upon your hand, and they shall be as frontlets between your eyes. Write them on the doorposts of your house and on your gates.

"And when the LORD your God brings you into the land which he swore to your fathers, Abraham, Isaac, and Jacob, to give you, a land with great and goodly cities, which you did not build, houses full of all good things, which you did not fill, cisterns hewn out, which you did not hew, and vineyards and olive trees, which you did not plant, and when you eat and are full, then take heed, lest you forget the LORD. You shall fear the LORD your God, serve him, and swear by his name. You shall not go after other gods, lest the anger of the LORD be kindled against you, and he destroy you.

"You shall not put the LORD your God to the test, as you tested him at Massah. Diligently keep his commandments, and do what is right and good in his sight.

"When your son asks, 'What is the meaning of the ordinances which the LORD our God has commanded you?' you shall say, 'We were Pharaoh's slaves in Egypt; and the LORD brought us out with a mighty hand, that he might give us the land which he swore to give to our fathers. And the LORD commanded us to do all these statutes, to fear the LORD our God, for our good always, that he might preserve us alive, as at this day.'

"When the LORD your God brings you into the land you are to possess, and gives many nations over to you, nations greater and mightier than yourselves, then you must utterly destroy them; make no covenant with them, and show no mercy to them. Do not make marriages with them, giving your daughters to their sons or taking their daughters for your sons. For they would turn away your sons to serve other gods; then the anger of the LORD would be kindled against you, and he would destroy you. But thus shall you deal with them: break down their altars and pillars, and burn their graven images.

"For you are a people holy to the LORD your God, who has chosen you for his own possession, out of all the peoples on earth. It was not because you were more numerous than others that the LORD chose you, for you were the fewest of all peoples; but it is because the LORD loves you, and is keeping the oath which he swore to your fathers, that he has redeemed you from the house of bondage of Pharaoh king of Egypt. Know therefore that the LORD your God is God, the faithful God who keeps covenant and steadfast love with those who love him and keep his commandments, to a thousand generations, and requites to their face those who hate him, by destroying them.

"And because you hearken to these ordinances, and keep them, the LORD will love you, bless you, and multiply you; he will bless the fruit of your body and the fruit of your ground, your grain, your wine, and your oil, the increase of your cattle and your flocks. You shall be blessed above all peoples; there shall not be male or female barren among you, or among your cattle. The LORD will take away from you all sickness and evil diseases, and will inflict them upon all who hate you. You shall destroy all the peoples that the LORD will give over to you, your eye shall not pity them; neither shall you serve their gods, for that would be a snare to you.

"If you say in your heart, 'These nations are greater than I; how can I dispossess them?' you shall remember what the LORD did to Pharaoh and all Egypt, the great trials, the signs, and the wonders; so will the LORD do to the peoples you fear. Moreover the LORD will send hornets among them, until those who hide themselves from you are destroyed. Do not be in dread of them; for the LORD is in the midst of you, a great and terrible God. The LORD will clear away these nations little by little; you may not make an end of them at once, lest the wild beasts grow too numerous for you. But the LORD will throw them into great confusion. He will give their kings into your hand, and their name shall perish from under heaven; not a man shall be able to stand against you. You shall burn the graven images of their gods, but do not covet the silver or gold on them, or take it for yourselves, lest you be ensnared; for it is an abomination to the LORD. Do not bring an abominable thing into your house, and become accursed like it; you shall utterly detest and abhor it.

"Remember the way the LORD your God has led you these forty years in the wilderness, testing you to know what was in your heart. He humbled you and let you hunger and fed you with manna, that he might make you know that man does not live by bread alone, but by everything that proceeds out of the mouth of the LORD. Your clothing did not wear out upon you, and your foot did not swell, these forty years. Know then in your heart that, as a man disciplines his son, the LORD your God disciplines you. So keep the commandments of the LORD, by walking in his ways and by fearing him. For the LORD is bringing you into a good land, a land of brooks, fountains, and springs, a land of wheat and barley, of vines, fig trees, and pomegranates, of olive trees and honey, a land in which you will lack nothing, a land whose stones are iron, and out of whose hills you can dig copper. You shall eat and be full, and you shall bless the LORD your God for the good land he has given you.

"Take heed lest, when you have eaten and are full, and when your herds and flocks, your silver and gold, and all that you have is multiplied, you say in your heart, 'My power and the might of my hand have gotten me this wealth.' Remember it is the LORD who gives you power to get wealth; that he may confirm his covenant which he swore to your fathers.

"Know that the LORD your God is not giving you this good land because of your righteousness; for you are a stubborn people. Do not forget how you provoked the LORD in the wilderness; from the day you came out of Egypt, until you came to this place, you have been rebellious. Even at Sinai you provoked the LORD to such wrath that he was ready to destroy you. I went up the mountain, and at the end of forty days and forty nights the LORD gave me the two tables of the covenant, and said, 'Arise, go down quickly; for your people have acted corruptly, turning aside from the way I commanded them; they have made themselves a molten image. This people is a stubborn people. Let me alone, that I may destroy them and blot out their name from under heaven; and I will make of you a nation mightier and greater than they.'

"So I came down from the mountain, the two tables of the covenant in my hands. I looked, and behold, you had made yourselves a molten calf. So I cast the two tables out of my hands, and broke them before your eyes. Then I took the sinful thing, the calf which you had made, and burned it and crushed it, grinding it fine as dust; and I threw the dust into the brook that descended out of the mountain.

"I lay prostrate before the LORD for forty days and forty nights; I neither ate bread nor drank water, because of the sin which you had committed. For I was afraid of the anger the LORD bore against you, so that he was ready to destroy you. 'O Lord GOD,' I prayed, 'destroy not thy people and thy heritage, whom thou hast brought out of Egypt with a mighty hand. Remember thy servants, Abraham, Isaac, and Jacob; do not regard the stubbornness, wickedness, or sin of this people, lest the inhabitants of the land from which thou didst bring them say, "Because the LORD was not able to bring them into the land which he promised them, and because he hated them, he has brought them out to slay them in the wilderness." For they are thy people and thy heritage, whom thou hast redeemed through thy greatness.'

"The LORD hearkened to me, and said, 'Hew two tables of stone like the first, make an ark of wood, and come up to me on the mountain.' So I made an ark of acacia wood, hewed two tables of stone like the first, and took them up the mountain. And the LORD wrote on the tables, as at the first writing, the ten commandments which he had spoken to you on the mountain out of the midst of the fire; and he gave them to me. I came down from the mountain, and put the tables in the ark I had made; and there they are, as the LORD commanded."

"AND NOW, ISRAEL," Moses said, "what does the LORD your God require of you, but to fear the LORD, to walk in all his ways, to love him and serve him with all your heart and with all your soul, and to keep his commandments and statutes, which I command you this day for your good? To the LORD your God belong the heavens, the earth with all that is in it; yet the LORD set his heart in love upon your fathers and chose their descendants after them, you above all peoples. Therefore be no longer stubborn. For the LORD your God is God of gods and Lord of lords, the great, the mighty, and the terrible God, who is not partial and takes no bribe. He executes justice for the fatherless and the widow, and loves the sojourner, giving him food and clothing. Love the sojourner therefore; for you were sojourners in the land of Egypt. Fear the LORD; serve him, cleave to him, and swear by his name. He is your praise; he is your God, who has done for you great and terrible things. Your fathers went down to Egypt seventy persons; and now the LORD your God has made you as the stars of heaven for multitude.

"You shall therefore love the LORD your God, and keep his commandments always, that you may live long in the land which the LORD swore to give to your fathers and their descendants, a land flowing with milk and honey. For the land you are entering is not like Egypt, where you sowed your seed and watered it with your feet, like a garden of vegetables. The land you are to possess is a land of hills and valleys, which drinks rain from heaven, a land which the LORD your God cares for; his eyes are always upon it, from the beginning to the end of the year. If you will love the LORD your God, as I command you this day, and serve him with all your heart and with all your soul, he will give rain for your land in its season, that you may gather in your grain, your wine, and your oil. He will give grass for your cattle, and you shall eat and be full. Take heed, lest your heart be deceived, and you worship other gods, kindling the anger of the LORD against you, and he shut up the heavens, so that there be no rain, and the land yield no fruit, and you perish quickly off the good land which the LORD gives you.

"When you dwell in the land of your inheritance, and you say, 'I will set a king over me, like the nations round about me'; you may indeed set as king over you him whom the LORD your God will choose, one from among your brethren, not a foreigner. Only he must not multiply horses for himself, or cause the people to return to Egypt to multiply horses, since the LORD has said to you, 'You shall never return that way again.' And he shall not multiply wives for himself, lest his heart turn away; nor shall he greatly multiply for himself silver and gold. And when he sits on the throne, he shall write for himself in a book a copy of this law. It shall be with him, and he shall read in it all the days of his life, that he may learn to fear the LORD, by keeping and doing all the words of these statutes; that his heart may not be lifted up above his brethren, and he and his children may continue long in his kingdom.

"In the land the LORD gives you, the Levitical priests shall have no inheritance with Israel; the LORD is their inheritance, as he promised them; they shall eat the offerings by fire to the LORD. From a sacrifice of ox or sheep, you shall give them the shoulder, two cheeks, and the stomach. And you shall give them the first fruits of your grain, your wine, and your oil, and the first fleece of your sheep. For the LORD has chosen them out of all your tribes, to minister in the name of the LORD for ever.

"When you come into the land the LORD gives you, do not follow the abominable practices of those nations you dispossess. There shall not be found among you any one who burns his son or daughter as an offering, or practices divination, a soothsayer, augur, sorcerer, charmer, medium, wizard, or necromancer. For whoever does these things is an abomination to the LORD; and because of these practices the LORD your God is driving those nations out before you. They give heed to soothsayers and diviners; but as for you, the LORD your God has not allowed you so to do. You shall be blameless before the LORD.

"The LORD your God will raise up a prophet like me from among you—him you shall heed. This you desired of the LORD at Sinai on the day of the assembly, when you said, 'Let me not hear again the voice of the LORD my God, or see this great fire any more, lest I die.' And the LORD said to me, 'They have rightly spoken. I will raise up a prophet like you from among their brethren; I will put my words in his mouth, and he shall speak to them all that I command. Whoever will not give heed to my words which he shall speak in my name, I myself will require it of him. But the prophet who presumes to speak a word in my name which I have not commanded, or who speaks in the name of other gods, that same prophet shall die.' You may say in your heart, 'How can we know the word which the LORD has not spoken?' When a prophet speaks in the name of the LORD, if the word does not come to pass, that is a word the LORD has not spoken; the prophet has spoken it presumptuously, you need not be afraid of him.

"When the LORD your God cuts off the nations whose land he gives you, and you dispossess them and dwell in their cities and houses, you shall set apart three cities of refuge, by dividing into three parts the area of the land which the LORD gives you, and preparing the roads, so that the manslayer who kills his neighbor unintentionally can flee to them. And if the LORD enlarges your border—provided you keep all this commandment, by loving the LORD your God and walking ever in his ways—then you shall add three other cities to these three, lest innocent blood be shed in the land of your inheritance, and the guilt of bloodshed be upon you. But if any man hates his neighbor, lies in wait for him, attacks, and wounds him mortally, and then flees into one of these cities, the elders of his city shall fetch him, and hand him over to the avenger of blood, so that he may die. Your eye shall not pity him, but you shall purge the guilt of innocent blood from Israel.

"In the land the LORD gives you, a single witness shall not prevail against a man for any crime or offense he has committed; only on the evidence of two or three witnesses shall a charge be sustained. If a malicious witness rises against any man to accuse him of wrongdoing, then both parties to the dispute shall appear before the

LORD, before the priests and judges who are in office. The judges shall inquire diligently, and if the witness has accused his brother falsely, then you shall do to him as he had meant to do to his brother; so you shall purge the evil from your midst. And the rest shall hear, and fear, and never again commit such evil. Your eye shall not pity; it shall be life for life, eye for eye, tooth for tooth, hand for hand, foot for foot.

"You shall not see your brother's ox or sheep go astray, and withhold your help; take it back to your brother. If he is not near, or if you do not know him, bring it home to your house, to be with you until he seeks it; then restore it to him. And so you shall do with his ass, his garment, or any lost thing of your brother's which you find. And if you see your brother's ass or ox fallen down by the way, help him to lift it up again. You may not withhold your help.

"A woman shall not wear anything that pertains to a man, nor shall a man put on a woman's garment; whoever does these things is an abomination to the LORD.

"If you chance upon a bird's nest, in a tree or on the ground, with the mother sitting upon the young or upon the eggs, you shall let the mother go, but the young you may take to yourself.

"When you build a new house, make a parapet for your roof, that you may not bring the guilt of blood upon your house, if any one fall from it.

"Do not sow your vineyard with two kinds of seed. Do not plow with an ox and an ass together. Do not wear a mingled stuff, wool and linen together.

"If any man takes a wife, goes in to her, and then spurns her, and charges her with shameful conduct, saying, 'I took this woman, and when I came near her, I did not find in her the tokens of virginity,' then the father and mother of the young woman shall bring out the tokens of her virginity and spread the garment before the elders of the city. And the father shall say, 'These are the tokens of my daughter's virginity.' Then the elders shall take the man and whip him; they shall fine him a hundred shekels of silver, to be given to the father of the young woman, because this man has brought an evil name upon a virgin of Israel; and she shall be his wife; he may not put her away all his days. But if the tokens of virginity are not found in the young woman, then she shall be brought to the door of her father's house, and the men of her city shall stone her to death, because she has wrought folly in Israel by playing the harlot in her father's house; so you shall purge evil from your midst.

"If a man is found lying with another man's wife, both the man who lay with her and the woman shall die; so you shall purge evil from Israel.

"If a man meets a betrothed virgin in the city and lies with her, bring them both out to the gate of that city, and stone them to death, the young woman because she did not cry for help though she was in the city, and the man because he violated his neighbor's wife. But if a man meets a betrothed young woman in the open country, seizes her, and lies with her, then only the man shall die. To the young woman you shall do nothing, for in the open country, though the woman cried for help, there was no one to rescue her.

"If a man meets a virgin who is not betrothed, seizes her, lies with her, and they are found, then he shall give to her father fifty shekels of silver, and she shall be his wife, because he has violated her; he may not put her away all his days.

"A man shall not take his father's wife, nor uncover her who is his father's.

"If a man takes a wife, and then she finds no favor in his eyes because he has found some indecency in her, let him put a bill of divorce in her hand, and send her out of his house. If she becomes another man's wife, and he also dislikes her and writes her a bill of divorce, or if he dies, then her former husband, who sent her away, may not take her again to be his wife, after she has been defiled; that is an abomination before the LORD, and you shall not bring guilt upon the land which the LORD gives you for an inheritance.

"A newly married man shall not go out with the army or be charged with any business; he shall be free at home one year, to be happy with his wife.

"If a man steals one of his brethren, and

treats him as a slave or sells him, then that thief shall die; so you shall purge evil from your midst.

"When you make your neighbor a loan, do not go into his house to fetch his pledge. Stand outside, and he shall bring the pledge out to you. If he is poor, and pledges his cloak, do not sleep in it; when the sun goes down, restore it to him that he may sleep in it and bless you; and this shall be righteousness to you before the LORD.

"You shall not oppress a poor and needy hired servant, whether he is one of your brethren or a sojourner in your land; give him his hire on the day he earns it, before the sun goes down (for he is poor, and sets his heart upon it); lest he cry against you to the LORD, and it be sin in you.

"The fathers shall not be put to death for the children, nor the children for the fathers; every man shall be put to death for his own sin.

"When you reap your harvest and forget a sheaf in the field, do not go back to get it; it shall be for the sojourner, the fatherless, and the widow; that the LORD your God may bless you in all the work of your hands. When you beat your olive trees, do not go over the boughs again; when you gather the grapes of your vineyard, do not glean it afterward; what is left shall be for the sojourner, the fatherless, and the widow. Remember that you were a slave in Egypt; therefore I command you to do this.

"If there is a dispute between men, and the guilty man is condemned to be beaten, the judge shall cause him to be beaten in his presence with a number of stripes in proportion to his offense. Not more than forty stripes may be given, lest your brother be degraded in your sight.

"You shall not muzzle an ox when it treads out the grain.

"If brothers dwell together, and one dies leaving no son, the widow shall not be married outside the family; her husband's brother shall take her as his wife, and perform the duty of a husband's brother to her. The first son she bears shall succeed to the name of the brother who is dead, that his name may not be blotted out of

Israel. If the man does not wish to take his brother's wife, she shall go to the elders of the city, and say, 'My husband's brother refuses to perpetuate his brother's name in Israel.' Then the elders shall speak to him; and if he persists, saying, 'I do not wish to take her,' then his brother's wife, in the presence of the elders, shall pull his sandal off his foot, spit in his face, and say, 'So shall it be done to the man who does not build up his brother's house.'

"You shall not have in your bag or in your house two kinds of measures, a large and a small. A full and just weight you shall have, a full and just measure, that your days may be prolonged in the land which the LORD your God gives you. For all who act dishonestly are an abomination to the LORD your God.

"Remember how Amalek attacked you as you came out of Egypt, when you were faint and weary. He cut off at your rear all who lagged behind you, and he did not fear God. Therefore when the LORD has given you rest from your enemies, in the land of your inheritance, you shall blot out the remembrance of Amalek from under heaven; you shall not forget."

Now Moses and the elders of Israel commanded the people, saying, "On the day you pass over the Jordan to the land which the Lord your God gives you, set up large stones on Mount Ebal. Plaster them, and write upon them all the words of this law very plainly. Then build an altar of unhewn stones to the Lord your God, and make offerings. Eat there, and rejoice before the Lord."

Moses charged the people, saying, "Behold, I set before you a blessing and a curse: the blessing, if you obey the commandments of the Lord, and the curse, if you do not obey, but turn aside to go after other gods. When you have passed over the Jordan, you shall set the blessing on Mount Gerizim and the curse on Mount Ebal. These shall stand upon Mount Gerizim to bless the people: Simeon, Levi, Judah, Issachar, Joseph, and Benjamin. And these shall stand upon Mount Ebal for the curse: Reuben, Gad, Asher, Zebulun, Dan, and Naphtali. And the Levites shall declare to all Israel with a loud voice:

" 'Cursed be the man who makes a graven or molten image, an abomination to the LORD, made by the hands of a craftsman, and sets it up in secret.

" 'Cursed be he who dishonors his father or his mother.

" 'Cursed be he who removes his neighbor's landmark.

" 'Cursed be he who misleads a blind man on the road.

" 'Cursed be he who perverts the justice due to the sojourner, the fatherless, and the widow.

" 'Cursed be he who lies with his father's wife, because he has uncovered her who is his father's.

" 'Cursed be he who lies with any kind of beast.

" 'Cursed be he who lies with his sister, whether the daughter of his father or of his mother.

" 'Cursed be he who lies with his mother-in-law.

" 'Cursed be he who slays his neighbor in secret.

" 'Cursed be he who takes a bribe to slay an innocent person.

" 'Cursed be he who does not confirm the words of this law by doing them.' And all the people shall say, 'Amen.'

"If you obey the voice of the LORD your God, being careful to do all his commandments, the LORD will set you high above all nations, and these blessings shall come upon you. Blessed shall you be in the city, and in the field. Blessed shall be the fruit of your body, and of your ground, the increase of your cattle, and the young of your flock. Blessed shall be your basket and your kneading-trough. Blessed shall you be when you come in, and when you go out. The LORD will cause your enemies to be defeated. He will establish you as a people holy to himself, if you walk in his ways. All the peoples of the earth shall see that you are called by the name of the LORD; and they shall be afraid of you. The LORD will make you abound in prosperity, and will open his good treasury, the heavens, to give rain to your land in its season and to bless the work of your hands. You shall lend to many nations, but you shall not borrow. And the LORD will make you the head, not the tail; you shall tend upward only, not downward; if you obey the commandments of the LORD your God, and do not turn aside to serve other gods.

"But if you will not obey the voice of the LORD your God, then all these curses shall come upon you. Cursed shall you be in the city, and in the field. Cursed shall be your basket and your kneading-trough. Cursed shall be the fruit of your body, and of your ground, the increase of your cattle, and the young of your flock. Cursed shall you be when you come in, and when you go out. The LORD will send upon you confusion and frustration in all that you undertake, until you perish, on account of your evil doings. The heavens over your head shall be brass, and the earth under you shall be iron. The LORD will make the rain of your land powder and dust; from heaven it shall come down upon you until you are destroyed.

"The LORD will cause you to be defeated before your enemies, and you shall be a horror to all the earth's kingdoms. Your dead body shall be food for birds and beasts; and there shall be no one to frighten them away. The LORD will smite you with the boils of Egypt, and with ulcers, scurvy, and itch, of which you cannot be healed. He will afflict you with madness, blindness, and confusion of mind; you shall grope at noonday, as the blind grope in darkness; you shall not prosper; you shall be oppressed and robbed continually, and no one shall help you. You shall betroth a wife, and another man shall lie with her; you shall build a house, and not dwell in it; you shall plant a vineyard, and not use its fruit. Your ox shall be slain before your eyes, and you shall not eat of it; your ass shall be violently taken away, and not be restored to you; your sheep shall be given to your enemies, and no one shall help you. Your sons and daughters shall be given to another people, while your eyes look on and fail with longing for them; and it shall not be in your power to prevent it. The sojourner among you shall mount above you higher and higher, and you shall come down lower and lower. He shall lend to you, and you shall not lend to him; he shall be the head and you shall be the tail. All these curses shall come upon you and destroy you, because you did not obey the voice of the LORD your God. They shall be upon you as a sign and a wonder, and upon your descendants for ever.

"Because you did not serve the LORD your God with joyfulness, by reason of the abundance of all things, therefore you shall serve your enemies in hunger, thirst, and nakedness. The LORD will bring a nation against you from afar, a nation of stern countenance, whose language you do not understand, who shall not regard the person of the old or show favor to the young, and shall eat the offspring of your cattle and the fruit of your ground. That nation shall besiege your towns, until your high fortified walls come down. In your distress you shall eat the offspring of your own body, the flesh of your sons and daughters. Whereas you were a multitude as the stars of heaven, you shall be left few in number. The LORD will scatter you among all peoples, from one end of the earth to the other; and there you shall serve other gods. Among these nations you shall find no ease, and have no assurance for your life. The LORD will give you a trembling heart, failing eyes, and a languishing soul; night and day you shall be in dread. In the morning you shall say, 'Would it were evening!' and at evening you shall say, 'Would it were morning!' because of the fear in your heart, and the sights your eyes shall see. And the LORD will bring you back in ships to Egypt, a journey I promised you should never make again; there you shall offer yourselves for sale to your enemies as slaves, but no man will buy you."

THESE ARE THE words of the covenant which the LORD commanded Moses to make with the people of Israel in the land of Moab, besides the covenant he had made with them at Sinai. Summoning all Israel, Moses said, "You have seen all that the LORD did before your eyes. The secret things belong to the LORD our God; but the things that are revealed belong to us and our children for ever, that we may do all the words of this law.

"And when all these things come upon you, the blessing and the curse, and you call them to mind among the nations where the LORD has driven you, and return to the LORD your God, you and your children, obeying his voice in all that I command you this day, then the LORD will restore your fortunes, have compassion upon you, and gather you again from where he has scattered you. From the uttermost parts of heaven he will fetch you, and bring you into the land which your fathers possessed. He will make you abundantly prosperous in all the work of your hand, and in the fruit of your body, your cattle, and your ground; for the LORD will again take delight in prospering you, if you keep his commandments and turn to him with all your heart and with all your soul.

"For this commandment is not too hard for you, neither is it far off. It is not in heaven, that you should say, 'Who will go up to heaven, and bring it to us, that we may hear it and do it?' Neither is it beyond the sea, that you should say, 'Who will go over the sea, and bring it to us, that we may hear it and do it?' But the word is very near you; it is in your mouth and in your heart, so that you can do it.

"See, I have set before you life and good, death and evil. If you obey the commandments of the LORD your God, by loving him and walking in his ways, then you shall live and multiply, and the LORD your God will bless you. But if your heart turns away, and you will not hear, but worship other gods, you shall perish; you shall not live long in the land which you are going over the Jordan to enter and possess. I call heaven and earth to witness this day, that I have set before you life and death, blessing and curse; therefore choose life, loving the LORD your God, obeying his voice, and cleaving to him, that you and your descendants may live long in the land which the LORD swore to your fathers, to Abraham, Isaac, and Jacob, to give them."

THEN MOSES SAID to all Israel, "I am a hundred and twenty years old this day; I am no longer able to go out and come in. The LORD has said to me, 'You shall not go over this Jordan.' The LORD your God himself will go over before you, destroying nations, so that you shall dispossess them; and Joshua will go over at your head. Be of good courage, for the LORD goes with you; he will not fail you or forsake you."

When Moses had finished writing the words of the law in a book, he said to the Levites, "Take this book of the law, and put it by the side of the ark of the covenant of the LORD your God, that it may be there for a witness against you. Every seven years, during the feast of booths, when all Israel appears before the LORD at the place which he will choose, you shall read this law. Assemble the people, men, women, little ones, and the sojourner within your towns, that they may hear and learn to fear the LORD, and do all the words of this law. For I know how rebellious and stubborn you are today, while I am yet with you; how much more after my death!"

And the LORD said to Moses, "Behold, the days approach when you must die; call Joshua, and present yourselves in the tent of meeting, that I may commission him." Moses and Joshua presented themselves, and the LORD appeared by the door of the tent of meeting in a pillar of cloud. The LORD commissioned Joshua, saying, "Be strong and of good courage; for you shall bring the children of Israel into the land which I swore to give them: I will be with you."

To Moses the LORD said, "You are about to sleep with your fathers; then this people will play the harlot after strange gods, and forsake me and break my covenant. My anger will be kindled against them, and many troubles will come upon them. 'Have not these evils come upon us,' they will say, 'because our God is not among us?' And I will surely hide my face in that day, because they have turned to other gods. Now therefore write this song, and teach it to the people; put it in their mouths, that it may be a witness for me against the people of Israel. For I know the purposes they are already forming, before I have brought them into the land flowing with milk and honey. When they have eaten and grown fat, they will despise me and break my covenant. And when many evils have come upon them, this song shall confront them as a witness, living unforgotten in the mouths of their descendants." So Moses wrote this song the same day, and taught it to the people of Israel, saying,

"Give ear, O heavens, and let the earth hear my words. May my speech distil as the dew, and my teaching drop as gentle rain upon the tender grass. For I will proclaim the name of the LORD. He is the Rock, his work is perfect; for all his ways are justice. A God of faithfulness is he, without iniquity.

"They have dealt corruptly with him; no longer his children because of their blemish, they are a perverse and crooked generation. Do you thus requite the LORD, you senseless people? Is he not your father, who created you? Remember the days of old; ask your elders, and they will tell you. When the Most High gave the nations their inheritance, he separated the sons of men, and fixed the bounds of the peoples according to the number of the sons of God. But the LORD's portion is his people, Jacob his allotted heritage.

"He found him in a desert land, a howling waste of wilderness; he encircled him, cared for him as the apple of his eye. Like an eagle that flutters over its young, spreading out its wings, catching them, bearing them on its pinions, the LORD alone did lead him; no foreign god was with him. He made him ride on the high places of the earth, eat the produce of the field, and suck honey out of the rock.

"But Israel waxed fat, grew thick, became sleek; then he forsook God who made him, and scoffed at the Rock of his salvation.

"The LORD saw it, and said, 'I will hide my face from them, and see what their end will be, for they are children in whom there is no faithfulness. They have provoked me with their idols. I will provoke them with a foolish nation. For a fire is kindled by my anger; it devours the earth, and sets on fire the foundations of the mountains. I will heap evils upon them; they shall be wasted with hunger, devoured with poisonous pestilence; I will send the teeth of beasts, the venom of crawling things against them. In the open the sword shall bereave, and in the chambers terror shall destroy young man and virgin, the sucking child, and the man of gray hairs. I would have said, "I will scatter them afar, and make remembrance of them cease among men," had I not feared, lest their adversaries should judge amiss, saying, "Our hand is triumphant, the LORD has not wrought all this." '

"For they are a nation void of counsel, with no understanding. If they were wise, they would discern their latter end! How should one chase a thousand, and two put ten thousand to flight, unless their Rock had sold them, and the LORD had given them up? For the rock of our enemies is not as our Rock. Their vine comes from the vine of Sodom, and the fields of Gomorrah; their grapes are grapes of poison; their wine is the cruel venom of asps. But the day of their calamity is at hand. For the LORD will vindicate his people and have compassion, when he sees that their power is gone. Then he will say, 'Where are the gods who ate the fat of your sacrifices, and drank the wine of your drink offering? Let them rise up and be your protection! See now that I, even I, am he, and there is no god beside me; I kill and I make alive; I wound and I heal; none can deliver out of my hand. For I lift up my hand to heaven, and swear, As I live for ever, I will take vengeance on my adversaries. I will make my arrows drunk with the blood of the slain and the captives, and my sword shall devour flesh.'

"Praise his people, O you nations; for he avenges the blood of his servants, and makes expiation for the land of his people."

When Moses had finished reciting this song to the people of Israel, he said, "Lay to heart all the words which I enjoin upon you this day, that you may command them to your children. For this law is no trifle for you; it is your life, and thereby you shall live long in the land you are going over the Jordan to possess."

THE LORD SAID to Moses that very day, "Ascend this mountain of the Abarim, Mount Nebo, in the land of Moab, opposite Jericho, and view the land of Canaan. Because you broke faith with me in the midst of the people of Israel at the waters of Meribah, and did not revere me as holy, you shall not go into the land I give to the people of Israel. You shall die on the mountain and be gathered to your people, as Aaron your brother died on Mount Hor."

This is the blessing with which Moses the man of God blessed the children of Israel before his death: "The LORD came from Sinai, and shone forth from Paran; he came from the ten thousands of holy ones. Yea, he loved his people; those consecrated to him were in his hand, following in his steps, receiving direction from him, when Moses commanded a law. Thus the LORD became king in Israel."

Of Reuben he said, "Let Reuben live, and not die, nor let his men be few." And this he said of Judah, "Hear, O LORD, the voice of Judah; bring him in to his people, and be a help against his adversaries." Of Levi he said, "Levi, who has observed thy word, and kept thy covenant, shall teach Israel thy law, and put incense and burnt offering upon thy altar. Bless, O LORD, his substance, and accept the work of his hands; crush those that hate him, that they rise not again." And of Benjamin he said, "The beloved of the LORD dwells in safety by him; the LORD encompasses him, and makes his dwelling between his shoulders."

Of Joseph he said, "Blessed by the LORD be his land, with the choicest gifts of heaven above, and of the deep that couches beneath, with the choicest fruits of the sun, the abundance of the everlasting hills, and the favor of him that dwelt in the bush. Let these come upon the head of Joseph, prince among his brothers. His firstling bull has majesty, and his horns are the horns of a wild ox; with them he shall push the peoples to the ends of the earth; such are the ten thousands of Ephraim, and the thousands of Manasseh."

Of Zebulun and Issachar he said, "Rejoice, Zebulun, in your going out; and Issachar, in your tents. They shall offer right sacrifices; for they suck the affluence of the seas and the hidden treasures of the sand." Of Gad he said, "Blessed be he who enlarges Gad! He chose the best of the land for himself, a commander's portion, and with Israel he executed the commands and just decrees of the LORD." Of Dan he said, "Dan is a lion's whelp, that leaps forth from Bashan." Of Naphtali he said, "O Naphtali, full of the blessing of the LORD, possess the lake and the south." And of Asher he said, "Blessed be Asher, favorite of his brothers; let him dip his foot in oil. Your bars shall be iron and bronze; and as your days, so shall your strength be.

"There is none like God, O Israel, who rides through the heavens to your help. The eternal God is your dwelling place, and underneath are the everlasting arms. He thrust out the enemy before you, and Israel dwelt in safety, in a land of grain and wine; yea, his heavens drop down dew. Happy are you, O Israel! Who is like you, a people saved by the LORD, the shield of your help, and sword of your triumph! Your enemies shall come fawning to you, and you shall tread upon their high places."

Then Moses went up from the plains of Moab to Mount Nebo, to the top of Pisgah, which is opposite Jericho. And the LORD showed him all the land, Gilead as far as Dan, all Naphtali, the land of Ephraim and Manasseh, all Judah as far as the Western Sea, the Negeb, and the valley of Jericho the city of palm trees, as far as Zoar. And the LORD said to him, "This is the land I swore to give to the descendants of Abraham, Isaac, and Jacob. I have let you see it, but you shall not go over there." So Moses the servant of the LORD died there, according to the word of the LORD, and the LORD buried him in the valley in the land of Moab; but no man knows the place of his burial to this day. Moses was a hundred and twenty years old when he died; his eye was not dim, nor his natural force abated. And the people of Israel wept for Moses in the plains of Moab thirty days; then the days of mourning ended.

And Joshua the son of Nun was full of the spirit of wisdom, for Moses had laid his hands upon him; so the people of Israel obeyed Joshua, as the LORD had commanded. There has not arisen a prophet since in Israel like Moses, whom the LORD knew face to face, none like him for all the signs and wonders which the LORD sent him to do in the land of Egypt, and for all the mighty power and all the great and terrible deeds which Moses wrought in the sight of all Israel.

JOSHUA

With the passing of Moses, Joshua assumes leadership of the Israelites. This book tells how, under Joshua, the land of Canaan is conquered and divided among the twelve tribes. It is thus a sequel to Deuteronomy, tracing the history of the Israelites up to the death of Joshua. Its better-known incidents are the hiding of Israelite spies in Jericho by Rahab the harlot, the miraculous crossing of the Jordan, the fall of Jericho, and the deception practiced by the Gibeonites in order to become allies of the Israelites. Just before his death, the aged Joshua gathers all Israel about him in a solemn assembly at Shechem, where the people take upon themselves a covenant with the Lord similar to the one their forebears accepted at Mount Sinai.

The general impression conveyed by the

book as a whole is that of a complete
conquest of Canaan by Israel within a
period of a few years. The Book of Judges,
however, suggests that in reality the conquest was somewhat slower, rather confused, and not complete. Although some of
the book's sources may date from the
ninth century B.C. or even earlier, it probably did not reach its present form until the
sixth century B.C. or later. Its compilers
were also the final editors of Judges, 1 and
2 Samuel, and 1 and 2 Kings.

―――――

AFTER THE DEATH of Moses the servant of
the LORD, the LORD said to Joshua the son
of Nun, Moses' minister, "Moses my servant is dead; now therefore arise, go over
this Jordan, you and all this people, into
the land which I am giving to them. Every
place that the sole of your foot will tread
upon I have given to you, as I promised to
Moses. From the wilderness and this Lebanon as far as the river Euphrates, to the
Great Sea toward the going down of the

sun shall be your territory. No man shall be able to stand before you all the days of your life; as I was with Moses, so I will be with you; I will not fail you or forsake you. Be strong and of good courage; for you shall cause this people to inherit the land which I swore to give them. Only be strong, and be careful to keep all the law which Moses my servant commanded you; turn not from it to the right hand or to the left. This book of the law shall not depart out of your mouth, but you shall meditate on it day and night, that you may be careful to do according to all that is written in it; for then you shall make your way prosperous, and then you shall have good success. Have I not commanded you? Be not frightened, neither be dismayed; for the LORD your God is with you wherever you go."

Joshua then sent two men secretly from Israel's camp at Shittim as spies. "Go, view the land," he said, "especially Jericho." The two went, and coming to the house of a harlot whose name was Rahab, they lodged there. When the king of Jericho heard that certain men of Israel had come as spies, he sent to Rahab, saying,

"Bring forth the men who entered your house; for they have come to search out the land." But the woman had hidden them. "True, men came to me," she said, "but I did not know where they came from, and when the gate was to be closed, at dark, they went out. Where they went I do not know; pursue them quickly, for you will overtake them." When the king's men left, Rahab went up to the roof where she had hidden the men with stalks of flax, and she said, "I know that the LORD has given you the land, and fear has fallen upon us, and all the inhabitants melt away before you. We have heard how the LORD dried up the water of the Red Sea when you came out of Egypt, and how you utterly destroyed the two kings beyond the Jordan, Sihon and Og. As soon as we heard it, our hearts melted, and there was no courage left in any man; for the LORD your God is he who is God in heaven above and on earth beneath. Now then, swear to me by the LORD that as I have dealt kindly with you, you also will deal kindly with my father's house, and spare my father and mother, my brothers and sisters, and all who belong to them." And the men said, "Our life for yours! If you do not tell this business of ours, we will deal kindly and faithfully with you when the LORD gives us the land."

She let them down by a rope through the window, for her house was built into the city wall. "Go into the hills," she said, "lest the pursuers meet you. Hide yourselves there three days; then you may go your way." The men said, "We will be guiltless with respect to the oath you have made us swear. Behold, when we come into the land, bind this scarlet cord in the window through which you let us down, and gather into your house all your father's household. If any one goes into the street, his blood shall be upon his head, and we shall be guiltless; but if a hand is laid upon any one who is with you in the house, his blood shall be on our head." She said, "According to your words, so be it," and she bound the scarlet cord in the window.

After three days in the hills, the men returned to Joshua, and told him all that had befallen them. "Truly the LORD has given the land into our hands," they said, "and moreover all the inhabitants are fainthearted because of us."

Early in the morning Joshua set out from Shittim, with the people of Israel; they came to the Jordan, and lodged there before they passed over. At the end of three days the officers went through the camp and commanded the people, "When you see the ark of the covenant of the LORD your God being carried by the Levitical priests, set out and follow it, that you may know the way you shall go, for you have not passed this way before. Keep a space between you and the ark, a distance of about a thousand yards; do not come near it." And Joshua said to the people, "Sanctify yourselves; for tomorrow the LORD will do wonders among you."

The LORD said to Joshua, "Command the priests who bear the ark, 'When you come to the brink of the waters, stand still in the Jordan.' "

Joshua said to the people, "Come hither, and hear the words of the LORD your God. Hereby you shall know that the living God is among you, and that he will without fail drive out the inhabitants of the land. Behold, the ark of the covenant of the Lord of all the earth is to pass before you into the Jordan. When the soles of the feet of the priests who bear the ark shall rest in the Jordan, the waters shall be stopped from flowing."

The people set out from their tents to pass over the Jordan, and when the feet of the priests were dipped in the water (the Jordan overflows all its banks throughout the time of harvest), the waters coming down from above rose up in a heap far off, at the city of Adam, and those flowing down toward the Salt Sea were wholly cut off. The people passed over opposite Jericho on dry ground, while the priests stood in the midst of the Jordan.

When all the nation had finished passing over, the LORD said to Joshua, "Appoint twelve men from the people, from each tribe a man, and command them, 'Take twelve stones from the midst of the Jordan, and carry them with you.'" Joshua appointed the twelve men, and said to them, "Pass into the midst of the Jordan, and take up each of you a stone upon his shoulder, according to the number of the tribes of the people of Israel." And the men of Israel did as Joshua commanded. Then the LORD said to Joshua, "Command the priests who bear the ark to come up out of the Jordan." When the priests came up, the waters of the Jordan returned to their place and overflowed its banks, as before. On that day the LORD exalted Joshua in the sight of all Israel; and they stood in awe of him, as they had stood in awe of Moses, all the days of his life.

The people came up out of the Jordan on the tenth day of the first month, and encamped in Gilgal on the east border of Jericho. There Joshua set up the twelve stones from the Jordan, saying, "When your children ask their fathers in time to come, 'What do these stones mean?' you shall say, 'Israel passed over this Jordan on dry ground.' For the LORD your God dried up the waters of the Jordan for you, as he dried up the Red Sea for us, so that all the peoples of the earth may know that the hand of the LORD is mighty; that you may fear the LORD your God for ever." While the people of Israel were encamped in Gilgal they kept the passover on the fourteenth day of the month at evening in the plains of Jericho. On the morrow they ate of the produce of the land, unleavened cakes and parched grain. The manna ceased, and the people ate of the fruit of the land of Canaan.

WHEN JOSHUA WAS by Jericho, he lifted up his eyes, and behold, a man stood before him with drawn sword. "Are you for us, or for our adversaries?" Joshua asked. "As commander of the army of the LORD I have now come," he said. Joshua fell on his face to the earth, and worshiped.

Now Jericho was shut up from within and without because of the people of Israel; none went out, and none came in. And the LORD said to Joshua, "See, I have given into your hand Jericho, with its king and mighty men of valor. All your men of war shall march around the city once, for six days. Seven priests shall bear seven trumpets of rams' horns before the ark; and on the seventh day you shall march around the city seven times, the priests blowing the trumpets. When they make a long blast with the ram's horn, all the people shall shout with a great shout; and the wall of the city will fall down flat." So Joshua commanded the priests and the people, and they went forward, the trumpets blowing continually. "You shall not let your voice be heard," Joshua commanded, "until the day I bid you shout; then you shall shout." So he caused the ark of the LORD to compass the city, going about it once, and thus they did for six days.

On the seventh day they rose at dawn, and marched around the city in the same manner seven times. At the seventh time, when the priests had blown a long blast with the trumpets, Joshua said to the people, "Shout; for the LORD has given you the city. All within it shall be devoted to the LORD for destruction; only Rahab the harlot and her household shall live, because she hid the messengers that we sent. But you, keep yourselves from the things devoted to destruction, lest you take any and bring trouble upon the camp of Israel. All silver and gold, and vessels of bronze and iron, are sacred to the LORD; they shall go into the LORD's treasury." So the people raised a great shout, and the wall fell down flat, and they went up into the city, and took it.

Then Joshua said to the two men who had spied out the land, "Go into the harlot's house, and bring out the woman, and all who belong to her, as you swore." So they brought out Rahab and her kindred, and set them outside the camp of Israel. Then they utterly destroyed all in the city, both men and women, young and old, oxen, sheep, and asses, with the edge of the sword, and they burned the city, and all within it. Only the silver and gold, and the vessels of bronze and iron, they put into the treasury of the house of the LORD. Thus Joshua saved Rahab and her kindred, and she dwelt in Israel, because she hid the spies whom Joshua sent. And Joshua pronounced an oath: "Cursed before the LORD be the man that rises up and rebuilds this city, Jericho. At the cost of his first-born shall he lay its foundation, and at the cost of his youngest son shall he set up its gates."

So the LORD was with Joshua; and his fame was in all the land.

BUT THE PEOPLE of Israel broke faith; for Achan the son of Carmi, son of Zabdi, son of Zerah, of the tribe of Judah, took some of the devoted things; and the anger of the LORD burned against Israel.

Joshua sent men from Jericho to Ai, east of Bethel, to spy out the land. On their return they said, "Let about two or three thousand men go up and attack Ai; do not make the whole people toil up there, for they are but few." So about three thousand went up; but they fled before the men of Ai, who killed about thirty-six of them, and chased them as far as Shebarim, and slew them. The hearts of the people melted, and became as water. Joshua rent his clothes, and fell upon his face before the ark, he and the elders of Israel; and they put dust upon their heads. "Alas, O Lord GOD," Joshua said, "why hast thou brought this people over the Jordan at all, to give us into the hands of our enemies? Would that we had been content to dwell beyond the Jordan! O LORD, what can I say, when Israel has turned their backs before their enemies! The Canaanites and all the inhabitants of the land will hear of

it, and will surround us, and cut off our
name from the earth; and what wilt thou
do for thy great name?"

The LORD said to Joshua, "Arise, why
have you thus fallen upon your face? Israel
has transgressed my covenant; they have
taken some of the devoted things. I will be
with you no more, unless you destroy the
devoted things from among you. Up, sanctify the people, and say, 'Thus says the
LORD, God of Israel, "There are devoted
things in the midst of you; you cannot
stand before your enemies, until you take
them away." In the morning therefore you
shall be brought near by your tribes and
families and households; and the household which the LORD chooses shall come
near, man by man. He who is found with
the devoted things shall be burned, he and
all that he has, because he has transgressed
the covenant of the LORD, and done a
shameful thing in Israel.' "

In the morning Joshua brought Israel
near, tribe by tribe, and the tribe of Judah
was chosen by the sacred lot; he brought
near the families of Judah, and the family
of the Zerahites was chosen; he brought

near the Zerahites, and the household of
Zabdi was chosen; he brought near his
household, man by man, and Achan the
son of Carmi was chosen. "My son," Joshua
said to Achan, "give glory to the LORD
God of Israel, and tell me now what you
have done; do not hide it from me."
Achan answered, "Of a truth I have sinned
against the LORD. When I saw among the
spoil a beautiful mantle from Babylon, and
two hundred shekels of silver, and a bar of
gold weighing fifty shekels, I coveted them,
and took them. They are hidden in the
earth inside my tent." Joshua sent messengers to the tent, and they found the devoted
things and brought them. Then Joshua,
and all Israel with him, took Achan, with
the silver, the mantle, the bar of gold, his
sons and daughters, his oxen, asses, and
sheep, his tent, and all that he had, and
they brought them to the Valley of
Achor. And Joshua said, "Why did you
bring trouble on us? The LORD brings
trouble on you today." And all Israel
stoned them and burned them. They
raised over Achan a great heap of stones
that remains to this day; then the

LORD turned from his burning anger.

The LORD said to Joshua, "Do not fear or be dismayed; take all the fighting men with you, and go up to Ai; see, I have given into your hand the king, and his people, his city, and his land; you shall do to Ai as you did to Jericho; only its spoil and its cattle you shall take as booty for yourselves. Lay an ambush against the city, behind it." So Joshua chose thirty thousand men, and sent them forth by night. "Lie in ambush against the city, behind it," he commanded. "Hold yourselves in readiness; I, and all the people who are with me, will approach the city. When they come out against us, as before, we shall flee, and they will come after us. Then you shall rise up from the ambush, and seize the city; for the LORD your God will give it into your hand. When you have taken the city, set it on fire, doing as the LORD has bidden." So they went to the place of ambush, to the west of Ai.

Early in the morning Joshua mustered the people, and they encamped on the north side of the city, with a ravine be-

tween them and Ai. When the king of Ai
saw this, he and his men hastened to
meet Israel in battle. Joshua and his men
made a pretense of being beaten, and
fled, so all in the city were called together
to pursue them. There was not a man left
in Ai, and they left the city open. Then
the LORD said to Joshua, "Stretch out
your javelin toward Ai; for I will give it
into your hand." Joshua stretched out his
javelin, and the men in ambush rose
quickly, taking the city and setting it on
fire. The men of Ai looked back, and saw
the smoke of the city rising to heaven;
but they had no power to flee this way or
that, for when Joshua and his men saw
the smoke, they turned back against the
men of Ai, and the others came forth
from the city against them. So they were
in the midst of Israel, some on this side,
and some on that side; and Israel smote
them until none survived or escaped. But
the king of Ai they took alive, and
brought to Joshua.

All Israel returned to Ai, and smote it
with the edge of the sword. Those who fell
that day, both men and women, were

twelve thousand, all the people of Ai. For Joshua did not draw back his javelin until he had utterly destroyed all the inhabitants. The cattle and the spoil Israel took as their booty, according to the word of the LORD. So Joshua burned Ai, and made it for ever a heap of ruins, as it is to this day. He hanged the king of Ai on a tree until evening, when they took his body down, and cast it at the entrance of the city, and raised over it a great heap of stones, which stands there to this day.

Then, on Mount Ebal, Joshua built an altar to the LORD of unhewn stones, as Moses had commanded, and they made burnt offerings, and sacrificed peace offerings. In the presence of the people, Joshua wrote upon the stones a copy of the law of Moses. All Israel, with elders, officers, and judges, stood on opposite sides of the ark, facing the Levitical priests who carried it. Half of them stood in front of Mount Gerizim and half of them in front of Mount Ebal, as Moses had commanded. Afterward Joshua read all the words of the law, the blessing and the curse, before the assembly of Israel.

WHEN THE INHABITANTS of Gibeon heard what Joshua had done to Jericho and to Ai, they acted with cunning. They made ready dry and moldy provisions, and put worn-out sacks and mended wineskins upon their asses. Wearing patched sandals and worn-out clothes, they went to Joshua in the camp at Gilgal. "We are your servants," they said. "Come now, make a covenant with us." But the men of Israel said, "Perhaps you live among us; then how can we make a covenant with you? Who are you? And where do you come from?" They replied, "From a very far country your servants have come, because we have heard all that the LORD your God did in Egypt, and all that he did to the two kings, Sihon and Og. Here is our bread. It was still warm when we took it from our houses, but now, behold, it is dry and moldy. These wineskins were new when we filled them, and behold, they are burst. These garments and shoes of ours are worn out from the very long journey." So the men of Israel partook of their provisions, and did not ask direction from the LORD. Joshua made peace with them, and a covenant, and the leaders of the congregation swore to them.

Then, three days later, the people of Israel heard that the Gibeonites were their neighbors. They set out and reached their cities on the third day, but they did not kill them, because the leaders had sworn to them by the LORD. When the congregation of Israel murmured, the leaders said, "We have sworn to them by the LORD, and now we may not touch them, lest wrath be upon us."

Summoning the inhabitants of Gibeon, Joshua said, "Why did you deceive us? Now therefore you are cursed, and some of you shall always be slaves, hewers of wood and drawers of water for the house of my God." They answered, "Because we were told for a certainty that the LORD your God had commanded his servant Moses to give you all the land, and to destroy all the inhabitants, we feared greatly for our lives. Now, behold, we are in your hand: do to us as it seems good and right in your sight." So Joshua made them hewers of wood and drawers of water for the house of the LORD.

WHEN ADONIZEDEK KING of Jerusalem heard how Joshua had taken Ai, and how the inhabitants of Gibeon had made peace with Israel, he feared greatly, because Gibeon was a great city, greater than Ai, and all its men were mighty. So he sent to the Amorite kings of Hebron, Jarmuth, Lachish, and Eglon, saying, "Come up and help me, and let us smite Gibeon; for it has made peace with the people of Israel." Then these five kings gathered their forces, and went up to make war against Gibeon.

The Gibeonites sent to Joshua at the camp in Gilgal for help. So, with all the mighty men of valor, he went up. And the LORD said to Joshua, "Do not fear them, for I have given them into your hands; there shall not a man of them stand before you." Having marched all night from Gilgal, Joshua came upon them suddenly. And the LORD threw them into a panic before Israel, who slew them with a great slaughter at Gibeon, and chased them by the way of the ascent of Beth-horon. As they fled, the LORD threw great stones from heaven upon them, and they died; more died because of the hailstones than by the sword.

Then Joshua spoke to the LORD in the sight of Israel, "Sun, stand thou still at Gibeon, and thou Moon in the valley of Aijalon." And the sun stood still, and the moon stayed, until the nation took vengeance on their enemies. Is this not written in the Book of Jashar? The sun stayed in the midst of heaven, and did not hasten to go down for about a whole day. There has been no day like it before or since, when the LORD hearkened to the voice of a man; for the LORD fought for Israel.

The five kings fled, and hid themselves in the cave at Makkedah. "Roll great stones against the mouth of the cave," Joshua said, "and set men to guard it. Then pursue your enemies, and do not let them enter their cities; for the LORD your God has given them into your hand." When Joshua and the men of Israel had finished slaying all of them, except the remnant which had entered into the fortified cities, they returned to Makkedah; not a man moved his tongue against any of the people of Israel.

Then Joshua said, "Bring those five

kings out to me from the cave," and he summoned all the men of Israel. To the chiefs of war he said, "Come near, put your feet upon the necks of these kings." They did so, and Joshua said, "Do not be afraid or dismayed; be strong and of good courage; for thus the LORD will do to all your enemies against whom you fight." Afterward Joshua put the kings to death, and hung them on five trees. At the going down of the sun, at Joshua's command, they took them down, threw them into the cave where they had hidden, and set great stones against the mouth of the cave, which remain to this very day. Then Joshua took Makkedah, and smote it and its king with the edge of the sword until none remained.

So Joshua defeated the southern hill country and utterly destroyed all that breathed, as the LORD God of Israel commanded. Then he returned, and all Israel with him, to the camp at Gilgal.

WHEN THE KING of Hazor heard of this, he sent to the kings in the northern hill country. They came out, with all their troops, a

great host, in number like the sand upon
the seashore, with very many horses and
chariots, and joined their forces at the waters of Merom, to fight with Israel. The
LORD said to Joshua, "Do not be afraid of
them, for tomorrow at this time I will give
over all of them, slain, to Israel; you shall
hamstring their horses, and burn their
chariots." So Joshua came suddenly with
all his people of war by the waters of Merom, and fell upon them. The LORD gave
them into the hand of Israel, who smote
them until they left none remaining. Joshua
did as the LORD bade; he hamstrung their
horses, and burned their chariots. Then he
took their cities, and smote them with the
edge of the sword, utterly destroying them,
as Moses had commanded. The people of
Israel took the spoil of these cities and the
cattle for their booty.

Joshua made war a long time; for there
was not a city that made peace with the
people of Israel, except Gibeon. It was the
LORD'S doing to harden their hearts that
they should come against Israel in battle,
in order that they should be utterly destroyed, and receive no mercy. At that time

Joshua came and wiped out the Anakim, a people great and tall, from the hill country. Only in Gaza, in Gath, and in Ashdod did some remain. So Joshua took the whole land, according to all that the LORD had spoken to Moses; and Joshua gave it for an inheritance to Israel. And the land had rest from war.

JOSHUA SUMMONED THE Reubenites, the Gadites, and the half-tribe of Manasseh, and said to them, "You have kept all that Moses and I have commanded you; you have not forsaken your brethren these many days, but have been careful to keep the charge of the LORD your God. Now the LORD has given rest to your brethren, as he promised them; therefore turn and go to your home in the land which Moses gave you on the other side of the Jordan. Take good care to observe the commandment and the law which Moses commanded you, to love the LORD your God, to walk in all his ways, to keep his commandments, to cleave to him, and to serve him with all your heart and with all your soul." So the Reubenites, the Gadites, and the half-tribe of Manasseh returned home, parting from the people of Israel at Shiloh, in Canaan, to go to Gilead, their own land.

When they came to the region about the Jordan, they built an altar of great size at the frontier, on the side that belongs to Israel. The people of Israel heard of it, and gathered at Shiloh, to make war. They sent Phinehas the son of Eleazar the priest, and with him ten chiefs, to say, "What is this treachery which you have committed, by building yourselves an altar in rebellion against the LORD? Have we not had enough of the sin at Peor from which even yet we have not cleansed ourselves, and for which there came a plague? If you rebel against the LORD today, he will be angry with the whole congregation of Israel to-morrow. But now, if your land is unclean, pass over into the LORD's land where the LORD's tabernacle stands, and take for yourselves a possession among us; only do not rebel, or make us as rebels by building yourselves an altar other than the altar of the LORD our God. Did not Achan break faith in the matter of the devoted things, and bring wrath upon all the congregation of Israel? And he did not perish alone for his iniquity."

Then the Reubenites, the Gadites, and the half-tribe of Manasseh said, "The Mighty One, God, the LORD! He knows; and let Israel itself know! If it was in rebellion or in breach of faith toward the LORD, spare us not today for building an altar; or if we did so to make offerings, may the LORD himself take vengeance. Nay, but we did it from fear that in time to come your children might say to our children, 'What have you to do with the LORD, the God of Israel? For the LORD has made the Jordan a boundary between us and you; you have no portion in the LORD.' So your children might make our children cease to worship the LORD. Therefore we said, 'Let us now build an altar, not for offerings or sacrifice, but to be a witness between us and you, and between the generations after us, that we do perform the service of the LORD in his presence.' If it should be said to us or to our descendants, 'You have no portion in the LORD,' we should say, 'Behold the copy of the altar of the LORD, which our fathers made, to be a witness between us and you.' Far be it from us that we should turn away from following the LORD by building an altar other than the altar of the LORD our God that stands before his tabernacle!"

When Phinehas and the others heard these words, it pleased them well. "Today we know that the LORD is in the midst of us," Phinehas said, "because you have not committed this treachery against the LORD; now you have saved the people of Israel from the hand of the LORD." Then Phinehas and the chiefs returned, and their report pleased the people, who blessed God and spoke no more of making war.

A LONG TIME afterward, when the LORD had given rest to Israel, Joshua summoned all the people, their elders, judges, and officers, and he said, "I am now well advanced in years; and you have seen all that the LORD your God has done to these nations for your sake. Behold, I have allotted to you as an inheritance those nations that remain, along with all the nations that I have already cut off, from the Jordan to the Great Sea in the west. The LORD will push them back before you, and you shall possess their land, as the LORD promised you. Therefore keep the law of Moses, turning aside from it neither to the right hand nor to the left; cleave to the LORD your God as you have done to this day. No man has been able to withstand you. One man of you puts to flight a thousand, since it is the LORD who fights for you, as he promised. Therefore love the LORD your God. For if you turn back, and join the remnant of these nations, and make marriages with them, know assuredly that the LORD will not continue to drive them out; but they shall be a snare and a trap for you, a scourge on your sides, and thorns in your eyes, till you perish from off this good land which the LORD has given you. Now I am about to go the way of all the earth, and you know in your hearts and souls, all of you, that not one thing has failed of all the good things which the LORD your God promised you."

THEN JOSHUA GATHERED the tribes of Israel to Shechem, and they presented themselves before God. And Joshua said to the

people, "Thus says the LORD, the God of
Israel, 'Your fathers lived of old beyond
the Euphrates, and they served other gods.
Then I took Abraham from beyond the
River and led him through all the land of
Canaan, and made his offspring many. I
gave him Isaac; and to Isaac I gave Jacob
and Esau. I gave Esau the hill country of
Seir to possess, but Jacob and his children
went down to Egypt. I sent Moses and
Aaron, and I plagued Egypt; and afterwards I brought you out. You lived in the
wilderness a long time. Then I brought you
to the land of the Amorites, who lived east
of the Jordan; they fought with you, and I
gave them into your hand, and you took
possession of their land. Then Balak king
of Moab arose and fought against Israel;
and he invited Balaam the son of Beor to
curse you, but I would not listen to Balaam; therefore he blessed you; so I delivered you out of his hand. You went over
the Jordan, and the inhabitants of the land
fought against you. I sent the hornet before
you, which drove them out; it was not by
your sword or by your bow. I gave you a
land on which you had not labored, and

cities which you had not built, and you dwell therein; you eat the fruit of vineyards and oliveyards which you did not plant.' Now therefore fear the LORD, and serve him in sincerity and in faithfulness. If you be unwilling to serve the LORD, choose this day whom you will serve, whether the gods your fathers served in the region beyond the River, or the gods of the peoples in whose land you dwell; but as for me and my house, we will serve the LORD."

The people answered, "Far be it from us that we should forsake the LORD, to serve other gods; for it is the LORD our God who brought us from the land of Egypt, out of the house of bondage, and who did those great signs in our sight, and preserved us in all the way that we went, and drove out before us all the peoples who lived in the land; therefore we also will serve the LORD, for he is our God." But Joshua said, "The LORD will not forgive your transgressions or your sins. If you forsake the LORD and serve foreign gods, he will turn and do you harm, and consume you, after having done you good."

The people said, "Nay; but we will serve the LORD." Then Joshua said, "You are witnesses against yourselves that you have chosen the LORD, to serve him." And they said, "We are witnesses." He said, "Then put away the foreign gods which are among you, and incline your heart to the LORD, the God of Israel." The people said, "The LORD our God we will serve, and his voice we will obey." So Joshua made a covenant with the people that day, and made statutes and ordinances for them at Shechem. He wrote these words in the book of the law of God; and he set up a great stone under the oak in the sanctuary of the LORD. "Behold," he said to the people, "this stone, which has heard all the words of the LORD, shall be a witness against you, lest you deal falsely with your God." Then he sent the people away, every man to his inheritance.

After these things Joshua the son of Nun, the servant of the LORD, died, being a hundred and ten years old. They buried him in his own inheritance at Timnath-serah in the hill country of Ephraim. Israel served the LORD all the days of Joshua, and all the days of the elders who outlived Joshua and had known all the work which the LORD did for Israel.

The bones of Joseph which the people of Israel brought up from Egypt were buried at Shechem. And Eleazar the son of Aaron died; and they buried him at Gibeah, the town of Phinehas his son, which had been given him in the hill country of Ephraim.

JUDGES

With the death of Joshua, the people of Israel are ruled for several centuries by a series of tribal patriots and religious reformers. They are known as judges (the traditional translation of the Hebrew word), but settling disputes is only a part of their task. Mainly, because the Israelites are so often under attack by their neighbors, the judges serve as war leaders. The book came into being when some unknown editor gathered colorful stories about these leaders and about the Israelites' early life in the Promised Land, and placed them within a religious framework. His primary concern is not with simple history but with driving home to the people a fundamental moral and theological lesson: The repeated sequence of sin, punishment, repentance, and deliverance demonstrates that obedience to the divine commands leads to national success, while disobedience leads to disaster. This same theme also appears in classical form in the Book of Deuteronomy.

———

AFTER THE DEATH of Joshua there arose another generation, who did not know the LORD or the work he had done for Israel. The people did what was evil in the sight of the LORD; they forsook the God of their fathers, who had brought them out of Egypt, and they bowed down to the gods of the peoples who were round about them. So the anger of the LORD was kindled against Israel, and he gave them over to plunderers, and sold them into the power of their enemies. Whenever they marched out, the hand of the LORD was against them for evil, as the LORD had warned; and they were in sore straits.

Then the LORD raised up judges, who saved Israel out of the power of those who plundered them. The LORD was with the judge, saving the Israelites from the hand of their enemies all the days of the judge; for the LORD was moved to pity by their groaning under those who afflicted and oppressed them. But whenever the judge died, they turned back and behaved worse than their fathers, serving other gods; they did not drop any of their practices or their stubborn ways. So the LORD said, "Because this people have transgressed my covenant which I commanded their fathers, I will not henceforth drive out before them any of the nations that Joshua left when he died. By them I will test Israel, whether they will take care to walk in the way of the LORD as their fathers did, or not." These are the nations which the LORD left, to test all in Israel who had no experience of any war in Canaan: the Philistines, the Canaanites, the Sidonians, and the Hivites who dwelt on Mount Lebanon. So the Israelites dwelt among the people of these nations. They took their daughters for wives, and their own daughters they gave to their sons; and they served their gods.

Therefore the anger of the LORD was kindled against Israel, and he sold them

into the hand of Cushan-rishathaim king of
Mesopotamia. The people of Israel served
Cushan-rishathaim eight years. But when
the people cried to the LORD, he raised up
a deliverer for them, Othniel the son of
Kenaz, Caleb's younger brother. The Spirit
of the LORD came upon him, and he
judged Israel; he went out to war, and the
LORD gave Cushan-rishathaim into his
hand. So the land had rest for forty years.
Then Othniel died.

THE PEOPLE OF Israel again did what was
evil in the sight of the LORD; and the LORD
strengthened Eglon king of Moab against
them. Eglon defeated Israel, and Israel
served him eighteen years. But when the
people of Israel cried to the LORD, the
LORD raised up for them a deliverer, Ehud,
a left-handed man, the son of Gera, the
Benjaminite. Israel sent tribute by him to
Eglon. Now Ehud had made for himself a
sword with two edges, a foot and a half in
length; and he girded it on his right thigh
under his clothes. Then he presented the
tribute to Eglon king of Moab. When he
had finished presenting the tribute, he sent

away the people that carried it, but he himself turned back and said, "I have a secret message for you, O king." Eglon commanded, "Silence," and all his attendants went out from his presence. Ehud came to him, as he was sitting alone in his cool roof chamber, and said, "I have a message from God for you." Now Eglon was a very fat man. He arose from his seat, and Ehud reached with his left hand, took the sword from his right thigh, and thrust it into Eglon's belly. The hilt went in after the blade, and the fat closed over the blade, for Ehud did not withdraw the sword. Then Ehud went out, closed the doors of the roof chamber, and locked them.

When he had gone, the servants came; and when they saw that the doors were locked, they thought, "He is only relieving himself in the closet." They waited till they were utterly at a loss; but when he still did not open the doors, they took the key and went in, and there lay their lord dead on the floor. While they delayed, Ehud escaped.

When he arrived in the hill country of

Ephraim, he sounded the trumpet, and the people of Israel came down from the hills. "Follow after me," Ehud said, "for the LORD has given your enemies the Moabites into your hand." So they went down after him, and seized the fords of the Jordan against the Moabites, and allowed none to pass over. They killed at that time about ten thousand of the enemy, all strong, able-bodied men; not a man escaped. So Moab was subdued that day under the hand of Israel. And the land had rest for eighty years.

THE PEOPLE OF Israel again did what was evil in the sight of the LORD, after Ehud died. And the LORD sold them into the hand of Jabin king of Canaan, who reigned in Hazor; the commander of his army was Sisera. The people of Israel cried to the LORD for help; for Sisera had nine hundred chariots of iron, and oppressed the people of Israel cruelly for twenty years.

Now Deborah, a prophetess, the wife of Lappidoth, was judging Israel at that time. She used to sit under the palm of Deborah in the hill country of Ephraim; and the people of Israel came up to her for judgment. She summoned Barak the son of Abinoam from Kedesh in Naphtali, and said to him, "The LORD, the God of Israel, commands you, 'Go, gather your men at Mount Tabor, taking ten thousand from the tribes of Naphtali and Zebulun. I will draw out Sisera to meet you by the river Kishon with his chariots and his troops; and I will give him into your hand.' " Barak said to Deborah, "If you will go with me, I will go; but if you will not go with me, I will not go." She said, "I will surely go with you; nevertheless, the road on which you are going will not lead to your glory, for the LORD will sell Sisera into the hand of a woman." Then Deborah arose, and went with Barak to Kedesh. Barak summoned Zebulun and Naphtali, and ten thousand men went up at his heels to Mount Tabor.

When Sisera was told that Barak had gone up to Mount Tabor, he called out his nine hundred chariots of iron, and all his men, to the river Kishon. Deborah said to Barak, "Up! For this is the day in which the LORD has given Sisera into your hand.

Does not the LORD go out before you?" So Barak and his men went down from Mount Tabor, and the LORD routed Sisera and all his chariots and all his army before them at the edge of the sword. Barak pursued the chariots and the army, and all the troops of Sisera fell by the edge of the sword; not a man was left.

But Sisera fled on foot to the tent of Jael, the wife of Heber the Kenite. Jael came out to meet Sisera, saying, "Turn aside, my lord, turn aside to me; have no fear." So he turned aside into the tent, and she covered him with a rug. "Pray, give me a little water to drink," he said, "for I am thirsty." So she opened a skin of milk and gave him a drink. "Stand at the door of the tent," he told her, "and if any man comes and asks you, 'Is any one here?' say, No." But later, as Sisera was lying fast asleep from weariness, Jael took a tent peg and a hammer in her hand, went softly to him, and drove the peg into his temple, till it went down into the ground. So he died. And behold, as Barak pursued Sisera, Jael went out to meet him, saying, "Come, I will show you the

man you seek." He went in to her tent;
and there lay Sisera dead, with the tent
peg in his temple.

So on that day God subdued Jabin the
king of Canaan. And the hand of the people of Israel bore harder and harder on
Jabin, until they destroyed him.

Then sang Deborah and Barak the son
of Abinoam on that day:

That the leaders took the lead in Israel,
    that the people offered themselves
        willingly,
    bless the LORD!
Hear, O kings; give ear, O princes;
    to the LORD I will sing,
    I will make melody to the LORD, the
        God of Israel.

LORD, when thou didst go forth from
        Seir,
    when thou didst march from the
        region of Edom,
the earth trembled,
    and the heavens dropped,
    yea, the clouds dropped water.
The mountains quaked before the LORD,

yon Sinai before the LORD, the God of
Israel.

In the days of Shamgar, son of Anath,
in the days of Jael, caravans ceased
and travelers kept to the byways.
The peasantry ceased in Israel, they
ceased
until you arose, Deborah,
arose as a mother in Israel.
When new gods were chosen,
then war was in the gates.
Was shield or spear to be seen
among forty thousand in Israel?
My heart goes out to the commanders of
Israel
who offered themselves willingly
among the people.
Bless the LORD.
Tell of it, you who ride on tawny asses,
you who sit on rich carpets,
and you who walk by the way.
To the sound of musicians at the
watering places,
there they repeat the triumphs of the
LORD,
the triumphs of his peasantry in Israel.

Then down to the gates marched the
    people of the LORD.

Awake, awake, Deborah!
    Awake, awake, utter a song!
Arise, Barak, lead away your captives,
    O son of Abinoam.

Then down marched the remnant of the
     noble;
    the people of the LORD marched
       down for him against the mighty.

The kings came, they fought;
    then fought the kings of Canaan,
at Taanach, by the waters of Megiddo;
    they got no spoils of silver.
From heaven fought the stars,
    from their courses they fought against
     Sisera.
The torrent Kishon swept them away,
    the onrushing torrent, the torrent
     Kishon.
    March on, my soul, with might!

Most blessed of women be Jael,
    the wife of Heber the Kenite,

of tent-dwelling women most blessed.
He asked water and she gave him milk,
   she brought him curds in a lordly
      bowl.
She put her hand to the tent peg
   and her right hand to the workmen's
      mallet;
she struck Sisera a blow,
   she crushed his head,
   she shattered and pierced his temple.
He sank, he fell,
   he lay still at her feet;
at her feet he sank, he fell;
   where he sank, there he fell dead.

Out of the window she peered,
   the mother of Sisera gazed through
      the lattice:
"Why is his chariot so long in coming?
   Why tarry the hoofbeats of his
      chariots?"
Her wisest ladies make answer,
   nay, she gives answer to herself,
"Are they not finding and dividing the
      spoil?—
   A maiden or two for every man;
spoil of dyed stuffs for Sisera,

spoil of dyed stuffs embroidered,
two pieces of dyed work embroidered
for my neck as spoil?"

So perish all thine enemies, O LORD!
But thy friends be like the sun as he
rises in his might.

And the land had rest for forty years.

THE PEOPLE OF Israel did what was evil in
the sight of the LORD; and the LORD gave
them into the hand of Midian for seven
years. Because of Midian the people of
Israel made for themselves dens in the
mountains, and caves and strongholds.
For whenever the Israelites put in seed
the Midianites and the Amalekites and
the people of the East would come up
and attack them; they would destroy the
produce of the land, as far as the neighborhood of Gaza, and leave no suste-
nance in Israel, and no sheep or ox or
ass. They would come up with their cattle and their tents, coming like locusts for
number, so that they wasted the land as
they came. Israel was brought very low

because of Midian; and the people of Israel cried for help to the LORD.

Now Gideon, the son of Joash of the clan of Abiezer, was beating out wheat in the wine press, to hide it from the Midianites. The LORD appeared to him and said, "The LORD is with you, you mighty man of valor." Gideon said, "If the LORD is with us, why then has all this befallen us? Where are all his wonderful deeds which our fathers recounted to us? Now the LORD has cast us off, and given us into the hand of Midian." And the LORD said, "Go and deliver Israel from the hand of Midian; do not I send you?" Gideon said, "Pray, Lord, how can I deliver Israel? My clan is the weakest in Manasseh, and I am the least in my family." The LORD said to him, "But I will be with you, and you shall smite the Midianites as one man."

Then all the Midianites, the Amalekites, and the people of the East came together, and crossing the Jordan they encamped in the Valley of Jezreel. But the Spirit of the LORD took possession of Gideon; he sounded the trumpet, and the Abiezrites were called out to follow him. He sent messengers throughout all Manasseh, and to Asher, Zebulun, and Naphtali; and they too went up.

Then Gideon said to God, "Behold, I am laying a fleece of wool on the threshing floor; if there is dew on the fleece alone, and it is dry on all the ground, then I shall know that thou wilt deliver Israel by my hand, as thou hast said." And it was so. When he rose early next morning and squeezed the fleece, he wrung enough dew from it to fill a bowl with water. Then Gideon said to God, "Let not thy anger burn against me; let me make trial this once more with the fleece; pray, let it be dry only on the fleece, and on all the ground let there be dew." And God did so that night; for it was dry on the fleece only, and on all the ground there was dew.

Then Gideon and all the people who were with him rose early and encamped beside the spring of Harod, south of the camp of Midian. The LORD said to Gideon, "The people with you are too many for me to give the Midianites into their hand, lest Israel vaunt themselves against me, saying, 'My own hand has delivered me.' Therefore proclaim in the ears of the people, saying, 'Whoever is fearful and trembling, let him return home.' " And Gideon tested them; twenty-two thousand returned, and ten thousand remained. The LORD said, "The people are still too many; take them down to the water and I will test them for you there." So Gideon brought the people down to the water; and the LORD said, "Every one that laps the water with his tongue, as a dog laps, you shall set by himself; likewise every one that kneels down to drink." The number of those that lapped, putting their hands to their mouths, was three hundred men; the rest of the people knelt down to drink. The LORD said, "With the three hundred men that lapped I will deliver you; let all the others go every man to his home." So Gideon sent all these home, but retained the three hundred men; and the camp of Midian was below him in the valley.

That same night the LORD said to him, "Arise, attack the camp; for I have given it into your hand. But if you fear to attack, go down to the camp with Purah your servant; you shall hear what they say, and afterward your hands shall be strengthened." So Gideon went down with Purah his servant to the outposts of the camp. The Midianites, the Amalekites, and the people of the East lay along the valley like locusts for multitude; their camels were without number, as the sand upon the seashore. When Gideon came, behold, a man was telling a dream to his comrade: "I dreamed a cake of barley bread tumbled into the camp of Midian, and struck the tent, and turned it upside down, so that the tent lay flat." His comrade answered, "This is no other than the sword of Gideon the son of Joash, a man of Israel; into his hand God has given Midian and all the host."

When Gideon heard the telling of the dream and its interpretation, he worshiped. Then he returned to the camp of Israel and said, "Arise; for the LORD has given the host of Midian into your hand." He divided the three hundred men into three companies, and put trumpets into their hands and empty jars, with torches inside the jars. "Look at me," he said, "and when I come to the outskirts of the camp, do as I do. When I blow the trumpet, then blow the trumpets also on every side of the camp, and shout, 'For the LORD and for Gideon.' "

So Gideon and the hundred men who were with him came to the outskirts of the camp at the beginning of the middle watch. The three companies blew the trumpets and smashed the jars, holding in their left hands the torches, and in their right hands the trumpets to blow; and they cried, "A sword for the LORD and for Gideon!" They stood every man in his place round about the camp, and all the army cried out and fled.

Then Gideon sent messengers throughout the hill country of Ephraim, saying, "Come down against the Midianites, as far as the Jordan." So all the men of Ephraim were called out. As they pursued Midian, they took the two princes, Oreb and Zeeb, and killed them; and they brought their heads to Gideon beyond the Jordan. "What is this that you have done to us," the men of Ephraim said, "not to call us when you went to fight with Midian?" And they upbraided him violently. "What have I done now in comparison with you?" Gideon replied. "Is not the gleaning of the grapes of Ephraim better than the vintage of Abiezer? God has given into your hands the princes of Midian, Oreb and Zeeb; what have I been able to do in comparison with you?" And their anger against him was abated. So Midian was subdued before the people of Israel, and the land had rest for forty years. And Gideon died in a good old age, and was buried in the tomb of Joash his father, at Ophrah of the Abiezrites.

THE PEOPLE OF Israel again did what was evil in the sight of the LORD, and served the Baals, the gods of Syria, of the Ammonites, and of the Philistines; they forsook the LORD, and did not serve him. The anger of the LORD was kindled against Israel, and he sold them into the hands of the Philistines and the Ammonites. For eighteen years they oppressed all the people of Israel that were beyond the Jordan in the land of the Amorites, which is in Gilead. And the Ammonites crossed the Jordan to fight also against Judah, Benjamin, and the house of Ephraim; so that Israel was sorely distressed.

The people cried to the LORD, saying, "We have sinned against thee, because we have forsaken our God and have served the Baals." The LORD said, "Did I not deliver you from the Egyptians? Yet you have forsaken me and served other gods; therefore I will deliver you no more. Cry to the gods whom you have chosen; let them deliver you in the time of your distress." The people said, "We have sinned; do to us whatever seems good to thee; only deliver us, we pray thee, this day." So they put away the foreign gods and served the LORD; and he became indignant over the misery of Israel.

Now Jephthah the Gileadite was a mighty warrior, but he was the son of a harlot. His father's wife also bore sons; and when the wife's sons grew up, they thrust Jephthah out, saying, "You shall not inherit in our father's house; for you are the son of another woman." Jephthah fled from his brothers, and dwelt in the land of Tob; and worthless fellows collected round Jephthah, and went raiding with him. When the Ammonites made war against Israel, the elders of Gilead went to bring Jephthah from the land of Tob. "Come and be our leader," they said, "that we may fight the Ammonites." But Jephthah said, "Did you not hate me, and drive me out of my father's house? Why have you come to me now when you are in trouble?" The elders said, "We have turned to you now, that you may go with us and fight the Ammonites, and be our head over all the inhabitants of Gilead." Jephthah said, "If you bring me home again to fight the Ammonites, and the LORD gives them over to me, I will be your head." The elders said, "The LORD will be witness between us; we will surely do as you say." So Jephthah went with the elders of Gilead, and the people made him leader over them; and Jephthah spoke all his words before the LORD at Mizpah.

Then Jephthah sent messengers to the king of the Ammonites and said, "What have you against me, that you come to fight against my land?" The king answered, "Because Israel on coming from Egypt took away my land; now therefore

restore it peaceably." Jephthah sent messengers again, who said, "Thus says Jephthah: Israel did not take away the land of
the Ammonites. When they came up from
Egypt, Israel sent messengers to Sihon
king of the Amorites, king of Heshbon,
and said, 'Let us pass, we pray, through
your land to our country.' But Sihon did
not trust Israel to pass through his territory;
so he gathered all his people together, and
fought with Israel. And the LORD, the God
of Israel, gave Sihon and his people into
the hand of Israel; so Israel took possession of the land of the Amorites, from the
Arnon to the Jabbok and from the wilderness to the Jordan. Then the LORD dispossessed the Amorites from before his people
Israel; and are you now to take possession
of them? Will you not possess what Chemosh your god gives you to possess? All
that the LORD our God has dispossessed
before us, we will possess. The LORD, the
Judge, decide this day between the people
of Israel and the people of Ammon." But
the king of the Ammonites did not heed
the message Jephthah sent him.

Then the Spirit of the LORD came upon

Jephthah, and he passed through Gilead and Manasseh, to where the Ammonites were encamped. Jephthah made a vow to the LORD, "If thou wilt give the Ammonites into my hand, then whoever comes forth from the doors of my house to meet me, when I return victorious, shall be the LORD'S, and I will offer him up for a burnt offering." Jephthah crossed over to the Ammonites to fight against them; and the LORD gave them into his hand. He smote twenty cities, with a very great slaughter.

As Jephthah came to his home at Mizpah, behold, his daughter came out to meet him with timbrels and with dances; she was his only child. When he saw her, he rent his clothes, and said, "Alas, my daughter! you have brought me very low; for I have opened my mouth to the LORD, and I cannot take back my vow." She said, "My father, do to me according to what has gone forth from your mouth, now that the LORD has avenged you on your enemies. But let this one thing be done for me. Let me alone two months, that I may go and wander on the mountains, I and my companions, and bewail that I must die a virgin." He said, "Go." She departed, with her companions, and bewailed her virginity upon the mountains. At the end of two months, she returned to her father, who did with her according to his vow. She had never known a man. And it became a custom that the daughters of Israel went year by year to lament the daughter of Jephthah the Gileadite four days in the year.

After the Ammonites were subdued, the men of Ephraim said to Jephthah, "Why did you cross over to fight against the Ammonites, and not call us to go with you? We will burn your house over you." Jephthah replied, "I and my people had a great feud with the Ammonites; and when I called you, you did not deliver me from them. Therefore I took my life in my hand, and crossed over against the Ammonites, and the LORD gave them into my hand; why then have you come this day, to fight against me?" Then Jephthah gathered all the men of Gilead and fought with Ephraim; and the men of Gilead smote Ephraim. They took the fords of the Jordan, and held them against the Ephraimites. When any fugitive of Ephraim said, "Let me go over," the men of Gilead said to him, "Are you an Ephraimite?" When he said, "No," they said, "Then say Shibboleth," and he said, "Sibboleth," for he could not pronounce it right; then they seized him and slew him at the fords of the Jordan. There fell at that time forty-two thousand of the Ephraimites.

Jephthah judged Israel six years. Then Jephthah died, and was buried in his city in Gilead.

THE PEOPLE OF Israel again did what was evil in the sight of the LORD; and the LORD gave them into the hand of the Philistines for forty years.

Now there was a certain man of the tribe of the Danites, whose name was Manoah; his wife was barren and had no children. The angel of the LORD appeared to her and said, "Behold, you are barren, but you shall conceive and bear a son. Therefore beware, and drink no wine or strong drink, and eat nothing unclean. No razor shall come upon the boy's head, for he shall be a Nazirite, consecrated to God from birth; and he shall begin to deliver

Israel from the hand of the Philistines."
The woman told her husband of the man,
and she said, "His countenance was like
the countenance of the angel of God, very
terrible; I did not ask him whence he was,
and he did not tell me his name." Now
they did not know that the man was the
angel of the LORD.

Then Manoah entreated the LORD, "I
pray thee, O LORD, let the man whom
thou didst send come again to us, and
teach us what we are to do with the boy
that will be born." God listened, and the
angel came again to the woman as she sat
in the field; but Manoah was not with her.
The woman ran in haste and told her husband, "Behold, the man has appeared to
me again." Manoah went with his wife and
said to the man, "When your words come
true, what is to be the boy's manner of life,
and what is he to do?" The angel said, "Of
all that I said to the woman let her beware.
She may not eat of anything that comes
from the vine, neither let her drink wine or
strong drink, or eat any unclean thing; all
that I commanded her let her observe."
Manoah said, "Pray, let us detain you, and

prepare a kid for you." The angel replied, "If you detain me, I will not eat of your food; but if you make ready a burnt offering, then offer it to the LORD." Manoah asked, "What is your name, so that, when your words come true, we may honor you?" The angel said, "Why do you ask my name, seeing it is wonderful?" So Manoah took the kid with the cereal offering, and offered it upon the rock to the LORD, to him who works wonders. When the flame went up toward heaven from the altar, the angel ascended in the flame while Manoah and his wife looked on; and they fell on their faces, and they knew that the man was the angel of the LORD. "We shall surely die," Manoah said, "for we have seen God." But his wife said, "If the LORD had meant to kill us, he would not have accepted an offering at our hands, or announced to us such things as these." And the woman bore a son, and called his name Samson; the boy grew, and the LORD blessed him. And the Spirit of the LORD began to stir him.

Samson went down to Timnah, and there he saw one of the daughters of the

Philistines. He asked his father and mother
to get her as his wife. "Is there not a
woman among your kin," they asked, "or
among all our people, that you must take a
wife from the uncircumcised Philistines?"
But Samson said, "Get her for me; for she
pleases me well." His father and mother
did not know that this request was from
the LORD; for he was seeking an occasion
against the Philistines, who had dominion
over Israel.

Then Samson went again to Timnah,
and in the vineyards a young lion roared
against him. The Spirit of the LORD came
mightily upon him, and although he had
nothing in his hand, he tore the lion asunder as one tears a kid. But he did not tell
his father or his mother what he had done.
Then he went down and talked with the
woman, and she pleased him well. After a
while, when he returned to marry her, he
turned aside to see the carcass of the lion,
and behold, there was a swarm of bees in
the body, and honey. He scraped the honey
into his hands, and went on, eating as he
went. When he came to his father and
mother, he gave some to them, and they

ate. But he did not tell them that he had taken the honey from the carcass of the lion.

Samson made a marriage feast in Timnah, and when the people saw him, they brought thirty companions to be with him. "Let me now put a riddle to you," Samson said. "If you can tell me what it is, within the seven days of the feast, I will give you thirty linen garments and thirty festal garments; but if not, then you shall give the same to me." They said, "Put your riddle, that we may hear it." And he said, "Out of the eater came something to eat. Out of the strong came something sweet." And they could not in three days tell what the riddle was.

On the fourth day they said to Samson's wife, "Have you invited us here to impoverish us? Entice your husband to tell us what the riddle is, lest we burn you and your father's house." Samson's wife wept before him. "You hate me," she said, "you do not love me; you have put a riddle to my countrymen, and you have not told me what it is." He said, "I have not told my father nor my mother, and shall I tell you?" She wept before him the seven days that their feast lasted; and on the seventh day he told her, because she pressed him hard. Then she told the riddle to her countrymen. On the seventh day before the sun went down they said to Samson, "What is sweeter than honey? What is stronger than a lion?" Samson said, "If you had not plowed with my heifer, you would not have found out my riddle." The Spirit of the LORD came mightily upon him, and he went down to Ashkelon and killed thirty men of the town, and took their spoil and gave the festal garments to those who had told the riddle. In hot anger he went back to his father's house, and his wife was given to his companion, who had been his best man.

After a while, at the time of wheat harvest, Samson went to visit his wife. "I will go in to my wife in the chamber," he said. But her father would not allow him to go in. "I really thought that you utterly hated her," he said, "so I gave her to your companion. Is not her younger sister fairer than she? Pray take her instead." Samson said, "This time I shall be blameless in regard to the Philistines, when I do them mischief." He caught three hundred foxes, and took torches; and he tied the foxes tail to tail, putting a torch between each pair. After setting fire to the torches, he let the foxes go into the standing grain of the Philistines, and burned up the shocks and the standing grain, as well as the olive orchards. "Who has done this?" the Philistines asked. And they were told, "Samson, the son-in-law of the Timnite, because he has given Samson's wife to his companion." Then the Philistines came and burned both her and her father. "If this is what you do," Samson said to them, "I swear I will be avenged upon you, and after that I will quit." He smote them hip and thigh with great slaughter, and went down and stayed in the cleft of the rock of Etam.

The Philistines came up and encamped in Judah, and made a raid on Lehi. "Why have you come up against us?" the men of Judah asked. "We have come up to bind Samson," they replied, "to do to him as he did to us." Then three thousand men of Judah went down to Etam, and they asked

Samson, "Do you not know that the Philistines are rulers over us? What is this that you have done?" Samson said, "As they did to me, so have I done to them." And they said, "We have come down to bind you, that we may give you into the hands of the Philistines." Samson said, "Swear to me that you will not fall upon me yourselves." They said, "No, we will only bind you and give you into their hands; we will not kill you." So they bound him with two new ropes, and brought him up from the rock.

At Lehi, the Philistines came shouting to meet him; and the Spirit of the LORD came mightily upon him. The ropes on his arms became as flax that has caught fire, and his bonds melted off his hands. He found a fresh jawbone of an ass, and seized it, and with it he slew a thousand men. And Samson said, "With the jawbone of an ass, heaps upon heaps, with the jawbone of an ass have I slain a thousand men." He was very thirsty, and called on the LORD, saying, "Thou hast granted this great deliverance by the hand of thy servant; and shall I now die of thirst, and fall into the hands of the uncircumcised?" God split open the hollow place that is at Lehi, and there came water from it; when he drank, his spirit returned, and he revived.

Samson went to Gaza where he saw a harlot, and he went in to her. When the Gazites were told, "Samson has come here," they surrounded the place and lay in wait for him at the gate of the city. All night they kept quiet, saying, "Let us wait till the light of the morning; then we will kill him." But at midnight Samson arose and took hold of the doors of the gate of the city and the two posts, and pulled them up, bar and all, and carried them on his shoulders to the top of the hill that is before Hebron.

After this he loved a woman in the valley of Sorek, whose name was Delilah. The lords of the Philistines came to her and said, "Entice him, and see wherein his great strength lies, and by what means we may overpower him; we will each give you eleven hundred pieces of silver." So Delilah said to Samson, "Please tell me wherein your great strength lies, and how you might be bound, that one could subdue you." Samson said, "Bind me with seven fresh bowstrings which have not been dried; then I shall be like any other man." The lords of the Philistines brought her seven such bowstrings, and she bound him. Now she had men lying in wait in an inner chamber. And she said to him, "The Philistines are upon you, Samson!" But he snapped the bowstrings, as a string of tow snaps when it touches the fire. So the secret of his strength was not known. "You have mocked me," Delilah said, "and told me lies; please tell me how you might be bound." Samson said, "Bind me with new ropes that have not been used; then I shall be like any other man." So Delilah took new ropes and bound him, and said, "The Philistines are upon you, Samson!" But he snapped the ropes off his arms like a thread. "Until now you have mocked me, and told me lies," she said. "Tell me how you might be bound." He said, "If you weave the seven locks of my head into the cloth on the loom and make it tight with the pin, then I shall become weak, and be like any other man." So while he slept, Delilah took the seven locks of his head and wove them into the cloth, and made them tight with the pin. Then she said to him, "The Philistines are upon you, Samson!" But he awoke from his sleep, and pulled away the pin, the loom, and the cloth.

"How can you say, 'I love you,' when your heart is not with me?" she asked. "You have mocked me these three times, and you have not told me wherein your great strength lies." When she pressed him hard with her words day after day, and urged him, his soul was vexed to death. He told her all his mind, and said, "A razor has never come upon my head; for I have been a Nazirite to God from my mother's womb. If I be shaved, then my strength will leave me." When Delilah saw that he had told her all his mind, she sent for the lords of the Philistines. They came, and brought the money in their hands. She made Samson sleep upon her knees; and she called a man to shave off the seven locks of his head, and his strength left him. "The Philistines are upon you, Samson!" she said. Waking from his sleep, he said, "I will go out as at other times, and shake

myself free." He did not know that the
LORD had left him. Then the Philistines
seized him and gouged out his eyes, and
they brought him down to Gaza. There
they bound him with bronze fetters, and
put him in prison, where he ground at the
mill. But the hair of his head began to
grow again.

Now the lords of the Philistines gathered
to rejoice, and to offer a great sacrifice to
Dagon their god; for they said, "Our god
has given Samson our enemy into our
hand." When the hearts of the people were
merry, they said, "Call Samson, to make
sport for us." So they called Samson out of
the prison, and he said to the lad who led
him by the hand, "Let me feel the pillars
on which the temple rests, that I may lean
against them." Now the temple was full of
men and women; all the lords of the Philistines were there, and on the roof there were
about three thousand men and women,
looking on. Samson called to the LORD,
"O Lord GOD, remember me, I pray, and
strengthen me only this once, that I may be
avenged upon the Philistines for one of my
two eyes." He grasped the two middle pil-

lars upon which the temple rested, and leaned his weight upon them, his right hand on the one and his left hand on the other. "Let me die with the Philistines," he said. Then he bowed with all his might; and the temple fell upon the lords and upon all the people that were in it. So those he slew at his death were more than those he had slain during his life. Then his family came down and took him and buried him in the tomb of Manoah his father. He had judged Israel twenty years.

Now THERE WAS a young man of Bethlehem in Judah, of the family of Judah, who was a Levite; and he departed from Bethlehem, to live where he could find a place. As he journeyed, he came to the hill country of Ephraim to the house of a man whose name was Micah. "From where do you come?" Micah asked him. "I am a Levite of Bethlehem in Judah, and I am going to sojourn where I may find a place," he replied. "Stay with me," Micah said, "and be to me a father and a priest. I will give you ten pieces of silver a year, a suit of apparel, and your living." The Levite was content to dwell with him, and became like one of his sons. "Now I know that the LORD will prosper me," Micah said, "because I have a Levite as priest." And Micah had a shrine with idols and a silver image.

In those days the tribe of the Danites was seeking for itself an inheritance to dwell in. Until then no inheritance among the tribes of Israel had fallen to them, for the Amorites did not allow them to come down to the plain, to the land Joshua had apportioned them. So the Danites sent five able men to spy out and explore the land. They came to the hill country of Ephraim, to the house of Micah, and lodged there. When they recognized the voice of the young Levite, they said to him, "What are you doing in this place?" He answered, "Micah has hired me, and I have become his priest." They said to him, "Inquire of God, we pray thee, that we may know whether our journey will succeed." The Levite said, "Go in peace. The journey on which you go is under the eye of the LORD."

The five men departed, and came to Laish, and saw that the people there dwelt in security, quiet and unsuspecting, lacking nothing that is in the earth, and possessing wealth; and they had no dealings with any one. Returning to their brethren, they said, "Arise, and let us go up against them; for we have seen the land, and behold, it is very fertile. Do not be slow to enter in and possess the land. You will come to an unsuspecting people. Yea, God has given into your hands a place where there is no lack of anything that is in the earth."

So six hundred armed men of the tribe of Dan set forth, and came to the hill country of Ephraim. "Do you know," the five spies said to their brethren, "that in one of these houses there are idols and a graven image of silver? Therefore consider what you will do." And the five men turned aside to Micah's house, and asked him of his welfare. Then they entered the house and took the idols and the silver image. The six hundred Danites stood by the entrance to the village with the Levite; and when the five men approached with the idols and the image, the Levite asked, "What are you doing?" They said, "Keep quiet, put your hand upon your mouth, and come with us, and be to us a father and a priest. Is it better for you to be priest to the house of one man, or to a tribe and family in Israel?" The priest's heart was glad. He took the idols and the graven image, and went with the Danites.

When they had gone a good way, the men in the houses near Micah's house were called out, and they overtook the Danites. They shouted to the Danites, who turned round and said to Micah, "What ails you that you come with such a company?" He said, "You take my gods, and the priest, and go away. What have I left? How then do you ask me, 'What ails you?' " The Danites said, "Do not let your voice be heard among us, lest angry fellows fall upon you, and you lose your life with the lives of your household." Then the Danites went their way; and Micah, seeing they were too strong for him, went back to his home.

The Danites came to Laish, to a people quiet and unsuspecting, and smote them with the edge of the sword, and burned the city. There was no deliverer because they had no dealings with any one. The Danites rebuilt the city, and dwelt in it, and named it Dan, after their ancestor, who was born to Jacob. The Danites set up the graven image for themselves; and Jonathan the son of Gershon, son of Moses, and his sons were priests to the tribe until the day of the captivity of the land.

IN THOSE DAYS, when there was no king in Israel, a certain Levite sojourning in the remote parts of the hill country of Ephraim took to himself a concubine from Bethlehem in Judah. She became angry with him, and went away to her father's house, and was there about four months. Then her husband went after her, to speak kindly to her and bring her back. He had with him his servant and a couple of asses. When he came to her father's house, the father came with joy to meet him, and made him stay; he remained with him three days. On the fourth day he arose early and prepared to go, but the father said, "Strengthen your heart with a morsel of bread, and after that you may go." So the two men sat and ate and drank together; and the girl's father said, "Be pleased to spend the night, and let your heart be merry." He urged him till he lodged there again. On the fifth day he arose early to depart, and the father said, "Strengthen your heart, and tarry until the day declines." So they ate. When the man and his concubine and his servant rose up to depart, the father said, "Behold, now the day has waned toward evening; pray tarry all night, and let your heart be merry; tomorrow you shall arise early and go home."

But the man would not spend the night; the three departed, and arrived opposite Jebus (that is, Jerusalem) when the day was far spent. "Come now," the servant said, "let us turn aside to this city of the Jebusites, and spend the night in it." His master said, "We will not turn aside into the city of foreigners, who do not belong to the people of Israel; but we will pass on to Gibeah or Ramah." They passed on, and the sun went down on them near Gibeah, which belongs to Benjamin, and they turned aside to spend the night there. But no man would take them into his house, so they sat down in the open square of the city.

At evening an old man was coming from his work in the field; he was from the hill country of Ephraim, but was sojourning in Gibeah, where the men were Benjaminites. Seeing the wayfarer in the square, he asked, "Where are you going? and whence do you come?" The wayfarer replied, "We are passing from Bethlehem in Judah back to my home in the hill country of Ephraim; and nobody takes us into his house. We have straw and provender for our asses, and bread and wine for us; there is no lack of anything." The old man said, "Peace be to you; I will care for all your wants; only do not spend the night in the square." He brought them into his house, and gave the asses provender; and they washed their feet, and ate and drank.

As they were making their hearts merry, behold, the men of the city, base fellows, beset the house round about, beating on the door; and they said to the old man, the master of the house, "Bring out the man who came into your house, that we may know him." The master went out to them and said, "No, my brethren, do not act so wickedly; seeing that this man has come into my house, do not do this vile thing. Behold, here are my virgin daughter and his concubine; let me bring them out now. Ravish them and do with them what seems good to you; but against this man do not do so vile a thing." But the men would not listen to him. So the Levite seized his concubine, and put her out to them; and they knew her, and abused her all night. As the dawn began to break, they let her go, and she came and fell down at the door of the house.

In the morning, when her master opened the door to go on his way, behold, there was his concubine lying with her hands on the threshold. "Get up," he said to her, "let us be going." But there was no answer; she was dead. He put her body upon an ass, and went away to his home. When he entered his house, he took a knife, and laying hold of his concubine he divided her, limb by limb, into twelve pieces, and sent the pieces throughout all the territory of Israel. All who saw it said, "Such a thing has never happened or been seen from the day that the people of Israel came up out of the land of Egypt until this day; consider it, take counsel, and speak."

Then the people of Israel came out, from Dan to Beer-sheba, including the land of Gilead, and the congregation assembled at Mizpah, four hundred thousand men on foot that drew the sword. (Now the Benjaminites heard that the people of Israel had gone up to Mizpah.) "Tell us," the Israelites said, "how was this wickedness brought to pass?" The husband of the woman who was murdered told what the Benjaminites of Gibeah had done, and asked, "People of Israel, all of you, give your advice and counsel."

The people arose as one man, saying, "None of us will go to his tent or return to his house. We will go up to requite Gibeah of Benjamin for the wanton crime which they have committed in Israel." So the men of Israel gathered, and sent men through all the tribe of Benjamin, saying, "What wickedness is this that has taken place among you? Give up the base fellows in Gibeah, that we may put them to death, and put away evil from Israel." But the Benjaminites would not listen to the voice of their brethren, and twenty-six thousand seven hundred men came to Gibeah, to go out to battle against Israel. Among these were seven hundred picked men who were left-handed; every one could sling a stone at a hair, and not miss.

Then the men of Israel went out to battle, and the Benjaminites came out of Gibeah and they felled on that day twenty-two thousand Israelites. The people of Israel went up and wept before the LORD until the evening; and they inquired of the LORD, "Shall we again battle against our brethren the Benjaminites?" The LORD said, "Go up against them." The people took courage, and again formed the battle line in the same place where they had formed it on the first day.

Benjamin went against them out of Gibeah the second day, and felled eighteen thousand Israelites. Then all the people of Israel, the whole army, wept; they sat before the LORD, and fasted until evening, and offered burnt offerings and peace offerings. And they inquired of the LORD, "Shall we yet again go out to battle against our brethren the Benjaminites, or shall we cease?" The LORD said, "Go up; for tomorrow I will give them into your hand."

So Israel set men in ambush round about Gibeah, and went up against the Benjaminites on the third day. The men of Israel gave ground to Benjamin, because they trusted to the men in ambush; and the Benjaminites were drawn away from the city. Then the men in ambush rushed upon Gibeah, and smote all the city with the edge of the sword. Now the appointed signal between the men of Israel and the men in ambush was that when they made a great cloud of smoke rise up out of the city, the men of Israel should turn in battle. Benjamin had begun to smite Israel; but when the signal began to rise out of the city in a column of smoke, they looked behind them; and behold, the whole of the city went up in smoke to heaven. Then the men of Israel turned, and the men of Benjamin were dismayed, for they saw that disaster was close upon them. They turned their backs before the men of Israel in the direction of the wilderness; but the battle overtook them. Eighteen thousand men of Benjamin fell. The rest turned and fled toward the rock of Rimmon; five thousand were cut down in the highways, and two thousand more were pursued hard to Gidom, where they were slain. But six hundred men fled to the rock of Rimmon, and abode there. So all of Benjamin who fell that day were twenty-five thousand men that drew the sword, all of them men of valor.

In those days there was no king in Israel; every man did what was right in his own eyes.

RUTH

Renowned in world literature as a master-piece of idyllic narrative, the Book of Ruth is from the hand of an unknown author. The incidents relate to the later days of the judges, before 1000 B.C., and this explains why in the English Bible the book follows immediately after the Book of Judges (in the Hebrew Bible it follows Proverbs). Linguistic features of the narrative, however, suggest a date of composition after the Babylonian Exile, that is, sometime in the sixth century B.C. Besides providing information about King David's ancestors, the story testifies that piety and trust in God will be rewarded, and that God's goodness is not constricted by nationalistic frontiers.

In the days when the judges ruled there was a famine in the land of Judah, and a certain man of Bethlehem named Elimelech went to sojourn in the country of Moab with his wife, Naomi, and his two sons, Mahlon and Chilion. But Elimelech died, and Naomi was left with her two sons in Moab. The sons took Moabite wives, one named Orpah and the other Ruth. They had lived there about ten years when Mahlon and Chilion died, so that Naomi was bereft of both husband and sons.

Then she heard that the LORD had visited his people in Judah and had given them food, so she set out to return to Bethlehem. Her two daughters-in-law went with her, but Naomi said, "Turn back, my daughters, return to your mothers. May the LORD deal kindly with you, as you have dealt with the dead and with me. May he grant that you find a home, each of you in the house of her husband!" She kissed them, and they lifted up their voices and wept, saying, "Let us return with you to your people." But Naomi said, "Why will you go with me? Have I yet sons in my womb to become your husbands? Would you refrain from marrying? No, my daughters, for it is bitter to me for your sake that the hand of the LORD has gone forth against me."

Then the daughters-in-law wept again, and Orpah kissed Naomi and returned to her people. But Ruth clung to her mother-in-law. "Entreat me not to leave you," she said, "or to return from following you. Where you go I will go, and where you lodge I will lodge; your people shall be my people, and your God my God; where you die I will die, and there will I be buried. May the LORD punish me if even death parts me from you." When Naomi saw that Ruth was determined, she said no more.

Naomi and Ruth went on till they came to Bethlehem, and there the whole town was stirred because of them. "Is this Naomi?" the women asked. She answered, "Do not call me Naomi, call me Mara, for the Almighty has dealt very bitterly with me." Now it happened that the two had come to Bethlehem at the beginning of barley harvest. "Let me go to the field," Ruth said, "and glean among the ears of grain." Naomi answered, "Go, my daughter."

Gleaning after the reapers, Ruth came by chance to the part of the field belonging to Boaz, a man of wealth, who was of the family of Elimelech, Naomi's husband. When Boaz saw her, he said to the servant in charge of the reapers, "Who is that maiden working in the field?" The servant answered, "It is the Moabite maiden who came back with Naomi. She asked to glean after the reapers, and she has continued without resting even for a moment."

To Ruth, Boaz said, "Now, listen, my daughter, keep close to my maidens in this field. I have charged the young men not to molest you. When you are thirsty, go to the vessels and drink. And when you are hungry, eat some bread and dip it into the wine." Ruth fell on her face, bowing to the ground. "You are most gracious, my lord," she said. "Why should you take notice of me, when I am a foreigner?"

"All that you have done for your mother-in-law," Boaz said, "since the death of your husband has been fully told me, and how you left your father and mother and came to a people that you did not know. A full reward be given you by the God of Israel, under whose wings you have come to take refuge!" When Ruth rose to glean, he instructed his young men, "Let her glean even among the sheaves, and do not reproach her. Also pull out some grain from the bundles, and leave it for her."

Ruth worked in the field until evening, then she beat out the barley she had gleaned, and it was about a bushel. She took it up and went into the city and showed it to her mother-in-law. "In whose field did you glean today?" Naomi asked. "Blessed be the man who took notice of you." Ruth answered, "In the field of a man named Boaz."

"Blessed be he by the LORD," Naomi said, "whose kindness has not forsaken the living or the dead! The man is a relative, one of our nearest kin."

Until the end of the barley and wheat harvests, Ruth gleaned in the field. Then Naomi said, "My daughter, should I not seek a home for you? Is not Boaz our kinsman? See, he is winnowing barley tonight. Therefore anoint yourself, put on your best clothes, and go down to the threshing floor. Do not make yourself known to the man, but when he lies down to sleep, go and uncover his feet and lie down, and he will tell you what to do."

So Ruth went to the threshing floor, and when Boaz fell asleep at the end of the heap of grain, she came softly, and uncovered his feet and lay down. At midnight he awoke, and behold, a woman lay at his feet! "Who is that?" he said. "Ruth, your maidservant," she answered. "Spread your cloak over me, for you are next of kin."

"My daughter," Boaz said, "you have made this last kindness greater than the first, in that you have not gone after younger men. Do not fear. I will do for you what you ask, for all the city knows that you are a woman of worth. But though it is true that I am a near kinsman, there is a kinsman nearer than I. Remain this night, and in the morning, I will ask him if he will do his part for you. If he is not willing, then, as the Lord lives, I will do it myself."

She lay at his feet until morning, but

they arose before dawn so that it should not be known that she had come to the threshing floor. "Bring your mantle," he said, "and hold it out." Pouring six measures of barley into the mantle, he said, "You must not go back empty-handed to your mother-in-law."

When Naomi heard all that Boaz had done for Ruth, she said, "Wait, my daughter. The man will not rest, but will settle the matter today."

And Boaz went up to the gate of the city, and when the next of kin came by, Boaz said, "Turn aside, friend, and sit down here." Then he took ten elders of the city, and asked them also to sit down. "Naomi, who has come back from the country of Moab," he said to the next of kin, "is selling the land which belonged to our kinsman Elimelech. If you will, buy it in the presence of the elders sitting here. But if you will not redeem it, tell me, so that I may redeem it myself, for I am next of kin after you." The man said, "I will redeem it." And Boaz said, "The day you buy the field, you are also buying Ruth, the widow of Mahlon, to restore the name of the dead to his inheritance." The next of kin answered, "Then I cannot redeem it, lest I impair my own inheritance." In former times in Israel, this was the custom: to confirm a transaction, a man drew off his sandal and gave it to the other. Saying, "Buy it for yourself," the next of kin drew off his sandal and gave it to Boaz.

"You are witnesses this day," Boaz said to the elders, "that I have bought the land that belonged to Elimelech. Also Ruth the Moabitess, the widow of Mahlon, I have bought to be my wife, to perpetuate the name of the dead."

"We are witnesses," the elders said. "May the LORD make the woman, who is coming into your house, be like Rachel and Leah, who together built up the house of Israel."

So Ruth became the wife of Boaz; and the LORD gave her conception, and she bore a son. To Naomi, the women of the neighborhood said, "Blessed be the LORD, who has not left you this day without next of kin! He shall be to you a restorer of life and a nourisher of your old age, for your daughter-in-law, who is more to you than seven sons, has borne him." Then Naomi laid the child in her bosom and became his nurse. And the women of the neighborhood gave him the name of Obed, saying, "A son has been born to Naomi." And Obed was the father of Jesse, who was the father of David.

1 SAMUEL

The two books of Samuel were originally a single book in Hebrew, which was first written down probably in the sixth century B.C., before the Babylonian Exile. Together they carry Israelite history from the era of the judges to the establishment of David's kingdom. Chief participants are the prophet Samuel, King Saul, and King David.

The first book is woven of two main literary strands, known as the Early Source and the Late Source. The Early Source, probably dating to the reign of Solomon, is of such exceptional historical and literary quality that its unknown author deserves to be called the father of history (a title usually given to the Greek writer Herodotus, who lived five hundred years later). A noble but tragic figure, King Saul wins remarkable victories but falls into conflict between his own self-will and obedience to the will of God. Eventually he is rejected, and shows symptoms of psychosis in his attitude toward David, whose popularity threatens to eclipse his own. Finally, defeated by his enemies, alienated from his associates as well as from his God, he dies in battle. The real hero is David, but he is a very human hero who is not above ignoble deeds. As so often in the Old Testament, the narrative insists that, despite sin and human failing, God's providence accomplishes its ends.

THERE WAS A certain man of Ramah, in the hill country of Ephraim, whose name was Elkanah. He had two wives, Hannah and Peninnah. Now Peninnah had children, but Hannah had none.

Elkanah and his family used to go every year to worship the LORD at Shiloh, where Eli and his two sons were priests. When Elkanah sacrificed, he would give many portions to Peninnah and her children to eat; but to Hannah, although he loved her, he could give only one portion, because the LORD had closed her womb. Peninnah used to provoke her sorely because of this, to irritate her, and so it went on year by year, as often as they went up to Shiloh. Hannah would weep and would not eat, and Elkanah would say to her, "Hannah, why is your heart sad? Am I not more to you than ten sons?"

At last Hannah went to the temple, deeply distressed and weeping bitterly. "O LORD of hosts," she prayed, "if thou wilt indeed look on the affliction of thy maidservant, and remember me, and give me a son, I will give him to the LORD all the days of his life." Now Eli the priest was sitting beside the doorpost of the temple, and as Hannah was praying, he observed her. She was speaking in her heart; her lips moved but her voice was not heard, and Eli took her to be a drunken woman. "How long will you be drunken?" he said. "Put away your wine from you."

"No, my lord," Hannah answered, "I am a woman sorely troubled. I have drunk neither wine nor strong drink, but I have been pouring out my soul before the LORD, speaking out of my great anxiety and vexation."

"Go in peace," Eli said, "and the God of Israel grant your petition." So she went her way, and was no longer sad. In the morning they rose and went back to Ramah, and Elkanah knew Hannah, and the LORD remembered her. In due time she bore a son, and she called him Samuel.

After she had weaned her son, she brought him to the house of the LORD at Shiloh, along with a three-year-old bull, a measure of flour, and a skin of wine. They slew the bull for a sacrifice, and then they brought the child to Eli. "Oh, my lord!" said Hannah. "I am the woman who was standing here in your presence, praying to the LORD. For this child I prayed, and the LORD has granted my petition. Therefore I have given him to the LORD for as long as he lives." Then she went home to Ramah, leaving Samuel at the temple. And the boy ministered to the LORD in the presence of Eli.

Now the sons of Eli, Hophni and Phine-

has, were worthless priests, with no regard
for the LORD; they treated his offering with
contempt. When any man offered sacrifice
at Shiloh, the priest's servant would come
while the meat was boiling and thrust a
three-pronged fork into the pot; all that
the fork brought up the priest took for
himself. Moreover, before the fat was
burned for the sacrifice, the servant would
come and say, "Give raw meat for the
priest to roast; if not, I will take it by
force." Thus their sin was great in the
sight of the LORD. When Eli heard all that
his sons were doing, he said, "My sons,
why do you do such things? If a man sins
against a man, God will mediate for him;
but if he sins against the LORD, who can
intercede for him?" But they would not
listen, for it was the will of the LORD to
slay them.

Now Samuel was ministering to the
LORD, a boy girded with a priestly apron.
Each year his mother would make a little
robe and take it to him when she went up
with Elkanah for the yearly sacrifice, and
the boy continued to grow in stature and
in favor with the LORD and with men. But

the word of the LORD came rarely in those days; there was no frequent vision.

At that time Eli, whose eyesight had grown dim, was lying down in his room; it was near dawn, and Samuel was sleeping within the temple, where the ark was. Then the LORD called, "Samuel! Samuel!"

"Here I am!" he said, and ran to Eli. "Here I am, for you called me." But Eli said, "I did not call; lie down again." So he went and lay down. The LORD called again, "Samuel!" And Samuel arose and went to Eli. "I did not call, my son," said Eli, "lie down again."

The LORD called Samuel the third time, and again he arose and went to Eli. Then Eli perceived that the LORD was calling the boy. "Lie down," he said, "and if he calls, you shall say, 'Speak, LORD, for thy servant hears.'" So Samuel lay down, and the LORD came forth, calling, "Samuel! Samuel!"

"Speak," said Samuel, "for thy servant hears."

"Behold," said the LORD, "I am about to do a thing at which the two ears of every one that hears it will tingle. I am about to punish Eli's house for ever, for he knew that his sons were blaspheming God, and he did not restrain them. Therefore I swear that the iniquity of Eli's house shall not be expiated by sacrifice or offering for ever." In the morning Samuel was afraid to tell the vision to Eli, but Eli called him. "My son," he said, "what was it he told you? Do not hide it from me." So Samuel told him everything. "It is the LORD," said Eli. "Let him do what seems good to him."

Samuel grew, and the LORD was with him, and he became acknowledged as a prophet. Year by year he went on a circuit to Bethel, Gilgal, and Mizpah, and he judged Israel in all those places. Then he would come back to Ramah, for his home was there.

Now ISRAEL WENT out to battle against the Philistines, and in the first fighting Israel was defeated. "Why has the LORD put us to rout today?" the elders of Israel said. "Let us bring the ark of the covenant of the LORD here from Shiloh, that he may save us from our enemies."

So the people brought the ark from Shiloh, and the two sons of Eli were with it. When the ark came into the camp, all Israel gave a mighty shout, so that the earth resounded, and the Philistines heard it. "What does this great shouting in the camp of the Hebrews mean?" they asked; and learning that the ark of the LORD had come, they were afraid. "Woe to us!" they said. "This is the god who smote the Egyptians with plagues. Take courage and acquit yourselves like men, O Philistines, lest you become slaves to the Hebrews." So the Philistines fought, and again Israel was defeated and fled, every man to his home. There was a great slaughter, the ark of God was captured, and the two sons of Eli were slain.

A man of the tribe of Benjamin ran from the battle and came to Shiloh the same day, with his clothes rent and earth upon his head. Eli was sitting upon his seat by the road watching, for his heart trembled for the ark of God. "I am come from the battle," the man said to Eli. "Israel has fled before the Philistines, your two sons are dead, and the ark of God has been captured." Hearing this, Eli fell over back-

ward from his seat; his neck was broken
and he died, for he was an old man, and
heavy. He had judged Israel forty years.

For seven months the ark of the LORD
was in the country of the Philistines. The
hand of God was very heavy there, and
there was a deathly panic, for he afflicted
both young and old with plague. Those
who did not die were stricken with tu-
mors, and at last the people said, "Send
away the ark of the God of Israel, and let it
return to its own place." So the Philistines
put the ark on a cart, and followed it as far
as the border at Beth-shemesh. The people
there were reaping their harvest, and when
they saw the ark, they rejoiced, and they
sent messengers to Kiriath-jearim, saying,
"The Philistines have returned the ark of
the LORD. Come and take it." So the men
of Kiriath-jearim came and took the ark,
and brought it to the house of Abinadab
on the hill.

THERE WAS A wealthy man of Benjamin
whose name was Kish. He had a son
named Saul, and there was not a man of
Israel handsomer than he, and he was

head and shoulders taller than any of them.

Now the asses of Kish were lost, so he said to Saul, "Take one of the servants and go and look for the asses." They passed through the land of Benjamin, and the hill country of Ephraim, but they did not find them. When they came to the land of Zuph, Saul said to his servant, "Come, let us go back, lest my father become anxious about us." But the servant said, "Behold, there is in Ramah a man of God who is held in honor; all that he says comes true. Let us go there; perhaps he can help us in our journey."

"If we go," Saul said, "what have we to bring for a present?"

"I have the fourth part of a shekel of silver," the servant answered, "and I will give it to him."

As they went toward the city, they met young maidens coming out to draw water. "Is the prophet here?" they asked.

"He is," the maidens answered, "but make haste, for the people have a sacrifice today on the high place, and they will not eat till he comes, since he must bless it."

As they were entering the city, they saw
Samuel coming toward them on his way to
the high place.

Now the day before, the LORD had revealed to Samuel: "Tomorrow I will send
you a man of Benjamin. You shall anoint
him to be prince over my people Israel,
and he shall save them from the Philistines." When Samuel saw Saul, the LORD
told him, "Here is the man who shall rule
over my people."

Now Saul approached Samuel, saying,
"Tell me where is the house of the
prophet?"

"I am the prophet," Samuel answered;
"go up before me to the high place, for
today you shall eat with me, and in the
morning I will tell you all that is on your
mind. As for your lost asses, do not set
your mind on them, for they have been
found."

Samuel brought Saul into the hall,
where he placed him at the head of those
who had been invited. To the cook, he
said, "Bring the portion I gave you to put
aside," and the cook set the leg and the
upper portion before Saul. "Eat," said

Samuel, "because it was kept for you that you might eat with the guests." When they came down into the city, a bed was spread for Saul on the roof, and he lay down to sleep. At dawn Samuel called to him, "Up, that I may send you on your way." So Saul arose, and they went to the outskirts of the city. "Tell the servant to pass on before us," said Samuel, "that I may make known to you the word of God."

Then Samuel took a vial of oil and poured it on Saul's head, and kissed him. "Has not the LORD anointed you to be prince over his people Israel?" he said. "You shall reign over them and save them from their enemies. And this shall be the sign to you: When you depart today, you will meet two men by Rachel's tomb at Zelzah, and they will say to you, 'The asses you went to seek are found, and now your father is anxious about you.' After that you shall come to Gibeah, where there is a garrison of the Philistines; and there you will meet a band of prophets, prophesying. The spirit of the LORD will come mightily upon you, and you shall prophesy with them. Now when these signs meet you, do whatever your hand finds to do, for God is with you."

When Saul left Samuel, God gave him another heart; and all these signs came to pass that day. When he came to Gibeah, a band of prophets met him; and the spirit of God came upon him, and he prophesied among them. When all who knew him before saw how he prophesied, they said to one another, "What has come over the son of Kish? Is Saul also among the prophets?" When he had finished prophesying, he came home.

Now Samuel called the people of Israel together at Mizpah. "You have asked for a king," he said. "Now therefore present yourselves before the LORD by your tribes and families." He brought all the tribes near, and the tribe of Benjamin was chosen by sacred lot. Family by family he brought the Benjaminites near, and the Matrites were chosen by lot; then, man by man, he brought the Matrites near, and Saul the son of Kish was chosen by lot; and when he stood among the people, he was head and shoulders taller than any. "Do you see him whom the LORD has chosen?" Samuel cried. "There is none like him." And the people shouted, "Long live the king!"

Samuel told the people the rights and duties of the kingship, and then sent them home. Saul went home to Gibeah, and with him went men of valor whose hearts God had touched. But some worthless fellows despised him and said, "How can this man save us?" But Saul held his peace.

Then Nahash the Ammonite besieged Jabesh-gilead. The men of Jabesh said, "Make a treaty with us, and we will serve you." Nahash replied, "On this condition I will make a treaty, that I gouge out all your right eyes." So the elders of Jabesh sent messengers throughout Israel for help. When they came to Gibeah and reported the matter, all the people wept aloud. Saul, who was coming from the field behind his oxen, asked, "What ails you, that you are weeping?" When they told him the tidings from Jabesh, the Spirit of God came upon him, and his anger was kindled. He killed two oxen, cut them in pieces, and sent them throughout Israel by messengers, saying, "Whoever does not come to Saul and

Samuel, so shall it be done to his oxen!"

The dread of the LORD fell upon the people, and they came out as one man. Saul mustered them at Bezek, across the Jordan valley from Jabesh-gilead, and they sent a message to the men of Jabesh: "To-morrow, by the time the sun is hot, you shall have deliverance." The men of Jabesh were glad, and said to Nahash, "Tomor-row we will give ourselves up to you, and you may do to us whatever seems good to you."

That night Saul put the people in three companies. They crossed the Jordan valley and came into the camp of the Ammonites in the morning watch, and cut them down until the heat of the day; of those who survived no two were left together. "Who was it who said, 'Shall Saul reign over us?' " the people cried. "Bring them, that we may put them to death."

"No man shall be put to death this day," Saul answered, "for today the LORD has wrought deliverance in Israel." Afterward Saul fought valiantly against his enemies on every side, against Moab, the Ammon-ites, Edom, the kings of Zobah, and the

Philistines. Wherever he turned he put them to the worse, and delivered Israel out of the hands of those who plundered her. But all his days he had hard fighting against the Philistines, and when he saw any strong man, he attached him to himself.

The sons of Saul were Jonathan, Ishbosheth, Abinadab, and Malchishua; the name of his first-born daughter was Merab, the name of the younger Michal. His wife was Ahinoam the daughter of Ahimaaz.

Now SAMUEL SAID to Saul, "The LORD sent me to anoint you king over Israel; now therefore hearken to his words. Thus says the LORD of hosts, 'I will punish what Amalek did to Israel when they came up out of Egypt. Now go and smite Amalek, and utterly destroy them; kill both man and woman, infant and suckling, ox and sheep, camel and ass.'" So Saul summoned the men, and they came to the city of Amalek and defeated the Amalekites. They destroyed all the people with the sword, except Agag the king, and they spared the best of the sheep and the oxen and all that was good.

Then the word of the LORD came in the night to Samuel: "I repent that I have made Saul king, for he has not performed my commandments." Samuel was angry, and he rose early and came to Saul. "Blessed be you to the LORD," Saul said; "I have performed his commandment."

"What then is this bleating of sheep and lowing of oxen in my ears?" said Samuel. "The people brought them from the Amalekites," Saul said, "for they spared the best of the sheep and oxen to sacrifice to the LORD; the rest we have utterly destroyed."

"Stop!" said Samuel. "Did not the LORD say to go and utterly destroy the Amalekites? Why then did you not obey? Why did you fear the people and allow them to take spoil, and do what was evil in the sight of the LORD?"

"I have obeyed the LORD," said Saul; "I have brought back Agag the king of Amalek, and I have utterly destroyed the Amalekites. But the people took the best of the spoil to sacrifice to the LORD in Gilgal."

"Has the LORD as great delight in sacrifice as in obedience?" said Samuel. "Because you have rejected the word of the LORD, he has also rejected you from being king." As Samuel turned to go, Saul seized the skirt of his robe, and it tore. "The LORD has torn the kingdom from you this day," said Samuel, "and has given it to one better than you."

"I have sinned," Saul said, "yet honor me now before Israel, and return with me to Gilgal, that I may worship the LORD." So Samuel turned back with him, and Saul worshiped the LORD. "Now bring me the king of the Amalekites," said Samuel, and Agag came to him cheerfully, saying, "Surely the bitterness of death is past."

"As your sword has made women childless," Samuel answered, "so shall your mother be childless among women." And he hewed Agag in pieces before the LORD in Gilgal.

Then Samuel went home to Ramah, grieving over Saul, and Saul went to his house in Gibeah. Now the LORD said to Samuel, "How long will you grieve over Saul? Fill your horn with oil, and go to

Jesse the Bethlehemite, for I have provided for myself a king among his sons."

"How can I go?" said Samuel. "If Saul hears it, he will kill me."

The LORD said, "Take a heifer with you, and say, 'I have come to sacrifice to the LORD,' and invite Jesse to the sacrifice; you shall anoint him whom I name to you." So Samuel came to Bethlehem, where he consecrated Jesse and seven of his sons, and invited them to the feast of the sacrifice. When they came, Jesse made his sons pass before Samuel. "The LORD has not chosen these," Samuel said to him. "Are all your sons here?"

"There remains the youngest," said Jesse. "He is keeping the sheep."

"Send and fetch him," said Samuel, "for we will not sit down till he comes." So Jesse sent and brought him in. Now David was ruddy, and had beautiful eyes, and was handsome. The LORD said to Samuel, "Arise, anoint him; for this is he." Samuel took the horn of oil and anointed him in the midst of his brothers; and from that day forward, the Spirit of the LORD came mightily upon David.

Now the Spirit of the LORD left Saul, and an evil spirit tormented him. His servants said to him, "Let our lord command his servants to seek out a man skilful in playing the lyre; and when the evil spirit is upon you, he will play, and you will be well." Saul agreed, and one of the young men said, "I have seen a son of Jesse the Bethlehemite, who is skilful in playing, prudent in speech, and a man of good presence." So Saul sent messengers to Jesse, saying, "Send me David your son." And David came to Saul, and entered his service. Saul loved him greatly, and when the evil spirit was upon him, David played the lyre; so Saul was refreshed, and the evil spirit left him.

Now the Philistines gathered their armies for battle in Judah, and Saul and the men of Israel drew up against them, with a valley between. Out from the Philistine camp, his shield-bearer going before him, came a champion named Goliath, of Gath, who was more than nine feet tall. He wore a bronze helmet and a heavy coat of mail. Upon his legs were bronze greaves, and a bronze javelin was slung between his shoulders; its shaft was like a weaver's beam, the head weighing fifteen pounds. "I defy the ranks of Israel," Goliath shouted. "Choose a man, and if he is able to fight with me and kill me, then we will be your servants; but if I prevail and kill him, then you shall serve us."

When Saul and all Israel heard this, they were dismayed. But David said to Saul, "Who is this uncircumcised Philistine, that he should defy the armies of the living God? Let no man's heart fail; your servant will go and fight him."

"You cannot go against this Philistine," said Saul; "you are but a youth, and he has long been a man of war."

"I used to keep sheep for my father," David answered, "and when a lion took a lamb from the flock, I went after him and smote him and delivered it; and if he attacked me, I caught him by his beard, and smote him and killed him. The LORD who delivered me from the lion will deliver me from this Philistine." So Saul said, "Go, and the LORD be with you!" He clothed David with his armor and put a helmet of bronze on his head. Girding the king's sword over the armor, David tried to go, but in vain, for he was not used to these things. "I cannot go with these," he said, and took them off.

Then David took his staff and his sling, and he chose five smooth stones from the brook. Putting them in his shepherd's bag, he drew near to the Philistine. When Goliath saw David, he disdained him. "Am I a dog," he said, "that you come to me with sticks?"

"I come to you in the name of the LORD of hosts," said David, "the God of the armies of Israel, whom you have defied." Then he put his hand in his bag and took out a stone, and slung it, and struck the Philistine on his forehead. The stone sank in and Goliath fell to the ground. David ran and stood over him, and took Goliath's sword out of its sheath and killed him, and cut off his head with it. When the Philistines saw that their champion was dead, they fled, and the men of Israel and Judah rose with a shout and pursued them as far as Gath and the gates of Ekron. When they came back, they plundered the Philistine camp.

As they were going home, the women came out of all the cities to greet King Saul with music and dancing and songs of joy. "Saul has slain his thousands," they sang to one another, "and David his ten thousands." Saul was very angry. "They have ascribed to David ten thousands," he said, "and to me only thousands; what more can he have but the kingdom?" And he eyed David from that day on, fearing him because the LORD was with him but had departed from Saul. So Saul removed David from his presence, and made him a troop commander of a thousand. David had success in all his undertakings, and when Saul saw this, he stood in awe of him.

Now Saul's daughter Michal loved David, and Saul thought, "Let me give her to him, that she may be a snare for him." So he commanded his servants to speak to David and say, "Behold, the king has delight in you; now then become the king's son-in-law." But David said, "Does it seem easy to you to become the king's son-in-law, seeing that I am a poor man and of no repute?"

This the servants of Saul reported, and Saul told them to reply, "The king desires no marriage present except a hundred foreskins of the Philistines, that he may be avenged of his enemies." For Saul thought to make David fall by the hand of the Philistines. But David was well pleased, and he went with his men and killed two hundred Philistines and brought their foreskins to the king. So Saul gave him his daughter Michal for a wife.

Now Saul saw that all Israel loved David, and he became his enemy continually. He spoke to Jonathan his son, and to his servants, that they should kill David. But the soul of Jonathan was knit to the soul of David, and Jonathan loved him as his own soul, for they had made a vow of friendship. "My father seeks to kill you," Jonathan said. "Hide yourself, and I will speak to him about you; if I learn anything I will tell you."

To Saul, Jonathan spoke well of David. "Let not the king sin against David," he said, "because he has not sinned against you, and he has been of good service to you; for he took his life in his hand and slew the Philistine. You saw it, and rejoiced; why then will you kill him without cause?" Saul hearkened to the voice of his son. "As the LORD lives," he swore, "he shall not be put to death." So Jonathan called David and brought him to Saul, and he was accepted in his presence as before.

Again the Philistines came out to battle, and David made a great slaughter among them, so that they fled before him. Then an evil spirit rushed upon Saul, and he raved within his house while David was playing the lyre, as he did day by day. Saul had his spear in his hand, and he cast it, seeking to pin David to the wall; but David eluded him, so that the spear struck into the wall. And David fled.

That night Saul sent messengers to David's house to watch him, that he might kill him in the morning. But Michal told David, "If you do not escape tonight, tomorrow you will be killed." She let him down from the window, then she laid an image on the bed and put a pillow of goats' hair at its head, and covered it with the bedclothes. When Saul's messengers came to take David, she said, "He is sick," and sent them away. But Saul said, "Bring him up to me in the bed, that I may kill him." When the messengers came in, behold, the image was in the bed, with the pillow of goats' hair at its head.

"Why have you deceived me thus," said Saul to Michal, "and let my enemy escape?" Michal answered, "He said to me, 'Let me go; why should I have to kill you?'"

DAVID FLED TO Nob, to Ahimelech the priest, the great-grandson of Eli, who met him with respect. "Why are you alone?" asked Ahimelech. "The king charged me with a secret matter," David replied. "I am to meet my men. What have you at hand? Give me five loaves of bread, or whatever is here."

"I have no common bread," said the priest, "but there is holy bread; if only the young men have kept themselves from women."

"Of a truth, women are kept from us even when it is a common expedition," David answered; "how much more today will their bodies be holy?" So the priest gave him the bread of the Presence, which

is removed from before the LORD and re-
placed by hot bread. "Do you have a spear
or a sword at hand?" asked David. "I did
not bring my weapons with me because
the king's business required haste."

"The sword of Goliath whom you killed
is here wrapped in a cloth," the priest replied. "There is none like that," David
said; "give it to me."

Now Doeg the Edomite, Saul's chief
herdsman, was there that day, serving in
the temple. So David departed and fled to
the cave of Adullam. When his brothers
and all his father's house heard it, they
went down there to him. And every one in
distress, every one in debt, and every one
who was discontented gathered to him;
and he became captain over them. And
there were with him about four hundred
men.

At Gibeah, Saul was sitting under the
tamarisk tree on the height, with his spear
in his hand and all his servants about him.
Doeg the Edomite stood with them. "I saw
the son of Jesse coming to Nob," he said to
Saul, "and Ahimelech gave him provisions
and the sword of Goliath the Philistine."

Then the king sent to summon Ahimelech and all his father's house, the priests who were at Nob; and all of them came to the king. "Why have you conspired against me," Saul said to Ahimelech, "you and the son of Jesse, in that you have given him bread and a sword, and have inquired of God for him, so that he has risen against me?"

"Who among all your servants," Ahimelech answered, "is so faithful as David who is the king's son-in-law, and captain over your bodyguard, and honored in your house? No! Let not the king impute anything to me, for I have known nothing of all this."

"You shall surely die, Ahimelech," said the king, "you and all your father's house." Then he said to the guards, "Turn and kill them, for they also are with David, and they knew that he fled, and did not disclose it to me." But the guards would not fall upon the priests of the LORD, so the king said to Doeg, "You turn and fall upon the priests." So Doeg the Edomite fell upon them, and he killed on that day eighty-five persons who wore the priestly apron. And in Nob, the city of the priests, he put men and women, children and sucklings, oxen, asses, and sheep to the sword.

But one of Ahimelech's sons, named Abiathar, escaped and fled after David, and told him that Saul had killed the priests. "I knew on that day, when Doeg the Edomite was there," said David, "that he would surely tell Saul. I have occasioned the death of all your father's house. Stay with me, fear not; for he that seeks my life seeks your life; with me you shall be safe."

David and his men were in the wilderness of Maon, south of Ziph, and Saul and his men went there to seek him. David was told, and he took refuge in the mountain there. Saul sought him on one side of the mountain, while David and his men were on the other side, but as Saul was closing in, a messenger came to him, saying, "Make haste and come; for the Philistines have made a raid upon the land." So Saul returned from pursuing David and went against the Philistines; therefore that place was called the Rock of Escape.

Now Samuel died; and all Israel assembled and mourned for him, and they buried him in his house at Ramah.

THERE WAS IN Maon a very rich man named Nabal; he had three thousand sheep and a thousand goats. His wife, Abigail, was of good understanding and beautiful, but the man, a Calebite, was churlish and ill-behaved.

David, in the wilderness, heard that Nabal was shearing his sheep at Carmel, so he chose ten young men and said, "Go to Nabal, and greet him in my name thus: 'Peace be to you, and to your house. I hear that you have shearers; now your shepherds have been with us, and we did them no harm, and they missed nothing, for we guarded them all the time they were in the wilderness. Ask your young men, and they will tell you. Therefore let my young men find favor in your eyes, for we come on a feast day. Pray, give whatever you have at hand to them and to your son David.' " The young men came to Nabal and said all this in the name of David; and then they waited. "Who is David?" Nabal answered.

"There are many servants nowadays who are breaking away from their masters. Shall I take my bread and wine and meat that I have killed for my shearers, and give it to men who come from I do not know where?" David's men came back and told him all this.

"This fellow has returned me evil for good," said David. "God punish me if by morning I leave alive so much as one male of all who belong to him." To his men, he said, "Every man gird on his sword!" Every man did so, and David also. He now had about six hundred men; four hundred went with him, while two hundred remained with the baggage.

But one of Nabal's young men told Abigail how her husband had received David's messengers. "Yet they were very good to us," he told her, "all the while we were with them. Consider what you should do; for evil is determined against our master, and he is so ill-natured one cannot speak to him."

Abigail made haste and took two hundred loaves, two skins of wine, five sheep ready dressed, five measures of parched grain, a hundred clusters of raisins, and two hundred cakes of figs. She laid them on asses and departed, but she did not tell Nabal. As she came near the mountain, behold, David and his men were coming down toward her. When she saw David, she alighted from the ass and fell before him to the ground.

"Upon me alone, my lord, be the guilt," she said; "pray hear the words of your handmaid. Let not my lord pay attention to this ill-natured fellow, Nabal, for folly is with him; but I your handmaid did not see the young men you sent. Now then, my lord, seeing that the LORD has restrained you from bloodguilt, and from taking vengeance with your own hand, let this present which your servant has brought be given to your young men. Pray forgive my trespass, for your life shall be in the care of the LORD your God, and the lives of your enemies he shall sling out as from the hollow of a sling. And when the LORD has dealt well with you, my lord, then remember your handmaid."

"Blessed be the God of Israel," David replied, "who sent you this day to meet me! Blessed be your discretion, and blessed be you, who have kept me from bloodguilt and from avenging myself with my own hand!" And he received from her what she had brought him. "Go in peace to your house," he said. "I have hearkened to you and granted your petition."

When Abigail returned, Nabal was holding a feast in his house, like the feast of a king. His heart was merry, for he was very drunk, so she told him nothing at all until the morning light. In the morning, when the wine had gone out of him, she told him these things, and his heart died within him, and he became as a stone. About ten days later he died.

When David heard that Nabal was dead, he wooed Abigail, sending his servants to her at Carmel to say, "David has sent us to take you to him as his wife." Abigail bowed with her face to the ground. "Behold," she said, "your handmaid is a servant to wash the feet of the servants of my lord." Then she rose and mounted an ass, and with five maidens attending her, she followed the messengers of David, and became his wife. David also took Ahinoam of Jezreel; and both of them became his wives. But Saul had given Michal to Paltiel the son of Laish when David became a fugitive.

THE ZIPHITES CAME to Saul at Gibeah, saying, "Is not David hiding himself on the mountain in the wilderness of Ziph?" So Saul arose and returned to the wilderness with three thousand chosen men of Israel, and encamped on the mountain. Hearing that Saul was coming after him, David sent out spies and learned of a certainty that Saul had come. He came close to Saul's encampment and saw where he was lodged with Abner, the commander of his army. "Who will go down with me into the camp of Saul?" said David to his men. "I will go with you," said Abishai the son of Zeruiah, David's sister.

So David and Abishai went down to the encampment by night. Saul was sleeping with his spear stuck in the ground at his head; and Abner and the army lay around him. "God has given your enemy into your hand this day," said Abishai; "let me pin him to the earth with one stroke of the spear."

"Do not destroy him," David said. "As the LORD lives, the LORD will smite him; or his day shall come to die; or he shall perish in battle. The LORD forbid that I should raise my hand against the LORD's anointed; but let us take now his spear and the jar of water and go." So David took the spear and the jar of water, and they went away. No man saw it, or knew it, nor did any awake.

Then David went to the other side, and stood afar off on top of the mountain, and he called to Saul's army, "Will you not answer, Abner?"

"Who are you that calls to the king?" Abner answered.

"Are you not a man?" said David. "Why have you not kept watch over your king, the LORD's anointed? As the LORD lives, you deserve to die. Where is the king's spear, and the jar of water that was at his head?"

Saul recognized David's voice. "Is this your voice, David?" he said.

"It is my voice," replied David. "Why

does my lord pursue his servant? What have I done? What guilt is on my hands? If it is the LORD who has stirred you up against me, may he accept an offering; but if it is men, may they be cursed before the LORD, for they have driven me out, and my lord has come to seek my life, like one who hunts a partridge in the mountains."

Then Saul said, "I have done wrong; return, my son David, for I will no more do you harm; I have played the fool, and have erred exceedingly."

"Here is the spear, O king!" David answered. "Let one of the young men come over and fetch it. As your life was precious this day in my sight, so may my life be precious in the sight of the LORD, and may he deliver me out of all tribulation."

"Blessed be you, my son David!" said Saul. "You will do many things and will succeed in them."

So David went his way, and Saul returned to Gibeah. But David said in his heart, "I shall perish one day by the hand of Saul; there is nothing better for me than to escape to the land of the Philistines; then Saul will despair of seeking me any longer." So he went over with his six hundred men to Achish, king of Gath; and they dwelt at Gath, and Saul sought him no more.

Now David and his men made raids upon the Amalekites and other inhabitants of the land from of old, as far as the land of Egypt. He smote the land and left neither man nor woman alive, but took away the livestock and the garments and came back to Achish. But when Achish asked, "Against whom have you made a raid today?" David would say, "Against the Negeb of Judah," and he spared neither man nor woman, lest they bring tidings to Gath. Such was David's custom while he dwelt with the Philistines, and Achish trusted him, thinking, "He has made himself utterly abhorred by Israel; therefore he shall be my servant always."

Then David said to Achish, "If I have found favor in your eyes, let me be given a country town to dwell in; for why should your servant dwell in the royal city with you?" So Achish gave him Ziklag, and to this day Ziklag has belonged to the kings of Judah.

IN THOSE DAYS the Philistines again gathered forces for war against Israel. "You and your men are to go out with me in the army," Achish said to David. "Very well," David replied, "you shall know what your servant can do."

When the Philistines assembled their forces at Shunem, David and his men were in the rear with Achish as the lords of the Philistines passed by with their men. "What are these Hebrews doing here?" they said. "Is not this David, the servant of Saul?" Achish replied. "Since he deserted to me I have found no fault in him." But the commanders were angry. "Send the man back," they said; "he shall not go down with us to battle, lest he become an adversary. For how could this fellow reconcile himself to his lord?"

So Achish called David. "As the LORD lives," he said, "you have been honest, and to me it seems right that you should march with me in the campaign. Nevertheless the lords do not approve of you. Go back now peaceably, that you may not displease them." So early in the morning David set out with his men to return to the land of the Philistines.

Now the Amalekites had made a raid upon Ziklag, and when David and his men came to the city on the third day, they found it burned, and their wives and sons and daughters taken captive. David wept, and he was greatly distressed; for the people were bitter in soul for their sons and daughters and spoke of stoning him. But David strengthened himself in the LORD his God, and inquired of the LORD, "Shall I pursue this band?" The LORD answered, "Pursue; for you shall surely overtake and surely rescue."

So David set out with his six hundred men. When they came to the brook Besor, two hundred men stayed behind, too exhausted to cross. But David and four hundred men went on with the pursuit. In the open country they found an Egyptian who had not eaten or drunk water for three days and nights. They gave him water and figs and raisins, and when he had eaten, his spirit revived. "Where are you from?" David asked him.

"I am an Egyptian," he replied, "servant to an Amalekite. My master left me behind because I fell sick three days ago. We had made a raid upon the Negeb, and we burned Ziklag."

"Will you take me to this band?" David said.

"Swear to me that you will not kill me," the man said, "or deliver me into the hands of my master, and I will." He took them to the band, and behold, the Amalekites were spread over the land, eating and drinking and dancing, because of all the spoil they had taken from the land of Judah. And David smote them, and not a man of them escaped, except some who mounted camels and fled. David recovered all that they had taken, including Ahinoam and Abigail, and he captured all their flocks and herds. The people drove those cattle before him, saying, "This is David's spoil."

When David came to the two hundred men who had been left at the brook Besor, he saluted them. Then the wicked fellows among the men who had gone with David said, "Because they did not go with us, we will not give them any of the spoil." But David said, "Not so, my brothers. The LORD has preserved us and given into our hand the band that came against us. As his share is who goes into battle, so shall his share be who stays by the baggage; they shall share alike." And from that day this was an ordinance for Israel.

When David came back to Ziklag, he sent part of the spoil to his friends, the elders of Judah, in all the places where he and his men had roamed.

Now SAUL GATHERED all Israel, and they encamped at Mount Gilboa. When he saw the army of the Philistines, he was afraid, and his heart trembled; but when he inquired of the LORD, the LORD did not answer him, either by dreams, or by the sacred lot, or by prophets. "Seek out a woman who is a medium," Saul said to his servants, "that I may go and inquire of her."

"Behold, there is a medium at Endor," they replied.

So Saul disguised himself and went with two men to the woman by night. "Tell me the future through a spirit," he said, "and bring up for me whomever I shall name to you."

"Whom shall I bring up?" the woman asked.

"Bring up Samuel for me," Saul said. But when the woman saw Samuel, she cried out with a loud voice.

"What do you see?" the king said to her.

"I see a spirit coming up out of the earth," she said, "like an old man wrapped in a robe." Saul knew that it was Samuel, and he bowed with his face to the ground and did obeisance.

"Why have you disturbed me by bringing me up?" Samuel said to Saul.

"I am in great distress," Saul answered, "for the Philistines are warring against me, and God has turned away and answers me no more, either by prophets or by dreams; therefore I have summoned you to tell me what to do."

"The LORD has done to you as he spoke through me," said Samuel, "for he has torn the kingdom out of your hand and given it to David because you did not obey him and carry out his fierce wrath against

Amalek. Moreover the LORD will give Israel into the hand of the Philistines, and tomorrow you and your sons shall be with me." Then Saul fell full length upon the ground, filled with fear, and there was no strength in him. But his servants, together with the woman, urged him; and he rose and went away.

The next day the Philistines fought against Israel, and the men of Israel fled before them, and fell slain on Mount Gilboa. The Philistines overtook Saul and slew Jonathan and Abinadab and Malchishua, his sons. The battle pressed hard upon Saul, and the archers found him, and he was badly wounded. "Draw your sword," he said to his armor-bearer, "and thrust me through with it, lest these uncircumcised come and make sport of me." But his armor-bearer would not; for he feared greatly. Therefore Saul took his own sword, and fell upon it.

Thus Saul died, and his sons, and all his men, on the same day together. When the people heard that the men of Israel had fled and that Saul and three of his sons were dead, they fled from their cities; and the Philistines came and dwelt in them.

On the morrow, when the Philistines came to strip the slain, they found Saul on Mount Gilboa. They cut off his head, and stripped off his armor, and sent messengers throughout their land to carry the good news to their gods and to the people. They put his armor in the temple of Astarte, and they fastened his body to the wall of Beth-shan. But when the inhabitants of Jabesh-gilead heard what the Philistines had done to Saul, the valiant men arose and went all night, and took Saul's body from the wall. Then they came back to Jabesh and burned the body, and buried the bones under the tamarisk tree in Jabesh, and they fasted seven days.

2 SAMUEL

The central figure of 2 Samuel is David, the successor to Saul, Israel's first king. David's reign begins at Hebron, at first over the kingdom of Judah only. Later, after a successful war against the house of Saul, it is established at Jerusalem, this time over all Israel. David's reign of forty years is not without many difficulties, and a considerable part of the book describes the domestic and political troubles that plague him. The unknown author of 2 Samuel derived most of his material from the Early Source (see 1 Samuel Introduction), and consequently the narrative is unified and easily followed. Theologically, the most significant contribution from the Late Source is the prophecy of Nathan promising David an everlasting dynasty.

This pronouncement becomes the basis for the development of royal messianism throughout the Bible.

After the death of Saul, when David had returned from the slaughter of the Amalekites, he remained two days in Ziklag. On the third day a man came from Saul's camp, his clothes rent and earth upon his head. When he came to David, he fell to the ground and did obeisance. "Where do you come from?" asked David.

"I have escaped from the camp of Israel at Gilboa," the man replied. "The people have fled from the battle, many have fallen, and Saul and his son Jonathan are dead."

Then David took hold of his clothes and rent them, and so did all the men who were with him. They mourned and wept and fasted for Saul and Jonathan and for the people of the Lord fallen by the sword. And David lamented: "Thy glory, O Israel, is slain upon thy high places! How are the mighty fallen! Tell it not in

Gath, publish it not in the streets of Ashkelon, lest the daughters of the Philistines rejoice. Ye mountains of Gilboa, let no dew or rain fall upon you, O treacherous fields; for there the shield of Saul was defiled. Saul and Jonathan, beloved and lovely! They were swifter than eagles; they were stronger than lions. How are the mighty fallen in the midst of the battle! Jonathan lies slain upon thy high places. I am distressed for you, my brother Jonathan; very pleasant have you been to me; your love to me was wonderful, passing the love of women. How are the mighty fallen, and the weapons of war perished!"

AFTER THIS, DAVID inquired of the LORD, "Shall I go up into the cities of Judah?" The LORD answered, "Go up to Hebron." So David went up, with his wives and all his men, every one with his household; and they dwelt in the towns of Hebron. Then the men of Judah came, and they anointed David king over the house of Judah.

When they told David, "It was the men of Jabesh-gilead who buried Saul," he sent messengers to them in Gilead, saying, "May you be blessed by the LORD for this loyalty to Saul your lord. I will do good to you because of this. Now therefore be strong; for Saul is dead, and the house of Judah has anointed me king over them." But Abner, Saul's cousin and commander of his army, had taken Saul's young son Ishbosheth, and brought him over to Mahanaim in Gilead; and he made him king over Gilead and Benjamin and all Israel north of Judah.

Now Abner and Ishbosheth's men marched from Mahanaim across the Jordan to Gibeon. So Joab, the son of David's sister Zeruiah, went out with David's men and met them at the pool of Gibeon. They sat down, Abner's company on one side of the pool and Joab's on the other. "Let the young men arise for single combat," said Abner to Joab. "Let them arise," Joab answered. So the young men arose, twelve on a side. Each caught his opponent by the hair and thrust his sword into his opponent, so that they all fell down together. The battle spread and became very fierce.

The three sons of David's sister Zeruiah

were there that day, Joab, Abishai, and
Asahel. Now Asahel was as swift of foot as
a wild gazelle, and he pursued Abner,
turning neither right nor left from following him. Abner looked back and said to
Asahel, "Turn aside, and seize one of the
young men." But Asahel would not, and
Abner said again, "Turn aside; why should
I smite you? How then could I lift up my
face to your brother Joab?" When Asahel
refused again, Abner smote him in the belly
with his spear, so that it came out at his
back; and Asahel fell there and died. And
all who came to that place stood still in
grief.

Joab and Abishai took up the pursuit of
Abner. As the sun was going down they
came to a hill in the wilderness of Gibeon.
Here Abner and his people took their
stand. "Shall the sword devour for ever?"
Abner called to Joab. "Do you not know
that the end will be bitter? How long before you bid your people turn from the
pursuit of their brethren?"

"As God lives," Joab replied, "if you
had not spoken, surely the men would
have continued until morning." Then he

blew the trumpet; and all his men stopped and pursued Abner no more. When Joab gathered his people together, there were missing nineteen besides Asahel; but they had slain three hundred and sixty of Abner's men. They took up Asahel and buried him in the tomb of his father at Bethlehem. Then they marched all night, and the day broke upon them at Hebron.

Now THERE WAS a long war between the house of Saul and the house of David. While David grew stronger and stronger, the house of Saul became weaker and weaker. And while there was war, Abner was making himself strong in the house of Saul.

Now Saul had a concubine, Rizpah, and Ishbosheth said to Abner, "Why have you gone in to my father's concubine?" Abner was very angry at this. "Am I a dog's head of Judah?" he said. "I show loyalty to the house of Saul, and have not given you over to David; and yet you charge me today with a fault concerning a woman. God punish me if I do not accomplish for David what the LORD has sworn to him, to set up his throne over Israel and Judah, from Dan to Beer-sheba." Then Abner sent word to David at Hebron, saying, "To whom does this land belong? Make your covenant with me, and my hand shall be with you to bring over all Israel to you."

"I will make a covenant with you," David replied. "But one thing I require: you shall not see my face unless you bring Michal, Saul's daughter, when you come." Then he sent messengers to Ishbosheth, saying, "Give me my wife Michal, whom I betrothed at the price of a hundred foreskins of the Philistines." So Ishbosheth took Michal from her husband Paltiel; and her husband went with her, weeping, until Abner commanded him to return.

And Abner conferred with the elders of Israel, saying, "For some time past you have been seeking David as king. Now then bring it about, for the LORD has promised David that he will save our people from the hand of all their enemies." Then Abner went to Hebron to tell David all that the elders of Israel thought good to do. David made a feast for him, and Abner said, "Now I will arise and go, and I will gather all Israel to my lord the king, that they may make a covenant with you." So Abner went away in peace.

Just then Joab arrived from a raid; and he was told that Abner had come to talk with the king and that the king had let him go. "Why have you sent Abner away in peace?" Joab said to the king. "You know that he came to deceive you and to know all that you are doing." When he came out from David's presence, Joab sent messengers after Abner, and they brought him back to Hebron. Joab and Abishai his brother took Abner into the inner part of the gate to speak with him privately, and because he had killed their brother Asahel in the battle at Gibeon, they smote him in the belly and he died.

When David heard of it, he said, "I and my kingdom are guiltless before the LORD for the blood of Abner. May it fall upon the head of Joab and upon all his father's house." Then to Joab and all the people who were with him he said, "Rend your clothes and mourn before Abner. Do you not know that a prince and a great man has fallen in Israel?" They buried Abner at

Hebron, and David lamented at his grave, saying, "Should Abner die as a fool dies? Your hands were not bound, your feet were not fettered; as one falls before the wicked, you have fallen." The people wept, and all Israel understood that it had not been the king's will to slay Abner.

When Ishbosheth heard that Abner had died, his courage failed, and all Israel was dismayed. Two brothers named Baanah and Rechab, both captains of raiding bands, set out for Mahanaim, and in the heat of the day they came to the house of Ishbosheth. The doorkeeper had grown drowsy and slept, so Rechab and Baanah slipped into his chamber. As Ishbosheth lay on his bed they smote him and beheaded him. Then they took his head and traveled all night through the Arabah, and brought it to David at Hebron. "Here is the head of Ishbosheth, the son of Saul, your enemy," they said to the king. "The LORD has avenged my lord the king this day on Saul and his offspring."

"When wicked men have slain a righteous man in his own house," David answered, "shall I not now require his blood at your hand and destroy you from the earth?" And he commanded his young men, and they hanged Rechab and Baanah beside the pool at Hebron. But they took the head of Ishbosheth and buried it in the tomb of Abner.

Then all the tribes of Israel came to David at Hebron, and said, "Behold, we are your bone and flesh. When Saul was king over us, it was you that led us out and brought us in, and the LORD said to you, 'You shall be prince over my people Israel.' " So David made a covenant with the elders of Israel before the LORD, and they anointed him king. He was thirty years old, and he had reigned over Judah seven years and six months. He reigned over both Israel and Judah thirty-three years.

NOW THE KING and his men went to Jerusalem against the Jebusites, the inhabitants of the land, and they took the stronghold of Zion. David dwelt there in the fortress and called it the city of David. And he became greater and greater, for the LORD, the God of hosts, was with him. Hiram king of Tyre sent cedar trees to him and carpenters and masons who built him a house. And David perceived that the LORD had exalted his kingdom for the sake of his people Israel.

Sons had been born to David at Hebron: his first-born was Amnon, by Ahinoam of Jezreel, and his second Chileab, by Abigail; then Absalom, the son of Maacah, daughter of the king of Geshur; and Adonijah, and Shephatiah, and Ithream. Now David took more concubines and wives from Jerusalem, and more sons and daughters were born to him.

When the Philistines heard that David had been anointed king over Israel, they went up in search of him in the valley of Rephaim. David inquired of the LORD, "Shall I go up against the Philistines?" The LORD said, "Go up; for I will certainly give the Philistines into your hand." And David defeated them and carried away their idols. Then the Philistines came up again. When David inquired of the LORD, he said, "You shall not go up; go around to their rear, and come upon them opposite the balsam trees. When you hear the sound of marching in the balsam trees, then bestir yourself; for the LORD has gone out before you to smite the army of the Philistines." And David did as the LORD commanded him.

Now David gathered the chosen men of Israel and went with them to Kiriath-jearim, to bring up from there the ark of the LORD of hosts. They brought the ark out of the house of Abinadab on the hill, and carried it, with shouting and the sound of the horn, on a cart to the city of David. David sacrificed an ox and a fatling, and he danced before the LORD with all his might, girded with a priestly apron.

As the ark of the LORD came into the city, Michal the daughter of Saul looked out of the window and saw King David leaping and dancing before the LORD; and she despised him in her heart. They set the ark in its place in the tent David had pitched for it, and he made burnt offerings before the LORD. Then he blessed the people in the name of the LORD of hosts, and distributed to each a portion of meat and a cake of raisins. When he returned to bless his own household, Michal came out to meet him. "How the king of Israel honored himself today," she said, "uncovering himself before his servants' maids, as vulgar fellows shamelessly do!"

"It was before the LORD," said David, "who chose me above your father and all his house as prince over Israel—and I will make merry before him. I will make myself yet more contemptible than this in your eyes. But by the maids of whom you have spoken I shall be held in honor." And Michal had no child to the day of her death.

Now when the king dwelt in his house and the LORD had given him rest from all his enemies round about, he said to Nathan the prophet, "See now, I dwell in a house of cedar, but the ark of God dwells in a tent."

That night the word of the LORD came to Nathan: "Go and tell my servant David, 'Thus says the LORD: Would you build me a house to dwell in? I have not dwelt in a house since the day I brought up the people of Israel from Egypt. Wherever I have moved with them, did I speak a word with any of the judges, saying, "Why have you not built me a house of cedar?" '

"Now therefore you shall say to my servant David, 'I took you from following the sheep to be prince over my people Israel, and I have been with you wherever you went; and I will make for you a great name, like the great ones of the earth. And I will appoint a place for my people Israel, that they may dwell there and be disturbed no more; and I will give you rest from all your enemies. Moreover the LORD declares to you that he will build you a house. When your days are fulfilled and you lie down with your fathers, I will raise up your son after you, who shall come forth from your body, and I will establish his kingdom. He shall build a house for my name. I will be his father, and he shall be my son. When he commits iniquity, I will chasten him with the rod of men; but I will not take my steadfast love from him, as I took it from Saul. And your kingdom shall be established for ever.' " In accordance with all these words, and in accordance with all this vision, Nathan spoke to David.

Then King David went in and sat before the LORD, and said, "Who am I, O LORD, and what is my family, that thou hast brought me thus far? And yet this was a small thing in thy eyes, O LORD; thou hast also shown me future generations. Because of thy promise, and according to thy own heart, thou hast wrought all this greatness. Thou hast said, 'I will build you a house'; therefore I have found courage to pray this prayer to thee. Thy words are true, and thou hast promised this good thing to thy servant; and now may it please thee to bless the house of thy servant, that it may continue for ever before thee."

AFTER THIS, DAVID did as the LORD commanded him, and subdued the Philistines from Gibeon to Gezer. And he defeated Moab, making them lie down on the ground in three lines; two lines he measured to be put to death, and one full line to be spared. David also defeated Hadadezer, son of the king of Zobah, as he went to restore his power at the river Euphrates. And David took from him a thousand and seven hundred horsemen, and twenty thousand foot soldiers. When the Syrians of Damascus came to help Hadadezer, David slew twenty-two thousand of their men. When he returned, he slew eighteen thousand Edomites in the Valley of Salt and put garrisons throughout Edom. And his enemies became David's servants and brought tribute.

The LORD gave victory to David wherever he went. And David took all the articles of silver, gold, and bronze that had been given to him as tribute and dedicated them to the LORD. So David reigned over all Israel and administered justice and equity to his people.

IN THE SPRING of the year, the time when kings go forth to battle, David sent Joab and the army against the Ammonites, and they besieged Rabbah. But David remained at Jerusalem.

It happened late one afternoon, when David arose from his couch and was walking upon the roof of his house, that he saw a woman bathing; and the woman was very beautiful. David sent and inquired about her. One servant said, "Is not this Bathsheba, the wife of Uriah the Hittite, who is with the army in Ammon?" So David sent messengers, and they brought Bathsheba to him, and he lay with her;

then she returned to her house. She conceived; and she sent and told David, "I am with child."

David sent word to Joab, "Send me Uriah the Hittite." When Uriah came, David asked how the people fared and how the war prospered. Then he said, "Go down to your house and rest." Uriah left, but he slept at the door of the king's house with the soldiers and did not go down to his house.

When they told David this, he said to Uriah, "Have you not come from a journey? Why did you not go down to your house?"

"The ark dwells in a tent," Uriah answered, "and my lord Joab and your soldiers are camping in the open field; shall I then go to my house to eat and to drink and to lie with my wife? As your soul lives, I will not do this thing."

"Then remain here today also," David said, "and tomorrow I will let you depart." Uriah remained in Jerusalem that day and the next. David invited him, and Uriah ate and drank in his presence, so that David made him drunk. But again in the evening

Uriah went out to lie on his couch with the soldiers, and he did not go down to his house.

In the morning David wrote a letter to Joab, and sent it by the hand of Uriah. "Set Uriah in the forefront of the hardest fighting," he wrote, "and then draw back from him, that he may be struck down and die." So Joab assigned Uriah to a place in the siege lines where he knew the foe had valiant men. The men of the city came out and attacked; some of David's soldiers fell, and Uriah the Hittite was slain also. Then Joab sent David all the news about the fighting; and he instructed the messenger, "If the king's anger rises and he says to you, 'Why did you go so near the city wall to fight?' you shall say, 'Your servant Uriah the Hittite is dead also.' "

The messenger came to David and said, "We drove the enemy back to the gate of the city. Then the archers shot at us from the wall; some of the king's servants are dead; and your servant Uriah the Hittite is dead also."

"Thus shall you say to Joab," David replied. " 'Do not let this matter trouble you, for the sword devours now one and now another; strengthen your attack upon the city, and overthrow it.' " When Bathsheba heard that Uriah her husband was dead, she made lamentation for him. But when the mourning was over, David brought her to his house, and she became his wife and bore him a son.

The thing David had done displeased the LORD, and he sent Nathan the prophet to him. "There were two men in a certain city," Nathan said to David, "one rich and the other poor. The rich man had many flocks and herds; but the poor man had nothing but one little ewe lamb. It grew up with his children; it used to eat of his morsel, and drink from his cup, and it was like a daughter to him. Now there came a traveler to the rich man, and he was unwilling to slaughter one of his own flock for the wayfarer, so he took the poor man's lamb and prepared it for the feast."

David's anger was greatly kindled. "As the LORD lives," he said to Nathan, "the man who has done this deserves to die because he had no pity."

"You are the man," said Nathan. "Thus

says the LORD, 'I anointed you king over Israel, and I delivered you from Saul; and I gave you the house of Israel and of Judah; and if this were too little, I would add to you as much more. Why have you despised the word of the LORD, to do what is evil in his sight? You have smitten Uriah the Hittite with the sword of the Ammonites, and have taken his wife to be your wife. Now therefore the sword shall never depart from your house.' Thus says the LORD, 'Behold, I will raise up evil against you out of your own house; and I will take your wives and give them to another, and he shall lie with them in the sight of this sun. For you did it secretly, but I will do this thing before all Israel.'"

"I have sinned against the LORD," said David.

"And the LORD has put away your sin," replied Nathan; "you shall not die. Nevertheless, because by this deed you have utterly scorned the LORD, the child that is born to you shall die." The LORD struck the child that Uriah's wife bore to David, and it became sick. David besought God for the child, and he fasted and went in and lay all night upon the ground. The elders of his house tried to raise him up; but he would not rise, nor did he eat food with them. On the seventh day the child died. The servants of David feared to tell him, for they said, "How can we say to him the child is dead? He may do himself some harm."

But when David saw them whispering together, he asked, "Is the child dead?" And they replied, "He is dead." David arose from the earth, and washed, and changed his clothes; and he went into the house of the LORD and worshiped; then he went to his own house, and when they set food before him, he ate.

"You fasted and wept for the child while it was alive," his servants said, "but when it died, you arose and ate food."

David answered, "I fasted and wept, for I said, 'Who knows whether the LORD will be gracious to me, that the child may live?' But now he is dead. Why should I fast? Can I bring him back again? I shall go where he is, but he will not return to me." Then David comforted his wife, Bathsheba, and went in to her and lay with her; and she bore a son, and he called his name Solomon. And the LORD loved him.

Now ABSALOM, DAVID's son, had a beautiful sister whose name was Tamar, and Amnon, David's eldest son, loved her. Amnon was so tormented that he made himself ill because of Tamar; for she was a virgin, and it seemed impossible to him to do anything to her. But Amnon had a friend, Jonadab, who said to him, "O son of the king, why are you so haggard morning after morning? Will you not tell me?" Amnon answered him, "I love Tamar, my brother Absalom's sister."

"Lie down on your bed," Jonadab said, "and pretend to be ill. When your father comes to see you, say to him, 'Let my sister Tamar come and prepare food in my sight, that I may eat it from her hand.'" Amnon pretended to be ill, and when the king came to see him, he spoke as Jonadab had told him. So David sent Tamar, and she took dough and kneaded it and baked cakes in Amnon's sight; but he refused to eat. "Send out every one from me," he said, "then bring the food into the chamber, that I may eat from your hand." When every one left, Tamar brought the cakes into the chamber. As she came near him, Amnon took hold of her and said, "Come, lie with me, my sister."

"No, my brother, do not force me," she answered him. "Where could I carry my shame? As for you, you would be as a wanton fool in Israel. Now therefore, I pray you, speak to the king, for he will not withhold me from you." But he would not listen to her; and being stronger than she, he forced her, and lay with her.

Then Amnon's hatred for Tamar became greater than his love for her. "Arise, be gone," he said. "No, my brother," she answered, "for sending me away is a greater wrong than the other which you did to me." But he would not listen, and to his servant he said, "Put this woman out of my presence, and bolt the door after her." Tamar put ashes on her head, and rent her long robe; and she laid her hand on her head, and went away, crying aloud. She dwelt, a desolate woman, in her brother Absalom's house.

When King David heard of all these things, he was very angry. But Absalom spoke to Amnon neither good nor bad, for he hated Amnon because he had forced his sister Tamar.

Two years later Absalom had sheepshearers at his lands at Baalhazor, and he invited all the king's sons. He came to the king and said, "Behold, your servant has sheepshearers; pray let the king and his household visit me."

"No, my son," replied the king, "let us not all go, lest we be burdensome."

Absalom pressed him, but the king would not go. "If not you," said Absalom, "pray let my brother Amnon go with us." And Absalom urged the king until he let Amnon and all his other sons go to Baalhazor. Then Absalom commanded his servants, "Mark when Amnon's heart is merry with wine, and when I say to you, 'Strike Amnon,' then kill him." So the servants did to Amnon as Absalom had commanded. Then the king's sons arose, and each mounted his mule and fled. When they brought the tidings to the king, they lifted up their voices and wept; and the king also and all his servants wept very bitterly.

Absalom fled to his grandfather Talmai king of Geshur and was there three years. David mourned for his son Amnon day after day, but he became comforted about him, seeing he was dead, and his spirit longed to go forth to Absalom. Now Joab perceived that the king's heart went out to Absalom, and he sent to Tekoa for a wise woman. "Behave like a woman who has been mourning many days for the dead," he said to her, "and go to the king and speak thus to him." So Joab put the words in her mouth.

When the woman of Tekoa came to the king, she fell on her face and did obeisance, and said, "Help, O king."

"What is your trouble?" the king asked.

"Alas," she said, "I am a widow, and I had two sons, and they quarreled with one another in the field. One struck the other and killed him. Now the whole family has risen against me, and they say, 'Give up your son, that we may kill him for the life of his brother.' And so they would destroy the heir also, and leave to my husband neither name nor remnant upon the face of the earth."

"Go to your house," the king said. "I will give orders about you."

"Pray let the king invoke the LORD," said the woman, "that the avenger of blood slay no more, and my son be not destroyed."

"As the LORD lives," the king replied, "not one hair of your son shall fall to the ground."

"Pray let your handmaid speak a word further to my lord the king," the woman said. "In giving this decision the king convicts himself, inasmuch as he does not bring his banished son home again. We must all die, we are like water spilt on the ground; but God will not take the life of him who brings home his banished one. Now I have come to say this because my lord the king is like the angel of God to discern good and evil." The king answered, "Do not hide anything from me. Is the hand of Joab with you in all this?"

"As surely as you live, my lord the king, one cannot hide anything from you. In order to change the course of affairs, your servant Joab put these words into my mouth."

Sending for Joab, the king said, "Behold now, I grant this; go, bring back the young man Absalom." Joab fell on his face and did obeisance, and blessed the king. Then he arose and went to Geshur, and brought Absalom to Jerusalem. "Let him dwell apart in his own house," said the king; "he is not to come into my presence." And so it was.

After Absalom had dwelt two full years in Jerusalem without coming into the king's presence, he sent for Joab, to intercede for him with the king. But Joab would not come. Absalom sent a second time, but still Joab would not come. Then Absalom said to his servants, "See, Joab's barley field is next to mine; go and set it on fire." So they set the field on fire. Then Joab went to Absalom. "Why have your servants set my field on fire?" he said. "Behold," Absalom answered, "I wanted to send you to the king to ask, 'Why have I come from Geshur? It would be better for me to be there still.' Now therefore let me go into his presence; and if there is guilt in me, let him kill me." Joab told the king, and David summoned Absalom. Coming to the king, Absalom bowed himself on his face to the ground before him; and the king kissed him.

IN ALL ISRAEL there was no one so much to be praised for his beauty as Absalom; from the sole of his foot to the crown of his head there was no blemish in him. And when he cut his hair (for at the end of every year he cut it when it was heavy on him), it weighed five pounds by the king's weight.

Now Absalom got himself a chariot and horses, and fifty men to run before him. He would rise early and stand by the gate, and when any man had a suit he wanted to bring before the king for judgment, Absalom would say to him, "See, your claims are good and right; but there is no man deputed by the king to hear you. Oh that I were judge in the land! Then every man might come to me, and I would give him justice." And whenever a man did obeisance to him, he would take hold of him, and kiss him. Thus Absalom did to all who

came to the king for judgment; so he stole
the hearts of the men of Israel.

After four years Absalom said to the
king, "While I dwelt at Geshur I vowed a
vow, saying, 'If the LORD will indeed bring
me back to Jerusalem, then I will offer
worship to the LORD.' Pray let me go and
pay my vow in Hebron." And the king
answered, "Go in peace." Absalom took
with him two hundred men from Jerusalem, invited guests, who went in their simplicity and knew nothing. But Absalom
sent secret messengers throughout Israel,
saying, "As soon as you hear the sound
of the trumpet, then say, 'Absalom is
king at Hebron!' " And while he was offering the sacrifices at Hebron, he sent
for Ahithophel, David's counselor. And
the conspiracy grew strong, and the people with Absalom kept increasing.

At last messengers came to David, saying, "The hearts of the men of Israel have
gone after Absalom." And David said to
all who were with him at Jerusalem,
"Arise, and let us flee, lest Absalom overtake us quickly, and smite the city with the
sword." So the king went forth with his

household, leaving ten concubines to keep the house. At the last house of the city he halted while all his servants and all the Cherethites and Pelethites, and all the six hundred Gittites who had followed him from Gath, passed on before him. Then the king crossed the brook Kidron, and all the country wept aloud as he passed on toward the wilderness.

Abiathar and Zadok the priests came up, bearing the ark of God, and they set it down until the people had all passed out of the city. Then the king said to Zadok, "Carry the ark of God back into the city. If I find favor in the eyes of the LORD, he will bring me back and let me see it. Go back to the city in peace, you and Abiathar, with Ahimaaz your son, and Jonathan the son of Abiathar. I will wait by the Jordan, at the fords of the wilderness, until word comes from you." So Zadok and Abiathar carried the ark of God back to Jerusalem; and they remained there.

But David, barefoot and weeping, climbed the Mount of Olives, and all the people with him covered their heads and wept. And it was told David that his coun-

selor Ahithophel was among the conspira-
tors. "O LORD," David said, "I pray thee,
turn the counsel of Ahithophel into fool-
ishness." When David came to the summit, behold, Hushai the Archite, his other
counselor, came to meet him with his coat
torn and earth upon his head. David said
to him, "If you go on with me, you will be
a burden to me. But if you return to the
city and say to Absalom, 'O king, as I have
been your father's servant in time past, so
now I will be your servant,' then you will
defeat for me the counsel of Ahithophel.
Are not Zadok and Abiathar the priests
with you there? Whatever you hear from
the king's house, tell it to them. By their
two sons you shall send me everything you
hear." So Hushai came into Jerusalem just
as Absalom was entering the city.

When King David came to Bahurim,
near the border, there came out a man of
the family of Saul whose name was Shimei.
As he came he cursed continually, threw
stones at David, and at all the mighty men
who were on his right hand and on his left.
"Begone, begone, you worthless fellow!"
Shimei shouted. "The LORD has avenged

upon you all the blood of the house of Saul and given the kingdom to your son Absalom. See, your ruin is on you, for you are a man of blood."

"Why should this dead dog curse my lord the king?" said Abishai. "Let me go over and take off his head."

"Behold," said the king, "my own son seeks my life; how much more now may this Benjaminite! Let him alone, and let him curse; for the LORD has bidden him. It may be that the LORD will look upon my affliction and repay me with good for this cursing of me today." So David and his men went on the road, while Shimei went along on the hillside opposite and cursed as he went and threw stones and dust at him. The king and the people with him arrived weary at the Jordan; and there he refreshed himself.

Now Absalom and his people, the men of Israel, came to Jerusalem, and Ahithophel with him. And Hushai, David's counselor, came to Absalom. "Long live the king! Long live the king!" he cried.

"Is this your loyalty to my father?" Absalom asked.

"He whom the LORD and all Israel have chosen, his I will be," Hushai answered. "As I have served your father, so I will serve you." Then Absalom said to Ahithophel, "Give your counsel. What shall we do?"

"Go in to your father's concubines," said Ahithophel, "and all Israel will hear that you have made yourself odious to him, and our hands will be strengthened." So they pitched a tent for Absalom upon the roof, and he went in to his father's concubines in the sight of all Israel.

In those days the counsel of Ahithophel was as if one consulted the oracle of God; it was so esteemed by both David and Absalom. Now Ahithophel said to Absalom, "Let me set out with twelve thousand men tonight and come upon David while he is weary and discouraged, and throw him and all his people into a panic. I will strike down the king only, and I will bring the people back to you as a bride comes home to her husband." The advice pleased Absalom and the elders of Israel. But Absalom said, "Call Hushai the Archite also, and let us hear what he has to say." When

Hushai came, Absalom said, "Thus has Ahithophel spoken; shall we do as he advises? If not, you speak."

"This time," said Hushai, "the counsel of Ahithophel is not good. Your father and his men are mighty men, and they are enraged, like a bear robbed of her cubs. Besides, your father is expert in war; he will not spend the night with the people. My counsel is that all Israel be gathered to you, from Dan to Beer-sheba, as the sand by the sea for multitude, and that you go to battle in person. So we shall come upon him as the dew falls on the ground; and of him and all his men not one will be left." And Absalom and the elders said, "The counsel of Hushai the Archite is better than the counsel of Ahithophel." When Ahithophel saw that his good counsel was not followed, he went off home to his own city. He set his house in order, and then he hanged himself and was buried in the tomb of his father.

But Hushai did not know that the LORD had ordained to defeat the counsel of Ahithophel. He said to Zadok and Abiathar, "Send quickly to your sons that they may tell David, 'Do not lodge tonight at the fords of the wilderness, but by all means pass over the water, lest you and all your people be swallowed up tonight.' " So David and all the people with him crossed the Jordan; and they came to Mahanaim in Gilead. And Absalom also crossed the Jordan with the men of Israel, and encamped in the land of Gilead, having set Amasa his cousin over his army.

Then David mustered his men and sent forth the army, one third under the command of Joab, one third under Joab's brother Abishai, and one third under Ittai the Gittite, who with the men of Gath had been loyal to David. "I myself will also go out with you," the king said. "You shall not go out," the men told him. "If half of us die, they will not care about us. But you are worth ten thousand of us; therefore it is better that you send us help from the city."

"Whatever seems best to you I will do," the king replied. So he stood by the gate at Mahanaim, while the army marched out by its hundreds and its thousands. "Deal gently for my sake with the young man

Absalom," the king ordered his three commanders. And all the people heard him.

So the army went out into the field against Absalom, and the battle was fought in the forest nearby. Absalom's men were defeated there by the servants of David, and the slaughter was great on that day. The battle spread over the face of all the country; the forest devoured more people than the sword.

Now Absalom was riding upon his mule, and the mule chanced to go under the thick branches of a great oak. Absalom's head caught fast in the branches, and he was left hanging between heaven and earth, while the mule under him went on. One of David's servants saw it, and told Joab. "What, you saw him!" cried Joab. "Why then did you not strike him there to the ground? I would have been glad to give you ten pieces of silver."

"Even for a thousand pieces of silver I would not put forth my hand against the king's son; for in our hearing the king commanded you to protect him."

"I will not waste time like this with you," said Joab. He took three darts and went and thrust them into Absalom's heart while he was still alive in the oak. Then ten of Joab's young men surrounded Absalom and struck him, and killed him. Joab blew the trumpet, and the troops came back from the pursuit. They took Absalom and threw him into a pit in the forest, and raised over him a great heap of stones; and his men fled every one to his own home.

AT MAHANAIM, DAVID was sitting by the gate. The watchman went up to the roof of the gate, and he called out to tell the king that he saw a man running alone. "If he is alone," said the king, "there are tidings in his mouth." The runner came apace, and drew near. Now the watchman called again and said, "See, another man running alone!"

"He also brings tidings," said the king.

"I think the running of the foremost is like the running of Ahimaaz the son of Zadok," the watchman said. "He is a good messenger," said the king, "and comes with good tidings."

Then Ahimaaz came and cried out to

the king, "All is well." And he bowed before the king with his face to the earth and said, "Blessed be the LORD, who has delivered up the men who raised their hand against my lord the king."

"Is it well with the young man Absalom?" the king asked.

"When Joab sent me, I saw a great tumult," Ahimaaz replied, "but I do not know what it was."

"Turn aside," the king said, "and stand here." So Ahimaaz turned aside, and stood still. Then the second messenger came. "Good tidings for my lord the king!" he cried. "For the LORD has delivered you this day from the power of all who rose up against you."

"Is it well with the young man Absalom?" asked the king.

"May the enemies of my lord the king, and all who rise up against you for evil, be like that young man," the messenger replied.

The king was deeply moved and went up to the chamber over the gate and wept; and as he went, he said, "O my son Absalom, my son, my son Absalom! Would I had died instead of you, O Absalom, my son, my son!"

So THE KING came back to the Jordan; and the men of Judah came to meet him and to bring him across the river. And all the people of Judah, and also half the people of Israel, brought him on his way.

Now there happened to be there a worthless fellow, Sheba, the son of Bichri, a Benjaminite; and he blew the trumpet and then said, "We have no portion in David, nor inheritance in the son of Jesse; every man to his tents, O Israel!" So all the men of Israel withdrew from David and followed Sheba. But the men of Judah followed their king steadfastly from the Jordan to Jerusalem.

When David came to his house there, he took the ten concubines he had left to care for it and put them in a house under guard. He provided for them, but did not go in to them, so they were shut up until the day of their death, living as if in widowhood. Then David said to Abishai, "Sheba the son of Bichri will do us more harm than Absalom; take the army and pursue him." So Abishai went out from Jerusalem with Joab his brother and all the mighty men, and they pursued Sheba northward through all the tribes of Israel to Abel of Beth-maacah; and they besieged him there. They cast up a mound against the rampart, and were battering the wall when a wise woman called from the city for Joab. He came near her, and the woman said, "Listen to the words of your maidservant. I am one of those who are peaceable and faithful in Israel. You seek to destroy a city which is a mother in Israel; why will you swallow up the heritage of the LORD?"

"Far be it from me that I should swallow up or destroy!" Joab answered. "But a man called Sheba has lifted up his hand against King David; give him up, and I will withdraw from the city."

"Behold," said the woman, "his head shall be thrown to you over the wall." She went to all the people of the city in her wisdom, and they cut off Sheba's head and threw it out. So Joab blew the trumpet; they dispersed from the city and returned to Jerusalem to the king.

NOW THE KING said to Joab and the commanders of the army, "Go through all the tribes of Israel, from Dan to Beer-sheba, and number the people, that I may know their number." But Joab said, "May the LORD add to the people a hundred times as many as they are, but why does my lord the king delight in this thing?" But David's word prevailed, so Joab and his commanders went out to number the people of Israel. When they had gone through all the land, they came to Jerusalem after nine months and twenty days, and Joab gave the sum of the numbering to the king: in Israel there were eight hundred thousand men who drew the sword, and the men of Judah were five hundred thousand. But David's heart smote him after he had numbered the people, and he said to the LORD, "I have sinned greatly, O LORD; I pray thee, take away the iniquity of thy servant; for I have done very foolishly."

So the LORD sent a pestilence upon Israel, and there died seventy thousand of the people from Dan to Beer-sheba. The angel of the LORD was by the threshing floor of Araunah the Jebusite, and he was stretching forth his hand to destroy Jerusalem when David spoke to the LORD. "Lo, I have sinned," he said, "and I have done wickedly; but these sheep, what have they done? Let thy hand, I pray thee, be against me." The prophet Gad came that day to David, and said, "Go up, rear an altar to the LORD on the threshing floor of Araunah the Jebusite." So David went up as the LORD commanded. When Araunah saw the king and his servants coming up, he did obeisance, asking, "Why has my lord the king come to his servant?"

"To buy the threshing floor of you," David replied, "in order to build an altar to the LORD, that the plague may be averted from the people."

"Let my lord the king take the oxen for the burnt offering," said Araunah, "and the threshing sledges and the yokes of the oxen for the wood. All this, O king, Araunah gives to the king."

"No," said the king; "but I will buy it of you for a price; I will not offer burnt offerings to the LORD which cost me nothing." So David bought the threshing floor and the oxen, and he built there an altar to the LORD, and offered burnt offerings and peace offerings. So the plague was averted.

THIS IS THE oracle of David, the son of Jesse, the oracle of the man who was raised on high, the anointed of the God of Jacob, the sweet psalmist of Israel: "The Spirit of the LORD speaks by me; his word is upon my tongue. The God of Israel has said to me: 'When one rules justly over men, ruling in the fear of God, he dawns on them like the morning light, like the sun shining forth upon a cloudless morning, like rain that makes grass to sprout.'
"Yea, does not my house stand so with God? For he has made with me an everlasting covenant, ordered in all things and secure. But godless men are all like thorns; for they cannot be taken with the hand, or a man touch them except with the shaft of a spear; and they must be destroyed with fire."

1 KINGS

In the two books of Kings, originally a single book in Hebrew, the history of Israel is continued. This book opens with the last days of King David, and continues with the reign of King Solomon and the building of the temple in Jerusalem. After Solomon's death, what had been a single nation splits into two separate kingdoms, Judah and Israel. Through the remainder of the book the successive rulers in each kingdom are treated alternately. While the author evidently had access to several purely historical sources, his main interest is religious. He ascribes a dominant role to the prophet Elijah, and he judges every king by his obedience to God's commandments and his rejection of idol worship. By that standard, all the kings of Israel fail, and only two kings of Judah are thoroughly good, Hezekiah and Josiah. The author's message, reflecting the theme of Deuteronomy, is that national success depends on obedience to the will of God, while abandonment of religious faith inevitably brings divine punishment. The bulk of 1 and 2 Kings seems to have been written about 600 B.C., with additions made some fifty years later.

––––––––––––

Now KING DAVID was old and advanced in years, and although they covered him with clothes, he could not get warm. Therefore his servants said to him, "Let a young maiden be sought to wait upon my lord the king and be his nurse; let her lie in your bosom, that you may be warm." So they sought throughout all Israel and found Abishag the Shunammite, and brought her to the king. She was very beautiful, and she became the king's nurse and ministered to him; but the king knew her not.

Now Adonijah the son of David, born

next after Absalom, exalted himself, saying, "I will be king." He was a very handsome man, and his father had never displeased him by asking, "Why have you done thus and so?" He prepared chariots and horsemen, with fifty men to run before him, and he conferred with Joab and with Abiathar the priest, and they followed him. But Zadok the priest, and Benaiah the commander of the king's bodyguard, and Nathan the prophet, and David's mighty men were not with him. Adonijah sacrificed sheep and oxen at En-rogel, outside Jerusalem, and he invited all his brothers except Solomon, and all the royal officials of Judah.

Then Nathan said to Bathsheba the mother of Solomon, "Have you not heard that Adonijah has become king and David does not know it? Go in at once to King David and say, 'Did you not swear to your maidservant, saying, "Solomon your son shall reign after me"? Why then is Adonijah king?' "

Bathsheba went to the king in his chamber, where Abishag was ministering to him. "My lord," she said, "you swore to your maidservant, saying, 'Solomon your son shall reign after me.' But now, behold, Adonijah is king. My lord the king, the eyes of all Israel are upon you, to tell them who shall sit on the throne after you. Otherwise, when my lord sleeps with his fathers, I and my son Solomon will be in danger."

"As the LORD lives," the king said, "as I swore to you that Solomon should reign after me, even so will I do this day." Then he summoned Zadok, Nathan, and Benaiah. "Take with you my bodyguard," he said, "and cause Solomon my son to ride on my own mule, and bring him down to Gihon; and let Zadok and Nathan there anoint him king over Israel; then blow the trumpet and say, 'Long live King Solomon!' For I have appointed him to be king over Israel and Judah in my stead."

"Amen!" said Benaiah. "May the LORD make his throne greater than the throne of my lord King David."

ADONIJAH AND HIS guests, as they finished feasting, heard playing on pipes and rejoicing. "What does this uproar in the city mean?" said Joab. While he was still speaking, Jonathan the son of Abiathar came. "Our lord King David has made Solomon king," he said. "Zadok and Nathan have anointed him at Gihon, and they have gone up from there rejoicing, so that the city is in an uproar. This is the noise that you have heard."

Then all the guests of Adonijah trembled and rose, and each went his own way. Adonijah feared Solomon, and he went to the tent of the LORD and caught hold of the horns of the altar, saying, "Let King Solomon swear to me that he will not slay me with the sword." And it was told Solomon, and he said, "If he prove to be a worthy man, not one of his hairs shall fall to the earth; but if wickedness is found in him, he shall die." Then they brought Adonijah down from the altar, and he came and did obeisance to the king; and Solomon said to him, "Go to your house."

When David's time to die drew near, he charged Solomon, saying, "I am about to go the way of all the earth. Be strong, and show yourself a man, and walk in the ways of the LORD and keep his commandments, as it is written in the law of Moses, that you may prosper in all that you do and that the LORD may establish his word concerning me, saying, 'If your sons take heed to their way, to walk before me in faithfulness with all their heart, there shall not fail you a man on the throne of Israel.' Moreover, you know what Joab did to me, how he murdered Abner, the commander of the army of Israel, avenging in time of peace blood which had been shed in war, and putting innocent blood upon me. Do not let his gray head go down to Sheol in peace." Then David slept with his fathers, and was buried in the city of David; and Solomon sat upon his throne.

Now Adonijah came to Bathsheba the mother of Solomon. "You know that the kingdom was mine," he said, "and that all Israel fully expected me to reign; however, the kingdom has turned about and become my brother's, for it was his from the LORD. And now I have one request to make of you; pray ask King Solomon—he will not refuse you—to give me Abishag the Shunammite as my wife."

"Very well," Bathsheba replied. "I will

speak for you to the king." She went to King Solomon, and the king rose and bowed to her; then he had a seat brought, and she sat on his right. "I have one small request to make of you," she said. "Let Abishag the Shunammite be given to Adonijah your brother as his wife."

"And why do you ask this for Adonijah?" King Solomon answered. "Ask for him the kingdom also; for he is my elder brother, and on his side are Abiathar and Joab. God punish me if this word does not cost Adonijah his life this day!" So King Solomon sent Benaiah, and Benaiah struck Adonijah down, and he died. To Abiathar Solomon said, "Go to your estate. You deserve death, but I will not at this time put you to death, because you bore the ark of the LORD before David my father, and because you shared in all his affliction." Solomon expelled Abiathar as priest to the LORD, thus fulfilling the word the LORD had spoken concerning the house of Eli.

When the news came to Joab, he fled to the tent of the LORD and caught hold of the horns of the altar. When it was told King Solomon, he summoned Benaiah,

saying, "Go, strike Joab down." So Benaiah came to the tent of the LORD. "The
king commands, 'Come forth,'" he said.
"No, I will die here," Joab replied. Benaiah
brought word of this to the king. "Do as
he has said," the king replied. "Strike him
down there, and thus take away from my
father's house the guilt for the blood
which Joab shed without cause." So Benaiah went back and struck Joab down and
killed him; and he was buried in his own
house in the wilderness. Then the king put
Benaiah over the army in place of Joab,
and Zadok the priest in the place of
Abiathar; and so the kingdom was firmly
established in the hand of Solomon.

SOLOMON MADE A marriage alliance with
Pharaoh king of Egypt; he brought Pharaoh's daughter into the city of David until he had finished building his own
house and the house of the LORD. Now
Solomon loved the LORD, walking in the
statutes of David his father; but because
no temple had yet been built for the
LORD, he sacrificed at the high places. He
went to Gibeon to sacrifice (for that was

the great high place), and there the Lord appeared to him in a dream by night. "Ask what I should give you," the Lord said.

"O Lord my God," Solomon answered, "thou hast made thy servant king in place of David my father, although I do not know how to go out or come in. Give thy servant therefore an understanding mind to govern thy great people, that I may discern between good and evil."

It pleased the Lord that Solomon had asked this. "Because you have not asked for yourself long life or riches or the life of your enemies," he said, "behold, I now give you a wise and discerning mind, so that none like you has been before and none shall arise after you. I give you also what you have not asked, both riches and honor, so that no other king shall compare with you all your days. And if you will walk in my ways, keeping my commandments, as your father David walked, then I will lengthen your days."

Solomon awoke, and behold, it was a dream. He came to Jerusalem, and stood before the ark of the Lord, and offered up burnt offerings, and made a feast for all his servants.

Then two harlots came to the king. "Oh, my lord," one of them said, "this woman and I dwell in the same house, and I gave birth to a child there. On the third day after I was delivered, this woman also gave birth; and we two were alone in the house. This woman's son died in the night, because she lay on it; so she arose at midnight, and took my son from beside me while I slept, and laid it in her bosom, and laid her dead son in my bosom. When I rose in the morning to nurse my child, behold, it was dead; but when I looked at it closely, it was not the child that I had borne."

"The living child is mine," said the other woman.

"No, the dead child is yours," said the first.

Then the king said, "Bring me a sword." So a sword was brought, and the king said, "Divide the living child in two, and give half to one woman and half to the other."

Then the heart of the first woman yearned for her son. "Oh, my lord," she said, "give her the child, and by no means slay it."

"It shall be neither mine nor yours," said the other. "Divide it."

Then the king answered and said, "Give the living child to the first woman, and by no means slay it; she is its mother." All Israel heard of the judgment the king had rendered, and they stood in awe of him, because they perceived that the wisdom of God was in him.

KING SOLOMON HAD twelve officers over the twelve districts of Israel; each man had to provide food for the king and his household for one month in the year. Solomon's provision for one day was three hundred and thirty bushels of fine flour, and six hundred and sixty bushels of meal, ten fat oxen, and twenty pasture-fed cattle, a hundred sheep, besides harts, gazelles, roebucks, and fatted fowl. King Solomon also had four thousand stalls of horses for his chariots. And those officers supplying provisions let nothing be lacking. Barley and straw for the horses they brought to the place where it was required.

Judah and Israel were as many as the sand by the sea; they ate and drank and were happy. They dwelt in safety, from Dan even to Beer-sheba, every man under his vine and under his fig tree; for Solomon ruled over all the kingdoms from the Euphrates to the border of Egypt; they brought tribute and served Solomon all the days of his life. Solomon's wisdom surpassed the wisdom of all the people of the east, so that his fame was in all the nations round about. He also uttered three thousand proverbs, and his songs were a thousand and five; and men came from all peoples to hear his wisdom.

HIRAM KING OF Tyre sent his servants to Solomon when he heard that he was anointed king in place of his father; for Hiram always loved David. Solomon sent word back, "You know that my father could not build a house for the name of the LORD his God because of the warfare with which his enemies surrounded him. But now the LORD has given me rest on every side; there is neither adversary nor misfortune. And so I purpose to build a house for his name, as the LORD foretold to David my father. Now therefore command that cedars of Lebanon be cut for me; and my servants will join your servants, and I will pay you for your servants such wages as you set; for you know that no one knows how to cut timber like the Sidonians."

When Hiram heard these words, he rejoiced greatly, and sent to Solomon, saying, "I am ready to do all you desire. My servants shall bring the cedar and cypress timber down to the sea; and I will make it into rafts to go by sea to the place you direct, and I will have them broken up there." Year by year Hiram supplied Solomon with all the timber that he desired, while Solomon gave Hiram wheat and beaten oil for his household.

Solomon also raised a levy of thirty thousand men out of all Israel and placed Adoniram in charge. He sent them to Lebanon as forced labor, ten thousand a month in relays. And he had seventy thousand burden-bearers and eighty thousand hewers of stone in the hill country, with three thousand three hundred officers over the work. They quarried out great, costly stones for the foundation of the house. And so, in the four hundred and eightieth year after the people of Israel came out of Egypt, in the fourth year of his reign, in the month of Ziv, which is the second month, Solomon began to build the house of the LORD.

The temple was ninety feet long, thirty feet wide, and forty-five feet high. Solomon lined the walls with boards of cedar and covered the floor with cypress. The inner sanctuary he prepared in the innermost part of the house, to set there the ark of the covenant. It was thirty feet long, thirty feet wide, and thirty feet high; and he overlaid it with pure gold. In it he placed two cherubim of olivewood, each fifteen feet high. The wings of the two cherubim were spread out so that a wing of each touched each wall, and their other wings touched in the middle. And he overlaid the cherubim with gold.

Solomon was seven years in building the house of the LORD, and in the eleventh year of his reign, in the month of Bul, which is the eighth month, it was finished in all its parts. Then he assembled in Jerusalem the elders of Israel and the heads of the tribes, to bring the ark of the covenant up from the city of David, which is Zion, to the temple. The priests took up the ark and brought it to its place in the inner sanctuary, in the most holy place, underneath the wings of the cherubim. There was nothing in the ark except the two tablets of stone which Moses put there at Sinai, where the LORD made a covenant with the people of Israel when they came out of Egypt. And when the priests came out of the holy place, a cloud filled the house of the LORD, so that the priests could not minister; for the glory of the LORD filled his house.

Then Solomon knelt before the altar in the presence of all the assembly of Israel, and spread forth his hands toward heaven and said, "O LORD, God of Israel, the highest heaven cannot contain thee; how much less this house which I have built! Yet hearken thou to the supplication of thy servant and of thy people Israel when they pray toward this place; yea, hear thou in heaven; and when thou hearest, forgive.

For thou didst separate thy people from among all the peoples of the earth to be thy heritage, as thou didst declare through Moses, thy servant, when thou didst bring our fathers out of Egypt, O Lord God." As Solomon finished, he arose and stood before the altar and blessed the assembly. Then he and all Israel with him offered sacrifice before the Lord of twenty-two thousand oxen and a hundred and twenty thousand sheep. So the king and all the people dedicated the house of the Lord. Solomon held the feast at that time, a great assembly before the Lord, seven days. On the eighth day he sent the people away; and they went to their homes joyful and glad of heart.

When Solomon had finished building the house of the Lord and his own house and all that he desired to build, the Lord appeared to him a second time, as he had at Gibeon. And the Lord said, "I have heard your prayer, and I have consecrated this house which you have built. As for you, if you will walk before me with integrity of heart and uprightness, keeping my statutes and my ordinances, then I will establish your royal throne over Israel for ever, as I promised David your father. But if you turn aside from following me, you or your children, and go and worship other gods, then I will cut off Israel from the land which I have given them. The house which I have consecrated for my name will become a heap of ruins, and Israel will become a proverb and a byword among all peoples."

Now WHEN THE queen of Sheba heard of the fame of Solomon, she came to test him with hard questions. With a great retinue she came to Jerusalem, with camels bearing spices, gold, and precious stones, and when she met Solomon, she told him all that was on her mind. Solomon answered all her questions; there was nothing he could not explain to her. When the queen had seen all his wisdom, the palace he had built, and his manner of life, she said to him, "I did not believe the reports of your prosperity and your wisdom until my own eyes had seen it; and, behold, the half was not told me. Happy are your wives! Happy are these your servants, who continually stand before you and hear your wisdom! Blessed be the LORD your God, who has delighted in you!" Then she gave the king a very great quantity of gold and precious stones, and an abundance of spices. And the king gave to the queen of Sheba all that she desired before she went back to her own land.

Now the weight of gold that came to Solomon in one year was six hundred and sixty-six talents, besides that which came from the traders and all the kings of Arabia and the governors of the land. All the king's drinking vessels were of gold; silver was not considered as anything in the days of Solomon. For the king had a fleet of ships of Tarshish at sea with the fleet of Hiram, and every three years it came bringing gold, silver, ivory, apes, and peacocks.

Now Solomon loved many foreign women from the nations round about, concerning which the LORD had said, "You shall not enter into marriage with them, for surely they will turn away your heart after their gods." But Solomon clung to them in love. He had seven hundred wives, princesses, and three hundred concubines; and when he was old, his wives turned away his heart after other gods, and he was not wholly true to the LORD his God, as was David his father. For Solomon built a high place for Chemosh the abomination of Moab, and for Molech the abomination of the Ammonites, on the mountain east of Jerusalem. And so he did for all his foreign wives who sacrificed to their gods.

So Solomon did what was evil in the sight of the LORD, and the LORD was angry, and said to him, "Since you have not kept my covenant and my statutes, I will surely tear the kingdom from you and will give it to your servant." Then the LORD raised up an adversary against Solomon, Jeroboam the son of Nebat. When Solomon saw that the man Jeroboam was very able and industrious, he gave him charge over the forced labor of the house of Joseph.

About that time Jeroboam went out of Jerusalem, and the prophet Ahijah the Shilonite found him on the road. The two of them were alone in the open country, and Ahijah, who had clad himself in a new cloak, laid hold of it and tore it into twelve pieces. "Take for yourself ten pieces," he said to Jeroboam; "for thus says the LORD, 'Behold, I am about to tear the kingdom from the hand of Solomon, because he has forsaken me and worshiped foreign gods. Nevertheless, for the sake of David my servant I will not take the whole kingdom out of his hand during the days of his life, but I will take it out of his son's hand, and will give it to you, ten tribes. Yet to his son I will give one tribe, that David may always have a lamp before me in Jerusalem. You shall be king over Israel, and if you will keep my statutes and my commandments, as David my servant did, I will be with you, and will build you an enduring house.' " Solomon sought therefore to kill Jeroboam; but Jeroboam fled to Shishak king of Egypt.

Now the rest of the acts of Solomon, and all that he did, and his wisdom, are they not written in the book of the acts of Solomon? After he had reigned over all Israel for forty years, Solomon slept with his fathers, and was buried in the city of David; and Rehoboam his son reigned in his stead.

REHOBOAM WENT TO SHECHEM, for the northern tribes had come there to make him king; and when Jeroboam heard of it, he returned from Egypt. And they sent and called him; and Jeroboam and all the assembly of Israel came and said to Rehoboam, "Your father made our yoke heavy. Now therefore lighten his hard service, and we will serve you." And he said, "Depart for three days, then come again to me." When the people went away, Rehoboam conferred with the old men, the counselors of Solomon his father. "How do you advise me to answer this people?" he asked them. "If you will be a servant to this people," they answered, "and speak good words to them, they will be your servants for ever."

Then he asked counsel of the young men who had grown up with him. "Thus shall you speak," they replied. " 'My little finger is thicker than my father's loins. And now, whereas my father laid upon you a heavy yoke, I will add to it. My father chastised you with whips, but I will chastise you with scorpions.' "

Jeroboam and all the people came to

Rehoboam the third day, as he had said. And the king spoke to them harshly, according to the counsel of the young men. Now when Israel saw that the king did not hearken to them, the people answered him, "What portion have we in David? We have no inheritance in the son of Jesse. To your tents, O Israel! Look now to your own house, David." So Israel departed to their tents.

Then King Rehoboam sent Adoniram to them, who was taskmaster over the forced labor; but they stoned him to death, and the king made haste to mount his chariot to flee to Jerusalem. So Rehoboam reigned over the people who dwelt in the cities of Judah, and so Israel has been in rebellion against the house of David to this day.

Now they called Jeroboam to the assembly and made him king over all Israel. None followed the house of David, but the tribe of Judah only.

When Rehoboam returned to Jerusalem, he assembled all the house of Judah to fight to restore Israel to his rule. But the word of God came to Shemaiah the man of God: "Say to Rehoboam, king of Judah, and to the rest of the people, 'Thus says the LORD: You shall not go up or fight against your kinsmen. Return every man to his home, for this thing is from me.' " So they hearkened to the word of the LORD and went home again.

THEN JEROBOAM DWELT in Shechem, in the hill country of Ephraim; and he said in his heart, "If this people go up to offer sacrifices in the house of the LORD at Jerusalem, their hearts will turn again to Rehoboam, and they will kill me and return to the house of David." So Jeroboam took counsel, and made two calves of gold; he set one in Bethel and the other in Dan. He also built temples on high places, and appointed priests who were not Levites. And this thing became a sin.

"You have gone up to Jerusalem long enough," Jeroboam said to the people. "Behold your gods, O Israel, who brought you up out of the land of Egypt." Then he ordained a feast for the people of Israel at Bethel, and he went up to the altar that he had made to burn incense. And behold, a man of God came out of Judah to Bethel, and the man cried against the altar and said, "O altar, altar, thus says the LORD: 'Behold, a son shall be born to the house of David, Josiah by name; and he shall sacrifice upon you the priests of the high places who burn incense upon you, and men's bones shall be burned upon you.' And this is the sign that the LORD has spoken: 'Behold, the altar shall be torn down, and the ashes that are upon it shall be poured out.' "

Jeroboam stretched out his hand against the man of God, saying, "Lay hold of him." But his hand dried up, so that he could not draw it back. The altar also was torn down, and the ashes poured out from it, according to the sign the man of God had given. Then the king said to the man, "Entreat now the favor of the LORD your God and pray for me, that my hand may be restored." So the man entreated the LORD; and the king's hand became as it was before. "Come home with me and refresh yourself," said the king, "and I will give you a reward."

"If you give me half your house," replied the man of God, "I will not go in with you, nor eat bread or drink water in this place; for so was it commanded me by the word of the LORD." So he departed.

Now Jeroboam did not turn from his evil way, but consecrated any from among the people who desired to be priests of the high places. And this thing became sin to the house of Jeroboam, so as to cut it off and destroy it from the face of the earth.

At that time Abijah the son of Jeroboam fell sick, and Jeroboam said to his wife, "Arise, and go to Shiloh to Ahijah the prophet, who said of me that I should be king over this people. Take with you ten loaves, some cakes, and a jar of honey; he will tell you what shall happen to the child." In Shiloh she came to the house of Ahijah. Now Ahijah could not see, for his eyes were dim from age, and the LORD said to him, "Behold, the wife of Jeroboam is coming to inquire concerning her son. Thus and thus shall you say to her."

When she came, she pretended to be another woman. But when Ahijah heard the sound of her feet at the door, he said,

"Come in, wife of Jeroboam; why do you pretend to be another? I am charged with heavy tidings for you. Go, tell Jeroboam, 'Thus says the LORD, the God of Israel: "I exalted you from among the people and made you leader over Israel; yet you have done evil above all that were before you and have made for yourself molten images, provoking me to anger. Therefore I will bring evil upon your house and will utterly consume it, as a man burns up dung until it is all gone." ' Arise therefore; go to your house. When your feet enter the city of Tirzah, the child shall die. Moreover, the LORD will smite the people of Israel and root them out of this good land which he gave to their fathers, and scatter them beyond the Euphrates, because of the sins of Jeroboam, and those which he made Israel to sin." Then Jeroboam's wife departed; and as she came to the threshold of her house, the child died, according to the word of the LORD.

Now the rest of the acts of Jeroboam, how he warred and how he reigned, are written in the Book of the Chronicles of the Kings of Israel. And the time that Jeroboam reigned was twenty-two years; and he slept with his fathers, and Nadab his son reigned in his stead.

Now REHOBOAM THE son of Solomon reigned seventeen years in Jerusalem. Judah provoked the LORD by their sins more than all that their fathers had done. For they also placed idols on the high places, and there were male cult prostitutes in the land. They did according to all the abominations of the nations which the LORD drove out before the people of Israel.

In the fifth year of King Rehoboam, Shishak king of Egypt came up against Jerusalem; he took away the treasures of the house of the LORD and of the king's house; he took away everything. And there was war between Rehoboam and Jeroboam continually.

Then Rehoboam slept with his fathers, and Abijam his son reigned in his stead. Abijam reigned for three years in Jerusalem, and he walked in all the sins which his father did before him. Nevertheless, for David's sake the LORD gave him a lamp in Jerusalem, setting up his son after him, because David did what was right in the eyes of the LORD all the days of his life, except in the matter of Uriah the Hittite.

NADAB THE SON of Jeroboam reigned over Israel two years, and walked in the sinful way of his father. Then Baasha, of the house of Issachar, conspired against him. Now Nadab and his army were laying siege to Gibbethon, which belonged to the Philistines; and Baasha killed him there and reigned at Tirzah in his stead. As soon as Baasha was king, he killed all the house of Jeroboam, leaving not one that breathed, until he had destroyed it according to the word of the LORD. Then Baasha slept with his fathers, and Elah his son reigned in his stead; but Zimri, commander of half his chariots, conspired against Elah. When Elah was at Tirzah, drinking himself drunk in the house of his chamberlain, Zimri came in and struck him down and killed him, and reigned in his stead for seven days.

Now the troops were again encamped against the Philistines at Gibbethon, and when they heard that Zimri had killed the king, they made Omri, the commander of the army, king over Israel that day in the camp. So Omri took the army and went up from Gibbethon and besieged Tirzah. When Zimri saw that the city was taken, he went into the king's house and burned it over him and died.

Omri reigned for twelve years over Israel, six years in Tirzah. Then he bought the hill of Samaria for two talents of silver; and he fortified it, and called the city which he built Samaria, after the name of Shemer, the owner of the hill. Omri did what was evil in the sight of the LORD, more than all who were before him. And he slept with his fathers, and was buried in Samaria; and Ahab his son reigned in his stead.

AHAB REIGNED OVER Israel in Samaria twenty-two years. As if it were a light thing for him to walk in the sins of Jeroboam, he also took for wife Jezebel the daughter of the king of the Sidonians, and he went and served Baal, and he built a temple for Baal in Samaria. Ahab did more to provoke the LORD to anger than all the kings of Israel who were before him. In his days Hiel of Bethel built Jericho; he laid its foundation at the cost of Abiram his first-born, and set up its gates at the cost of his youngest son Segub, according to the word of the LORD, which he spoke by Joshua the son of Nun.

Now Elijah the prophet said to Ahab, "As the LORD the God of Israel lives, there shall be neither dew nor rain these years, except by my word." Then the word of the LORD came to Elijah, "Depart from here and hide yourself by the brook Cherith, east of the Jordan. You shall drink from the brook, and I have commanded the ravens to feed you there." So Elijah went and dwelt by the brook Cherith, and the ravens brought him bread and meat in the morning and in the evening. After a while the brook dried up, because there was no rain in the land; and again the word of the LORD came, "Arise, go to Zarephath, which belongs to Sidon, and dwell there. Behold, I have commanded a widow there to feed you." So Elijah went, and at the gate of Zarephath a widow was gathering sticks.

"Bring me a little water in a vessel," he

called to her, "and bring me also a morsel of bread."

"As the LORD lives," she said, "I have nothing baked, only a handful of meal in a jar, and a little oil in a cruse; and now I am gathering sticks, that I may go in and prepare it for myself and my son."

"Fear not," Elijah replied. "Go and do as you have said; but first make a little cake for me, and afterward make for yourself and your son. For thus says the LORD, 'The jar of meal shall not be spent, and the cruse of oil shall not fail, until the day the LORD sends rain upon the earth.' " The woman did as Elijah said; and she, and he, and her household ate for many days.

After this the son of the woman became ill, so that there was no breath left in him. "What have you against me, O man of God?" she cried to Elijah. "You have come to me to bring my sin to remembrance, and to cause the death of my son!"

"Give me your son," Elijah said; and he took up the child and laid him upon his own bed. Then he stretched himself upon the child three times. "O LORD my God," he cried, "let this child's soul come into him again." The LORD hearkened to the voice of Elijah; and the soul of the child came into him again. Then Elijah brought him to the widow. "See, your son lives," he said. "Now I know that you are a man of God," she said, "and that the word of the LORD in your mouth is truth."

In the third year of the drought the word of the LORD came to Elijah, saying, "Go, show yourself to Ahab; and I will send rain upon the earth." So Elijah went to show himself to Ahab. The famine was severe in Samaria, and Ahab called Obadiah, who was over his household. (Obadiah revered the LORD greatly; and when Jezebel persecuted the prophets of the LORD, Obadiah took a hundred of them and hid them in a cave, and fed them with bread and water.) "Go through the land," said Ahab. "Go to all the springs of water and to all the valleys; perhaps we may find grass to keep the horses and mules alive." As Obadiah was on the way, behold, Elijah met him. Obadiah recognized him and fell on his face. "Is it you, my lord Elijah?" he said.

"It is I. Go, tell your lord, 'Behold, Elijah is here.' "

"Wherein have I sinned," Obadiah replied, "that you would give me into the hand of Ahab, to kill me? As the LORD lives, there is no nation whither Ahab has not sent to seek you; and now you say, 'Go, tell your lord that Elijah is here.' As soon as I have left you, the Spirit of the LORD will carry you whither I know not; and when Ahab cannot find you, he will kill me, although I have revered the LORD from my youth."

"As the LORD lives," Elijah replied, "I will surely show myself to him today." So Obadiah told Ahab; and Ahab went to meet Elijah. "Is it you, you troubler of Israel?" Ahab said when he saw Elijah.

"I have not troubled Israel," Elijah answered, "but you have, because you have forsaken the LORD and followed Baal. Now therefore send and gather all Israel to me at Mount Carmel, and the prophets of Baal, who eat at Jezebel's table." So Ahab gathered all the people and the prophets together at Mount Carmel. "How long will you go limping about with two different opinions?" Elijah cried to them. "If the LORD is God, follow him; but if Baal, then follow him." The people did not answer him a word.

Then Elijah said, "Only I am left a prophet of the LORD, but Baal's prophets are four hundred and fifty. Let two bulls be brought; and let them choose one and cut it in pieces and lay it on the wood, but put no fire to it; and I will prepare the other bull and lay it on the wood, and put no fire to it. And you call on your god and I will call on the LORD; the God who answers by fire, he is God."

"It is well spoken," the people answered.

The prophets of Baal took a bull and prepared it, and called on the name of Baal from morning until noon, saying, "O Baal, answer us!" But there was no voice, and no one answered.

"Cry aloud," Elijah mocked them, "for he is a god; either he is musing, or he is on a journey, or perhaps he is asleep and must be awakened." They raved on, and cut themselves after their custom until the blood gushed out, but there was no voice; no one heeded.

Then Elijah said to the people, "Come

near to me." And taking twelve stones, according to the number of the tribes of Israel, he built an altar in the name of the LORD, and made a trench about it. He put the wood in place, and cut the bull in pieces and laid it on the wood. "Fill four jars with water," he said, "and pour it on the offering, and on the wood." He had them do it a second time, and a third time, so that the water ran round about the altar, and filled the trench also.

Then Elijah came near and said, "O LORD, God of Abraham, Isaac, and Israel, let it be known this day that thou art God in Israel, and I am thy servant, and that I have done all these things at thy word. Answer me, O LORD, that this people may know thou art God." Then the fire of the LORD fell, and consumed the burnt offering, and the wood, and the stones, and licked up the water in the trench. And when the people saw it, they fell on their faces. "The LORD, he is God," they cried. "The LORD, he is God."

"Seize the prophets of Baal," Elijah told them; "let not one escape." And the people seized the prophets and brought them down to the brook Kishon, and killed them there.

Then Elijah went up to the top of Carmel and bowed himself down upon the earth. "Go up now," he said to his servant, "look toward the sea." The servant went up and looked. "There is nothing," he said. "Go again seven times," said Elijah. At the seventh time the servant said, "Behold, a little cloud like a man's hand is rising out of the sea." "Go up," said Elijah, "and say to Ahab, 'Prepare your chariot and go down, lest the rain stop you.'" In a little while the heavens grew black with clouds and wind, and there was a great rain. Ahab rode to Jezreel; but the hand of the LORD was on Elijah, and he girded up his loins and ran before Ahab to the entrance of the city.

AHAB TOLD HIS wife Jezebel all that Elijah had done, and how he had slain all the prophets of Baal. Jezebel sent a messenger to Elijah, saying, "May the gods punish me if I do not make your life as the life of the prophets of Baal by this time tomorrow." Then Elijah was afraid, and he arose and went for his life, and came to Beer-sheba, in Judah, and left his servant there.

But he himself went a day's journey into the wilderness, and came and sat under a broom tree; and he asked that he might die, saying, "It is enough; now, O LORD, take away my life; for I am no better than those who came before me." He lay down and slept; and behold, an angel touched him, and said, "Arise and eat." At his head there was a cake baked on hot stones and a jar of water. He ate and drank, and lay down again. The angel came a second time, and touched him, and said, "Arise and eat, else the journey will be too great for you." So he arose, and ate and drank, and went in the strength of that food forty days and forty nights to Sinai, the mount of God. He came to a cave, and lodged there; and behold, the word of the LORD came to him, saying, "What are you doing here, Elijah?"

"I have been very jealous for the LORD, the God of hosts," Elijah answered; "for the people of Israel have forsaken thy covenant, thrown down thy altars, and slain thy prophets with the sword; and I, even I only, am left; and they seek my life, to take it away." The LORD said, "Go forth, and stand upon the mount before me."

And behold, the LORD passed by, and a great and strong wind rent the mountains, but the LORD was not in the wind; and after the wind an earthquake, but the LORD was not in the earthquake; and after the earthquake a fire, but the LORD was not in the fire; and after the fire a still small voice. When Elijah heard it, he wrapped his face in his mantle.

"Go," the LORD said to him, "return on your way to Damascus; when you arrive, you shall anoint Hazael king over Syria; and Jehu the son of Nimshi you shall anoint king over Israel; and Elisha the son of Shaphat you shall anoint to be prophet in your place. And him who escapes from the sword of Hazael shall Jehu slay; and him who escapes from the sword of Jehu shall Elisha slay. Yet I will leave seven thousand in Israel, all the knees that have not bowed to Baal, and every mouth that has not kissed him."

So Elijah departed, and found Elisha the

son of Shaphat, who was plowing with twelve yoke of oxen; and he cast his mantle upon him. Elisha left the oxen and ran after Elijah. "Let me kiss my father and my mother," he said, "and then I will follow you." And Elijah replied, "Go back." So Elisha went back and took a yoke of oxen, and slew them, and boiled their flesh, and gave it to the people, and they ate. Then he arose and went after Elijah, and ministered to him.

Now NABOTH THE Jezreelite had a vineyard in Jezreel, beside the country palace of Ahab king of Samaria. "Give me your vineyard," Ahab said to him, "that I may have it for a vegetable garden, because it is near my house; and I will give you a better vineyard for it; or, if it seems good to you, I will give you its value in money." Naboth replied, "The LORD forbid that I should give you the inheritance of my fathers."

So Ahab went into his house vexed and sullen, and he lay down on his bed, and turned away his face, and would eat no food. "Why is your spirit so vexed?" asked Jezebel. When Ahab told her, she said,

"Do you govern Israel or not? Arise and eat, and let your heart be cheerful; I will give you Naboth's vineyard." She wrote letters in Ahab's name and sealed them with his seal, and she sent them to the elders of Jezreel. She wrote in the letters, "Proclaim a fast, and set Naboth on high among the people; then set two base fellows opposite him, and let them bring a charge against him, saying, 'You have cursed God and the king.' Then take him out and stone him to death." And the elders did as Jezebel had written. Then they sent to Jezebel, saying, "Naboth is dead." As soon as Jezebel heard this, she said to Ahab, "Arise, take possession of Naboth's vineyard, for he is dead." And Ahab did so.

Then the word of the LORD came to Elijah, saying, "Arise, go to meet Ahab king of Israel, who is in the vineyard of Naboth, where he has gone to take possession. And you shall say to him, 'Thus says the LORD: "Have you killed, and also taken possession? In the place where dogs licked up the blood of Naboth shall dogs lick your own blood." ' "

So Elijah went down to meet the king. "Have you found me, O my enemy?" said Ahab. "I have found you," Elijah answered, "because you have sold yourself to do what is evil in the sight of the LORD. Behold, I will utterly sweep you away; I will destroy every son of the house of Ahab for the anger you have provoked in me. And the LORD also has said, 'The dogs shall eat Jezebel within the bounds of Jezreel.'" For there was none who sold himself to do what was evil in the sight of the LORD like Ahab, whom Jezebel incited.

Now JEHOSHAPHAT THE great-grandson of Rehoboam began to reign over Judah in the fourth year of Ahab king of Israel. He did what was right in the sight of the LORD, although the people still sacrificed on the high places. He also made peace with the king of Israel and came to visit him. Then Ahab said to his servants, "Do you know that Ramoth-gilead belongs to us, yet we keep quiet and do not take it from the king of Syria?" And he said to Jehoshaphat, "Will you go with me to battle at Ramoth-gilead?"

"I am as you are," Jehoshaphat replied, "my people as your people, my horses as your horses. But inquire first for the word of the LORD." Gathering the prophets together, Ahab asked them, "Shall I go to battle against Ramoth-gilead, or shall I forbear?"

"Go up," they replied; "for the LORD will give it into the hand of the king." But Jehoshaphat said, "Is there not here another prophet of the LORD of whom we may inquire?"

"There is yet one man," said the king, "but I hate him, for he never prophesies good concerning me." Then he summoned an officer and said, "Bring quickly Micaiah the son of Imlah." Now Ahab and Jehoshaphat were sitting on their thrones, arrayed in their robes, outside the gate of Samaria; and all the prophets were prophesying before them, saying, "Go up to Ramoth-gilead and triumph; the LORD will give it into the hand of the king." The messenger who went to summon Micaiah said to him, "Behold, the words of the prophets with one accord are favorable to the king; let your word be like theirs, and speak favorably."

"As the LORD lives," Micaiah answered, "what the LORD says to me, that I will speak." When he came to King Ahab, the king said to him, "Micaiah, shall we go to Ramoth-gilead to battle, or shall we forbear?"

"Go up and triumph," Micaiah answered him. "The LORD will give it into the hand of the king."

"How many times shall I adjure you to speak nothing but the truth in the name of the LORD?" the king said.

Now Micaiah answered, "I saw Israel scattered upon the mountains, as sheep that have no shepherd; and the LORD said, 'These have no master; let each return to his home in peace.' "

"Did I not tell you," Ahab said to Jehoshaphat, "that he would not prophesy good concerning me, but evil?"

"Therefore hear the word of the LORD," Micaiah continued. "I saw the LORD sitting on his throne, and all the host of heaven standing on his right hand and on his left; and the LORD said, 'Who will entice Ahab, that he may go up and fall at Ramoth-gilead?' And a spirit came forward, saying, 'I will entice him. I will be a lying spirit in the mouth of all his prophets.' And the LORD said, 'Go forth and entice him.' Now therefore, behold, the LORD has put a lying spirit in the mouth of all these your prophets; the LORD has spoken evil concerning you."

Then Zedekiah the son of Chenaanah came near and struck Micaiah on the cheek, and said, "How did the Spirit of the LORD go from me to speak to you?" Micaiah answered, "You shall see on that day when you go into an inner chamber to hide yourself." And the king cried, "Seize Micaiah. Take him back to the city, and put him in prison, and feed him on bread and water until I return in peace."

"If you ever return in peace," Micaiah answered, "the LORD has not spoken by me." And he added, "Hear, all you peoples!"

The kings of Israel and Judah went up to Ramoth-gilead, and Ahab said to Jehoshaphat, "I will disguise myself to go into battle, but you shall wear your royal robes." So the king of Israel disguised himself, and they went into battle. Now the king of Syria had commanded his captains, "Fight with neither small nor great, but only with the king of Israel." When the captains saw Jehoshaphat in his robes, they said, "It is surely the king of Israel," and they turned to fight against him. But Jehoshaphat cried out, and when the captains saw that he was not the king of Israel, they turned away. Then a certain man drew his bow at a venture, and, unknowing, struck King Ahab between the joints of his armor. "Turn about," Ahab said to his chariot driver, "and carry me out of the battle, for I am wounded."

The battle grew hot that day. The king was propped up in his chariot facing the Syrians; the blood of his wound flowed into the bottom of the chariot, until at evening he died. And about sunset a cry went through the army, "Every man to his city!" King Ahab was brought to Samaria and buried there. They washed out the chariot by the pool of Samaria, and the dogs licked up his blood, according to the word of the LORD.

Now the rest of the acts of Ahab, all that he did, and the ivory house and the cities which he built, are they not written in the Book of the Chronicles of the Kings of Israel? So Ahab slept with his fathers; and Ahaziah his son reigned in his stead.

2 KINGS

The first part of the book describes the miracles performed by the prophet Elisha, successor to Elijah, among them cleansing a Syrian commander of leprosy. Elisha also directs Jehu to grasp the throne of Israel from the house of King Ahab and his Baal-worshiping queen, Jezebel. In Judah, where Baal-worship had been extended by Ahab's daughter, Athaliah, the rightful heir, King Joash, restores the worship of God in the temple.

The latter part of the book continues the story of the Hebrew monarchies. Assyria, growing in power, constantly threatens Israel, until at last King Shalmaneser conquers it in 721 B.C. Judah is also threatened in the time of King Hezekiah, but through the intervention of the prophet Isaiah, Jerusalem is wonderfully preserved.

And though King Josiah reforms and puri-
fies religious practice, the short-lived kings
who come after him are unable to hold out
against Egypt and Babylon. Finally, Judah
is conquered in 586 B.C. and its people are
exiled to Babylon.

Now Ahaziah fell through the lattice in
his upper chamber in Samaria and lay in-
jured; so he sent messengers, telling them,
"Go, inquire of Baal-zebub, the god of Ekron, whether I shall recover." But the angel of the Lord said to Elijah the prophet,
"Arise, go up to meet the messengers of
the king of Samaria, and say to them, 'Is it
because there is no God in Israel that you
are going to inquire of Baal-zebub?' Now
therefore thus says the Lord, 'You shall
not come down from the bed to which you
have gone, but you shall surely die.'" So
Elijah went.

The messengers returned to the king,
and they told him what had happened.
"What kind of man was he who told you
these things?" King Ahaziah asked. "He

wore a garment of haircloth," they replied, "with a girdle of leather about his loins." And the king said, "It is Elijah the Tishbite."

Then the king sent a captain and fifty men to Elijah, who was sitting on top of a hill. "O man of God," said the captain, "the king says, 'Come down.'" Elijah answered, "If I am a man of God, let fire come down from heaven and consume you." Then fire came down from heaven and consumed the captain and his fifty. The king sent another captain with his fifty, but again the fire of God came down and consumed them. Then the king sent a third captain with his fifty. But this captain fell on his knees before Elijah and entreated him, "I pray you, O man of God, let my life and the lives of these servants of yours be precious in your sight." Then the angel of the LORD said to Elijah, "Go down with him; do not be afraid of him." So Elijah arose and went down with the captain to King Ahaziah, and he said to the king, "Thus says the LORD, 'Because you have sent to inquire of Baal-zebub—is it because there is no God in Israel?—therefore you shall not come down from your bed, but you shall surely die.' " So Ahaziah died according to the word of the LORD, and Joram his brother became king of Israel in his stead, because Ahaziah had no son.

WHEN THE LORD was about to take Elijah up to heaven, he and Elisha were on their way from visiting the prophets in Gilgal. "Tarry here, I pray you," Elijah said to Elisha, "for the LORD has sent me as far as Bethel." Elisha answered, "As the LORD lives, and as you yourself live, I will not leave you." So they went down to Bethel, and there the prophets came out to Elisha. "Do you know," they said to him, "that today the LORD will take your master away from you?" And he answered, "Yes, I know it. Hold your peace."

Again Elijah said, "Elisha, tarry here, I pray you; for the LORD has sent me on to Jericho." But Elisha replied, "As the LORD lives, I will not leave you." So they came to Jericho, and the prophets there drew near to Elisha, and said, "Do you know that today the LORD will take your master away from you?" And he answered,

"Yes, I know it. Hold your peace."

Then Elijah said to him, "Tarry here, I pray you; for the LORD has sent me to the Jordan." But Elisha said, "As the LORD lives, I will not leave you." So the two of them went on. Fifty of the prophets also went, and stood at some distance from them as they were standing by the river Jordan. Then Elijah took his mantle and rolled it up and struck the water, and the water was parted, so that the two of them could go over on dry ground. When they had crossed, Elijah said to Elisha, "Ask what I should do for you, before I am taken from you."

"I pray you," said Elisha, "let me inherit a double share of your spirit."

"You have asked a hard thing," said Elijah; "yet, if you see me as I am being taken from you, it shall be so. But if you do not see me, it shall not be so."

As they went on, behold, a chariot of fire and horses of fire separated the two of them, and Elijah went up by a whirlwind into heaven. Elisha saw it. "My father, my father!" he cried; "the chariots of Israel and its horsemen!" And he saw Elijah no more. Then Elisha rent his clothes, and he took up the mantle of Elijah that had fallen from him, and he went back to the river Jordan. He struck the water with the mantle, saying, "Where is the LORD, the God of Elijah?" And the water was parted, and Elisha returned to the other side. When the prophets of Jericho saw him on their side, they said, "The spirit of Elijah rests on Elisha." And they bowed to the ground before him.

Now the men of the city said to Elisha, "Behold, the situation of this city is pleasant, as my lord sees; but the water is bad, and the land is unfruitful." Elisha said, "Bring me a new bowl, and put salt in it." When they had brought it, he went to the spring and threw salt in it. "Thus says the LORD," he said, "I have made this water wholesome; henceforth neither death nor miscarriage shall come from it." So the spring has been wholesome to this day, according to the word which Elisha spoke.

NOW THE WIFE of one of the prophets cried to Elisha, "Your servant my husband is dead. You know that he feared the LORD, but the creditor has come to take my two children to be his slaves."

"What shall I do for you?" Elisha asked. "Tell me, what have you in the house?" She answered, "I have nothing in the house, except a jar of oil." Then Elisha said, "Go outside; borrow empty vessels of all your neighbors—and not too few. Then go in and shut the door upon yourself and your sons, and pour into all these vessels; and when one is full, set it aside." She went from him and shut the door upon herself and her sons; and as she poured they brought the vessels to her. When all of them were full, the oil stopped flowing, and the woman came and told the man of God. "Go," he said, "sell the oil and pay your debts, and you and your sons can live on the rest."

One day Elisha went to Shunem. A wealthy woman who lived there urged him to eat some food. Whenever he passed that way, he would turn in at her house. She said to her husband, "Behold now, I perceive that this is a holy man of God. Let us make a small chamber on the roof, and put there for him a bed, a table, a chair, and a lamp, so that when he comes to us, he can go in there." One day Elisha came and turned into the chamber and rested there. "Call this Shunammite woman," he said to his servant Gehazi. When she stood before him, he said to her, "See, you have taken all this trouble for us; what is to be done for you? Shall I speak a word on your behalf to the king or to the commander of the army?"

"I dwell among my own people," she answered. "I am content." Later Elisha said to Gehazi, "What then is to be done for her?" Gehazi answered, "Well, she has no son, and her husband is old."

"Call her," said Elisha. And when she stood in the doorway, he said, "At this season, when the year comes round again, you shall embrace a son."

"No, my lord, O man of God," she said, "do not lie to your maidservant." But the woman conceived, and she bore a son about that time the following spring, as Elisha had said. When the child had grown, he went out one day to his father among the reapers. "Oh, my head, my head!" the child cried to his father. "Carry him to his mother," the father said to a servant. And when the servant brought him to his mother, the child sat on her lap till noon, and then he died.

The woman went up and laid him on the bed of the man of God, and shut the door upon him. Then she called to her husband, "Send me a servant and one of the asses, that I may quickly go to the man of God and come back again." She saddled the ass, and did not slacken her pace until she came to the man of God at Mount Carmel.

When Elisha saw her coming, he said to Gehazi, "Yonder is the Shunammite; run at once to meet her, and say, 'Is it well with you? Is it well with the child?' " She answered, "It is well." But when she came to the mountain to the man of God, she caught hold of his feet. Gehazi came to thrust her away. But the man of God said, "Let her alone, for she is in bitter distress; and the LORD has hidden it from me." Then the woman said, "Did I ask my lord for a son? Did I not say, 'Do not deceive me'?"

Elisha told Gehazi, "Take my staff in

your hand, and go with the woman and lay my staff upon the face of the child." But the mother said to Elisha, "As the LORD lives, I will not leave you." So he arose and followed her. Gehazi went on ahead and laid the staff upon the face of the child, but there was no sound or sign of life. He returned and told Elisha, "The child has not awaked."

When Elisha went into the chamber where the child was lying dead on his bed, he shut the door and prayed to the LORD. Then he lay upon the child, putting his mouth upon the child's mouth, his eyes upon his eyes, and his hands upon his hands; and as he stretched himself upon the child, its flesh became warm. Elisha got up and walked once to and fro in the house, and then he stretched himself again upon the child. The child sneezed seven times and opened his eyes. Elisha summoned Gehazi, saying, "Call this Shunammite." When she came to him, he said, "Take up your son." She fell at his feet, bowing to the ground; then she took up her son and went out.

When Elisha came again to Gilgal, there was famine in the land, and as the prophets were sitting before him, he said to his servant, "Set on the great pot, and boil pottage for the prophets." One of them went out into the field and gathered wild gourds and cut them up into the pot, not knowing what they were. Then they poured out pottage, but while they were eating, the prophets cried out, "O man of God, there is death in the pot!" And they could not eat it. "Then bring meal," Elisha said. He threw the meal into the pot, and said, "Pour out for the men, that they may eat." And now there was no harm in the pot.

A man came bringing bread of the first fruits, twenty loaves of barley, and fresh grain in his sack. "Give to the men, that they may eat," Elisha said. But the servant asked, "How am I to set this before a hundred men?" Elisha repeated, "Give it to them, for thus says the LORD, 'They shall eat and have some left.'" So the servant set it before them, and they ate, and had some left, according to the word of the LORD.

NAAMAN, COMMANDER OF the Syrian army, was in high favor with his master the king, because through him the LORD had given victory to Syria. He was a mighty man of valor, but he was a leper. Now the Syrians on one of their raids had carried off a little maid from the land of Israel, and she waited on Naaman's wife. "Would that my lord were with the prophet Elisha who is in Samaria!" she said to her mistress. "He would cure him of his leprosy." So Naaman told his lord, "Thus and so spoke the maiden from Israel." And the king of Syria said, "Go now, and I will send a letter to the king of Israel." Naaman went, taking with him talents of silver and shekels of gold and festal garments, and the letter to the king of Israel, which read, "I have sent to you Naaman my servant, that you may cure him of his leprosy."

When the king of Israel read the letter, he rent his clothes. "Am I God, to kill and to make alive," he said, "that this man sends word to me to cure a man of his leprosy? Only consider, and see how he is seeking a quarrel with me!" But when Elisha heard of this, he sent to the king, saying, "Why have you rent your clothes? Let Naaman come now to me, that he may know that there is a prophet in Israel." So Naaman came with his horses and chariots to the door of Elisha's house, and Elisha sent a messenger to him, saying, "Go and wash in the Jordan seven times, and your flesh shall be restored."

Naaman turned and went away in a rage. "Behold," he said, "I thought he would surely come out and call on the name of his God, and wave his hand over the place, and cure the leper. Are not the rivers of Damascus better than all the waters of Israel? Could I not wash in them and be clean?"

His servants came near and said to him, "My father, if the prophet had commanded you to do some great thing, would you not have done it? How much rather, then, when he says to you, 'Wash, and be clean'?" So Naaman went down and dipped himself seven times in the Jordan, and his flesh was restored like the flesh of a little child.

Then he and all his company returned and stood before Elisha. "Behold," he said,

"I know that there is no God in all the earth but in Israel; so accept now a present from your servant." And Elisha answered, "As the LORD lives, whom I serve, I will receive none." Then Naaman said, "If not, I pray you, let me have two mules' burden of earth; for henceforth I will not offer sacrifice to any god but the LORD. And when my master goes into the house of Rimmon to worship, leaning on my arm, and I bow myself there, may the LORD pardon your servant in this matter." Elisha answered, "Go in peace."

When Naaman had gone a short distance, Gehazi, Elisha's servant, said to himself, "See, my master has spared this Syrian in not accepting the gift that he brought. As the LORD lives, I will run after him and get something from him." When Naaman saw someone running after him, he alighted from the chariot. "Is all well?" he said. Gehazi answered, "All is well, but my master has sent me to say, 'There have just come to me from the hill country of Ephraim two young prophets; pray, give them a talent of silver and two festal garments.'" Naaman tied up the silver and garments in two bags, and laid them upon two of his servants; and they carried them before Gehazi. Near Elisha's house, Gehazi took them from their hands and sent the men away. Then he went in and stood before his master.

"Where have you been, Gehazi?" said Elisha. Gehazi said, "Your servant went nowhere." Elisha answered, "Did I not go with you in spirit when Naaman turned from his chariot to meet you? Was it a time to accept money and garments? Because of this, the leprosy of Naaman shall cleave to you and to your descendants for ever." So Gehazi went out from Elisha's presence a leper, as white as snow.

Now the prophets said to Elisha, "See, the place where we dwell under your charge is too small for us. Let us go to the Jordan and each of us get there a log, and let us make a place for us to dwell there." So Elisha went with them, and when they came to the Jordan, they cut down trees. But as one was felling a log, his axe head fell into the water; and he cried, "Alas, my master! It was borrowed." Then the man of God said, "Where did it fall?" When he showed him the place, Elisha cut off a stick, and threw it in there, and made the iron float. "Take it up," he said. So the young man reached out his hand and took it.

WHEN THE KING of Syria was warring against Israel, Elisha would send word to the king of Israel, "Beware that you do not pass such and such a place, for the Syrians are going down there." And the king of Israel more than once thus saved himself.

The king of Syria was greatly troubled because of this, and he said to his servants, "Show me who of us is for the king of Israel." One of them answered, "None, my lord; but Elisha the prophet tells the king of Israel the words you speak in your bedchamber." The king said, "Go and see where he is, that I may send and seize him."

It was told him that Elisha was in Dothan, to the north of Samaria; so he sent there horses and chariots and a great army; and they came by night, and surrounded the city. When Elisha's servant rose early in the morning and went out, behold, an army was round about the city. "Alas, my master!" he cried; "what shall we do?" Elisha answered, "Fear not, for those who are with us are more than those with them." Then he prayed, "O LORD, open his eyes that he may see." So the LORD opened the eyes of the servant, and he saw that the mountain was full of horses and chariots of fire round about Elisha.

When the Syrians came down against him, Elisha prayed again to the LORD, and said, "Strike this people, I pray thee, with blindness." So the LORD struck them with blindness, and Elisha said to them, "This is not the way; follow me, and I will bring you to the man whom you seek." He led them to Samaria, and as soon as they entered the city, the LORD opened their eyes; and lo, they were in the midst of Samaria. When the king of Israel saw them, he asked Elisha, "My father, shall I slay them?" Elisha answered, "You shall not slay them. Would you slay those whom you have taken captive with your sword? Set food before them, that they may eat and drink and go to their master." So the king prepared for them a great feast; and when they had eaten and drunk, he sent them back to their master. And for some time the Syrians came no more on raids into Israel.

AFTERWARD BEN-HADAD KING of Syria mustered his entire army and went up and besieged Samaria. There was a great famine there, until an ass's head was sold for eighty shekels of silver and a portion of dove's dung for five shekels. Now as the king of Israel was passing by upon the wall, a woman cried out to him, saying, "Help, my lord, O king!" The king said, "If the LORD will not help you, whence shall I help you? What is your trouble?" She answered, "This woman said to me, 'Give your son, that we may eat him today, and we will eat my son tomorrow.' So we boiled my son, and ate him. And on the next day I said to her, 'Give your son, that we may eat him'; but she has hidden her son."

When the king heard these words, he rent his clothes, and the people saw that he wore sackcloth beneath them. "May God punish me," he said, "if the head of Elisha remains on his shoulders today."

Elisha was sitting in his house with the elders when the king came down to him. "This trouble is from the LORD!" the king said. "Why should I wait for him any longer?" But Elisha answered, "Thus says the LORD, 'Tomorrow about this time a measure of fine meal shall be sold for a shekel, and two measures of barley for a shekel, at the gate of Samaria.'" Then a captain of the king said to Elisha, "If the LORD himself should make windows in heaven, could this thing be?" And Elisha said to him, "You shall see it with your own eyes, but you shall not eat of it."

Now there were four lepers at the entrance to the gate. "Why do we sit here till we die?" they said to one another. "If we enter the city, the famine is there and we shall die there; and if we sit here, we die also. So let us go over to the camp of the Syrians; if they spare our lives we shall eat, and if they kill us we shall but die." They arose at twilight; but when they came to the edge of the camp of the Syrians, behold, there was no one there. For the LORD had made the Syrians hear the sound of the chariots and horses of a great army, so that they said to one another, "Behold, the king of Israel has hired the king of Egypt to come against us." So they fled for their lives, and forsook their tents, their horses, and their asses, leaving the camp as it was.

When the lepers came to the camp, they went into a tent and ate and drank, and carried off silver and gold and clothing, and so with another tent. But then they said to one another, "We are not doing right. This is a day of good news. If we are silent until the morning light, punishment will overtake us. Now therefore let us go and tell the king's household." So they came back and told the city gatekeepers, and the gatekeepers called out. When it was told within the king's household, the king said to his servants, "The Syrians know that we are hungry. Therefore they have gone to hide themselves in the open country, thinking, 'When the people come out of the gate, we shall take them alive and get into the city.' " One of the servants said, "Let us send and see," so the king sent two mounted men after the Syrians. They went as far as the Jordan, and lo, all the way was littered with garments and equipment which the Syrians had thrown away in their haste.

Then the people went out and plundered the Syrian camp. So a measure of fine meal was sold for a shekel at the gate of Samaria, and two measures of barley for a shekel, according to the word of the LORD. But the captain whom the king had placed in charge of the gate was trod upon by the people, so that he died, as Elisha had foretold when he said to him, "You shall see it with your own eyes, but you shall not eat of it."

IN THE FIFTH year of Joram the son of Ahab, king of Israel, Jehoram the son of Jehoshaphat began to reign in Judah. Jehoram was thirty-two years old when he became king, and he reigned eight years in Jerusalem. He walked in the way of the kings of Israel, as the house of Ahab had done, for the daughter of Ahab was his wife. And he did what was evil in the sight of the LORD. Yet the LORD did not destroy Judah, for the sake of David his servant, since he promised to give a lamp to him and to his sons for ever.

In his days Edom revolted from the rule of Judah, and set up a king of their own. Then the city of Libnah revolted at the same time. When Jehoram slept with his fathers, he was buried in the city of David; and Ahaziah his son reigned in his stead.

It was in the twelfth year of Joram the son of Ahab, king of Israel, that Ahaziah began to reign in Jerusalem. His mother was Athaliah, daughter of Ahab, and he did what was evil in the sight of the LORD, as the house of Ahab had done. Ahaziah went with King Joram and all Israel to make war against the Syrians, who were threatening Ramoth-gilead. Joram was wounded, and he returned to be healed in Jezreel. Ahaziah went down to see him there.

Now Elisha called one of the young prophets. "Gird up your loins," he said to him, "and take this flask of oil and go to Ramoth-gilead. Look there for Jehu the son of Jehoshaphat and go in and lead him to an inner chamber. Then take the flask of oil and pour it on his head, and say, 'Thus says the LORD, I anoint you king

over Israel.' Then open the door and flee.
Do not tarry."

When the young prophet went to
Ramoth-gilead, the commanders of the
army were in council there. "I have an
errand to you, O commander," the prophet
said. "To which of us all?" said Jehu. "To
you," the prophet replied.

Jehu arose and went into the house; and
the young man poured the oil on his head,
saying, "Thus says the LORD the God of
Israel, I anoint you king over Israel. You
shall strike down the house of Ahab, that I
may avenge on Jezebel the blood of my
prophets. The whole house of Ahab shall
perish, and the dogs shall eat Jezebel in
Jezreel and none shall bury her." Then he
opened the door and fled.

When Jehu came out, the commanders
asked him, "Why did this mad fellow
come to you?" Jehu answered, "He spoke
to me, saying, 'Thus says the LORD, I
anoint you king over Israel.' " Then in
haste every man of them took his cloak
and put it under Jehu on the bare steps,
and they blew the trumpet and proclaimed, "Jehu is king." Thus Jehu con-

spired against Joram. "If this is your mind," he said to the commanders, "let no one slip away to tell the news in Jezreel." Then he mounted his chariot and went to Jezreel, where Joram lay wounded and Ahaziah king of Judah had come to visit him.

Now the watchman standing on the tower in Jezreel spied the company of Jehu as he came. "I see a company," he cried. "Send a horseman to meet them," Joram commanded, "and let him say, 'Is it peace?' " But Jehu answered the horseman, "What have you to do with peace? Turn round and ride behind me."

The watchman on the tower reported, "The messenger reached them, but he is not coming back. And the driving is like the driving of Jehu, for he drives furiously."

"Make ready," Joram ordered, and they made ready his chariot. Then Joram and Ahaziah set out, each in his chariot, and they met Jehu at the vineyard of Naboth the Jezreelite. "Is it peace, Jehu?" Joram asked. "What peace can there be," answered Jehu, "so long as the harlotries and the sorceries of your mother Jezebel are so many?" Then Joram reined about and fled, saying, "Treachery, O Ahaziah!"

Jehu drew his bow with his full strength and shot Joram between the shoulders, so that the arrow pierced his heart, and he sank in his chariot. "Take him up," Jehu told his aide, "and cast him on the plot of ground belonging to Naboth, in accordance with the word of the LORD." When Ahaziah king of Judah saw this, he fled south. Jehu pursued him and shot him in his chariot at the ascent of Gur. Ahaziah fled to Megiddo and died there. Then his servants carried him in a chariot to Jerusalem and buried him with his fathers in the city of David.

When Jehu came to Jezreel, Jezebel heard of it. She painted her eyes and adorned her head. As Jehu entered the gate, she looked out of the window and said, "Is it peace, you murderer of your master?" Jehu lifted up his face. "Who is on my side? Who?" he called. Two or three eunuchs looked out at him. "Throw her down," he ordered. So they threw her down; and some of her blood spattered on the wall and on the horses, and they trampled on her.

Then Jehu went in and ate and drank. "Now bury this cursed woman," he ordered, "for she is a king's daughter." But when they went to bury her, they found no more of her than the skull and the feet and the palms of her hands. "This is the word of the LORD," Jehu said, "which he spoke by his servant Elijah the prophet: 'In the territory of Jezreel the dogs shall eat the flesh of Jezebel, and her corpse shall be as dung upon the face of the field, so that no one can say, This is Jezebel.'"

Thus Jehu wiped out Baal from Israel, but he did not turn aside from the sins of Jeroboam, which he made Israel to sin—the golden calves that were in Bethel and in Dan. And in those days the LORD began to cut off parts of Israel. Hazael king of Syria defeated them throughout their territory from the Jordan eastward, all the land of Gilead and Bashan.

Jehu reigned over Israel for twenty-eight years. Then he slept with his fathers, and Jehoahaz his son reigned in his stead.

WHEN ATHALIAH THE mother of Ahaziah, king of Judah, saw that her son was dead, she arose and destroyed all his sons except Joash, whom Ahaziah's sister stole away. She was the wife of Jehoiada the priest, and Joash remained with her six years, hid in the house of the LORD, while Athaliah reigned over the land. But in the seventh year Jehoiada had the captains of the guards come to him in the house of the LORD. Then he brought out Joash and put the crown upon him; and they proclaimed him king, and anointed him, and clapped their hands, and said, "Long live the king!"

When Athaliah heard the noise, she went into the house of the LORD; and when she looked, there was the king standing by the pillar, according to the custom. Athaliah rent her clothes. "Treason! Treason!" she cried. Then Jehoiada commanded the captains, "Bring her out between the ranks, but let her not be slain in the house of the LORD." So they laid hands on her; and she went through the horses' entrance to the king's house, and there she was slain. So Joash took his seat on the throne of the kings, and all the people of the land rejoiced.

Joash was seven years old when he began to reign in the seventh year of Jehu king of Israel, and he reigned forty years in Jerusalem. He did what was right in the eyes of the LORD all his days, as Jehoiada the priest instructed him. Nevertheless the high places were not taken away; the people continued to sacrifice there.

At that time Hazael king of Syria went up and took Gath, and then he set his face to go up against Jerusalem. But Joash took all the votive gifts that his fathers, the kings of Judah, had dedicated and all the gold that was found in the temple and in the king's house, and sent these to Hazael. Then Hazael went away from Jerusalem.

Now the servants of Joash arose and made a conspiracy and struck him down, so that he died. They buried him with his fathers in the city of David, and Amaziah his son reigned in his stead.

IN THE TWENTY-THIRD year of Joash king of Judah, Jehoahaz the son of Jehu began to reign over Israel in Samaria, and he reigned seventeen years. In the thirty-seventh year of Joash king of Judah, Jehoash the grandson of Jehu began to reign over Israel in Samaria. He also did what was evil in the sight of the LORD; he did not depart from the sins of Jeroboam, which he made Israel to sin. So the anger of the LORD was kindled against Israel, and he gave them continually into the hand of Hazael king of Syria and of Ben-hadad his son. For there was not left to Israel an army of more than fifty horsemen and ten chariots and ten thousand footmen; the king of Syria had destroyed them and made them like the dust at threshing.

Now when Elisha had fallen sick with the illness of which he was to die, Jehoash went down to him and wept before him, crying, "My father, my father! The chariots of Israel and its horsemen!"

"Take a bow and arrows," Elisha said; so he took a bow and arrows. "Draw the bow"; and he drew it. Then Elisha laid his hands upon the king's hands. "Open the window eastward," he said; and he opened it. Then Elisha said, "Shoot"; and he shot. "The LORD's arrow of victory," Elisha

cried. "The arrow of victory over Syria! For
you shall fight the Syrians until you have
made an end of them." Then he said,
"Take the arrows and strike the ground
with them"; so the king struck three times,
and stopped. But the man of God was
angry with him. "You should have struck
five or six times," he said; "then you would
have made an end of it, but now you will
strike down Syria only three times." So
Elisha died, and they buried him.

When Hazael king of Syria died, Jehoash
took back from Ben-hadad his son the cities which had been taken in war. Three
times Jehoash defeated him and recovered
the cities of Israel.

So Jehoash slept with his fathers and
was buried in Samaria with the kings of
Israel; and Jeroboam II, his son, reigned in
his stead.

In the second year of Jehoash, Amaziah
the son of Joash began to reign in Jerusalem, and he did what was right in the eyes
of the LORD, yet not like David. As soon as
the royal power was firmly in his hand,
Amaziah killed those who had slain his
father, King Joash.

In Jerusalem they made a conspiracy against Amaziah, and he fled to Lachish. But they sent after him to Lachish and slew him there. They brought him upon horses, and he was buried in Jerusalem with his fathers in the city of David. And all the people of Judah took Uzziah his son, and made him king.

In the twenty-seventh year of Jeroboam II, king of Israel, Uzziah the son of Amaziah, king of Judah, began to reign. He was sixteen years old, and he reigned fifty-two years in Jerusalem. He did what was right in the eyes of the LORD, according to all that his father Amaziah had done. Nevertheless the high places were not taken away; the people still sacrificed and burned incense there. And the LORD smote the king, so that he was a leper to the day of his death, and he dwelt in a separate house. Jotham his son was over the household, governing the people of the land. And when Uzziah slept with his fathers, Jotham reigned in his stead.

IN THE FIFTEENTH year of Amaziah king of Judah, Jeroboam II began to reign in Samaria, and he reigned forty-one years. Although he did what was evil in the sight of the LORD, he restored the border of Israel from Damascus as far as the Sea of the Arabah, according to the word of the LORD, which he spoke by his servant Jonah the prophet. For the LORD saw that the affliction of Israel was very bitter, and that there was none to help them; so he saved them by the hand of Jeroboam II.

When Jeroboam II slept with his fathers, Zechariah his son reigned in his stead, and he reigned over Israel six months. Shallum the son of Jabesh conspired against him, and struck him down and killed him, and reigned in his stead. (This was the promise which the LORD gave to Jehu, "Your sons shall sit upon the throne of Israel to the fourth generation." And so it came to pass.) But Shallum reigned only one month in Samaria, for Menahem the son of Gadi came up from Tirzah and struck him down and slew him. At that time Menahem sacked the towns around Tirzah because they did not open to him, and he ripped up all the women there who were with child.

Menahem began to reign over Israel in the thirty-ninth year of Uzziah king of Judah, and he reigned ten years in Samaria. He did what was evil in the sight of the LORD. The king of Assyria came against the land, and Menahem gave him a thousand talents of silver, that he might help him to confirm his hold of the royal power, exacting the money from all the wealthy men of Israel. So the king of Assyria turned back, and did not stay there in the land.

Then Menahem slept with his fathers, and Pekahiah his son reigned in his stead. Pekahiah reigned two years in Samaria; but Pekah the son of Remaliah, Pekahiah's captain, conspired against him with fifty men of Gilead, and slew him in the citadel of the king's house, and reigned in his stead.

In the fifty-second year of Uzziah king of Judah, Pekah began to reign over Israel in Samaria. He reigned twenty years, and he did what was evil in the sight of the LORD. Now Tiglath-pileser king of Assyria came and captured Gilead and Galilee and Syria, and he carried the people captive to Assyria.

Now Hoshea the son of Elah made a conspiracy against Pekah, and struck him down and slew him, and reigned in his stead.

Hoshea began to reign over Israel in the twelfth year of Ahaz king of Judah. He did what was evil in the sight of the LORD, yet not as the kings who were before him. Against him came Shalmaneser king of Assyria. Hoshea became his vassal and paid him tribute. But Shalmaneser found treachery in Hoshea, for he had sent messengers to the king of Egypt and offered no tribute, as he had done year by year. Therefore Shalmaneser shut Hoshea up in prison. Then he invaded all the land and came to Samaria, and for three years he besieged it. In the ninth year of Hoshea he captured it, and he carried the Israelites away to Assyria and placed them on the river Habor and in the cities of the Medes.

This was so, because the people of Israel had sinned against the LORD their God, who had brought them up out of Egypt. They had feared other gods and burned incense on all the high places. They would not listen when the LORD warned them by every prophet and seer. They despised his statutes, and his covenant that he made with their fathers, and the warnings which he gave them. They went after false idols, and made for themselves molten images of two calves. They burned their sons and their daughters as offerings, and used divination and sorcery. They sold themselves to do evil, provoking the LORD to anger. Therefore he removed them out of his sight to Assyria. None was left but the tribe of Judah only.

The king of Assyria also brought people from Babylon and Syria, and they took possession of Samaria and dwelt in its cities. At the beginning of their dwelling there, they did not fear the LORD. Therefore the LORD sent lions among them. The king of Assyria was told, "The nations which you have placed in the cities of Samaria do not know the law of the god of the land; therefore he sent lions among them, and behold, the lions are killing them." Then the king of Assyria commanded, "Send there one of the priests whom you carried away, and let him go and dwell there and teach them the law of the god of the land." So one of the priests came back and dwelt in Bethel and taught them how they should fear the LORD.

But every nation still made gods of its own; so these nations feared the LORD, but also served their own graven images; their children likewise, and their children's children—as their fathers did, so they do to this day.

WHEN AHAZ KING of Judah slept with his fathers, Hezekiah his son reigned in his stead. He did what was right in the eyes of the LORD, according to all that David his father had done. He removed the high places, and he broke in pieces the bronze serpent of Moses, for until those days the people of Israel had burned incense to it. He trusted in the LORD the God of Israel; so that there was none like him among all the kings of Judah. And the LORD was with him; wherever he went forth, he prospered. In those days Hezekiah became sick and was at the point of death. And Isaiah the prophet, the son of Amoz, came to him and said, "Thus says the LORD, 'Set your house in order, for you shall die; you shall not recover.' " Then Hezekiah turned his face to the wall, and prayed to the LORD, saying, "Remember, O LORD, I beseech thee, how I have walked before thee in faithfulness and with a whole heart, and have done what is good in thy sight." And he wept bitterly.

Then the word of the LORD came to Isaiah the prophet: "Go and say to Hezekiah, 'Thus says the LORD: I have heard your prayer, I have seen your tears; behold, I will heal you; on the third day you shall go up to the house of the LORD. And I will add fifteen years to your life.' " When he had spoken thus to Hezekiah, Isaiah said, "Bring a cake of figs. And let them take and lay it on the boil, that he may recover."

"What shall be the sign that the LORD will heal me?" Hezekiah asked. Isaiah replied, "This is the sign to you from the LORD: shall the shadow on the dial of Ahaz go forward ten steps, or go back ten steps?" And Hezekiah answered, "It is an easy thing for the shadow to lengthen ten steps; rather let the shadow go back ten steps." Then Isaiah the prophet cried to the LORD; and he brought the shadow back ten steps, by which the sun had declined on the dial of Ahaz.

Now in the fourteenth year of King Hezekiah he rebelled against the king of Assyria and would not serve him. So Sennacherib king of Assyria came up against all the fortified cities of Judah and took them. Then he sent the Rabshakeh, his chief of staff, with a great army to Jerusalem. When they arrived, they came and stood by the water conduit from the upper pool and called for King Hezekiah. There came out to them Eliakim the son of Hilkiah, who was over the household.

The Rabshakeh said to him, "Say to Hezekiah, 'Thus says the great king Sennacherib: On what do you rest this confidence of yours, that you have rebelled against me? Do you think mere words are strategy and power? Behold, you are relying now on Egypt, that broken reed of a staff, which will pierce the hand of any man who leans on it. How then can you repulse the least of my captains? But if you say to me, "We rely on the LORD our God," is it without the LORD that I have come up against this place to destroy it? The LORD said to me, Go up against this land, and destroy it.' "

"Pray, speak to your servant in the Aramaic language," said Eliakim, "for I understand it. Do not speak in the language of Judah within hearing of the people on the wall." The Rabshakeh replied, "Has my master sent me to speak these words to your master and not to the men sitting on the wall, who are doomed with you to eat their own dung and to drink their own urine?"

Then the Rabshakeh stood and called out in a loud voice in the language of Judah: "Hear the word of the great king, the king of Assyria! Thus says the king: 'Do not let Hezekiah deceive you, for he will not be able to deliver you out of my hand. And do not listen when he misleads you by saying, "The LORD will surely deliver us." Has any of the gods of the nations ever delivered his land out of the hand of the king of Assyria? Where are the gods of Samaria? Have they delivered Samaria out of my hand, that the LORD should deliver Jerusalem?' "

But Eliakim was silent, for the king's command was, "Do not answer him." Then he came to Hezekiah and told him the words of the Rabshakeh. Hezekiah rent his clothes and covered himself with sackcloth and went into the house of the LORD. He sent Eliakim and the senior priests, covered with sackcloth, to the prophet Isaiah. "Thus says Hezekiah," they said to him, " 'It may be that the LORD your God heard all the words of the Rabshakeh, whom the king of Assyria has sent to mock the living God, and will rebuke them; therefore lift up your prayer for the remnant of Israel that is left.' "

Isaiah replied, "Say to your master, 'Thus says the LORD concerning the king of Assyria: He shall not come into this city or shoot an arrow there, or come before it with a shield or cast up a siege mound against it. By the way he came, by the same he shall return, says the LORD, and I will cause him to fall by the sword in his own land. For I will defend this city to save it, for my own sake and for the sake of my servant David.' "

That night the angel of the LORD went

forth and slew a hundred and eighty-five thousand in the camp of the Assyrians; and when men arose early in the morning, behold, these were all dead bodies. Then Sennacherib king of Assyria departed and went home to Nineveh. And as he was worshiping in the house of his god, two of his sons slew him with the sword, and escaped into Ararat. And Esarhaddon his son reigned in his stead.

THEN HEZEKIAH SLEPT with his fathers, and Manasseh his son reigned. For fifty-five years Manasseh reigned in Jerusalem, and he did what was evil in the sight of the LORD. He rebuilt the high places which his father had destroyed; and he erected new altars for Baal in the house of the LORD, of which the LORD had said to David and to Solomon his son, "In this house and in Jerusalem I will put my name." Manasseh also practiced soothsaying and augury, and dealt with mediums and with wizards, provoking the LORD to anger. Moreover he shed much innocent blood, till he had filled Jerusalem from one end to another.

And the LORD said by his prophets, "Because Manasseh has committed these abominations and has made Judah to sin with his idols, therefore thus says the LORD: Behold, I am bringing upon Jerusalem such evil that the ears of every one who hears of it will tingle. I will stretch over Jerusalem the measuring line of Samaria, and the plummet of the house of Ahab; and I will wipe Jerusalem as one wipes a dish, wiping it and turning it upside down. And I will cast off the remnant of my heritage, and they shall become a prey to all their enemies, because they have done what is evil in my sight."

When Manasseh slept with his fathers, Amon his son reigned two years in Jerusalem. But his servants conspired against him and killed him, and the people of the land made Josiah his son king in his stead.

JOSIAH WAS EIGHT years old when he began to reign, and he reigned thirty-one years in Jerusalem. He did what was right in the eyes of the LORD, and walked in all the ways of David his father, and he did not turn aside to the right hand or to the left.

In the eighteenth year King Josiah sent

Shaphan the secretary to the temple. "Go up to Hilkiah the high priest," he said, "that he may reckon the amount of money the people have brought into the house of the LORD, and let it be given to the workmen who are repairing the house." To Shaphan, Hilkiah said, "I have found a book of the law in the house of the LORD," and he gave the book to Shaphan. After reading it, Shaphan returned to the king, saying, "Your servants have delivered the money that was found in the temple into the hand of the workmen." Then he said, "Hilkiah the priest has given me a book," and he read the book before the king.

When the king heard the words of the book of the law, he rent his clothes. "Go," he commanded Hilkiah and Shaphan, "inquire of the LORD for me and for all Judah concerning the words of this book. Great is the wrath of the LORD against us, because our fathers have not obeyed its words."

They went to Huldah the prophetess, who dwelt in Jerusalem in the Second Quarter, and she said to them, "Thus says the LORD: 'Tell the man who sent you, Behold, I will bring evil upon this place and upon its inhabitants. Because they have forsaken me and have burned incense to other gods, therefore my wrath will be kindled against them, and it will not be quenched.' But as to the king of Judah, thus shall you say to him: 'Because your heart was penitent, and you humbled yourself before me when you heard how I spoke against this place, and you have rent your clothes and wept before me, I also have heard you,' says the LORD. 'Therefore, behold, I will gather you to your fathers in peace, and your eyes shall not see all the evil which I will bring upon this place.' "

Then the king went up to the house of the LORD, and with him the priests and the prophets and all the people, both small and great; and he read in their hearing the book of the law which had been found in the house of the LORD. And the king stood by the pillar and made a covenant before the LORD, to walk after him and to keep his commandments and his statutes with all his heart and all his soul; and all the people joined in the covenant.

Commanding Hilkiah to bring out of the

temple all the vessels made for Baal, King Josiah burned them outside Jerusalem and carried their ashes to Bethel. And he broke down the houses of the male cult prostitutes which were in the house of the LORD, and defiled the high places where the priests had burned incense, from Geba to Beer-sheba. And he removed the horses that the kings of Judah had dedicated to the sun, and burned the chariots of the sun with fire. And he defiled the high places east of Jerusalem, which Solomon had built for Ashtoreth the abomination of the Sidonians, and for Milcom the abomination of the Ammonites.

Moreover he pulled down and broke in pieces the altar at Bethel, the high place erected by Jeroboam the son of Nebat, crushing its stones to dust. As he turned he saw the tombs on the mountain, and he said, "What is yonder monument?"

"It is the tomb of the man of God who came from Judah and predicted these things you have done against the altar at Bethel," the men of the city told him. "Let him be," Josiah said; "let no man move his bones." And he removed all the high places in the cities of Samaria which kings of Israel had made. Then he returned to Jerusalem where he commanded the people, "Keep the passover to the LORD your God, as it is written in this book of the covenant." For no such passover had been kept since the days of the judges, nor during all the days of the kings of Israel or of Judah.

Josiah put away the mediums and the wizards and all the abominations that were seen in the land of Judah, that he might establish the words of the law. Before him there was no king like him, who turned to the LORD with all his heart and with all his soul and with all his might, according to the law of Moses; nor did any like him arise after him. Still the LORD did not turn from the fierceness of his great wrath against Judah, because of all the provocations of Manasseh.

Now IN THE days of Josiah, Pharaoh Neco of Egypt went up to the river Euphrates to help the king of Assyria against Babylon. King Josiah went to meet him; and Pharaoh Neco slew him in battle at Megiddo. His servants carried him dead in a chariot to Jerusalem, and buried him there; and the people took Jehoahaz his son and made him king in his father's stead.

Jehoahaz reigned only three months in Jerusalem, for Pharaoh Neco took him away in bonds to Egypt and made his brother Jehoiakim king in his place. Jehoiakim reigned eleven years in Jerusalem, and he did what was evil in the sight of the LORD. He gave tribute to Pharaoh, but he exacted silver and gold from the people, from every one according to his assessment.

In the days of Jehoiakim, Nebuchadnezzar king of Babylon came up against the king of Egypt, and took all that belonged to Pharaoh from the Brook of Egypt to the river Euphrates. Jehoiakim became the servant of Nebuchadnezzar three years; then he turned and rebelled against him. And the LORD sent against him bands of the Babylonians, and the Syrians, and the Moabites, and the Ammonites—sent them against Judah to destroy it, according to the word of the LORD which he spoke by his prophets. Then Jehoiakim slept with his fathers, and Jehoiachin his son reigned in his stead.

Jehoiachin was eighteen years old when he became king, and he reigned three months in Jerusalem. He did what was evil in the sight of the LORD, and at that time Nebuchadnezzar sent his army and besieged Jerusalem, so that Jehoiachin gave himself up. Nebuchadnezzar carried him away to Babylon; the king's mother, the king's wives, his princes, and his officials he also took into captivity in Babylon. And he made Zedekiah, Jehoiachin's uncle, king in his stead.

Zedekiah was twenty-one years old when he became king, and he reigned eleven years in Jerusalem. He did what was evil in the sight of the LORD, and because of the anger of the LORD it came to the point in Jerusalem and Judah that he cast them out from his presence.

Zedekiah rebelled against the king of Babylon, and in the ninth year of his reign Nebuchadnezzar came with all his army and laid siege to Jerusalem. So the city was besieged till the eleventh year of King Zedekiah. The famine was so severe in the city that there was no food for the people.

Then a breach was made in the walls, and the king with all his men of war fled by night by way of the king's garden, though the Babylonians were around the city. They fled in the direction of the Arabah, but the Babylonians pursued them and overtook the king in the plains of Jericho, and scattered his army. Capturing the king, they brought him up to Nebuchadnezzar at Riblah in Syria. When Nebuchadnezzar had passed sentence upon him, they slew Zedekiah's sons before his eyes. Then they put out his eyes and bound him in fetters and took him to Babylon.

In the fifth month of the eleventh year, on the seventh day of the month, Nebuzaradan, the captain of the bodyguard of King Nebuchadnezzar, came to Jerusalem with an army. And he burned the house of the LORD and the king's house and all the houses of Jerusalem; and the army broke down the walls around Jerusalem. The pillars of bronze and the bronze sea that Solomon had made for the temple, they broke in pieces and carried to Babylon, along with the dishes for incense and all the vessels used in the temple service. What was of gold they cut in pieces and took away as so much gold, and what was of silver, as so much silver.

The people were carried into exile, though Nebuzaradan left some of the poorest in the land to be vinedressers and plowmen. Seraiah the chief priest, the three keepers of the threshold, five men of the king's council, and sixty of the men of the land were brought to the king of Babylon at Riblah. And Nebuchadnezzar smote them and put them to death. So Judah was taken into exile out of its land.

IN THE THIRTY-SEVENTH year of the exile of Jehoiachin king of Judah before his uncle Zedekiah, Evil-merodach king of Babylon, in the year that he began to reign, graciously freed Jehoiachin from prison. He spoke kindly to him and gave him a seat above the seats of the other kings who were with him in Babylon. So Jehoiachin put off his prison garments, and every day of his life he dined at the king's table. And an allowance was given him by the king, every day as long as he lived.

1 CHRONICLES

The two books of Chronicles, also originally a single book, cover the same period of history as 1 and 2 Kings. But some events and personages are left out (the prophets Elijah and Elisha, for example), while other materials and a more religious emphasis have been added. In 1 Chronicles the long rule of King David is described, with the author underlining his glory and omitting the less praiseworthy episodes in his life. Much attention is also given to David's preparations for the building of the temple in Jerusalem and his establishment of the proper rituals to be conducted there. Because of the Chronicler's concern with the role of Levites and singers, it is thought that he himself may have been a Levite and a singer. The date usually assigned to his work is the latter part of the fourth century B.C.

ADAM, SETH, METHUSELAH, Noah; the sons of Noah: Shem, Ham, and Japheth.

The sons of Shem: Elam, Asshur, and Arpachshad. Arpachshad was the father of Shelah, and Shelah of Eber. To Eber were born two sons, Peleg and Joktan. Among the descendants of Peleg was Terah; and Terah was the father of Abram, that is, Abraham.

Abraham was the father of Isaac. The sons of Isaac: Esau and Israel (Jacob).

These are the sons of Israel: Reuben, Simeon, Levi, Judah, Issachar, Zebulun, Dan, Joseph, Benjamin, Naphtali, Gad, and Asher.

Judah became strong among his brothers. He had five sons in all: three by Bathshua the Canaanitess, and his daughter-in-law Tamar also bore him Zerah and Perez.

The descendants of Perez were Hezron, Ram, and Amminadab, and Amminadab was the father of Nahshon, prince of the sons of Judah. Nahshon was the father of Salma, Salma of Boaz, Boaz of Obed, Obed of Jesse; and Jesse was the father of David.

Now MEN CAME to David at Ziklag while he could not move about freely because of Saul the son of Kish; and they were among the mighty men who helped him in war. They were bowmen, and could shoot arrows and sling stones with either the right or the left hand; they were Benjaminites, Saul's kinsmen.

From the Gadites there went over to David at the stronghold in the wilderness mighty and experienced warriors, expert with shield and spear, whose faces were like the faces of lions and who were swift as gazelles upon the mountains. David went out to meet them. "If you have come in friendship to help me," he said, "my heart will be knit to you; but if to betray me to my adversaries, then may the God of our fathers see and rebuke you."

Then the Spirit came upon Amasai, chief of the warriors, and he said, "We are yours, O David, and with you, O son of Jesse! Peace, peace to you, and peace to your helpers! For your God helps you." David received them and made them officers of his troops.

Some of the men of Manasseh deserted to David when he came with the Philistines to Gilboa for the battle against Saul. (Yet he did not help the Philistines, for they took counsel and sent him away, saying, "At peril to our heads he will desert to his master Saul.") From day to day mighty men of valor kept coming to David, until there was a great army, like an army of God.

NOW THE PHILISTINES fought against Israel, and the men of Israel fled before them, and fell slain on Mount Gilboa. The Philistines overtook Saul and slew Jonathan and Abinadab and Malchishua, his sons. The battle pressed hard upon Saul, and the archers found him and wounded him. "Draw your sword," he said to his armor-bearer, "and thrust me through with it, lest these uncircumcised come and make sport of me." But his armor-bearer would not; for he feared greatly. Therefore Saul took his own sword and fell upon it.

Thus Saul died, and his sons, and all his men. When the men of Israel down in the valley saw that their army had fled and that Saul and his sons were dead, they forsook their cities, and the Philistines came and dwelt in them.

On the morrow, when the Philistines came to strip the slain, they found Saul and his sons fallen on Mount Gilboa. They stripped Saul and took his head and his armor and sent messengers throughout their land to carry the good news to the people. They put his armor in the temple of their gods and fastened his head in the temple of Dagon. But when Jabesh-gilead heard what the Philistines had done, the valiant men arose and took the bodies of Saul and his sons from the battlefield and brought them to Jabesh. They buried their bones under the oak in Jabesh and fasted seven days.

So Saul died for his unfaithfulness, in that he did not keep the command of the LORD and also consulted a medium, seeking guidance. Therefore the LORD slew him and turned the kingdom over to David the son of Jesse.

ALL ISRAEL GATHERED to David at Hebron, and said, "Behold, we are your bone and flesh. Even when Saul was king it was

you that led us out and brought us in, and
the LORD said to you, 'You shall be shepherd of my people Israel, and prince over
my people Israel.' " So the elders of Israel
came to Hebron with full intent to make
David king. David made a covenant with
them before the LORD, and they anointed
him king over all Israel, according to the
word of the LORD by Samuel. They were
there with David for three days, eating
and drinking, for their brethren had
made preparation for them, bringing
abundant provisions of meal, cakes of
figs, clusters of raisins, and wine and
oil, oxen and sheep; for there was joy in
Israel.

After this, David went to Jerusalem,
where the Jebusites were, the inhabitants
of the land. "You will not come in here!"
they told David. Nevertheless David took
the stronghold of Zion. Then he said,
"Whoever shall smite the Jebusites first
shall be chief and commander." And Joab
the son of Zeruiah, David's sister, went up
first, so he became chief. David took the
stronghold of Zion, and then dwelt there;
and it was called the city of David. And

David became greater and greater, for the LORD of hosts was with him.

Now these are the chiefs of David's mighty men, who gave him strong support to make him king. Jashobeam was chief of the three; he wielded his spear against three hundred whom he slew at one time. Next to him was Eleazar the son of Dodo. At Pas-dammim against the Philistines, David's men had fled, but Eleazar took his stand in the midst of a plot of barley and slew the Philistines; and the LORD saved them by a great victory.

Abishai the brother of Joab was the most renowned of the thirty mighty men and became their commander, but he did not attain to the three. And Benaiah was a valiant man, a doer of great deeds. He went down and slew a lion in a pit on a day when snow had fallen. He also slew an Egyptian, a man of great stature, who had in his hand a spear like a weaver's beam; but Benaiah snatched it out of his hand and slew him with his own spear. Benaiah was renowned among the thirty, and David set him over his bodyguard.

DAVID CONSULTED WITH the commanders, and with every leader; then he said to the assembly of Israel, "If it seems good to you, let us send abroad to our brethren in all the land of Israel, and to the priests and Levites, that we may bring again the ark of our God to us; for we neglected it in the days of Saul." And the thing was right in the eyes of all the people. So David assembled all Israel from the border of Egypt to Syria, and they went up to Kiriath-jearim to bring up from there the ark of the LORD. They carried the ark upon a new cart from the house of Abinadab upon the hill, and Uzzah his son was driving the cart. David and all Israel were making merry before God with all their might, with song and lyres and tambourines and trumpets. But it happened that the oxen stumbled, and Uzzah put out his hand to hold the ark. The anger of the LORD was kindled against him, and he smote him because he had touched the ark; and Uzzah died there before God. David was afraid, because the LORD had broken forth upon Uzzah, and he said, "How can I bring the ark of God home to me?" So he did not take the ark into the city of David, but took it aside to the house of Obed-edom the Gittite. And the ark of God remained there three months; and the LORD blessed the household of Obed-edom and all that he had.

WHEN THE PHILISTINES heard that David had been anointed king over all Israel, they went in search of him. David heard of it and went out against them. Now the Philistines made a raid in the valley of Rephaim, and David inquired of God, "Shall I go up against the Philistines?" and the LORD said, "Go up, and I will give them into your hand." David went up to Baal-perazim, and defeated them there; the Philistines left their gods behind, and David gave command, and they were burned.

The Philistines made another raid in the valley. When David again inquired of God, God said, "You shall not go up after them; go around and come upon them opposite the balsam trees. When you hear the sound of marching in the tops of the trees, then go out to battle; for God has gone out before you to smite the army of the

Philistines." David did as God commanded, and they smote the Philistine army from Gibeon to Gezer. The fame of David went out into all lands, and the LORD brought the fear of him upon all nations.

HIRAM KING OF Tyre sent messengers to David, and cedar trees, also masons and carpenters. David built houses for himself in the city of David; and he prepared a place for the ark of God and pitched a tent for it. Then he said, "No one but the Levites may carry the ark of God, for the LORD chose them to carry it and to minister to him for ever."

Now David assembled all Israel at Jerusalem, to bring up the ark of the LORD to the place he had prepared for it; and he summoned the priests and the Levites. "Sanctify yourselves, you and your brethren," he said, "so that you may bring up the ark of the LORD to the place that I have prepared for it. Because you did not carry it the first time, the LORD broke forth upon us." The priests and the Levites sanctified themselves, and the Levites carried the ark of God upon their shoulders with the poles, as Moses had commanded according to the word of the LORD. David also commanded the Levites to appoint their brethren as the singers who should play on harps and lyres and cymbals, to raise sounds of joy.

David and the elders of Israel went to bring up the ark of the covenant from the house of Obed-edom with rejoicing, and they sacrificed seven bulls and seven rams. David was clothed with a robe of fine linen, and he wore a priestly apron. All Israel brought up the ark of the LORD with shouting, to the sound of the horn, trumpets, and cymbals, and made loud music on harps and lyres. They set the ark inside the tent which David had pitched for it; and David offered burnt offerings and peace offerings before God. When he had finished, he blessed the people and distributed to each a loaf of bread, a portion of meat, and a cake of raisins.

Moreover he appointed certain of the Levites as ministers before the ark of the LORD, to invoke, to thank, and to praise the LORD. Asaph was the chief; he was to sound the cymbals, and Benaiah and Jahaziel the priests were to blow trumpets continually before the ark of the covenant. On that day David first appointed that thanksgiving be sung to the LORD by Asaph and his brethren. Then all the people said "Amen!" and praised the LORD.

Now WHEN DAVID dwelt in his house, he said to Nathan the prophet, "Behold, I dwell in a house of cedar, but the ark of the LORD is under a tent."

That same night the word of the LORD came to Nathan, "Go and tell my servant David, 'Thus says the LORD: You shall not build me a house. For I have not dwelt in a house since the day I led Israel from Egypt. In all places where I have moved with Israel, did I speak a word with any of the judges, saying, "Why have you not built me a house of cedar?" ' Now therefore shall you say to my servant David, 'Thus says the LORD of hosts, I took you from following the sheep, that you should be prince over my people Israel, and I have been with you wherever you went; and I will make for you a name like the great ones of the earth. When your days are fulfilled, I will raise up one of your own sons, and he shall build a house for me. I will be his father, and he shall be my son; I will not take my steadfast love from him, as I took it from Saul, but his throne shall be established for ever.' " In accordance with all these words, Nathan spoke to David.

Then King David went in and sat before the LORD, and said, "Who am I, O LORD God, and what is my family, that thou hast brought me thus far? And what more can David say to thee? For thou knowest thy servant. For thy servant's sake, O LORD, and according to thy own heart, thou hast wrought all this greatness. Thou hast revealed to him that thou wilt build a house for him; therefore I have found courage to pray before thee. May it please thee to bless the house of thy servant, that it may continue for ever before thee."

AFTER THIS, DAVID defeated the Philistines and subdued them; and he defeated Moab, and the Moabites became his servants and brought tribute. David also defeated Hadadezer king of Zobah, toward Hamath in the north, and when the Syrians came to help Hadadezer, David slew twenty-two thousand of them, and put garrisons in Damascus; and the Syrians became his servants and brought tribute. From the cities of Hadadezer David took very much bronze; with it Solomon made the bronze sea and the pillars and the vessels of bronze for the temple.

Also Abishai the son of Zeruiah slew eighteen thousand Edomites in the Valley of Salt, and the Edomites became David's servants. And the LORD gave victory to David wherever he went. So David reigned over all Israel; and he administered justice and equity to all his people. Joab the brother of Abishai was over the army; and Zadok the son of Ahitub, and Ahimelech the son of Abiathar were priests; and Benaiah was over the Cherethites and the Pelethites of the bodyguard; and David's sons were the chief officials in the service of the king.

AFTER NAHASH THE king of the Ammonites died, David said, "I will deal loyally with Hanun the son of Nahash, for his father dealt loyally with me." So David sent messengers to console Hanun concerning his father.

But the princes of the Ammonites said to Hanun, "Do you think that David is honoring your father? Have not his servants come to spy out the land?" So Hanun took David's servants and shaved them and cut off their garments at their hips and sent them away. When David was told, he sent to meet the men, for they were greatly ashamed. "Remain at Jericho until your beards have grown," he told them, "and then return."

In the spring of the year, the time when kings go forth to battle, Joab led out the army. He ravaged the country of the Ammonites, and came and smote Rabbah, their chief city, and overthrew it. And David took Hanun's crown from his head, and it was placed on David's head. And he brought forth the spoil of the city, and the people who were in it, and set them to labor with saws and picks and axes. Thus David did to all the cities of the Ammonites. Then he returned to Jerusalem.

SATAN STOOD UP against Israel and incited David to number the people. "Go, number Israel from Beer-sheba to Dan," David said to Joab, "and bring me a report."

"May the LORD add to his people a hundred times as many as they are!" Joab replied. "Are they not all of them my lord's servants? Why then should my lord require this? Why should he bring guilt upon Israel?"

But the king's word prevailed, so Joab departed and went throughout all Israel, and came back to Jerusalem and gave the number of the people to David. In all Israel there were one million one hundred thousand men who drew the sword, and in Judah four hundred and seventy thousand. But Joab did not include Levi and Benjamin in the numbering, for the king's command was abhorrent to him.

God was displeased with this thing, and he smote Israel. David said to God, "I have sinned greatly in doing this, but now, I pray thee, take away the iniquity of thy servant."

And the LORD spoke to Gad, David's seer, saying, "Go and say to David, 'Thus says the LORD, Three things I offer you; choose one, that I may do it to you.' " So Gad came to David and said, "Thus says the LORD, 'Take which you will: either three years of famine; or three months of devastation by the sword of your enemies; or three days of pestilence upon the land, and the angel of the LORD destroying throughout all Israel.' Now decide what answer I shall return to him who sent me."

"Let me fall into the hand of the LORD," David replied, "for his mercy is very great; but let me not fall into the hand of man."

So the LORD sent a pestilence upon Israel, and there fell seventy thousand men. God sent the angel to Jerusalem to destroy it, and the angel of the LORD was standing by the threshing floor of Ornan the Jebusite. David lifted his eyes and saw the destroying angel standing between earth and heaven, and in his hand a drawn sword stretched out over Jerusalem. Then David and the elders, clothed in sackcloth, fell upon their faces, and David said to God, "It is I who have sinned by numbering the people; but these sheep, what have they done? Let thy hand, I pray thee, O Lord my God, be against me and my father's house; but let not the plague be upon thy people." The Lord repented of the evil; and he said to the destroying angel, "It is enough; now stay your hand."

Then the angel of the Lord commanded Gad the seer to say to David that David should go up and rear an altar to the Lord on the threshing floor of Ornan. So David went up at Gad's word, which he had spoken in the name of the Lord. Now Ornan was threshing wheat; he turned and saw the angel, and his four sons who were with him hid themselves. Then Ornan looked and saw David coming, and he went forth and did obeisance to David with his face to the ground.

"Give me the site of the threshing floor," said David, "that I may build on it an altar to the Lord, that the plague may be averted from the people."

"Take it," said Ornan, "and let my lord the king do what seems good to him; see, I give the oxen for burnt offerings, and the threshing sledges for the wood, and the wheat for a cereal offering. I give it all."

"No," answered King David, "but I will buy it for the full price; I will not take for the LORD what is yours, or offer burnt offerings which cost me nothing." So David paid Ornan six hundred shekels of gold for the site, and he built there an altar to the LORD and presented burnt offerings and called upon the LORD; and the LORD answered him with fire from heaven upon the altar. Then the LORD commanded the angel to put his sword back into its sheath.

When David saw that the LORD had answered him, he said, "Here shall be the house of the LORD God and here the altar of burnt offering for Israel." Then he called for Solomon his son. "My son," he said, "I had it in my heart to build a house to the name of the LORD my God. But the LORD said, 'You shall not build a house to my name, because you have waged great wars and shed much blood upon the earth. Behold, a son shall be born to you, a man of peace. His name shall be Solomon, and I will give him peace from all his enemies round about. He shall build a house for my name, and I will establish his royal throne in Israel for ever.' Now, my son, the LORD be with you, so that you may succeed in building the house of the LORD your God. Only, may the LORD grant you discretion and understanding, that when he gives you charge over Israel you may observe his statutes and ordinances. Be strong, and fear not; be not dismayed. Arise and be doing! The LORD be with you!"

Then David commanded the aliens who were in the land of Israel to prepare dressed stones for building the temple. He also provided great stores of iron, as well as bronze in quantities beyond weighing, and cedar timbers without number. For David said, "Solomon my son is young and inexperienced, and the house that is to be built for the LORD must be exceedingly magnificent, of fame and glory throughout all lands." David also commanded the leaders of Israel to help Solomon, saying, "Arise and build the sanctuary of the LORD God, so that the ark of the covenant and the holy vessels of God may be brought into a house built for the name of the LORD."

And he assembled all the leaders of Israel and the priests and the Levites, saying,

"The LORD has given peace to his people, and he dwells in Jerusalem for ever, so the Levites no longer need to carry the tabernacle or any of the things for its service; but their duty shall be to assist the sons of Aaron for the service of the temple, having the care of the courts and the chambers, the cleansing of all that is holy, and any work for the service of the temple; to assist also with the showbread, the wafers of unleavened bread, the baked offering, and the offering mixed with oil. And they shall stand every morning and evening, thanking and praising the LORD, and whenever burnt offerings are offered on sabbaths, new moons, and feast days. Thus they shall keep charge of the sanctuary, and shall attend the sons of Aaron, their brethren, for the service of the temple."

Now King David assembled at Jerusalem all the officials of Israel and of the tribes, all the mighty men, and all the seasoned warriors. Then he rose to his feet. "Hear me, my brethren and my people," he said. "I had it in my heart to build a house for the ark of the covenant of the LORD, but God said to me, 'You may not build a house for my name, for you are a warrior and have shed blood. It is Solomon your son who shall build my house, and I will establish his kingdom for ever if he keeps my commandments and my ordinances.' Now therefore in the sight of all Israel and in the hearing of our God, observe all the commandments of the LORD, that you may possess this good land, and leave it for an inheritance to your children for ever. And you, Solomon my son, take heed now, for the LORD has chosen you to build a house for the sanctuary; be strong, and do it."

Then David gave Solomon the plan of the vestibule of the temple, and of its treasuries, its upper rooms, and its inner chambers, and of the room for the mercy seat; and the plan of all that he had in mind for the divisions of the priests and Levites in the service of the temple; also his plan for the golden chariot of the cherubim that spread their wings and covered the ark of the covenant. All this he made clear by an edict from the hand of the LORD, and all the work was to be done according to the plan.

And David said to the assembly, "Now I

have provided for the house of my God, so far as I was able, the gold for the things of gold, the silver for the things of silver, the bronze, the iron, and the wood, besides great quantities of precious stones and marble. Who then will offer willingly, consecrating himself today to the LORD?" Then all made their freewill offerings for the service of the temple, and the people rejoiced, for with a whole heart they had offered freely to the LORD.

David also rejoiced greatly, and he blessed the LORD in the presence of all the assembly, saying, "Blessed art thou, O LORD, the God of Israel our father, for ever and ever. Thine is the greatness, and the power, and the glory, and the victory, and the majesty; for thine is the kingdom, O LORD, and thou art exalted as head above all. And now we thank thee, our God, and praise thy glorious name.

"But who am I, and what is my people, that we should be able thus to offer willingly? For we are strangers before thee, and sojourners, as all our fathers were; our days on the earth are like a shadow, and there is no abiding. O LORD our God, all this abundance that we have provided for building thee a house for thy holy name comes from thy hand and is all thy own. I know that thou triest the heart and hast pleasure in uprightness; in the uprightness of my heart I have freely offered all these things, and now I have seen thy people here offering freely and joyously to thee. O LORD, the God of Abraham, Isaac, and Israel, our fathers, keep for ever such purposes and thoughts in the hearts of thy people, and direct their hearts toward thee."

Then David said to all the assembly, "Bless the LORD your God." And all the assembly blessed the LORD, the God of their fathers, and bowed their heads, and worshiped the LORD, and did obeisance to the king. And they performed sacrifices to the LORD, and on the next day offered burnt offerings to the LORD, a thousand bulls, a thousand rams, and a thousand lambs, with their drink offerings, and sacrifices in abundance for all Israel; and they ate and drank before the

LORD on that day with great gladness.

When David was old, he made Solomon his son king over Israel. All the leaders and the mighty men, and also the other sons of King David, pledged their allegiance to King Solomon. He prospered, and all Israel obeyed him, and the LORD gave him great repute. David had reigned over Israel forty years, and he died in a good old age, full of riches and honor.

2 CHRONICLES

This book begins by describing the grandeur of the reign of David's son Solomon, emphasizing his zeal in constructing the temple and instituting its services. Most of the book deals with the period of the divided monarchy that followed Solomon's death. The unknown author, however, writes as little as possible about the northern kingdom, since to him the apostasy of the ten tribes from the worship of God means that they no longer represent the true Israel. Though the people of the southern kingdom of Judah sometimes go badly astray, suffering divine punishment for their sins, they still remain God's chosen people even as they are led into exile. The author accepts the view of Deuteronomy that national calamity is the result of national sin, and he emphasizes the blessings that come from respect for the law of God.

SOLOMON THE SON of David established himself in his kingdom, and the LORD was with him and made him exceedingly great.

Solomon spoke to all Israel, to the commanders, to the judges, and the heads of fathers' houses. He, and all the assembly with him, went to the high place at Gibeon, for there stood the tabernacle of God which Moses had made in the wilderness. They sought the LORD, and Solomon went up to the bronze altar and offered a thousand burnt offerings upon it.

In that night God appeared to him, and said, "Ask what I should give you."

"O LORD God, thou hast made me king over a people as many as the dust of the earth," Solomon answered. "Give me wisdom and knowledge to rule them."

God answered, "Because you have not asked possessions, wealth, honor, or the life of those who hate you, wisdom and knowledge are granted to you. I will also give you riches and honor surpassing those of other kings."

WHEN SOLOMON DECIDED to build a temple for the name of the LORD and a royal palace for himself, he sent word to Hiram king of Tyre: "Behold, I am about to build a house for the name of the LORD my God, for the burning of sweet spices and burnt offerings before him. It will be great and wonderful, for our God is greater than all gods, and even heaven cannot contain him. Send me a man skilled to work in gold, silver, bronze, and iron, and in purple, crimson, and blue fabrics, trained also in engraving, to be with the craftsmen in Judah whom David my father provided. Send me also cedar and cypress from Lebanon. My servants will be with your servants to prepare timber in abundance, and I will give for your servants two hundred and twenty thousand bushels of crushed wheat, two hundred and twenty thousand bushels of barley, a hundred and eighty thousand gallons of wine, and a hundred and eighty thousand gallons of oil."

Hiram answered in a letter, "Because

the LORD loves his people he has made you king over them. Now I have sent a man, endowed with understanding and trained to execute with your craftsmen any design that may be assigned him. Therefore the wheat and barley, oil and wine, of which my lord has spoken, let him send them to Lebanon; and we will cut whatever timber you need and bring it to you in rafts by sea to Joppa."

Solomon took a census of all the aliens who were in the land of Israel, and there were found a hundred and fifty-three thousand six hundred. Seventy thousand of them he assigned to bear burdens, eighty thousand to quarry in the hill country, and three thousand six hundred as overseers to make the people work. Then in the second month of the fourth year of his reign, Solomon began to build the house of the LORD in Jerusalem on Mount Moriah, where the angel had appeared to David his father on the threshing floor of Ornan the Jebusite. He adorned the house with settings of precious stones, lined it with gold, and carved cherubim on the walls.

In the inner sanctuary he placed two

cherubim of wood and overlaid them with gold. The cherubim stood together facing the nave. Their wings extended thirty feet: one wing of each touched opposite walls of the house, and the other wings joined in the middle. Solomon made the veil of blue and purple and crimson fabrics and fine linen, and worked cherubim on it. In front of the temple he set two high pillars; one on the south he called Jachin, the other on the north Boaz. He made all the things that were in the temple: the golden altar, the tables for the bread of the Presence, the lamps to burn before the inner sanctuary, the tongs, snuffers, basins, and firepans, all of purest gold.

When the work for the house of the LORD was finished, Solomon assembled the elders of Israel and the heads of the tribes in Jerusalem to bring up the ark of the covenant out of the city of David, which is Zion. The king and all the congregation were before the ark, sacrificing so many sheep and oxen that they could not be counted. Then the Levites took up the ark and brought it to its place in the inner sanctuary, in the most holy place, underneath the wings of the cherubim. There was nothing in the ark except the two tablets which Moses put there at Sinai, where the LORD made a covenant with Israel after they came out of Egypt.

When the priests came out of the holy place, a song in praise to the LORD was raised by the Levitical singers, with lyres, harps, trumpets, and cymbals. The temple was filled with a cloud, so that the priests could not stand to minister, for the glory of the LORD filled his house.

Then Solomon stood before the altar in the presence of all the assembly of Israel, and spread forth his hands. "O LORD, God of Israel," he said, "behold, heaven and the highest heaven cannot contain thee— how much less this house which I have built! Yet hearken thou to the supplications of thy people Israel when they pray toward this place; yea, hear thou from heaven thy dwelling place; and when thou hearest, forgive." When Solomon had ended his prayer, fire came down from heaven and consumed the burnt offering and the sacrifices, and the glory of the LORD filled the temple. And the children of Israel bowed down with their faces to the earth and gave thanks to the LORD. Then Solomon held a feast for seven days, and on the eighth day he sent the people away to their homes, joyful and glad of heart.

The LORD appeared to Solomon in the night and said to him, "I have heard your prayer, and have chosen this place for myself as a house of sacrifice. When I shut up the heavens so that there is no rain, or command the locust to devour the land, if my people seek my face and turn from their wicked ways, I will forgive their sin and heal their land. My ears will be attentive to the prayer that is made in this place. As for you, if you walk before me as David your father walked, keeping my statutes and my ordinances, I will establish your royal throne, as I covenanted with David, saying, 'There shall not fail you a man to rule Israel.' But if you turn aside and serve other gods, then I will pluck you up from the land I have given you; and this house, which I have consecrated for my name, I will cast out of my sight, and will make it a proverb and a byword among all peoples."

AT THE END of twenty years, during which he had built the house of the LORD and his own palace, Solomon rebuilt the cities which Hiram had given to him, and settled the people of Israel in them. He built Tadmor in the wilderness and store-cities in Hamath. He also built fortified cities with walls and gates, and cities for his chariots and for his horsemen. He built whatever he desired in Jerusalem, in Lebanon, and in the whole of his dominion. Solomon made a forced levy of all the people in the land who were not of Israel, and so they are to this day. But of the people of Israel, Solomon made no slaves for his work; they were soldiers and officers, commanders of chariots, and horsemen.

When the queen of Sheba heard of the fame of Solomon, she came to Jerusalem to test him with hard questions, bringing a very great retinue and camels bearing spices and much gold and precious stones. She told Solomon all that was on her mind, and he answered all her questions; there was nothing he could not explain to her. When the queen had seen his wisdom, the house he had built, and his manner of living, she said to him, "I did not believe the reports of your affairs and your wisdom until my own eyes had seen it; and behold, half your greatness was not told me. Happy are your wives! Happy are these your servants, who continually stand before you and hear your wisdom! Blessed be the LORD your God, who has delighted in you and set you on his throne as king." Then she gave the king a very great quantity of gold, spices, and precious stones before she went back to her own land.

Now the weight of gold that came to Solomon in one year was fifty thousand pounds, besides that which the traders and merchants and all the kings of Arabia brought. The king made a great ivory throne overlaid with pure gold; the like of it was never made in any kingdom. It had six steps and a footstool of gold attached to the throne, and on each side of the seat were arm rests and two lions standing beside the arm rests. Lions also stood on the ends of each of the six steps. All the king's drinking vessels were of gold; silver was not considered as anything in his days. For his ships went to Tarshish with the servants of Hiram, and once every three years they used to come bringing gold, silver, ivory, apes, and peacocks.

Thus King Solomon excelled all the kings of the earth in riches and in wisdom. Every one of them sought his presence and brought him articles of silver and gold, myrrh, spices, horses, and mules, so much year by year. He had four thousand stalls for horses and chariots, and twelve thousand horsemen, whom he stationed in the chariot cities and in Jerusalem. And he ruled over all the kings from the Euphrates to the border of Egypt. After Solomon had reigned over all Israel forty years, he slept with his fathers and was buried in the city of David; and Rehoboam his son reigned in his stead.

REHOBOAM WENT TO Shechem, for the northern tribes had come there to make him king. When Jeroboam the son of Nebat heard of it (for he was in Egypt, whither he had fled from King Solomon), he returned to Israel; and they sent and called him to Shechem. Then he and all Israel came to Rehoboam. "Your father made our yoke heavy," they said. "Now therefore lighten his hard service and we will serve you."

"Come to me again in three days," King Rehoboam said. Then he conferred with the old men who had counseled Solomon his father. "How do you advise me to answer this people?" he asked them. "If you will be kind to this people," they answered, "and speak good words to them, they will be your servants for ever."

Now Rehoboam took counsel with the young men who had grown up with him. "What do you advise that I answer this people?" he said. "Thus shall you speak to them," they replied. " 'My little finger is thicker than my father's loins, and whereas my father chastised you with whips, I will chastise you with scorpions.' "

Jeroboam and the people of Israel came to Rehoboam the third day, as he had said. But the king forsook the counsel of the old men. He answered them harshly, saying, "My father made your yoke heavy, but I will add to it." When the people saw that the king did not hearken to them, they answered him, "What portion have we in

David? We have no inheritance in the son of Jesse. Each of you to your tents, O Israel! Look now to your own house, David." So all Israel departed to their tents.

Then King Rehoboam sent Adoram, the taskmaster over forced labor, to them. But the people of Israel stoned him to death, and King Rehoboam made haste to mount his chariot to flee to Jerusalem. Rehoboam reigned only over the people who dwelt in the cities of Judah, and Israel has been in rebellion against the house of David to this day.

In Jerusalem, Rehoboam assembled the house of Judah to fight against Israel and restore it to his rule. But the word of the LORD came to Shemaiah the man of God: "Say to Rehoboam, king of Judah, and to the rest of the people, 'Thus says the LORD, You shall not fight against your brethren. Return every man to his home, for this thing is from me.' " So they hearkened to the word of the LORD, and did not go against Jeroboam in Israel.

Rehoboam dwelt in Jerusalem, and he made fortresses in Bethlehem and other cities in Judah and Benjamin. The priests and the Levites of all Israel left their holdings and came to Jerusalem from wherever they lived, because Jeroboam had cast them out from serving as priests of the LORD. He had appointed his own priests for the high places and for the golden calves which he had made. So those from all the tribes of Israel who had set their hearts to seek the LORD strengthened the kingdom of Judah. For three years they made Rehoboam secure, because they walked in the way of David and Solomon.

Rehoboam took eighteen wives and sixty concubines, but he loved above all Maacah the granddaughter of Absalom, who bore him Abijam. He appointed Abijam chief prince among his brothers, for he intended to make him king. But when the rule of Rehoboam was established and strong, he forsook the law of the LORD. Because the people of Judah had been unfaithful to the LORD, Shishak king of Egypt came and took their fortified cities and came up against Jerusalem; he took away the treasures of the temple and the king's house; he took away everything. But when Rehoboam humbled himself, the wrath of the

LORD turned from him, so as not to make a complete destruction; moreover, conditions were good in Judah.

King Rehoboam reigned seventeen years in Jerusalem, and there were continual wars between him and Jeroboam. Then Rehoboam slept with his fathers, and was buried in the city of David; and Abijam his son reigned in his stead.

In the eighteenth year of King Jeroboam, Abijam began to reign over Judah. Now there was war between the two kings. Abijam went out to battle in the hill country of Ephraim with an army of valiant men. Jeroboam drew up his line of battle against him with twice as many mighty warriors. Then Abijam stood up and called, "Hear me, O Jeroboam and all Israel! Ought you not to know that the LORD gave the kingship over Israel for ever to David and his sons by a covenant of salt? Yet Jeroboam, a servant of Solomon, rose up and rebelled against his lord; and certain worthless scoundrels gathered about him and defied Rehoboam the son of Solomon when he was young and irresolute. And now you think to withstand the sons of David, because you are a great multitude and have with you the golden calves of Jeroboam. Have you not driven out the priests of the LORD and made priests for yourselves like the peoples of other lands? But as for us, we keep the charge of the LORD. Behold, his priests are at our head with their trumpets to sound the call to battle against you. O sons of Israel, do not fight against the LORD, the God of your fathers, for you cannot succeed."

Now Jeroboam had sent an ambush around behind them, and when Judah looked, behold, his troops were before and behind them. They cried to the LORD, and the priests blew the trumpets. When they raised the battle shout, the men of Israel fled, and Abijam and his people slew them with a great slaughter. Thus Judah prevailed, because it relied upon the LORD.

Jeroboam did not recover his power in the days of Abijam; and the LORD smote him, and he died. But Abijam grew mighty; and he took fourteen wives, and had twenty-two sons and sixteen daughters. When he slept with his fathers, they buried him in the city of David.

Now JEHOSHAPHAT THE grandson of Abijam reigned in Jerusalem and strengthened himself against Israel. The LORD was with him, because he walked in his commandments. Therefore the LORD established the kingdom in his hand, and all Judah brought him tribute. The fear of the LORD fell upon all the kingdoms round about Judah, so that they made no war against Jehoshaphat. Some of the Philistines brought him silver for tribute, and the Arabs brought him more than seven thousand rams and seven thousand he-goats.

Jehoshaphat made a marriage alliance with Ahab king of Israel, and after some years he went down to visit the king in Samaria. Ahab killed an abundance of sheep and oxen for him and asked him to go up with him against the Syrians at Ramoth-gilead. "I am as you are; my people are as your people," Jehoshaphat answered. "But inquire first for the word of the LORD." Ahab gathered the prophets together. "Shall we go to battle against Ramoth-gilead," he asked them, "or shall I forbear?"

"Go up," they said, "for God will give it into the hand of the king." But Jehoshaphat said, "Is there not here another prophet of the LORD of whom we may inquire?"

"There is yet one," King Ahab replied, "but I hate him, for he never prophesies good concerning me." Then he summoned an officer and said, "Bring quickly Micaiah the son of Imlah."

Now the kings were sitting on their thrones, arrayed in their robes, outside the gate of Samaria; and all the prophets were prophesying before them, saying, "Go up to Ramoth-gilead and triumph; the LORD will give it into the hand of the king." When Micaiah came before them, King Ahab said to him, "Micaiah, shall we go to Ramoth-gilead to battle, or shall I forbear?" Micaiah answered, "Go up; the Syrians will be given into your hand."

"How many times shall I adjure you that you speak to me nothing but the truth in the name of the LORD?" King Ahab said.

Then Micaiah replied, "I saw all Israel scattered upon the mountains, as sheep that have no shepherd; and the LORD said,

'These have no master; let each return to his home in peace.' "

"Did I not tell you," said Ahab to Jehoshaphat, "that he would not prophesy good concerning me, but evil?"

"Therefore hear the word of the LORD," Micaiah continued. "I saw the LORD sitting on his throne, and all the host of heaven standing on his right hand and on his left; and the LORD said, 'Who will entice Ahab that he may go up and fall at Ramoth-gilead?' And a spirit came forward, saying, 'I will entice him. I will be a lying spirit in the mouth of all his prophets.' And the LORD said, 'Go forth and entice him.' Now therefore behold, the LORD has put a lying spirit in the mouth of these your prophets."

Then Zedekiah the son of Chenaanah came near and struck Micaiah on the cheek. "How did the Spirit of the LORD go from me to speak to you?" he said. "Behold," Micaiah replied, "you shall see on that day when you go into an inner chamber to hide yourself."

"Seize Micaiah," the king cried, "and put him in prison, and feed him with scant fare of bread and water until I return in peace."

"If you return in peace," Micaiah answered, "the LORD has not spoken by me." And he added, "Hear, all you peoples!"

So the kings of Israel and Judah went up to Ramoth-gilead. Ahab said to Jehoshaphat, "I will disguise myself to go into battle, but you shall wear your royal robes." And thus they went into battle.

Now the king of Syria had commanded his captains, "Fight with neither small nor great, but only with King Ahab of Israel." So when the captains saw King Jehoshaphat, they said, "It is the king of Israel," and they turned to fight against him. But Jehoshaphat cried out, and the LORD helped him, drawing them away. But a certain man drew his bow at a venture, and, unknowing, struck King Ahab between the scales of his armor. "Turn about," Ahab said to his chariot driver, "and carry me out of the battle, for I am wounded." The battle grew hot that day. King Ahab propped himself up in his chariot facing the Syrians until evening; then at sunset he died.

Jehoshaphat returned in safety to his house in Jerusalem. But Jehu the son of Hanani went out to meet him, and said, "Should you help the wicked and love those who hate the LORD? Because of this, wrath has gone out against you from the LORD." So Jehoshaphat went out again among the people, from Beer-sheba to the hill country of Ephraim, and brought them back to the LORD, the God of their fathers. Moreover, in Jerusalem he appointed certain Levites and priests to give judgment for the LORD and to decide disputed cases; and he charged them to deal in faithfulness, and in fear of the LORD.

After this the Moabites and Ammonites, and with them some of the men of Mount Seir, came against Jehoshaphat for battle. Jehoshaphat feared, and he stood in the assembly of Judah in the house of the LORD and said, "O LORD, God of our fathers, we are powerless against this great multitude that is coming against us. We do not know what to do, but our eyes are upon thee."

Meanwhile all the men of Judah stood before the LORD, with their little ones and their wives. And the Spirit of the LORD came upon Jahaziel the son of Zechariah in the midst of the assembly. And he said, "Hearken, all Judah and King Jehoshaphat: Thus says the LORD, 'Be not dismayed at this great multitude; for the battle is not yours but God's. Behold, tomorrow they will come up by the ascent of Ziz, at the end of the valley. You will not need to fight; take your position, stand still, and see the victory of the LORD on your behalf.' Fear not; go out against them, and the LORD will be with you." Then Jehoshaphat bowed his head to the ground, and all Judah fell down before the LORD.

They rose early in the morning and went out into the wilderness of Tekoa; and Jehoshaphat appointed those who were to praise the LORD in holy array as they went before the army, saying, "Give thanks to the LORD, for his steadfast love endures for ever." When they began to sing, the LORD set an ambush against those who had come against Judah, so that they were routed. The men of Ammon and Moab rose against the inhabitants of Mount Seir, destroying them utterly; and then they all turned to attack one another.

When Jehoshaphat and his people came to the watchtower of the wilderness, they beheld only dead bodies lying on the ground; none had escaped. They were three days in taking the spoil, for they found cattle in great numbers, goods, and precious things. On the fourth day they returned to Jerusalem with joy. And the fear of God came on all the kingdoms when they heard that the LORD had fought against the enemies of Judah. So the realm of Jehoshaphat was quiet, for his God gave him rest round about. Jehoshaphat reigned twenty-five years in Jerusalem. Then he slept with his fathers, and was buried in the city of David; and Jehoram his son reigned in his stead.

When Jehoram was established, he slew all his brothers with the sword, and also some of the princes of Israel. And he walked in the way of the kings of Israel, for Athaliah the daughter of Ahab was his wife, and he did what was evil in the sight of the LORD. Yet the LORD would not destroy the house of David because of the covenant he had made with David.

But a letter came to Jehoram from Elijah the prophet, saying, "Thus says the LORD, 'Because you have walked in the way of the kings of Israel, and have led Judah into unfaithfulness, behold, the LORD will bring a great plague on your people, and you yourself will have a severe sickness, until your bowels come out because of it, day by day.'"

After this the LORD smote him in his bowels, and at the end of two years he died in great agony. His people made no fire in his honor, like the fires made for his fathers, and he departed with no one's regret. They buried him in the city of David, but not in the tombs of the kings, and they made Ahaziah his son king in his stead.

AHAZIAH REIGNED ONE year in Jerusalem. His mother was Athaliah, the daughter of Ahab and Jezebel. He did what was evil in the sight of the LORD, for his mother was his counselor. He even followed her advice and went with Joram the son of Ahab to make war against Syria at Ramoth-gilead. The Syrians wounded Joram, and he returned to be healed in Jezreel, and Ahaziah went down to see him there.

It was ordained by God that the downfall of Ahaziah should come about through this visit. At Jezreel he went out with Joram to meet Jehu the son of Nimshi, whom the LORD had anointed to destroy the house of Ahab. When Jehu was executing judgment upon the house of Ahab, he captured Ahaziah and put him to death.

Now when Athaliah saw that her son was dead, she arose and destroyed all his sons except Joash, whom Ahaziah's sister stole away. She was the wife of Jehoiada the priest, and Joash remained with them six years, hid in the house of God, while Athaliah reigned over the land. But in the seventh year Jehoiada the priest took courage and entered into a compact with the captains of the army; and they went about through Judah and gathered the Levites from all the cities, and the heads of fathers' houses; and they came to the house of God in Jerusalem.

"Behold, Joash the king's son!" Jehoiada said to them. "Let him reign, as the LORD spoke concerning the sons of David. The

Levites shall surround him, each with his weapons in his hand; and whoever enters the house of the LORD shall be slain." Then he brought out Joash the king's son, and put the crown upon him. The Levites and all Judah proclaimed him king, and Jehoiada anointed him, and they cried, "Long live the king!"

When Athaliah heard the people praising the king, she went into the house of the LORD; and when she looked, there was Joash standing by the king's pillar with the captains and the trumpeters. All the people were rejoicing, and the singers with their musical instruments led in the celebration. "Treason! Treason!" Athaliah cried, and she rent her clothes.

Then Jehoiada brought out the captains of the army. "Bring Athaliah out between the ranks," he said to them. "Do not slay her in the house of the LORD." So they laid hands on her and took her into the entrance of the horse gate of the king's house, and they slew her there.

Then all the people went to the house of Baal and tore it down. Baal's altars and images they broke in pieces, and they slew his priest before the altar. Jehoiada posted watchmen for the house of the LORD under the direction of the priests and the Levites, as it is written in the law of Moses. Then he and all the people of the land brought the king down to the king's house and set him upon the royal throne. The people rejoiced, and the city was quiet.

JOASH WAS SEVEN years old when he began to reign, and he reigned forty years in Jerusalem. He did what was right in the eyes of the LORD all the days of Jehoiada the priest.

Now Joash decided to restore the house of the LORD; for the sons of Athaliah, that wicked woman, had broken into the temple, and used all the dedicated things for the Baals. He said to the priests and the Levites, "Go out to the cities of Judah and gather money to repair the house of your God, and see that you hasten the matter." Then they made a chest and set it outside the gate of the house of the LORD; and proclamation was made throughout Judah to bring in the tax for the LORD. And whenever the Levites saw that there was much money in the chest, the king's secretary and Jehoiada would give it to those who had charge of the repair. They hired masons and carpenters to restore the house of the LORD to its proper condition, and they made burnt offerings there continually all the days of Jehoiada.

When he was a hundred and thirty years old, Jehoiada died and they buried him among the kings, because he had done good in Israel. After this, King Joash and the princes of the people forsook the God of their fathers and served idols. The LORD sent prophets among them to bring them back to him, but they would not give heed.

Then the Spirit of God took possession of Zechariah the son of Jehoiada, and he stood up among the people. "Thus says God," he said. " 'Why do you transgress the commandments of the LORD, so that you cannot prosper? Because you have forsaken the LORD, he has forsaken you.' " But by the command of King Joash the people stoned Zechariah in the court of the temple. "May the LORD see and avenge!" he said as he was dying.

At the end of the year the Syrian army

came up against Joash. They destroyed all the princes of the people and sent their spoil to Damascus. Though the Syrians had come with few men, the LORD delivered Judah into their hand, because they had forsaken the God of their fathers.

When the Syrians had departed, leaving Joash severely wounded, his servants conspired against him and slew him on his bed because of the blood of Zechariah. They buried him in the city of David, but not in the tombs of the kings; and Amaziah his son reigned in his stead.

AMAZIAH WAS TWENTY-FIVE years old when he began to reign in Jerusalem, and he did what was right in the eyes of the LORD, yet not with a blameless heart. As soon as the royal power was firmly in his hand, he killed those who had slain his father. He turned away from the LORD, and they made a conspiracy against him in Jerusalem and slew him. Then the people of Judah took Uzziah his son, who was sixteen years old, and made him king instead.

Uzziah built Elath and restored it to Judah, and he did what was right in the eyes of the LORD; and as long as he sought the LORD, he prospered. He made war against the Philistines, and God helped him. The Ammonites paid him tribute and his fame spread even to the border of Egypt. He built towers in the wilderness and hewed out many cisterns. He had large herds in the plain, and he had farmers and vine-dressers in the fertile lands, for he loved the soil. In Jerusalem he made engines, invented by skilful men, to shoot arrows and great stones. And Uzziah's fame spread far, for he was marvelously helped, till he was strong.

But when he was strong he grew proud, to his destruction. He was false to the LORD and entered the temple to burn incense on the altar. Azariah the priest went in after him with eighty priests who were men of valor; and they said to King Uzziah, "It is not for you, Uzziah, to burn incense to the LORD, but for the priests the sons of Aaron. Go out of the sanctuary, for you have done wrong."

Because Uzziah became angry with the priests, the LORD smote him with leprosy on his forehead, and the priests thrust him quickly from the temple. And King Uzziah was a leper to the day of his death, and dwelt in a separate house, excluded from the house of the LORD. Jotham his son was over the king's household, governing the people of the land.

When Uzziah slept with his fathers, Jotham his son reigned in his stead. He prevailed against the Ammonites and became mighty, because he ordered his ways before the LORD his God.

After Jotham slept with his fathers, his son Ahaz reigned sixteen years in Jerusalem. He did not do what was right in the eyes of the LORD, but walked in the ways of the kings of Israel. He made molten images for the Baals; he sacrificed on the high places, and on the hills, and under every green tree; and he even burned his sons as an offering. Therefore the LORD gave him into the hands of the king of Syria and of Pekah king of Israel, who defeated him with great slaughter.

The men of Israel took captive two hundred thousand of their kinsfolk in Judah, women, sons, and daughters; they also took much spoil and brought it to Samaria. Oded a prophet of the LORD went out to meet the army and said to them, "Behold, because the LORD, the God of your fathers, was angry with Judah, he gave them into your hand; but you have slain them in a rage which has reached up to heaven. And now you intend to subjugate the people of Judah as your slaves. Have you not sins of your own against the LORD? Now hear me, and send back the kinsfolk whom you have taken, for your guilt is already great."

So the men of Israel rose and clothed with the spoil all that were naked among the captives, provided them with food and drink, and anointed them. Carrying the feeble among them on asses, they brought them to their kinsfolk at Jericho, the city of palm trees.

At that time King Ahaz sent to Tiglath-pileser king of Assyria for help, for the Edomites had again invaded Judah and carried away captives, and the Philistines had made raids and taken Beth-shemesh. Tiglath-pileser came against Ahaz instead of strengthening him. Ahaz gave tribute, but it did not help him.

In the time of his distress he became yet more faithless to the LORD—this same King Ahaz. For he said, "Because the gods of the kings of Syria helped them, I will sacrifice to them, that they may help me." But they were the ruin of Ahaz, and of all Judah, for he cut in pieces the vessels of the temple, and he shut up its doors; and he made himself heathen altars in every corner of Jerusalem, provoking the LORD to anger.

WHEN AHAZ SLEPT with his fathers, Hezekiah his son reigned in his stead. Hezekiah reigned twenty-nine years in Jerusalem, and he did what was right in the eyes of the LORD, according to all that David his father had done. In the first month of his reign he opened the doors of the temple and repaired them, and he assembled the priests and the Levites in the square on the east. "Hear me, Levites!" he said to them. "Now sanctify yourselves, and carry out the filth from the holy place. For our fathers have been unfaithful and have done what was evil in the sight of the LORD; therefore his wrath has come on Judah and

Jerusalem. He has made them an object of horror, of astonishment, and of hissing, as you see with your own eyes. Our fathers have fallen by the sword, and our children and our wives are in captivity for this. Now it is in my heart to make a covenant with the LORD, that his fierce anger may turn away from us. My sons, do not now be negligent, for the LORD has chosen you to stand in his presence and to be his ministers."

Then the Levites arose and sanctified themselves and went in as the king had commanded to cleanse the house of the LORD. They began on the first day of the month, and on the sixteenth day they finished. Then they went in to Hezekiah and said, "We have cleansed all the house of the LORD, and we have made ready all the utensils which King Ahaz discarded."

Then Hezekiah rose early and gathered the officials of the city and went up to the temple. They brought seven bulls, seven rams, seven lambs, and seven he-goats, and Hezekiah commanded the priests to offer them for a sin offering for all Israel on the altar of the LORD. So they killed the bulls, and the priests received the blood and threw it against the altar; and so with the rams, and the lambs, and the he-goats.

Then the king stationed the Levites in the temple with cymbals, harps, and lyres, according to the commandment of David. When the burnt offering began, the song to the LORD began also, and continued until the offering was finished. Thus the service of the house of the LORD was restored. And Hezekiah and the people rejoiced because of what God had done for them; for the thing came about suddenly.

Now the king and all the assembly in Jerusalem decreed to make a proclamation that the people should come and keep the passover at Jerusalem. Couriers went throughout all Israel and Judah with letters from the king, saying, "O people of Israel, return to the LORD, the God of Abraham, Isaac, and Israel, that he may turn again to the remnant of you who have escaped from the hand of the kings of Assyria. Do not now be stiff-necked as your fathers were, but yield yourselves to the LORD, and come to his sanctuary, that his fierce anger may turn away from you. For if you return to the LORD, your brethren and your children will find compassion with their captors and return to this land. The LORD is merciful and will not turn away his face from you if you return to him."

Sojourners out of Israel and Judah came together in Jerusalem to keep the feast of unleavened bread, a very great assembly. There were many who had not sanctified themselves; therefore the Levites had to kill the passover lamb for every one who was not clean, to make it holy to the LORD. And Hezekiah prayed for them, saying, "The good LORD pardon every one who sets his heart to seek the LORD, even though not according to the sanctuary's rules of cleanness." The LORD heard Hezekiah and healed the people. There was great joy in Jerusalem, for there had been nothing like this since the time of Solomon.

Thus Hezekiah did what was good and right before the LORD. But after these acts of faithfulness, Sennacherib king of Assyria came and invaded Judah and encamped against the fortified cities, thinking to win them for himself. Hezekiah built up the wall of Jerusalem and raised towers upon it. He also made weapons in abundance and set combat commanders over the people. Then he gathered the people together in the square at the gate of the city. "Be strong and of good courage," he said to them. "Do not be dismayed before the king of Assyria and his horde, for with us there is one greater than he; with us is the LORD, to help us and to fight our battles." And the people took confidence from his words.

After this, Sennacherib, who was besieging Lachish, sent his servants to Jerusalem. "Thus says Sennacherib king of Assyria," they said. " 'On what are you relying, that you stand siege in Jerusalem? Is not Hezekiah misleading you when he tells you, "The LORD will deliver us"? Do you not know what I and my fathers have done to the peoples of other lands? Were the gods of those nations able to deliver their lands out of my hand? How much less will your God be able to deliver you! Now therefore do not let Hezekiah deceive you in this fashion.' " His servants shouted with a loud voice in the language of Judah to the people upon the wall in order to frighten them.

Then Hezekiah and Isaiah the prophet, the son of Amoz, prayed to heaven, and the LORD sent an angel who cut off all the mighty warriors in the Assyrian camp. So Sennacherib returned with shame of face to his own land, and when he came into the house of his god, some of his own sons struck him down with the sword. Thus the LORD saved Hezekiah and Jerusalem from the hand of the Assyrians, and he gave them rest on every side.

Hezekiah had very great riches and honor, and flocks and herds in abundance. This same Hezekiah closed the upper outlet of the waters of Gihon and directed them down to the west side of the city of David. And he prospered in all his works. Then he slept with his fathers, and all Judah did him honor at his death; and Manasseh his son reigned in his stead.

MANASSEH REIGNED FIFTY-FIVE years in Jerusalem, and he did what was evil in the sight of the LORD. For he rebuilt the high places which his father had broken down, and erected an altar to Baal in the house of God. And he burned his sons as an offering and practiced soothsaying and sorcery. Manasseh seduced Judah, so that they did more evil than the nations whom the LORD drove out before the people of Israel.

The LORD spoke to Manasseh and to his people, but they gave no heed. Therefore the LORD brought upon him the army of the king of Assyria, who took Manasseh with hooks and bound him with fetters and brought him to Babylon. In his distress Manasseh entreated the favor of the LORD and humbled himself greatly before the God of his fathers. He prayed to him, and God heard his supplication and brought him again to Jerusalem into his kingdom. Then Manasseh knew that the LORD was God.

Afterwards he took away the foreign gods from the house of the LORD, and he threw them outside of the city. He also restored the altar of the LORD and offered upon it sacrifices of thanksgiving; and he commanded Judah to serve the LORD God of Israel.

When Manasseh slept with his fathers,

Amon his son reigned for two years in Jerusalem. He did what was evil in the sight of the LORD, and his servants conspired against him and killed him, and the people of the land made Josiah his son king in his stead.

JOSIAH WAS EIGHT years old when he began to reign, and he reigned thirty-one years in Jerusalem. He did what was right in the eyes of the LORD and walked in the ways of David his father; he did not turn aside to the right or to the left. For in the twelfth year of his reign he began to purge Judah of the high places and the molten images. He also burned the bones of their priests and hewed down all the incense altars throughout the land.

Now in the eighteenth year of his reign he sent Shaphan the secretary to Hilkiah the high priest to see to the repair of the temple, which the kings of Judah had let go to ruin. While Shaphan was bringing out the money that had been collected, Hilkiah the priest found the book of the law of the LORD given through Moses. "I have found the book of the law in the house of the LORD," he told Shaphan, and he gave the book to him.

Shaphan reported to the king, "Hilkiah has given me a book." And Shaphan read it before the king.

When the king heard the words of the law he rent his clothes. "Go, inquire of the LORD for me concerning the words of the book that has been found," he commanded Hilkiah and Shaphan. "Great is the wrath of the LORD on us, because our fathers have not done according to its words."

So Hilkiah and Shaphan went to Huldah the prophetess, who dwelt in Jerusalem in the Second Quarter, and spoke to her. "Thus says the LORD, the God of Israel," she replied. " 'Behold, I will bring evil upon this place and upon its inhabitants, all the curses that are written in the book which was read before the king. Because they have forsaken me and have burned incense to other gods, therefore my wrath will be poured out upon them. But to the king of Judah, thus shall you say to him: Because your heart was penitent and you humbled yourself and wept before God when you heard his words against this place, I also have heard you, says the LORD. Behold, I will gather you to your fathers in peace, and your eyes shall not see all the evil which I will bring upon this place and its inhabitants.' " And they brought back this word to the king.

Then the king sent and gathered together all the elders of Judah. He went up to the house of the LORD with them and all the people both great and small; and he read in their hearing the book which had been found in the house of the LORD. And the king stood in his place and made a covenant before the LORD, to walk after him and to keep his commandments with all his heart and soul. Then he made all who were present promise to adhere to it. And Josiah took away all the abominations from the territory of Israel, and all his days the people did not turn away from following the LORD.

IN THE EIGHTEENTH year of the reign of Josiah he said to the Levites, who were holy to the LORD, "Now serve the LORD your God and his people Israel. Kill the passover lamb, and sanctify yourselves, and prepare for your brethren, to do according to the word of the LORD by Moses."

Then Josiah contributed as passover offerings lambs and kids from his own flock to the number of thirty thousand. When the service had been prepared, the priests, the sons of Aaron, stood in their place, and the Levites in their divisions according to the directions of David king of Israel. The Levites killed the passover lambs, and the sons of Aaron sprinkled the blood which they received from them. And the priests distributed the burnt offerings to the lay people to sacrifice to the LORD, as it is written in the book of Moses. The singers were in their place, according to the command of David, and the gate-keepers were at each gate; they did not need to depart from their service, for their brethren the Levites prepared burnt offerings for them. So the people of Israel kept the passover that day, and the feast of unleavened bread seven days, according to the command of King Josiah. No passover like it had been kept since the days of Samuel the prophet.

After all this, Neco king of Egypt went up to fight at Carchemish on the Euphrates, and Josiah went out against him. But Neco sent envoys to him, saying, "What have we to do with each other, king of Judah? I am not coming against you this day, but against the house with which I am at war; and God has commanded me to make haste. Cease opposing God, who is with me, lest he destroy you."

Nevertheless Josiah did not listen to the words of Neco from the mouth of God, but joined battle with him in the plain of Megiddo. And the archers shot him, and he said to his servants, "Take me away, for I am badly wounded." So his servants carried King Josiah in his chariot to Jerusalem, and he died and was buried with his fathers. All Judah mourned for Josiah. Jeremiah the prophet also uttered a lament for him; and all the singing men and women have spoken of Josiah in their laments to this day.

THE PEOPLE TOOK Jehoahaz the son of Josiah and made him king in his father's stead. But Jehoahaz reigned only three months in

Jerusalem, for the king of Egypt deposed him and took him to Egypt and made Jehoiakim his brother king in his place.

Jehoiakim reigned eleven years in Jerusalem, and he did what was evil in the sight of the LORD. Nebuchadnezzar king of Babylon came up against him, and bound him in fetters to take him to Babylon; and Jehoiachin his son reigned in his stead.

Jehoiachin was eighteen years old when he began to reign, and he reigned three months and ten days in Jerusalem. In the spring of the year King Nebuchadnezzar sent and brought him to Babylon, and made his brother Zedekiah king over Judah.

Zedekiah reigned eleven years in Jerusalem. He did what was evil in the sight of the LORD, and did not humble himself before Jeremiah the prophet, who spoke from the mouth of the LORD. He also rebelled against King Nebuchadnezzar, and he hardened his heart against turning to the LORD. All the leading priests and the people likewise were exceedingly unfaithful, following all the abominations of the nations. The LORD sent persistently to them by his messengers, but they kept scoffing at his prophets. So the wrath of the LORD rose against his people, till there was no remedy.

Therefore he brought up against them Nebuchadnezzar king of Babylon. He slew their young men with the sword in their sanctuary, and had no compassion on young man or virgin, old man or aged. The LORD gave them all into his hand. And all the treasures of the house of God, and the treasures of the king, all these he brought to Babylon. And they burned the house of God, and broke down the wall of Jerusalem, and burned all its palaces with fire. Nebuchadnezzar took into exile in Babylon those who had escaped from the sword, and they became servants to him and to his sons until the establishment of the kingdom of Persia, to accomplish the word of the LORD by the mouth of Jeremiah. All the days that the land lay desolate it kept sabbath, to fulfil seventy years.

NOW IN THE first year of Cyrus king of Persia, that the word of the LORD by the mouth of Jeremiah might be accomplished, the LORD stirred up the spirit of Cyrus, so that he made a proclamation throughout all his kingdom: "Thus says Cyrus king of Persia, 'The LORD, the God of heaven, has given me all the kingdoms of the earth, and he has charged me to build him a house at Jerusalem, which is in Judah. Whoever is among you of all his people, may the LORD his God be with him. Let him go up.' "

EZRA

The books of Ezra and Nehemiah, which in Hebrew form a single book, are a continuation of the books of Chronicles, telling about the return of the Jews from exile in Babylon. In 586 B.C. the Babylonians conquered Judah, but they in turn were conquered by Cyrus, king of Persia. In 538, Cyrus issued an edict permitting the Jews to leave Babylon. Many do so, and under the leadership of Sheshbazzar they begin to rebuild the temple in Jerusalem. Because of local opposition, however, the temple has to be left unfinished. During the reign of Darius I (521–485 B.C.) a second returning group, led by Zerubbabel and Jeshua, and encouraged by the prophets Haggai and Zechariah, manages in the face of opposition to complete the temple by the spring of 515 B.C. Still later another large group of Jews returns, under the leadership of Ezra, a Jewish scribe. With him Ezra brings a codification of the Mosaic law, and he also introduces reforms, notably in the matter of mixed marriages. Because of intermarriage with Gentiles, he charges, the Jews are in danger of blending with the nations around them. He therefore requires the eviction of Gentile wives from Jewish families.

IN THE FIRST year of Cyrus king of Persia, that the word of the LORD by the mouth of Jeremiah might be accomplished, the LORD stirred up the spirit of the king, so that he made a proclamation throughout all his kingdom:

"Thus says Cyrus king of Persia: The LORD, the God of heaven, has given me all the kingdoms of the earth, and he has charged me to build him a house at Jerusalem, which is in Judah. Whoever is among you of all his people, let him go up and rebuild the house of the LORD, the God of

Israel—he is the God who is in Jerusalem; and let each survivor be assisted by the men of his place with silver and gold, with goods and with beasts."

Then rose up the heads of the families of Judah, and the priests and the Levites, every one whose spirit God had stirred to go up to rebuild the temple in Jerusalem; and all who were about them aided them with vessels of silver, with gold, with goods, with beasts, and with costly wares. Cyrus also brought out the vessels of the temple, which Nebuchadnezzar had carried away from Jerusalem, and the treasurer counted them out to Sheshbazzar the prince of Judah. The vessels of gold and of silver were five thousand four hundred and sixty-nine. All these did Sheshbazzar bring up to Jerusalem.

When the seventh month came, and the sons of Israel were back in the towns, the people gathered as one man to Jerusalem, and they built the altar of the God of Israel for burnt offerings, as it is written in the law of Moses. For fear was upon them because of the peoples of the lands round about, and they made burnt offerings to the LORD daily, morning and evening. And they kept the feast of booths, as it is written. But the foundation of the temple was not yet laid, so they gave money to the masons and the carpenters, and food, drink, and oil to the Sidonians and the Tyrians to bring cedar trees from Lebanon by sea to Joppa.

When the builders laid the foundation of the temple, the priests in their vestments came forward with trumpets, and the Levites with cymbals, to praise the LORD, according to the directions of David the king; and they sang responsively, praising and giving thanks to the LORD: "For he is good, for his steadfast love endures for ever toward Israel." And all the people shouted with a great shout when they praised the LORD, because the foundation of his house was laid. But many of the old men who had seen the first house wept when they saw the foundation being laid, though many shouted aloud for joy; so that the people could not distinguish the sound of the joyful shout from that of the people's weeping, and the sound was heard afar.

Now when the Samaritans heard that the returned exiles were building a temple to the LORD, they approached them and said, "Let us build with you; for we worship your God as you do, and we have been sacrificing to him ever since Esarhaddon king of Assyria brought us here." But all Israel said to them, "You have nothing to do with us in building a house to our God; we alone will build to the God of Israel, as King Cyrus has commanded us."

Then the Samaritans discouraged the people of Judah, and made them afraid to build, and hired counselors against them at court to frustrate their purpose, all the days of Cyrus. So the work on the house of God in Jerusalem ceased until the second year of the reign of Darius king of Persia.

That year the prophets Haggai and Zechariah the son of Iddo prophesied to the Jews in Jerusalem in the name of the God of Israel. Then Zerubbabel the son of She-alti-el and Jeshua the son of Jozadak arose and began to rebuild the temple, the prophets helping them.

At the same time Tattenai the governor of the province Beyond the River came and spoke to them thus: "Who gave you a decree to build this house and to finish this structure?" But the eye of their God was upon the Jews, and Tattenai did not stop them till a report should reach Darius and answer be returned. His report read as follows:

"To Darius the king, all peace. Be it known to the king that we went to the province of Judah, to the house of the great God. It is being built with huge stones, and timber is laid in the walls; this work goes on diligently and prospers. We spoke to the elders thus: 'Who gave you a decree to build this house and to finish this structure?' This was their reply: 'We are the servants of the God of heaven and earth, and we are rebuilding the house built many years ago by a great king of Israel. But because our fathers had angered the God of heaven, he gave them into the hand of Nebuchadnezzar king of Babylon, who destroyed this house and carried away the people to Babylonia. However, in the first year of Cyrus the king, Cyrus made a decree that this house of God should be rebuilt. And he delivered the gold and silver vessels, which Nebuchadnezzar had taken out of the temple in Jerusalem and brought to Babylon, to one Sheshbazzar, whom he had made governor, saying, "Take these vessels to Jerusalem, and let the temple be rebuilt on its site." Then this Sheshbazzar came and laid the foundations of the temple in Jerusalem; and it is not yet finished.' Therefore, if it seem good to the king, let search be made in the royal archives for such a decree issued by Cyrus. And let the king send us his pleasure in this matter."

Then Darius the king had search made, and a record was found: "In the first year of Cyrus the king, he issued a decree: Concerning the house of God at Jerusalem, let the house be rebuilt, and let the cost be paid from the royal treasury. Also let the gold and silver vessels of the temple, which Nebuchadnezzar brought to Babylon, be restored and brought back to Jerusalem."

"Now therefore," Darius decreed, "Tattenai, governor of the province Beyond the River, keep away; let the governor and the elders of the Jews rebuild this temple on its site. Moreover, the cost is to be paid in full and without delay from the royal revenue, the tribute of the province Beyond the River. And whatever is needed—young bulls, rams, or sheep for burnt offerings to the God of heaven, wheat, salt, wine, or oil, as the priests at Jerusalem require—let that be given to them day by day without fail, that they may offer pleasing sacrifices to the God of heaven, and pray for the life of the king and his sons. If any one alters this edict, a beam shall be pulled out of his house, and he shall be impaled upon it, and his house shall be made a dunghill. I Darius make a decree; let it be done with all diligence."

Then Tattenai did with all diligence what Darius had ordered; and the Jews built and prospered, through the prophesying of Haggai and Zechariah. They finished their building by command of the God of Israel and by decree of Cyrus and Darius; and the temple was finished on the third day of the month of Adar, in the sixth year of the reign of Darius.

The people of Israel, the priests and the Levites, and the rest of the returned exiles celebrated the dedication of this temple with joy. They offered sacrifices: one hundred bulls, two hundred rams, four hundred lambs, and as a sin offering twelve he-goats, according to the number of the tribes of Israel. And they set the priests and the Levites in their divisions for the service of God, as it is written in the book of Moses.

On the fourteenth day of the first month the returned exiles kept the passover. The priests and the Levites killed the passover lamb for all the exiles, for their fellow priests, and for themselves; it was eaten by them, and also by every one who had separated himself from the pollutions of the peoples of the land to worship the God of Israel. And they kept the feast of unleavened bread seven days with joy; for the LORD had made them joyful, and had turned to them the heart of the king of Persia.

Now IN THE seventh year of the reign of Artaxerxes king of Persia, Ezra the son of Seraiah went up from Babylonia to Jerusalem. He was a scribe skilled in the law of

Moses, and the king granted him all that he asked, for the hand of the LORD was upon him. Ezra had set his heart to study the law of the LORD, and to do it, and to teach his statutes and ordinances in Israel. King Artaxerxes gave him this letter: "Artaxerxes, king of kings, to Ezra the priest, the scribe of the law of the God of heaven. Now I make a decree that any of the people of Israel who freely offer to go to Jerusalem may go with you. For you are sent by the king and his seven counselors to make inquiries about Judah and Jerusalem according to the law of your God, which is in your hand, and also to convey the silver and gold which the king and his counselors have freely offered to the God of Israel, whose dwelling is in Jerusalem. With this money, then, you shall with all diligence buy bulls, rams, and lambs, and you shall offer them upon the altar of the temple. And whatever else is required for the house of your God, you may provide it out of the king's treasury.

"And I, Artaxerxes the king, make a decree to all the treasurers in the province Beyond the River: Whatever Ezra the priest, the scribe of the law, requires of you, be it done with all diligence, lest the wrath of the God of heaven be against the realm of the king and his sons.

"And you, Ezra, according to the wisdom of your God which is in your hand, appoint magistrates and judges who may judge all the people in the province Beyond the River such as know the laws of your God; and those who do not know them, you shall teach. Whoever will not obey the law of your God and the law of the king, let judgment be strictly executed upon him, for death or banishment or confiscation of goods or imprisonment."

BLESSED BE THE LORD, the God of our fathers, who put it into the heart of the king to beautify the temple in Jerusalem, and who extended to me his steadfast love before all the king's mighty officers. I took courage, for the hand of the LORD was upon me, and I gathered leading men from Israel to go up with me from Babylonia. I gathered them to the river that runs to Ahava, and there we encamped three days.

I proclaimed a fast, that we might humble ourselves before our God, to seek from him a straight way for ourselves, our children, and all our goods. For I was ashamed to ask the king for soldiers to protect us on our way, since we had told him, "The hand of our God is for good upon all that seek him, and the power of his wrath is against all that forsake him." So we fasted and besought our God for this, and he listened to our entreaty.

Then I set apart twelve of the leading priests, and I weighed out to them the silver and the gold and the vessels which the king had offered for the temple.

"You are holy to the LORD," I said to them, "and the vessels are holy, and the silver and the gold are a freewill offering to the LORD. Guard them and keep them until you weigh them before the chief priest at Jerusalem, within the chambers of the temple." So the priests took the silver and the gold and the vessels, to bring them to Jerusalem.

Then we departed from the river on the twelfth day of the first month, to go to Jerusalem; the hand of our God was upon us, and he delivered us from the enemy and from ambushes by the way. We came to Jerusalem on the first day of the fifth month. On the fourth day, within the temple, the silver and the gold and the vessels were weighed into the hands of Meremoth the priest, and the weight of everything was recorded. At that time those who had come from captivity offered burnt offerings to the God of Israel. They also delivered the king's commissions to the governors of the province Beyond the River, and they aided the people and the house of God.

THE OFFICIALS APPROACHED me and said, "The people of Israel and the priests and the Levites have not separated themselves from the peoples of the lands round about, with their abominations. For they have taken their daughters to be wives for themselves and for their sons, so that the holy race has mixed itself with the peoples of the lands. And in this faithlessness the chief men have been foremost."

When I heard this, I rent my garments and pulled hair from my head and beard, and sat appalled until evening. At the evening sacrifice I rose from my fasting, and fell upon my knees and spread out my hands to the LORD my God, saying: "O my God, I am ashamed to lift my face to thee, for our iniquities have risen higher than our heads, and our guilt has mounted to the heavens. From the days of our fathers to this day we have been in great guilt; and for our iniquities we, our kings, and our priests have been given to the sword, to captivity, to plundering, and to utter shame, as at this day. But now for a brief moment favor has been shown by the LORD to leave us a remnant, and to give us a secure hold within his holy place, that he may brighten our eyes and grant us a little reviving in our bondage. We are bondmen; yet our God has not forsaken us in our bondage, but has extended to us his steadfast love before the kings of Persia, to set up the house of our God, to repair its ruins, and to give us protection in Judea.

"And now, O our God, what shall we say after this? For we have forsaken thy commandments, which thou didst command by the prophets, saying, 'The land you are entering to possess is a land unclean with the pollutions of its peoples, whose abominations have filled it from end to end. Therefore give not your daughters to their sons, neither take their daughters for your sons, and never seek their peace or prosperity, that you may be strong, and eat the good of the land, and leave it for an inheritance to your children for ever.' And after all that has come upon us for our evil deeds, and seeing that thou, our God, hast punished us less than our iniquities deserved, shall we break thy commandments again and intermarry with the peoples who practice these abominations? Wouldst thou not be angry with us till thou wouldst consume us, so that there should be no remnant, nor any to escape? O LORD, thou art just. Behold, we are before thee in our guilt, for none can stand before thee because of this."

While Ezra prayed, weeping and casting himself down before the house of God, a very great assembly of men, women, and children gathered to him out of Israel, and the people wept bitterly. Shecaniah the son of Jehiel addressed Ezra: "We have broken faith with our God and have married foreign women, but even now there is hope for Israel in spite of this. Therefore let us make a covenant with our God to put away all these wives and their children, according to the counsel of my lord; and let it be done according to the law. Arise, for it is your task, and we are with you; be strong and do it."

Then Ezra arose and made all Israel take oath that they would do as had been said. Then he withdrew from before the temple and went to the chamber of Jehohanan the son of Eliashib, where he spent the night, neither eating bread nor drinking water; for he was mourning over the faithlessness of the exiles. And a proclamation was made throughout Judah that all the returned exiles should assemble at Jerusalem. Any one who did not come within three days should be banned from the congregation of the exiles, and all his property forfeited.

All the men of Judah came within the three days. On the twentieth day of the ninth month they sat in the open square before the temple, trembling because of this matter and because of heavy rain.

Then Ezra the priest stood up. "You have trespassed and married foreign women," he said to them, "and so increased the guilt of Israel. Now then make confession to the LORD, and do his will; separate yourselves from the foreign wives."

"It is so," the assembly answered; "we must do as you have said. But the people are many, and it is a time of heavy rain; we cannot stand in the open. Nor is this a work for one day or for two; for we have greatly transgressed in this matter. Let our officials stand for the whole assembly; let all in our cities who have taken foreign wives come at appointed times, and with them their elders and judges, till the fierce wrath of our God over this matter be averted from us."

This the returned exiles did. Ezra selected heads of fathers' houses, and on the first day of the tenth month they sat down to examine the matter. By the first day of the first month they had come to the end of all the men who had married foreign women. These pledged themselves to put away their wives, and they put them away with their children.

NEHEMIAH

The Book of Nehemiah embodies the first-person "memoirs" of this Jewish leader of the postexilic period. Nehemiah, cup-bearer to the Persian king Artaxerxes (465–424 B.C.), is allowed to visit Jerusalem in order to assist with the city's restoration. His narrative contains stirring accounts of conflicts with enemies who plot against the rebuilding of the city walls. Despite this opposition, the work of restoration is finally completed, and the people then enter into a covenant to observe God's law as given by Moses. Nehemiah also tells of Ezra reading the Mosaic law to a great assembly of the people, while the Levites interpret the law to them, after which Ezra leads the assembly in a confession of sins and in the worship of God. Both books, Ezra and

Nehemiah, were written by the same man (who was probably also the author of the books of Chronicles), sometime between 350 and 300 B.C.

———

THE WORDS OF Nehemiah the son of Hacaliah. Now it happened in the month of Chislev, in the nineteenth year of King Artaxerxes, as I was in Susa the winter capital, that Hanani, one of my brethren, came with certain men out of Judah; and I asked them concerning the Jews that survived, who had escaped exile, and concerning Jerusalem.

"The survivors are in great trouble and shame," they replied. "The wall of Jerusalem is broken down, and its gates are destroyed by fire."

When I heard these words, I sat down and wept, and mourned for days, fasting and praying before the God of heaven. "O LORD," I said, "the great and terrible God who keeps covenant and steadfast love with those who love him and keep his commandments; hear thy servant confessing the sins of the people of Israel. We have acted very corruptly against thee, and have not kept the ordinances thou didst command thy servant Moses, saying, 'If you are unfaithful, I will scatter you among the peoples; but if you keep my commandments and do them, though your exiles be under the farthest skies, I will bring them thence to the place I have chosen, to make my name dwell there.' They are thy servants and thy people, whom thou hast redeemed by thy great power and strong hand."

Now I was cupbearer to the king. In the month of Nisan, I took up wine and gave it to him. I had not been sad before in his presence, and the king said to me, "Why is your face sad, seeing you are not sick? This is nothing else but sadness of the heart."

Then I was very much afraid. "Let the king live for ever!" I said. "Why should not my face be sad, when the city, the place of my fathers' sepulchres, lies waste, and its gates have been destroyed by fire?"

"For what do you make request?" the king asked.

So I prayed to the God of heaven, "O LORD, let thy ear be attentive to the prayer of thy servant, and give him success today, and grant him mercy in the sight of this man." Then I said to the king, "If it pleases the king, and if your servant has found favor in your sight, send me to Jerusalem, that I may rebuild it."

"How long will you be gone, and when will you return?" the king said to me (the queen sitting beside him).

So it pleased him to send me; and I set him a time. "If it pleases the king," I said, "let letters be given me to the governors of the province Beyond the River, that they may let me pass through to Judah; and a letter to Asaph, the keeper of the king's forest, that he may give me timber to make beams for the wall of the city, and for the house I shall occupy." The king granted what I asked, for the good hand of my God was upon me.

Then I came to the governors of the province Beyond the River and gave them the king's letters; but when Sanballat the governor of Samaria heard this, it displeased him greatly that some one had come to seek the welfare of the children of Israel.

I came to Jerusalem. After three days there, I arose in the night, I and a few men with me. Telling no one what my God had put into my heart to do for Jerusalem, I went out by night by the Valley Gate, and inspected the walls of Jerusalem which were broken down and its gates which had been destroyed. I went on to the Fountain Gate and to the King's Pool, and entered again by the Valley Gate. The officials did not know where I had gone or what I was doing; and I had not yet told the Jews, the priests, the nobles, and the rest that were to do the work.

"You see the trouble we are in," I then said to the Jews, "how Jerusalem lies in ruins with its gates burned. Come, let us rebuild the wall, that we may no longer suffer disgrace." And I told them how the hand of my God had been upon me for good, and also the words the king had spoken to me.

"Let us rise up and build," they said. So they strengthened their hands for the good work.

Then Eliashib the high priest rose up with his brethren the priests and they built the Sheep Gate; and next to him the men of Jericho built. Joiada the son of Paseah repaired the Old Gate; he laid its beams and set its doors, its bolts, and its bars. And Hanun and the inhabitants of Zanoah repaired the Valley Gate and fifteen hundred feet of the wall, as far as the Dung Gate. Others repaired opposite their houses.

So we built the wall; and all the wall was joined together to half its height. For the people had a mind to work.

When Sanballat and Tobiah the Ammonite and Geshem the Arab heard of it, they derided us. "What is this thing that you are doing?" they asked. "Are you rebelling against the king?"

"The God of heaven will make us prosper," I replied to them, "and we his servants will arise and build; but you have no portion or right or memorial in Jerusalem."

Sanballat ridiculed us in the presence of his brethren. "What are these feeble Jews doing?" he cried. "Will they restore things? Will they finish up in a day? Will they revive the stones out of the heaps of rubbish, and burned ones at that?"

Tobiah said, "Yes, what they are building—if a fox goes up on it, he will break down their stone wall!"

Hear, O our God, for we are despised; turn back their taunt upon their own heads, and give them up to be plundered in a land where they are captives. Do not cover their guilt.

Sanballat and Tobiah and the Arabs were very angry; they all plotted to fight against Jerusalem and to cause confusion in it. We prayed to our God, and set a guard against them day and night.

But the Jews said, "The strength of the burden-bearers is failing, and there is much rubbish; we are not able to work on the wall." Our enemies said, "They will not know or see till we come into the midst of them and kill them and stop the work." The Jews who lived near them came and said to us ten times, "From all the places where they live they will come up against us."

So in open places behind the wall I stationed the people according to their families, with their swords, their spears, and their bows. "Do not be afraid of them," I said to the nobles and the people. "Remember the Lord, who is great and terrible, and fight for your brethren, your sons, your daughters, your wives, and your homes."

Our enemies heard that their plan was known to us and that God had frustrated it. We all returned to the wall, each to his work. From that day on, half of my servants worked on construction, and half held the spears, shields, bows, and coats of mail; and the leaders stood behind all who were building on the wall. Those who carried burdens were laden in such a way that each held his weapon in one hand, and each of the builders had his sword girded at his side while he built. The trumpeter was beside me. "The work is great and widely spread," I said to the people, "and we are separated on the wall, far from one another. In the place where you hear the sound of the trumpet, rally to us there. Our God will fight for us."

So we labored at the work, and half held the spears from the break of dawn till the stars came out. I also had every man and his servant pass the night within Jerusalem, that they might be a guard for us by night and labor by day. So neither I nor my brethren nor the men of the guard took off our clothes; each kept his weapon in his hand.

Now THERE AROSE a great outcry of the people against their Jewish brethren: "We are mortgaging our fields, our vineyards, and our houses to get grain because of the famine." Others said, "We have borrowed money upon our fields and our vineyards to pay the king's tax. Our flesh is as the flesh of our brethren, our children are as their children; yet we are forcing our sons and daughters to be slaves, and some of our daughters have already been enslaved, that we may buy grain in order to live; but it is not in our power to help it, for our brethren have our fields and our vineyards."

I was very angry when I heard their outcry. I took counsel with myself, and I brought charges against the nobles and officials. "You are exacting interest, each from his brother," I said to them; and I held a great assembly against them. "We, as far as we are able, have bought back our Jewish brethren who have been sold to the nations," I told them; "but you even sell your brethren that they may be sold back to us!" They were silent, finding not a word to say.

"What you are doing is not good," I said. "Ought you not to walk in the fear of our God to prevent the taunts of our enemies? Leave off this interest. Return to your brethren this very day their fields, their vineyards, their olive orchards, and their houses, and the hundredth of money, grain, wine, and oil which you have been exacting of them each month."

"We will restore these and require nothing from them," they replied. "We will do as you say."

Then I called the priests, who took an oath of them. I also shook out my lap and said, "So may God shake out every man from his house who does not perform this promise. May he be shaken out and emptied." All the assembly said "Amen" and praised the LORD. And the people did as they had promised.

Moreover from the time I was appointed governor of Judah, from the twentieth year to the thirty-second year of Artaxerxes the king, twelve years, neither I nor my brethren took the food allowance of the governor. Former governors laid heavy burdens upon the people, and took from them food and wine, besides forty shekels of silver. Even their servants lorded it over the people. But I did not do so, because of the fear of God. I also held to the work on the wall, and acquired no land; and all my servants were gathered there for the work. Moreover there were at my table a hundred and fifty Jews who came to us from the nations about us. There was prepared for one day one ox and six choice sheep, and fowls likewise, and every ten days skins of wine in abundance; yet with all this I did not demand the food allowance of the governor, because the servitude was heavy upon this people. Remember for my good, O my God, all that I have done for this people.

Now WHEN IT was reported to Sanballat and to Geshem the Arab that I had built the wall and that there was no breach left in it (although I had not yet set up the doors in the gates), they sent to me, saying, "Come and let us meet together." But they intended to do me harm, so I sent messengers to them, saying, "I am doing a great work, and why should the work stop while I leave it and come down to you?" They sent to me four times in this way.

Then Sanballat for the fifth time sent his servant to me with an open letter in his hand. In it was written, "It is reported among the nations that you and the Jews intend to rebel; that is why you are building the wall; and you wish to become their king. You have set up prophets to proclaim you in Jerusalem, 'There is a king in Judah.' It will be reported to the king. So now come, and let us take counsel together."

"No such things as you say have been done," I replied to him, "for you are inventing them out of your own mind." They wanted to frighten us, thinking, "Their hands will drop from the work, and it will not be done." But now, O God, strengthen thou my hands.

Now when I went into the house of Shemaiah, who had pronounced a prophecy against me, he said, "Let us meet together in the house of God, within the temple, and close the doors; for they are coming to kill you; at night they are coming to kill you."

"Should such a man as I flee?" I answered. "And what man such as I could go into the temple and live? I will not go in." I understood that God had not sent him, but that Tobiah and Sanballat had hired him, so that I should be afraid and act in this way and sin, so they could give me an evil name. Remember Tobiah and Sanballat, O my God, according to these things that they did, and also the rest of the prophets who wanted to make me afraid.

So the wall was finished on the twenty-fifth day of the month Elul, in fifty-two days. When our enemies heard of it they were afraid, for they perceived that this work had been accomplished with the help of our God.

Now when the wall had been built and I had set up the doors, and the gatekeepers had been appointed, I gave my brother Hanani charge over Jerusalem, for he was a more faithful and God-fearing man than many.

"Let not the gates of Jerusalem be opened until the sun is hot," I told him, "and while they are still standing guard in the evening, let them shut and bar the doors. Appoint guards from among the inhabitants of Jerusalem, each to a station opposite his own house." The city was wide and large, but the people within it were few and no new houses had been built. The people who came up out of captivity had returned each to his town.

Then God put it into my mind to assemble the nobles and the people to consult together. After this the leaders of the people came to live in Jerusalem; the rest of the people cast lots to bring one out of ten to live in the holy city, while nine tenths remained in the other towns. The people blessed all who willingly offered to live in Jerusalem.

Then they sought the Levites in all their places, to bring them to celebrate the dedication of the wall with thanksgivings and singing, with cymbals, harps, and lyres. The priests and the Levites purified themselves; then they purified the people and the gates and the wall. I brought up the princes of Judah upon the wall, and appointed two great companies which went in procession upon the wall. One went to the right. The other, which I followed with half of the people, went to the left, and we came to a halt at the Gate of the Guard. Then both companies went and stood in the house of God, and they offered great sacrifices that day and rejoiced with great joy; the women and children also rejoiced, and the joy of Jerusalem was heard afar off.

IN THE THIRTY-SECOND year of King Artaxerxes, I went back to Babylon. After some time I again asked leave of the king and returned to Jerusalem. I found that while I was not there, the portions of the Levites, who did the work, had not been given to them, so that they had fled each to his field. So I remonstrated with the officials: "Why is the House of God forsaken?" I gathered the Levites together to set them in their stations. Then all Judah brought the tithes of grain, wine, and oil, and I appointed faithful treasurers over the storehouses, whose duty was to distribute to their brethren.

I also discovered that Eliashib the priest, who was connected with Tobiah the Ammonite, had prepared for Tobiah a large chamber in the temple where they had previously put the frankincense, the vessels, and the tithes of grain, wine, and oil for the Levites and the priests. I was very angry, and I threw all the household furniture of Tobiah out. Then I gave orders, and they cleansed the chamber, and I brought back thither the vessels of the temple, with the frankincense.

Remember me, O my God, concerning this, and wipe not out my good deeds that I have done for the house of my God and for his service.

In those days I saw in Judah men treading wine presses on the sabbath, and bringing in heaps of grain and loading them on asses; also wine, grapes, and figs, which they brought into Jerusalem on the sabbath day. Men of Tyre also, who lived in the city, brought in fish and all kinds of wares and sold them on the sabbath. Then

I remonstrated with the nobles of Judah: "What is this evil thing you are doing, profaning the sabbath day? Did not your fathers act in this way, and did not our God bring evil on us and on this city? Yet you bring more wrath upon Israel."

Before the sabbath, when it began to be dark, I gave orders that the gates should be shut and not opened until after the sabbath. Then the merchants lodged outside the gates once or twice; but I said to them, "Why do you lodge before the wall? If you do so again, I will lay hands on you." From that time on, they did not come on the sabbath. Remember this also in my favor, O my God, and spare me according to the greatness of thy steadfast love.

In those days also I saw Jews who had married foreign women, and half of their children could not speak the language of Judah. I contended with them and cursed them and beat some of them and pulled out their hair; and I made them take oath in the name of God, saying, "You shall not give your daughters to their sons, or take their daughters for your sons or for yourselves. Did not Solomon king of Israel sin on account of such women? Among the nations there was no king like him, and he was beloved by his God, who made him king over all Israel; nevertheless foreign women made even him to sin. Shall we then act treacherously against our God by marrying foreign women?"

And one of the grandsons of Eliashib the high priest was the son-in-law of Sanballat; therefore I chased him from me. Remember them, O my God, because they have defiled the covenant of the priesthood and the Levites.

Thus I cleansed them from everything foreign, and I established the duties of the priests and Levites. Remember me, O my God, for good.

Because of all this we now make a firm covenant and write it, and our princes, our Levites, and our priests set their seal to it. The rest of the people, all who have knowledge and understanding, join with their brethren and enter into a curse and an oath to walk in God's law given by Moses, and to observe all his commandments. We will not give our daughters to the peoples of the land or take their daughters for our sons; nor will we buy from the peoples on the sabbath; and we will forego the crops of the seventh year and the exaction of every debt.

We also lay upon ourselves the yearly obligation of the third part of a shekel for the service of the temple. We have likewise cast lots for the wood offering, to bring it into the temple to burn upon the altar of the LORD, as it is written in the law. We obligate ourselves to bring the first fruits of our ground and of every tree, year by year, to the house of the LORD; also the first-born of our sons and of our cattle, as it is written in the law, and to bring our contributions of fruit and wine and oil to the priests, and the tithes to the Levites, for it is the Levites who collect the tithes in all our rural towns. We will not neglect the house of our God.

WHEN THE SEVENTH month had come, all the people gathered as one man into the square before the Water Gate; and they told Ezra the scribe to bring the book of the law of Moses which the LORD had given to Israel. So Ezra brought the law before the assembly on the first day of the seventh month. He stood on a wooden pulpit which they had made for the purpose, and when he opened the book in the sight of all, the people stood. He read from it, facing the square from early morning until midday, in the presence of both men and women; and they were attentive to the law.

Ezra blessed the LORD, the great God; and all the people answered, "Amen, Amen," lifting up their hands; and they bowed their heads and worshiped the LORD with their faces to the ground. The Levites helped the people to understand the law, giving the sense so that they understood the reading.

"This day is holy to the LORD your God," said Ezra to the people; "do not mourn or weep." For all the people wept when they heard the words of the law. "Go your way, eat the fat and drink sweet wine and send portions to him for whom nothing is prepared; for this day is holy to our LORD; and do not be grieved, for the joy of the LORD is your strength."

So the people went their way to eat and drink and to send portions and to make great rejoicing, because they had understood the reading.

On the second day the heads of families, with priests and the Levites, came to Ezra the scribe to study the words of the law. They found it written that the LORD had commanded by Moses that the people of Israel should dwell in booths during the feast of the seventh month, and that they should go out to the hills and bring branches of olive, myrtle, palm, and other leafy trees to make booths. So the people went out and brought them and made booths for themselves, each on his roof, and in the courts of the temple, and in the square at the Water Gate. All those who had returned from the captivity made booths and dwelt in them, and there was very great rejoicing. Day by day, from the first day to the last day, Ezra read from the book of the law of God. They kept the feast seven days; and on the eighth day there was a solemn assembly, according to the ordinance.

Now ON THE twenty-fourth day of the ninth month, the people of Israel were assembled with fasting and in sackcloth, and with earth upon their heads; they separated themselves from all foreigners, and stood and confessed their sins and the iniquities of their fathers. They stood and listened to the book of the law for a fourth of the day; for another fourth they made confession and worshiped the LORD.

Then Ezra said: "Thou art the LORD, thou alone; thou hast made the heavens with all their host, the earth and all that is on it, the seas and all that is in them; and thou preservest all of them; and the host of heaven worships thee. Thou art the God who didst choose Abram and bring him forth out of Ur of the Chaldeans and give him the name Abraham; and thou didst find his heart faithful before thee, and didst make with him the covenant to give to his descendants the land of Canaan; and thou hast fulfilled thy promise, for thou art righteous.

"And thou didst see the affliction of our fathers in Egypt and hear their cry at the Red Sea, and didst perform signs and wonders against Pharaoh and all his people. Thou didst divide the sea before them, so that they went through the midst of the sea on dry land; and thou didst cast their pursuers into the depth, as a stone into mighty waters. By a pillar of cloud thou didst lead them in the day, and by a pillar of fire in the night to light their way. Thou didst come down upon Mount Sinai, and speak with them and give them right ordinances and good statutes and commandments by Moses thy servant. Thou didst give them bread from heaven for their hunger and bring forth water from the rock for their thirst, and tell them to go in to possess the land which thou hadst sworn to give them.

"But they and our fathers acted presumptuously and did not obey thy commandments, and were not mindful of the wonders thou didst perform among them. But thou art a God gracious and merciful, slow to anger and abounding in steadfast love, and thou didst not forsake them. Even when they had made for themselves a molten calf and said, 'This is your God who brought you up out of Egypt,' and had committed great blasphemies, thou in thy great mercies didst not forsake them in the wilderness; the pillar of cloud which led them did not depart from them by day, nor the pillar of fire by night. Forty years didst thou sustain them in the wilderness, and they lacked nothing; their clothes did not wear out and their feet did not swell. Thou didst multiply their descendants as the stars of heaven, and bring them into the land thou hadst told their fathers to possess. So the descendants went in and captured fortified cities and a rich land, and took possession of houses full of all good things, cisterns hewn out, vineyards, olive orchards and fruit trees in abundance; so they ate, and were filled and became fat, and delighted themselves in thy great goodness.

"Nevertheless they were disobedient and cast thy law behind their back and killed thy prophets, and they committed great blasphemies. Therefore thou didst give them into the hand of the peoples of the lands. Yet thou didst not make an end of them; for thou art a gracious and merciful God.

"Now therefore, our God, the great and mighty and terrible God, who keepest cov-

enant and steadfast love, let not all the
hardship that has come upon us seem little
to thee. Yet thou hast been just in all that
has come upon us, for we have acted wickedly, and behold, we are slaves this day; in
the land thou gavest our fathers, behold,
we are slaves. Its rich yield goes to the
kings whom thou hast set over us because
of our sins; they have power also over our
bodies and over our cattle at their pleasure, and we are in great distress."

ESTHER

During the reign of the Persian king Ahasuerus (that is, Xerxes I, 486–465 B.C.),
the Jews are so hated by the grand vizier,
Haman, that he schemes to have them all
put to death by the king's order. Esther
hears of the plot through Mordecai, her
cousin, and is able, at some risk to herself, to turn the tables on the plotter.
Although there may be a historical basis
for the story, in its present form it seems
to be a popular romance. The book does
not mention God or religion, and the
probable reason for its inclusion in the
canon of the Old Testament was that it
describes the institution of Purim, an annual feast still kept by Jews. Nothing is
known of the book's author or date.
There are no quotations from it in the

New Testament, nor have any fragments of it been found among the Biblical manuscripts at Qumran.

IN THE DAYS of Ahasuerus, the Ahasuerus who reigned from India to Ethiopia over one hundred and twenty-seven provinces, in those days when King Ahasuerus sat on his royal throne in Susa the capital, in the third year of his reign he gave a banquet for all his princes and servants, the army chiefs of Persia and Media, and the nobles and governors of the provinces. For a hundred and eighty days he showed his riches and the splendor of his majesty. When these days were completed, he gave for all the people in Susa a banquet lasting seven days, in the garden court of the palace. There were white cotton curtains and blue hangings caught up with cords of fine linen; also couches of gold and silver on a mosaic pavement of marble, mother-of-pearl, and precious stones. The royal wine was lavished according to the bounty of the king, and served in golden goblets.

Queen Vashti also gave a banquet for the women.

On the seventh day, when the king's heart was merry with wine, he commanded his chamberlains to bring Queen Vashti before him, in order to show the peoples and the princes her beauty. But she refused to come. At this the king was enraged. "According to the law," he asked his wise men, seven princes versed in law and judgment, "what is to be done to Queen Vashti, who has not performed my command?" Memucan, one of the princes, answered, "Not only to the king has Queen Vashti done wrong, but also to all the peoples who are in all the provinces of the king. For her deed will be made known to all women, causing them to look with contempt upon their husbands. They will say, 'King Ahasuerus commanded Queen Vashti to be brought before him, and she did not come.' If it please the king, let a royal order be written among the laws of the Persians and the Medes so that it may not be altered, that Vashti is to come no more before King Ahasuerus, and let the king give her royal position to another who is better than she. When the decree is proclaimed throughout the kingdom, all women will honor their husbands, high and low." This advice pleased the king, and he did as Memucan proposed.

Then the king's servants said, "Let officers be appointed in all the provinces to gather beautiful young virgins to the harem in Susa, under custody of Hegai the eunuch in charge of the women. Let the maiden who pleases the king be queen instead of Vashti." This also pleased the king, and he did so.

Now there was a Jew in Susa named Mordecai, the son of Jair, son of Shimei, son of Kish, a Benjaminite, who had been carried away from Jerusalem among the captives taken by King Nebuchadnezzar of Babylon. Mordecai had brought up Hadassah, that is Esther, the daughter of his uncle, for her father and mother had died. Esther was beautiful, so when the king's order was proclaimed, she was one of the maidens taken into the palace and put in Hegai's custody. But she did not make known her people, for Mordecai had charged her not to. She won Hegai's favor, and he provided her with seven chosen maids and advanced her to the best place in the harem. And every day Mordecai walked in front of the harem court to learn how Esther fared.

Each maiden was to go in turn to King Ahasuerus after twelve months of beautifying: six months with oil of myrrh and six months with spices and ointments. In the evening she went to the palace, and in the morning she came back to the second harem in custody of Shaashgaz the eunuch in charge of the concubines. She did not go in to the king again, unless he delighted in her and she was summoned by name.

Now Esther found favor in the eyes of all who saw her, and when she was taken to the king, in the seventh year of his reign, he loved her more than all others, so he set the royal crown on her head and made her queen. Then he gave a great banquet in her honor, granted a remission of taxes to the provinces, and gave gifts with royal liberality.

One day, as Mordecai was sitting at the king's gate, it came to his knowledge that Bigthana and Teresh, two of the king's eunuchs who guarded the threshold, sought to lay hands on King Ahasuerus. He told Queen Esther, and she told the king in the name of Mordecai. When the affair was investigated and found to be so, the men were hanged. It was recorded in the Book of the Chronicles in the king's presence.

AFTER THESE THINGS King Ahasuerus promoted Haman the Agagite, son of Hammedatha, above all the princes. The servants at the king's gate bowed down to Haman, for the king had so commanded. But Mordecai did not bow down, and when Haman saw this, he was filled with fury. He had been told that the people of Mordecai were Jews, but he disdained to lay hands on Mordecai alone, and sought to destroy all Jews throughout the kingdom.

In the first month, in the twelfth year of King Ahasuerus, they cast Pur, that is the lot, before Haman, and the lot fell on the twelfth month, the month of Adar. Then Haman said to King Ahasuerus, "There is a certain people dispersed in your kingdom whose laws are different from those of every other people. They do not keep the

king's laws, so it is not for the king's profit
to tolerate them. Let it be decreed that
they be destroyed, and I will pay ten thousand talents of silver into the king's treasuries." The king took off his signet ring
and gave it to Haman, saying, "The money
is given to you, the people also. Do with
them as it seems good to you."

On the thirteenth day of the first month,
secretaries were summoned. An edict, according to all that Haman commanded,
was written to the governors and princes
of the provinces, to slay all Jews in one
day, the thirteenth day of the twelfth
month, the month of Adar, and to plunder
their goods. The edict was written in the
name of King Ahasuerus and sealed with
his ring, and a copy of it was to be issued
as a decree in every province and in Susa
the capital.

When Mordecai learned all that had
been done, he rent his clothes and put on
sackcloth and ashes, and went through the
city, wailing loudly. He went only as far as
the entrance of the king's gate, for no one
might enter clothed with sackcloth. In every province, wherever the king's com-

mand came, there was mourning among the Jews.

Esther's maids came and told her, and the queen was deeply distressed. She ordered Hathach, one of the eunuchs who attended her, to go to Mordecai to learn why this was. Mordecai gave Hathach a copy of the decree, that he might show it to Esther and charge her to entreat the king for her people. Hathach did so, and Esther gave him a message for Mordecai, saying, "If any man or woman goes to the king inside the inner court without being called, there is but one law; all alike are to be put to death, unless the king holds out the golden scepter. I have not been called to the king these thirty days."

Mordecai answered, "Think not that in the king's palace you will escape any more than the other Jews. For if you keep silence at such a time as this, deliverance will rise for the Jews from another quarter, but you and your father's house will perish. And who knows whether you have not come to the kingdom for such a time as this?" Esther replied, "Go, gather all the Jews in Susa, and hold a fast on my behalf for three days. I will also fast. Then I will go to the king, though it is against the law; and if I perish, I perish." Mordecai then did as Esther had ordered.

On the third day Esther put on her royal robes and stood in the inner court, opposite the king's hall. The king was sitting on his throne, and when he saw Queen Esther, she found favor in his sight and he held out the golden scepter. Esther approached and touched the top of the scepter. "What is your request?" said the king. "It shall be given you, even to the half of my kingdom." Esther said, "If it please the king, let him come this day with Haman to a dinner that I have prepared." So the king and Haman came to the dinner, and as they were drinking wine, the king said to Esther, "What is your petition? It shall be granted you." Esther said, "If it please the king, let him come again with Haman tomorrow to the dinner which I will prepare, and tomorrow I will answer."

Haman went out glad of heart. But when he saw Mordecai in the king's gate, that he neither rose nor trembled before him, he was filled with wrath. He went home, and recounted to his friends and his wife the riches and promotions with which the king had honored him. "Even Queen Esther," he added, "let no one come with the king to the banquet she prepared but myself. Tomorrow also I am invited. Yet all this does me no good, so long as I see Mordecai the Jew sitting at the king's gate." Then his wife and his friends said, "Let a gallows be made, and in the morning tell the king to have Mordecai hanged upon it; then go merrily to the dinner." This counsel pleased Haman, and he had the gallows made. That night the king could not sleep, and he ordered that the book of memorable deeds, the chronicles, be read to him. It was found written how Mordecai had told about Bigthana and Teresh, who had sought to lay hands upon the king. "What honor or dignity has been bestowed on Mordecai for this?" the king asked, and his servants told him nothing had been done.

When Haman entered the court to speak to the king about having Mordecai hanged, the king said to him, "What shall be done to the man whom the king delights to honor?" Haman, thinking to himself, "Whom more than me would the king delight to honor?" said, "Let royal robes be brought, which the king has worn, and the horse which the king has ridden, and let one of the king's most noble princes array the man and conduct him on horseback through the open square of the city, proclaiming: 'Thus shall it be done to the man whom the king delights to honor.' " The king said, "Make haste, and do as you have said to Mordecai the Jew. Leave out nothing that you have mentioned." So Haman arrayed Mordecai and made him ride through the open square of the city, proclaiming, "Thus shall it be done to the man whom the king delights to honor." When Mordecai returned to the king's gate, Haman hurried to his house, mourning, and told his wife and his friends what had befallen him. They said, "If Mordecai, before whom you have begun to fall, is of the Jewish people, you will not prevail against him, but will surely fall before him." While they were talking, the king's eunuchs arrived and brought Haman in haste to the banquet that Esther had prepared.

The king and Haman feasted with Esther, and as they were drinking wine, the king said, "What is your petition, Queen Esther? It shall be fulfilled." Esther answered, "O king, let my life be given me at my petition, and my people at my request. For we are sold, to be slain and to be annihilated."

"Who is he, and where is he, that would presume to do this?" asked the king. "A foe and enemy!" Esther said. "This wicked Haman!" Then Haman was in terror. The king rose in wrath and went into the garden; but Haman stayed to beg his life from Queen Esther, for he saw that the king determined evil against him. The king returned as Haman was falling on the couch where Esther was. "Will he even assault the queen in my own house?" said the king. Then Harbona, one of the king's attendants, said, "Haman has prepared a gallows for Mordecai, whose word saved the king. It is standing at his house." The king said, "Hang him on that." So they hanged Haman on the gallows he had prepared for Mordecai, and King Ahasuerus gave Esther the house of Haman.

That day Mordecai came before the king, for Esther had told what he was to her. The king took off his signet ring, which he had taken from Haman, and gave it to Mordecai, and Esther set Mordecai over the house of Haman. Then she fell at the king's feet and besought him with tears to avert the evil plot which Haman had devised against the Jews. The king held out the golden scepter to her, and she rose and stood before him. "If it please the king," she said, "let the edict which Haman wrote to destroy the Jews be revoked. For how can I endure to see the destruction of my people?"

"I have given Esther the house of Haman," King Ahasuerus said to Esther and to Mordecai, "and they have hanged him on the gallows, because he would lay hands on the Jews. You may write as you please with regard to the Jews, in the name of the king, and seal it with the king's ring, for an edict so written cannot be revoked."

The king's secretaries were summoned, and an edict was written according to all that Mordecai commanded, and sent by couriers riding on swift horses to the governors and princes of all the provinces, and also to the Jews. The writing was in the name of King Ahasuerus and sealed with his ring. It allowed the Jews to defend their lives, to annihilate any armed force that might attack them, with their children and women, and to plunder their goods, upon one day, the thirteenth day of the twelfth month, the month of Adar.

Mordecai went out from the king's presence in royal robes, with a golden crown, while the city of Susa rejoiced. Wherever the king's edict came, there was gladness among the Jews. And many declared themselves Jews, for fear of the Jews had fallen upon them.

On the thirteenth day of Adar, the very day when the enemies of the Jews had hoped to get mastery over them, the Jews gathered to lay hands on such as sought their hurt. No one could stand against them. The royal officials also helped the Jews, for fear of Mordecai, who grew more and more powerful. In Susa the capital itself the Jews slew five hundred men, also the ten sons of Haman; but they laid no hand on the plunder.

When this was reported to the king, he said to Queen Esther, "Now what is your petition? It shall be granted." Esther said, "If it please the king, let the Jews in Susa be allowed tomorrow also to do according to this day's edict. And let the bodies of Haman's sons be hanged on the gallows." So the king commanded this to be done.

The Jews in the provinces slew seventy-five thousand of their enemies, but laid no hands on the plunder. This was on the thirteenth day of Adar, and on the four-teenth they rested. But the Jews in Susa gathered on the thirteenth day and the fourteenth, and rested on the fifteenth, making that a holiday. Mordecai recorded these things, and sent letters to all the Jews, enjoining them that they should keep the fourteenth day of Adar and the fif-teenth, year by year, as the days on which the Jews got relief from their ene-mies; that they should make them days of feasting and gladness, days for sending choice portions to one another and gifts to the poor. The Jews called these days Purim, after the term Pur, and they ordained that without fail the commemoration of these two days should never cease among their descendants. The command of Queen Esther fixed these practices of Purim, and it was recorded in writing.

The full account of the high honor of Mordecai, to which King Ahasuerus advanced him, is it not written in the Book of the Chronicles of the kings of Media and Persia? For Mordecai the Jew was next in rank to King Ahasuerus, and he was great among the Jews and popular with the multitude of his brethren, for he sought their welfare and spoke peace to all his people.

JOB

Why do good people, the righteous and the innocent, sometimes suffer great sorrow and affliction? In the Book of Job this age-old problem, perhaps the deepest mystery of human life, is brilliantly and movingly discussed.

Job, a good man who is greatly afflicted, rejects the traditional view that suffering is the result of sin, for he has no doubt about his innocence. But he is thoroughly perplexed why God should have sent such calamity upon him, since he does not doubt that God is just. After a searching dialogue between Job and his friends, God himself speaks out of a whirlwind, reminding Job that the universe and the creatures in it are really beyond the understanding of mortals. How then can they presume to argue with God about what he chooses to do? No explicit solution to the problem is offered, but Job is satisfied by an experience of immediate communion with God (*"now my eye sees thee"*), his humility and trust deepened by his sufferings. The book's historical background is uncertain, and the author is unknown. Modern opinion favors a date of composition in the fifth century B.C.

―――――――

THERE WAS A man in the land of Uz, whose name was Job; and that man was blameless and upright, one who feared God, and turned away from evil. There were born to him seven sons and three daughters. He had seven thousand sheep, three thousand camels, five hundred yoke of oxen, five hundred she-asses, and very many servants; so that this man was the greatest of all the people of the east. His sons used to hold a feast, each in turn in his own house, and they would invite their sisters to eat and drink with them. When the days of the feast had run their course, Job would send and sanctify them, and he would rise early and offer burnt offerings according to the number of them all; for he said, "It may be that my sons have sinned, and cursed God in their hearts." Thus Job did continually.

Now there was a day when the sons of God came to present themselves before the LORD, and Satan also came among them. The LORD said to Satan, "Whence have you come?" Satan answered, "From going to and fro on the earth, and from walking up and down on it." And the LORD said, "Have you considered my servant Job, that there is none like him on the earth, a blameless and upright man, who fears God and turns away from evil?" Satan answered, "Does Job fear God for nought? Hast thou not put a hedge about him on every side? Thou hast blessed the work of his hands, and his possessions have increased in the land. But put forth thy hand and touch all that he has, and he will curse thee to thy face." And the LORD said, "Behold, all that he has is in your power; only upon himself do not put your hand." So Satan went forth from the presence of the LORD.

Now there was a day when Job's sons and daughters were eating and drinking wine in their eldest brother's house. A messenger came to Job, and said, "The oxen were plowing and the asses feeding beside them; the Sabeans fell upon them and took them, and slew the servants; and I alone have escaped to tell you." While he was yet speaking, there came another, and said, "The fire of God fell from heaven and burned up the sheep and the servants; and I alone have escaped to tell you." Then came another, saying, "The Chaldeans made a raid upon the camels and took them, and slew the servants; and I alone have escaped to tell you." While he was yet speaking, there came one other, and said, "Your sons and daughters were feasting in their eldest brother's house; and behold, a great wind struck the four corners of the house, and it fell upon the young people, and they are dead; and I alone have escaped to tell you."

Then Job rent his robe, and shaved his head, and fell upon the ground and worshiped. "Naked I came from my mother's womb," he said, "and naked shall I return;

the LORD gave, and the LORD has taken away; blessed be the name of the LORD." In all this Job did not sin or charge God with wrong.

Again there was a day when the sons of God came before the LORD, and Satan also came among them. The LORD said to Satan, "Whence have you come?" and Satan answered, "From going to and fro on the earth, and from walking up and down on it." And the LORD said, "Have you considered my servant Job, that there is none like him? He still holds fast his integrity, although you moved me against him, to destroy him without cause." Satan answered, "Skin for skin! All that a man has he will give for his life. But touch his bone and his flesh, and he will curse thee." And the LORD said to Satan, "Behold, he is in your power; only spare his life."

So Satan went forth, and afflicted Job with loathsome sores from the sole of his foot to the crown of his head. And Job took a potsherd with which to scrape himself, and sat among the ashes. "Do you still hold fast your integrity?" his wife said to him. "Curse God, and die." But Job said,

"You speak as a foolish woman. Shall we receive good at the hand of God and not receive evil?" In all this Job did not sin with his lips.

Now when Job's three friends, Eliphaz the Temanite, Bildad the Shuhite, and Zophar the Naamathite, heard of all that had come upon him, they made an appointment together to go and comfort him. When they saw him from afar, they did not recognize him; and they wept, and rent their robes, and sprinkled dust upon their heads. They sat with him on the ground seven days and seven nights, and no one spoke a word to him, for they saw that his suffering was very great.

After this, Job opened his mouth and cursed the day of his birth, saying, "Let the day perish wherein I was born, and the night which said, 'A man-child is conceived.' Let that day be darkness! Yea, let that night be barren; let no joyful cry be heard in it. Let the stars of its dawn be dark; let it hope for light, but have none, nor see the eyelids of the morning; because it did not shut the doors of my mother's womb.

"Why did I not die at birth? Why did the knees receive me? Or why the breasts, that I should suck? For then I should have slept, and been at rest with kings and counselors of the earth. Or why was I not as a hidden untimely birth, as infants that never see the light? There the wicked cease from troubling, and the weary are at rest. The small and the great are there, and the slave is free from his master.

"Why is light given to him that is in misery, and life to the bitter in soul, who long for death and who rejoice exceedingly when they find the grave? Why is light given to a man whose way is hid, whom God has hedged in? For my groanings are poured out like water, and what I dread befalls me. I am not at ease, I have no rest; but trouble comes."

THEN ELIPHAZ THE Temanite answered:

"If one ventures a word with you, will you be offended? Yet who can keep from speaking? Behold, you have instructed many. Your words have upheld him who was stumbling, and you have made firm the feeble knees. But now it has come to you, and you are impatient; it touches you, and you are dismayed. Is not your fear of God your confidence, and the integrity of your ways your hope? Think now, who that was innocent ever perished? As I have seen, those who sow trouble reap the same. By the blast of God's anger they are consumed. The teeth of the young lions are broken. The strong lion perishes for lack of prey, and the whelps of the lioness are scattered.

"Now a word was brought to me stealthily. Amid thoughts from visions of the night, when deep sleep falls on men, dread came upon me, and trembling made all my bones shake. A spirit glided past my face; the hair of my flesh stood up. It stood still, but I could not discern its appearance. Then I heard a voice: 'Can mortal man be righteous before God? Can a man be pure before his Maker? Even in his servants he puts no trust, and his angels he charges with error; how much more those who dwell in houses of clay, whose foundation is in the dust, who are crushed before the moth. Between morning and evening they are destroyed; they perish for ever without any regarding it. If their tent-cord is plucked up within them, do they not die, and that without wisdom?'

"Call now; is there any one who will answer you? To which of the holy ones will you turn? Surely vexation kills the fool, and jealousy slays the simple. I have seen the fool taking root, but his sons are far from safety; they are crushed in the gate, and there is no one to deliver them. His harvest the hungry eat, and the thirsty pant after his wealth. For affliction does not come from the dust, nor does trouble sprout from the ground; but man is born to trouble as the sparks fly upward.

"As for me, I would seek God, and to him commit my cause. He sets on high those who are lowly, and those who mourn are lifted to safety. He takes the wise in their own craftiness, and the schemes of the wily are brought to a quick end. But he saves the needy from the hand of the mighty. So the poor have hope, and injustice shuts her mouth.

"Behold, happy is the man whom God reproves; despise not the chastening of the Almighty. For he wounds, but his hands heal. He will deliver you from six troubles; in seven shall no evil touch you. In famine he will redeem you from death, and in war from the sword. You shall be in league with the stones of the field, and the beasts of the earth shall be at peace with you. You shall know that your tent is safe; you shall inspect your fold and miss nothing. You shall know also that your descendants shall be many. And you shall come to your grave in ripe old age, as grain comes up to the threshing floor in its season. Lo, this we have searched out; it is true."

THEN JOB ANSWERED:

"Oh, that my vexation were weighed, and all my calamity laid in the balances! It would be heavier than the sand of the sea; therefore my words have been rash. For the arrows of the Almighty are in me; my spirit drinks their poison; the terrors of God are arrayed against me. Does the wild ass bray when he has grass? Can that which is tasteless be eaten without salt? Oh, that God would grant my desire; that it would please him to crush me, to let loose his hand and cut me off! This would be my consolation; I would even exult in pain unsparing; for I have not denied the words of the Holy One. What is my end, that I should be patient? Is my strength the strength of stones, or is my flesh bronze?

"He who withholds kindness from a friend forsakes the fear of the Almighty. My brethren are treacherous as a torrent bed, as streams that pass away when it is hot, vanishing from their place. Caravans turn aside from their course, go up into the waste, and perish. They look for water, and are disappointed because they were confident. Such you have now become to me; you see my calamity, and are afraid. Have I said, 'Make me a gift,' or 'Offer a bribe for me,' or 'Ransom me from oppressors'? Teach me, and I will be silent; make me understand how I have erred. Be pleased to look at me; for I will not lie to your face. My vindication is at stake. Is there any wrong on my tongue?

"Has not man a hard service upon earth? Like a slave who longs for the shadow, or a hireling who looks for his wages, so I am allotted months of emptiness and nights of misery. When I lie down

I say, 'When shall I arise?' But the night is long, and I am full of tossing till the dawn. My flesh is clothed with worms and dirt; my skin hardens, then breaks out afresh. My days are swifter than a weaver's shuttle, and come to their end without hope.

"Remember, O God, that my life is a breath; my eye will never again see good. While thy eyes are upon me, I shall be gone. As the cloud fades and vanishes, so he who goes down to Sheol does not come up; he returns no more to his house. Therefore I will not restrain my mouth; I will speak in the anguish of my spirit: Am I the sea, or a sea monster, that thou settest a guard over me? When I say, 'My bed will comfort me,' then thou dost terrify me with dreams. I loathe my life; I would not live for ever. What is man, that thou dost make so much of him, and set thy mind upon him, dost visit him every morning, and test him every moment? How long wilt thou not look away from me, nor let me alone till I swallow my spittle? If I sin, what do I do to thee, thou watcher of men? Why hast thou made me thy mark? Why dost thou not pardon my transgression and take away my iniquity? For now I shall lie in the earth; thou wilt seek me, but I shall not be."

THEN BILDAD THE Shuhite answered:

"How long will you say these things, and the words of your mouth be a great wind? Does God pervert justice? If your children have sinned against him, he has delivered them into the power of their transgression. If you will seek God, if you are pure and upright, surely then he will reward you with a rightful habitation. And though your beginning was small, your latter days will be very great.

"Inquire, I pray you, of bygone ages, and consider what the fathers have found. Will they not teach you out of their understanding? Can papyrus grow where there is no marsh? Can reeds flourish where there is no water? While yet in flower, they wither. Such are the paths of all who forget God. The hope of the godless man shall perish; his confidence breaks, and his trust is a spider's web. He thrives before the sun, his shoots spread over his garden, his roots twine about the stoneheap. But if he is destroyed from his place, it will deny him, saying, 'I have never seen you,' and out of the earth others will spring. Behold, God will not reject a blameless man, nor take the hand of evildoers. He will yet fill your mouth with laughter. Those who hate you will be clothed with shame, and the tent of the wicked will be no more."

THEN JOB ANSWERED:

"Truly I know that it is so. But how can a man be just before God? If one wished to contend with him, one could not answer him once in a thousand times. He is wise in heart and mighty in strength—who has hardened himself against him and succeeded?—he who overturns mountains in his anger; who shakes the earth out of its place; who commands the sun and it does not rise; who seals up the stars; who alone stretched out the heavens and trampled the waves of the sea; who does marvelous things without number. Lo, he passes by me, and I see him not. Behold, he snatches away; who can hinder him? Who will say to him, 'What doest thou'? God will not turn back his anger. How then can I answer him? Though I am innocent, I cannot; I must appeal for mercy to my accuser. If I summoned him and he answered me, I would not believe he was listening to my voice. For he crushes me with a tempest, and multiplies my wounds without cause; he will not let me get my breath, but fills me with bitterness. Though I am innocent, my own mouth would condemn me; though I am blameless, he would prove me perverse. Therefore I say, he destroys both the blameless and the wicked. When disaster brings sudden death, he mocks at the calamity of the innocent. The earth is given into the hand of the wicked, and he covers the faces of its judges. If it is not he, who then is it?

"My days are swifter than a runner; they go by like an eagle swooping on the prey. If I say, 'I will forget my complaint and put off my sad countenance,' I become afraid of all my suffering, for I know thou wilt not hold me innocent. I shall be condemned; why then do I labor in vain? If I wash myself with snow, and cleanse my hands with lye, yet thou wilt plunge me into a pit, and my own clothes will abhor me.

"For he is not a man, as I am, that I might answer him, that we should come to trial together. There is no umpire between us, who might lay his hand upon us both. Let him take his rod away from me, and let not dread of him terrify me. Then I would speak without fear of him.

"I will give free utterance to my complaint. I will say to God, Let me know why thou dost contend against me. Hast thou eyes of flesh? Dost thou see as man sees? Are thy days as the days of man, that thou dost seek out my iniquity, although thou knowest I am not guilty, and there is none to deliver out of thy hand? Remember that thou hast made me of clay; wilt thou turn me to dust again? Didst thou not pour me out like milk and curdle me like cheese? Thou didst clothe me with skin and flesh, and knit me together with bones and sinews. Thou hast granted me life and steadfast love; and thy care has preserved my spirit. Yet these things thou didst hide in thy heart; I know that this was thy purpose. If I sin, thou dost not acquit me. If I am righteous, I am filled with disgrace. If

I lift myself up, thou dost hunt me like a lion. Why didst thou bring me forth from the womb? Would that I had died before any eye had seen me. Are not the days of my life few? Let me alone, that I may find a little comfort before I go whence I shall not return, to the land of gloom and chaos, where light is as darkness."

THEN ZOPHAR THE Naamathite answered: "Should a multitude of words go unanswered, and a man full of talk be vindicated? Should your babble silence men, and when you mock, shall no one shame you? For you say, 'My doctrine is pure, and I am clean in God's eyes.' But oh, that God would open his lips to you and tell you the secrets of wisdom! Know that God exacts of you less than your guilt deserves. Can you find out the deep things of God? Can you find out the limit of the Almighty? It is higher than heaven—what can you do? Deeper than Sheol—what can you know? Its measure is longer than the earth, and broader than the sea. If he passes through, and calls to judgment, who can hinder him? If you set your heart aright, you will stretch out your hands toward him. Surely then you will lift up your face without blemish; you will forget your misery, and your life will be brighter than the noonday. You will have confidence, because there is hope. You will lie down, and none will make you afraid."

THEN JOB ANSWERED:

"No doubt you are the people, and wisdom will die with you. But I have understanding as well as you. Who does not know such things as these? I am a laughingstock to my friends; I, who called upon God and he answered me, am a laughingstock. In the thought of one who is at ease there is contempt for misfortune; it is ready for those whose feet slip. The tents of robbers are at peace, and those who provoke God are secure. But ask the beasts and the birds, or the plants and the fish, and they will tell you. Who among all these does not know that the hand of the LORD has done this? In his hand is the life of every living thing. Does not the ear try words as the palate tastes food? Is wisdom with the aged, and understanding in length of days? With God are wisdom and might. If he tears down, none can rebuild; if he shuts a man in, none can open. The deceived and the deceiver are his. He leads counselors away stripped, and judges he makes fools. He pours contempt on princes, and looses the belt of the strong. He makes nations great, and he destroys them. He takes away understanding from the chiefs of the people, and makes them wander in a pathless waste.

"Lo, my eye has seen all this, my ear has heard and understood it. What you know, I also know. But I would speak to the Almighty; I desire to argue my case with God. As for you, you whitewash with lies; worthless physicians are you all. Oh, that you would keep silent, and it would be your wisdom! Hear now my reasoning. Will you speak falsely for God? Will you show partiality toward him, will you plead the case for him? Will it be well with you when he searches you out? Or can you deceive him, as one deceives a man? He will surely rebuke you if in secret you show partiality. Will not his majesty terrify you? Your maxims are proverbs of ashes, your defenses are defenses of clay. Let me have silence, and I will speak; let come on me what may. I will take my life in my hand. Behold, he will slay me. I have no hope; yet I will defend my ways to his face. This will be my salvation, that a godless man shall not come before him. Listen carefully to my words. I have prepared my case; I know I shall be vindicated.

"Only grant two things, O God, then I will not hide myself from thy face: withdraw thy hand far from me, and let not dread of thee terrify me. Then call, and I will answer; or let me speak, and do thou reply. How many are my iniquities? Make me know my sin. Why dost thou hide thy face, and count me as thy enemy? Wilt thou frighten a driven leaf? For thou writest bitter things against me, and makest me inherit the iniquities of my youth. Thou puttest my feet in the stocks, and watchest all my paths; thou settest a bound to the soles of my feet.

"Man that is born of a woman is of few days, and full of trouble. He comes forth like a flower, and withers; he flees like a shadow. And dost thou open thy eyes upon such a one and bring him into judgment with thee? Who can bring a clean thing out of an unclean? There is not one. Since the number of his days is with thee, and thou hast appointed his bounds, look away from him, and desist, that he may enjoy, like a hireling, his day. For there is hope for a tree, if it be cut down, that it will sprout again. But man dies, and is laid low; man breathes his last, and where is he? As waters fail from a lake, and a river wastes away and dries up, so man lies down and rises not again; till the heavens are no more he will not awake, or be roused out of his sleep. Oh, that thou wouldst hide me in Sheol until thy wrath be past, and appoint me a set time, and remember me! If a man die, shall he live again? All the days of my service I would wait till my release should come. Thou wouldst call, and I would answer; thou wouldst long for the work of thy hands. For then thou wouldst number my steps, and not keep watch over my sin; my transgression would be sealed up in a bag, and thou wouldst cover over my iniquity. But the mountain falls and crumbles; the waters wear away the stones; the torrents wash away the soil of the earth; so thou destroyest the hope of man. Thou prevailest for ever against him, and he passes. His sons come to honor, and he does not know it; they are brought low, and he perceives it not. He feels only the pain of his own body, and he mourns only for himself."

THEN ELIPHAZ THE Temanite answered:

"Should a wise man fill himself with the east wind? Should he argue in words with which he can do no good? You are doing away with the fear of God, hindering meditation before him. For you choose the tongue of the crafty. Your own mouth condemns you, not I. Are you the first man that was born? Have you listened in the council of God? And do you limit wisdom to yourself? What do you understand that is not clear to us? Both the gray-haired and the aged are among us, older than your father. Are the consolations of God too small for you, or the word that deals gently with you? Why does your heart carry you away, why do your eyes flash, that you turn your spirit against God, and let such words out of your mouth? What is man born of a woman, that he can be righteous? Behold, God puts no trust in his holy ones, and the heavens are not clean in his sight; how much less one who is abominable and corrupt, who drinks iniquity like water!

"Hear me; what I have seen I will declare. The wicked man writhes in pain all his days. Terrifying sounds are in his ears; in prosperity the destroyer will come upon him. He wanders abroad for bread, saying, 'Where is it?' He knows a day of darkness is at hand. Because he has stretched forth his hand against God, running stubbornly against him; because he has lived in houses destined to become ruins, his wealth will not endure, nor will he strike root in the earth; the flame will dry up his shoots, and his blossom will be swept away by the wind. Let him not trust in emptiness, deceiving himself; for emptiness will be his recompense. It will be paid in full before his time, and his branch will not be green. He will shake off his unripe grape, like the vine. For the company of the godless is barren. They conceive mischief and bring forth evil, and their heart prepares deceit."

THEN JOB ANSWERED:

"I have heard many such things; miserable comforters are you all. Shall windy words have an end? Or what provokes you that you answer? I also could speak as you do, if you were in my place; I could join words together against you, and shake my head at you. But I would strengthen you with my mouth, and the solace of my lips would assuage your pain.

"If I speak, my pain is not assuaged, and if I forbear, how much of it leaves me? Surely now God has worn me out; he has shriveled me up, which is a witness against me. He has torn me in his wrath, and hated me; my adversary sharpens his eyes against me. Men have gaped at me, and struck me on the cheek; they mass together against me. God gives me up to the ungodly. I was at ease, and he seized me by the neck and dashed me to pieces; he set me up as his target, his archers surround me. He slashes open my kidneys; he pours out my gall on the ground. I have sewed sackcloth on my skin, and laid my strength in the dust. My face is red with weeping, and on my eyelids is deep darkness; although there is no violence in my hands, and my prayer is pure.

"O earth, cover not my blood, and let my cry find no resting place. Even now, behold, my witness is in heaven, and he that vouches for me is on high. My friends scorn me; my eye pours out tears to God, that he would maintain the right of a man with God, like that of a man with his neighbor. For when a few years have come, I shall go the way whence I shall not return. My spirit is broken; the grave is ready for me. Surely there are mockers about me, and my eye dwells on their provocation.

"Lay down a pledge for me with thyself; who is there that will give surety for me? Since thou hast closed their minds to understanding, therefore thou wilt not let them triumph. He who informs against his friends, the eyes of his children will fail.

"I am made a byword, one before whom men spit. My eye has grown dim from grief, and all my members are like a

shadow. Upright men are appalled at this.
Yet the righteous holds to his way, and he
that has clean hands grows stronger and
stronger. Come on again, all of you, and I
shall not find a wise man among you. My
days are past, my plans are broken off. If I
look for Sheol as my house and spread my
couch in darkness, if I say to the pit, 'You
are my father,' and to the worm, 'My
mother,' or 'My sister,' where then is my
hope? Who will see my hope? Will it go
down to the bars of Sheol? Shall we descend together into the dust?"

THEN BILDAD THE Shuhite answered:
"How long will you hunt for words?
Why are we counted as cattle, stupid in
your sight? You who tear yourself in your
anger, shall the earth be forsaken for you?
"Yea, the light of the wicked is put out;
it is dark in his tent. His strong steps are
shortened; he is cast into a net by his own
feet. A trap seizes him by the heel, a rope
is hid for him in the ground. He is torn
from the tent in which he trusted, and
brought to the king of terrors. Brimstone is
scattered upon his habitation. His roots

dry up and his branches wither. His memory perishes from the earth; he has no name in the street, and no survivor where he used to live. They of the west are appalled at his day, and horror seizes them of the east. Surely such is the place of him who knows not God."

THEN JOB ANSWERED:

"How long will you torment me? Are you not ashamed to wrong me? If it be true that I have erred, my error remains with myself. If you make my humiliation an argument against me, know then that God has put me in the wrong, and closed his net about me. Behold, I cry out, 'Violence!' but I am not answered. He has walled up my way, so I cannot pass; he has stripped from me my glory; he breaks me down on every side, and my hope has he pulled up like a tree. He counts me as his adversary. His troops have cast up siegeworks against me, and encamp about my tent. He has put my brethren far from me. My kinsfolk and close friends have failed me; the guests in my house have forgotten me; my maidservants count me a stranger. I am repulsive to my wife, loathsome to the sons of my own mother; even young children despise me. My bones cleave to my flesh, and I have escaped by the skin of my teeth. Have pity on me, have pity on me, O you my friends, for the hand of God has touched me! Why do you, like God, pursue me? Why are you not satisfied with my flesh?

"Oh, that my words were inscribed in a book! Oh, that with an iron pen they were graven in the rock for ever! For I know that my Redeemer lives, and at last he will stand upon the earth; and after my skin has been thus destroyed, then from my flesh I shall see God on my side. My heart faints within me! If you say, 'How we will pursue him!' and, 'The root of the matter is found in him'; be afraid, for wrath brings the punishment of the sword, that you may know there is a judgment."

THEN ZOPHAR THE Naamathite answered:

"My thoughts hasten within me. I hear censure which insults me, and out of my understanding a spirit answers me. Do you not know, since man was placed upon earth, that the exulting of the wicked is short? Though his head reach to the clouds, he will perish like his own dung. He will be chased away like a vision of the night. Though wickedness is sweet in his mouth, though he hides it under his tongue, yet his food is turned in his stomach; it is the gall of asps within him. He swallows down riches and vomits them up again; from the profit of his trading he will get no enjoyment. For he has crushed the poor, he has seized a house which he did not build. Because his greed knew no rest, he will not save anything in which he delights. All the force of misery will come upon him. A bronze arrow will strike him through; the glittering point comes out of his gall; terrors come upon him. The heavens will reveal his iniquity, and the earth will rise up against him. The possessions of his house will be dragged off in the day of God's wrath. This is the wicked man's portion from God."

THEN JOB ANSWERED:
"Listen carefully to my words, and let this be your consolation to me. Bear with

me, and after I have spoken, mock on. As for me, is my complaint against man? Why should I not be impatient? Look at me, and be appalled. When I think of it, shuddering seizes my flesh. Why do the wicked live, reach old age, and grow mighty in power? Their children are established in their presence, their houses are safe from fear, and no rod of God is upon them. Their bull breeds without fail; their cow does not cast her calf. Their children dance to the tambourine and the lyre, and rejoice to the sound of the pipe. They spend their days in prosperity, and in peace they go down to Sheol. They say to God, 'Depart from us! We do not desire the knowledge of thy ways. What is the Almighty, that we should serve him? What profit do we get if we pray to him?' Behold, is not their prosperity in their hand? The counsel of the wicked is far from me.

"How often is it that the lamp of the wicked is put out? That their calamity comes upon them? That God distributes pains in his anger? You say, 'God stores up their iniquity for their sons.' Let him recompense it to themselves, that they may know it; let their own eyes see their destruction, for what do they care for their houses after them? Will any teach God knowledge, seeing that he judges those that are on high? One dies in full prosperity, wholly at ease, his body fat and the marrow of his bones moist. Another dies in bitterness of soul, never having tasted of good. They lie down alike in the dust, and the worms cover them.

"Have you not asked those who travel the roads, and do you not accept their testimony that the wicked man is spared in the day of calamity, that he is rescued in the day of wrath? Who requites him for what he has done? When he is borne to the grave, watch is kept over his tomb. The clods of the valley are sweet to him; all men follow after him, and those who go before him are innumerable. How then will you comfort me with empty nothings? There is nothing left of your answers but falsehood."

THEN ELIPHAZ THE Temanite answered:
"Can a man be profitable to God? Surely he who is wise is profitable to himself. Is

it any pleasure to the Almighty if you are righteous? Is it for your fear of him that he reproves you? There is no end to your iniquities. You have exacted pledges of your brothers for nothing, stripped the naked of their clothing, withheld bread from the hungry, sent widows away empty. Therefore snares are round about you, and sudden terror overwhelms you; your light is darkened, so that you cannot see, and a flood of water covers you. Is not God high in the heavens? See the highest stars, how lofty they are! Therefore you say, 'What does God know? Can he judge through the deep darkness? Thick clouds enwrap him, so that he does not see, and he walks on the vault of heaven.' Will you keep to the old way which wicked men have trod? They were snatched away before their time; their foundation was washed away. The righteous see it and are glad, the innocent laugh them to scorn, saying, 'Surely our adversaries are cut off, and what they left the fire has consumed.'

"Agree with God, and be at peace; thereby good will come to you. Lay up his words in your heart. If you return to the

Almighty and humble yourself, if you remove unrighteousness from your tents, if you lay gold in the torrent bed, and if the Almighty is your gold, then you will delight yourself in the Almighty and lift up your face to God. You will make your prayer, and he will hear you. For God abases the proud, but he saves the lowly. He delivers the innocent man; you will be delivered through the cleanness of your hands."

THEN JOB ANSWERED:

"Today also my complaint is bitter, his hand is heavy in spite of my groaning. Oh, that I knew where I might find him, that I might come even to his seat! I would lay my case before him and learn what he would answer me. He would give heed to me; an upright man could reason with him, and I should be acquitted for ever by my judge.

"Behold, I go forward, but he is not there, and backward, but I cannot perceive him; on the left hand I seek him, and on the right, but I cannot see him. But he knows the way that I take; when he has tried me, I shall come forth as gold. My foot has held fast to his steps, and I have treasured in my bosom the words of his mouth. But who can turn him? What he desires, that he does. For he will complete what he appoints for me, and many such things are in his mind. Therefore, when I consider, I am in dread of him. God has made my heart faint.

"Why are not times of judgment kept by the Almighty, and why do those who know him never see his days? Men remove landmarks, seize flocks and pasture them, drive away the ass of the fatherless, take the widow's ox for a pledge, and thrust the poor off the road. The poor hide themselves, seeking prey in the wilderness as food for their children; they lie all night naked in the cold; they are wet with the rain of the mountains, and cling to the rock for want of shelter. From out of the city the dying groan, and the soul of the wounded cries for help. Yet God pays no attention to their prayer.

"There are those who rebel against the light and do not stay in its paths. The murderer rises in the dark, that he may kill the poor and needy. The eye of the adulterer also waits for the twilight, and he disguises his face. In the dark they dig through houses, by day they shut themselves up, for deep darkness is morning to all of them. You say, 'Their portion is cursed in the land. Drought and heat snatch away the snow; so does Sheol those who have sinned.' Yet God prolongs the life of the mighty. He gives them security, and his eyes are upon their ways. If it is not so, who will prove there is nothing in what I say?"

THEN BILDAD THE Shuhite answered:

"Dominion and fear are with God; he makes peace in his high heaven. Is there any number to his armies? Upon whom does his light not arise? How then can man be righteous before God? Behold, even the moon is not bright and the stars are not clean in his sight; how much less man, who is a worm!"

THEN JOB ANSWERED:

"How you have helped him who has no power! How you have counseled him who has no wisdom! With whose help have you uttered words, and whose spirit has come forth from you?

"The shades below tremble before God. He stretches out the north over the void, and hangs the earth upon nothing. He binds up the waters in his thick clouds, and covers the face of the moon. He has described a circle upon the waters at the boundary between light and darkness. By his power he stilled the sea; by his wind the heavens were made fair; his hand pierced the fleeing serpent. Lo, these are but the outskirts of his ways.

"As God lives, who has made my soul bitter, as long as my breath is in me, and the spirit of God is in my nostrils, my tongue will not utter deceit. Far be it from me to say that you are right. Till I die I will not put away my integrity from me; my heart does not reproach me for any of my days.

"Surely there is a mine for silver, and a place for gold which they refine. Iron is taken out of the earth, and copper is smelted from the ore. Men search out to the farthest bound the ore in gloom and deep darkness. They open shafts in a valley away from where men live; forgotten by travelers, they hang afar from men, they swing to and fro. As for the earth, out of it comes bread; but underneath it is turned up as by fire. Its stones are the place of sapphires, and it has dust of gold. Man puts his hand to the flinty rock, and over-turns mountains by the roots. He cuts out channels in the rocks, and his eye sees every precious thing. He binds up the streams so that they do not trickle, and the thing that is hid he brings forth to light.

"But where shall wisdom be found? And where is the place of understanding? Man does not know the way to it, and it is not found in the land of the living. The deep says, 'It is not in me,' and the sea says, 'It is not with me.' It cannot be got-ten for gold, and silver cannot be weighed as its price. It cannot be valued in precious onyx or sapphire, nor can it be exchanged for jewels. The price of wisdom is above pearls. Whence then comes wisdom? Where is the place of understanding? It is hid from the eyes of all living, and con-cealed from the birds of the air.

"But God understands the way to it, for he sees everything under the heavens. When he gave to the wind its weight, and measured out the waters; when he made a decree for the rain, and a way for the lightning and thunder; then he saw it and declared it; he established it, and searched it out. And he said to man, 'Behold, the fear of the Lord, that is wisdom; and to depart from evil is understanding.'"

And Job again took up his discourse, saying, "Oh, that I were as in the months of old when God watched over me, when his lamp shone upon my head, when my children were about me, when my steps were washed with milk, and the rock poured out for me streams of oil! At the gate of the city, or when I sat in the square, the young men withdrew, and the aged stood; the princes refrained from talking, the voice of the nobles was hushed. The blessing of him who was about to perish came upon me, and I caused the widow's heart to sing for joy. I put on righteousness, and it clothed me. I was eyes to the blind, and feet to the lame. I was a father to the poor, and I searched out the cause of him whom I did not know. I broke the fangs of the unrighteous, and made him drop his prey from his teeth. Then I thought, 'I shall die in my nest, and I shall multiply my days as the sand, my glory fresh with me, and my bow ever new in my hand.' Men listened to my counsel. After I spoke they did not speak again; my word dropped upon them. They waited for me, and opened their mouths as for the spring rain. I smiled on them when they had no confidence, and the light of my countenance they did not cast down. I chose their way, and dwelt like a king among his troops, like one who comforts mourners.

"But now they make sport of me, men who are younger than I, whose fathers I would have disdained to set with the dogs of my flock. I have become their song, a byword to them. They do not hesitate to spit at the sight of me. Because God has humbled me, the rabble rise against me. As through a wide breach they come. My honor is pursued as by the wind, and my prosperity has passed away like a cloud. And now my soul is poured out within me;

the pain that gnaws me takes no rest; it binds me about like the collar of my tunic. God has cast me into the mire.

"I cry to thee and thou dost not heed me. Thou hast turned cruel to me; thou liftest me up on the wind, thou makest me ride on it. Yea, I know that thou wilt bring me to death, to the house appointed for all living.

"Yet does not one in a heap of ruins stretch out his hand for help? Did not I weep for him whose day was hard? Was not my soul grieved for the poor? But when I looked for good, evil came. My heart is in turmoil; I go about blackened, but not by the sun. I am a brother of jackals. My skin turns black and falls from me, and my bones burn with heat.

"I have made a covenant with my eyes; how then could I look upon a virgin? What would be my portion from God above? Does not he see my ways, and number all my steps? If I have walked with falsehood, if my step has turned aside from the way, and my heart has gone after my eyes; if any spot has cleaved to my hands, then let me sow, and another eat;

and let what grows for me be rooted out. If my heart has been enticed to a woman, and I have lain in wait at my neighbor's door, then let my wife grind for another. For that would be a heinous crime to be punished by the judges, a fire which would burn all my increase to the root.

"If I have withheld anything that the poor desired, or caused the eyes of the widow to fail, or eaten my morsel alone, and the fatherless has not eaten of it; if I have seen any one perish for lack of clothing; if I have raised my hand against the fatherless because I saw help in the gate, then let my arm be broken from its socket. For I was in terror of God and could not have faced his majesty.

"If I have made gold my trust; if I have looked at the sun when it shone, or the moon moving in splendor, and my heart has been secretly enticed; this also would be an iniquity to be punished by the judges, for I should have been false to God above. If I have rejoiced at the ruin of him that hated me, or exulted when evil overtook him; if the men of my tent have not said, 'Who is there that has not been filled with his meat?'; if I have concealed my transgressions from men because I stood in fear of the multitude so that I kept silence, and did not go out of doors— Oh, that I had one to hear me! Let the Almighty answer me! Oh, that I had the indictment written by my adversary! Surely I would carry it on my shoulder, I would bind it on me as a crown; I would give him an account of all my steps; like a prince I would approach him. If my land has cried out against me, and its furrows have wept together; if I have eaten its yield without payment, let thorns grow instead of wheat, and foul weeds instead of barley."

The words of Job are ended.

So THESE THREE men ceased to answer Job, because he was righteous in his own eyes. Then Elihu the son of Barachel the Buzite, of the family of Ram, became angry. He was angry at Job because he justified himself rather than God, and at Job's friends because they had found no answer, although they had declared Job to be wrong. Elihu had waited to speak because they were older than he.

Now Elihu answered:

"I am young in years, and you are aged; therefore I was afraid to declare my opinion. But it is the spirit in a man, the breath of the Almighty, that makes him understand. It is not the old that are wise. Therefore I say, 'Listen to me.' While you searched out what to say, I waited. And, behold, there was none among you that confuted Job. Beware lest you say, 'We have found wisdom; God may vanquish him, not man.' Job has not directed his words against me, and I will not answer him with your speeches. But I am full of words. My heart is like wine that has no vent; like new wineskins, it is ready to burst. I must speak, that I may find relief. I will not show partiality to any person or use flattery toward any man. For I do not know how to flatter, else would my Maker soon put an end to me.

"Now hear my speech, O Job. My words declare the uprightness of my heart; for the spirit of God has made me, and his breath gives me life. Answer me, if you can; take your stand. Behold, I am toward God as you are; I too was formed from a piece of clay. No fear of me need terrify you; my pressure will not be heavy upon you.

"Surely, I have heard you say, 'I am pure, and there is no iniquity in me; yet God finds occasions against me, he counts me as his enemy; he puts my feet in the stocks, and watches all my paths.' In this you are not right. I answer that God is greater than man. Why do you contend against him, saying, 'He will answer none of my words'? For God speaks in one way, and in two, though man does not perceive it. In a dream, while they slumber, he opens the ears of men, and terrifies them with warnings, that he may turn man aside from his deed, and cut off his pride; and he keeps back his soul from the Pit.

"Man is also chastened with pain upon his bed, so that his life loathes bread. His flesh wastes away and his bones stick out. His soul draws near the Pit, and his life to those who bring death. If there be for him an angel, a mediator, to declare to man what is right for him; if he is gracious to him, and says, 'Deliver him from the Pit, I have found a ransom, let his flesh become fresh with youth'; then man prays to God, and he accepts him, he comes into his presence with joy, and he sings before men: 'I sinned, and perverted what was right, and it was not requited to me. He has redeemed my soul, and my life shall see the light.'

"Behold, God does all these things, twice, three times, with a man, to bring back his soul from the Pit, that he may see the light of life. Give heed, O Job. If you have anything to say, speak, for I desire to justify you. If not, be silent, and I will teach you wisdom."

Then Elihu said, "Hear my words, you wise men. Let us determine among ourselves what is good. For Job has said, 'I am innocent, and God has taken away my right; my wound is incurable, though I am without transgression.' What man is like Job, who drinks up scoffing like water and walks with evildoers? For he has said, 'It profits a man nothing that he should take delight in God.' Therefore, hear me, you men of understanding. Far be it from God that he should do wrong. For according to the work of a man he will requite him. Of a truth, the Almighty will not pervert justice. Who gave him charge over the whole world? If he should take back his spirit, and gather his breath to himself, all flesh would return to dust.

"If you have understanding, O Job, listen. Shall one who hates justice govern? Will you condemn him who is righteous and mighty, who says to a king, 'Worthless one,' and shows no partiality to princes, nor regards the rich more than the poor? They are all the work of his hands. In a moment they die; at midnight the people pass away, and the mighty are taken by no human hand. For his eyes are upon the ways of a man, and there is no darkness where evildoers may hide. For he has not appointed a time for any man to go before him in judgment. He shatters the mighty without investigation and sets others in their place. Knowing their works, he overturns them in the night, and they are crushed because they turned aside from his ways and caused the cry of the afflicted to come to him. When he is quiet, who can condemn? When he hides his face, who can behold him, whether it be a nation or a man? For has any one said to God, 'I

have borne chastisement; I will not offend
any more; teach me what I do not see; if I
have done iniquity, I will do it no more'?
Will he then make requital to suit you?
You must choose, not I; declare what you
know. The wise man who hears me will
say: 'Job speaks without knowledge, his
words are without insight.' Would that Job
were tried to the end, because he answers
like wicked men. For he adds rebellion to
his sin; he claps his hands among us, and
multiplies his words against God.

"Do you think this to be just? Do you
say, 'It is my right before God,' that you
ask, 'How am I better off than if I had
sinned?' I will answer you and your friends
with you. Look at the heavens and behold
the clouds, which are higher than you. If
you have sinned, what do you accomplish
against him? If you are righteous, what do
you give to him? Your wickedness concerns a man like yourself, and your righteousness a son of man.

"Because of the multitude of oppres-
sions people cry for help; but none says,
'Where is God my Maker, who gives songs
in the night, who teaches us more than the

beasts of the earth, and makes us wiser than the birds of the air?' They cry out, but he does not answer, because of the pride of evil men. Surely God does not regard an empty cry. How much less when you say that you do not see him, that the case is before him, and you are waiting for him! And now, because his anger does not punish, Job opens his mouth in empty talk, he multiplies words without knowledge.

"Bear with me, for I have yet something to say on God's behalf. I will fetch my knowledge from afar, and ascribe righteousness to my Maker. For truly my words are not false; one who is perfect in knowledge is with you. Behold, God is mighty, and does not despise any; he does not keep the wicked alive, but gives the afflicted their right. He does not withdraw his eyes from the righteous, but with kings he sets them for ever. And if they are caught in the cords of affliction, he declares to them their transgressions, and commands that they return from iniquity. If they hearken, they complete their years in pleasantness. But if they do not, they die without knowledge.

"But you are full of the judgment on the wicked. Beware lest wrath entice you into scoffing; and let not the greatness of the ransom turn you aside. Will your cry avail to keep you from distress? Take heed, do not turn to iniquity, for this you have chosen rather than affliction. Behold, God is exalted in his power; who is a teacher like him? Who has prescribed for him his way, or who can say, 'Thou hast done wrong'? Remember to extol his work, of which men have sung.

"Behold, God is great, and we know him not; the number of his years is unsearchable. Can any one understand the spreading of the clouds, the thunderings of his pavilion? He scatters his lightning about him, and commands it to strike the mark. Its crashing declares concerning him, who is jealous with anger against iniquity. At this my heart trembles, and leaps out of its place. God thunders wondrously with his voice; he does great things which we cannot comprehend. To the snow he says, 'Fall on the earth'; and to the rain, 'Be strong.' He seals up the hand of every man, that all men may know his work; and then the beasts go into their lairs and remain there. From its chamber comes the whirlwind, and cold from the scattering winds. By the breath of God ice is given. He loads the thick clouds with moisture; they turn round and round by his guidance, to accomplish all that he commands them on the face of the habitable world. Whether for correction, or for his land, or for love, he causes it to happen.

"Hear this, O Job; stop and consider the wondrous works of God. Can you, like him, spread out the skies, hard as a molten mirror? Teach us what we shall say to him; we cannot draw up our case because of darkness. Shall it be told him that I would speak? Did a man ever wish that he would be swallowed up? The Almighty— we cannot find him; he is great in power and justice, and abundant righteousness he will not violate. Therefore men fear him; he does not regard any who are wise in their own conceit."

THEN THE LORD answered Job out of the whirlwind:

"Who is this that darkens counsel by

words without knowledge? Gird up your loins like a man; I will question you, and you shall declare to me. Where were you when I laid the foundation of the earth? Tell me, if you have understanding. Who determined its measurements—surely you know! On what were its bases sunk, or who laid its cornerstone, when the morning stars sang together, and all the sons of God shouted for joy? Who shut in the sea with doors, when it burst forth from the womb; when I made clouds its garment and thick darkness its swaddling band, and prescribed bounds for it, and said, 'Thus far shall you come, and no farther; here shall your proud waves be stayed'?

"Have you commanded the morning since your days began, and caused the dawn to know its place, that it might take hold of the skirts of the earth, and the wicked be shaken out of it? Have you entered into the springs of the sea, or walked in the recesses of the deep? Have the gates of death been revealed to you? Have you comprehended the expanse of the earth? Declare, if you know all this. Where is the way to the dwelling of light, and where is the place of darkness, that you may discern the paths to its home? You know, for you were born then, and the number of your days is great!

"Have you entered the storehouses of the snow, or seen the hail, which I have reserved for the time of trouble, the day of war? What is the way to the place where the east wind is scattered? Who has cleft a channel for the torrents, and a way for the thunderbolt, to bring rain on the desert, and make the ground put forth grass? Has the rain a father, or who has begotten the drops of dew? From whose womb did the ice and the hoarfrost come forth?

"Can you bind the chains of the Pleiades, or loose the cords of Orion? Do you know the ordinances of the heavens? Can you establish their rule on the earth? Can you lift up your voice to the clouds, that a flood of waters may cover you? Can you send forth lightnings, that they may say to you, 'Here we are'? Who has put wisdom in the clouds? Who can number them? Or who can tilt the waterskins of the heavens, when the dust runs into a mass and the clods cleave fast together?

"Can you hunt the prey for the lion, or satisfy the appetite of the young lions, when they lie in wait in their covert? Who provides for the raven its prey, when its young ones cry to God, and wander about for lack of food? Do you know when the mountain goats bring forth? Do you observe the calving of the hinds? Their young become strong, grow up in the open, go forth, and do not return to them.

"Who has let the wild ass go free, the swift ass to whom I have given the steppe for his home? He scorns the tumult of the city; he hears not the shouts of the driver. He ranges the mountains as his pasture, and searches after every green thing. Is the wild ox willing to serve you? Will he spend the night at your crib? Can you bind him in the furrow with ropes, will he harrow the valleys after you? Will you depend on him because his strength is great, and will you leave to him your labor? Do you have faith that he will return, and bring your grain to your threshing floor?

"The wings of the ostrich wave proudly; but are they the pinions and plumage of love? For she leaves her eggs to be warmed on the ground, forgetting that a wild beast may trample them. She deals cruelly with her young, as if they were not hers; though her labor be in vain, yet she has no fear because God has given her no share in understanding. When she rouses herself to flee, she laughs at the horse and his rider.

"Do you give the horse his might? Do you clothe his neck with strength? Do you make him leap like the locust? His majestic snorting is terrible. He paws in the valley, and exults in his strength; he goes out to meet the weapons. He laughs at fear. Upon him rattle the quiver, the flashing spear, and the javelin. With rage he swallows the ground; he cannot stand still at the sound of the trumpet. He says 'Aha!' and smells the battle from afar, the thunder of the captains, and the shouting.

"Is it by your wisdom that the hawk soars, and spreads his wings toward the south? Is it at your command that the eagle mounts up and makes his nest on high? On the rock he dwells and makes his home in the fastness of the rocky crag. Thence he spies out the prey; his eyes behold it afar off. His young ones suck up blood; and where the slain are, there is he."

And the LORD said to Job, "Shall a fault-finder contend with the Almighty? He who argues with God, let him answer it."

THEN JOB ANSWERED the LORD:
"Behold, I am of small account; what shall I answer thee? I lay my hand on my mouth. I have spoken once, and I will not answer; twice, but I will proceed no further."

THEN THE LORD answered Job out of the whirlwind:
"Gird up your loins like a man; I will question you, and you declare to me. Will you even put me in the wrong? Will you condemn me that you may be justified? Have you an arm like God, and can you thunder with a voice like his? Deck your-self with majesty and dignity; clothe your-self with glory. Pour forth your anger; look on every one that is proud, and bring him low; tread down the wicked where they stand. Hide them all in the dust together;

bind their faces in the world below. Then will I also acknowledge that your own right hand can give you victory.

"Behold Behemoth, which I made as I made you; he eats grass like an ox. Behold his strength in his loins and in the muscles of his belly. He makes his tail stiff like a cedar; his bones are tubes of bronze, his limbs like bars of iron. He is the first of the works of God; let him who made him bring near his sword! For the mountains yield food for him where all the wild beasts play. In the covert of the reeds he lies; for his shade the lotus trees cover him, and the willows of the brook surround him. Behold, if the river is turbulent he is not frightened; he is confident though Jordan rushes against his mouth. Can one take him with hooks, or pierce his nose with a snare?

"Can you draw out Leviathan with a fishhook, or put a rope in his nose? Will you play with him as with a bird, or put him on leash for your maidens? Can you fill his skin with harpoons, or penetrate his double coat of mail? Who can open the doors of his face? Round about his teeth is terror. His back is made of rows of shields, shut up closely as with a seal. Out of his mouth go flaming torches, and out of his nostrils comes forth smoke. He makes the deep boil like a pot; behind him he leaves a shining wake. Upon earth there is not his like, a creature without fear. He is king over all the sons of pride. Behold, the hope of a man is laid low even at the sight of him.

"Who then is he that can stand before me? Who has given to me, that I should repay him? Whatever is under the whole heaven is mine."

THEN JOB ANSWERED the LORD:
"I know that thou canst do all things, and that no purpose of thine can be thwarted. Thou hast said, 'Who is this that hides counsel without knowledge?' Therefore I have uttered what I did not understand, things too wonderful for me, which I did not know. Thou hast said, 'Hear, and I will speak; I will question you, and you declare to me.' I had heard of thee by the hearing of the ear, but now my eye sees thee; therefore I despise myself, and repent in dust and ashes."

AFTER THE LORD had spoken to Job, he said to Eliphaz the Temanite: "My wrath is kindled against you and against your two friends; for you have not spoken of me what is right, as my servant Job has. Now take seven bulls and seven rams, and go to Job, and offer up for yourselves a burnt offering. Job shall pray for you, for I will accept his prayer not to deal with you according to your folly." So Eliphaz, Bildad, and Zophar did what the LORD told them. And the LORD restored the fortunes of Job, when he had prayed for his friends, giving him twice as much as he had before. Then all his brothers and sisters and all who had known him came and ate bread with him, and comforted him for the evil the LORD had brought upon him; and each of them gave him a piece of money and a ring of gold. And the LORD blessed the latter days of Job more than his beginning; he had fourteen thousand sheep, six thousand camels, a thousand yoke of oxen, and a thousand she-asses. He had also seven sons and three daughters. He named the first daughter Jemimah, the second Keziah, and the third Keren-happuch. In all the land there were no women so fair as Job's daughters, and he gave them inheritance among their brothers. After this, Job lived a hundred and forty years, and saw his sons, and his sons' sons, four generations. And Job died, an old man, and full of days.